›

Lecture Notes of the Institute for Computer Sciences, Social Informatics and Telecommunications Engineering

361

More information about this series at http://www.springer.com/series/8197

Rafik Zitouni · Amreesh Phokeer ·
Josiah Chavula · Ahmed Elmokashfi ·
Assane Gueye · Nabil Benamar (Eds.)

Towards new e-Infrastructure and e-Services for Developing Countries

12th EAI International Conference, AFRICOMM 2020
Ebène City, Mauritius, December 2–4, 2020
Proceedings

 Springer

Editors
Rafik Zitouni ⓘ
ECE Paris, INSEEC U. Research Center
Paris, France

Josiah Chavula ⓘ
University of Cape Town
Rondebosch, South Africa

Assane Gueye ⓘ
CMU-Africa
Kigali, Rwanda

Amreesh Phokeer ⓘ
African Network Information Center
Ebène, Mauritius

Ahmed Elmokashfi ⓘ
(org. 984648855)
Simula Research Laboratory
Fornebu, Norway

Nabil Benamar ⓘ
Universite Moulay Ismail De Meknes
Meknes, Morocco

ISSN 1867-8211   ISSN 1867-822X   (electronic)
Lecture Notes of the Institute for Computer Sciences, Social Informatics
and Telecommunications Engineering
ISBN 978-3-030-70571-8   ISBN 978-3-030-70572-5   (eBook)
https://doi.org/10.1007/978-3-030-70572-5

This Springer imprint is published by the registered company Springer Nature Switzerland AG
The registered company address is: Gewerbestrasse 11, 6330 Cham, Switzerland

Preface

It is our utmost pleasure to introduce the proceedings of the 12th European Alliance for Innovation (EAI) International Conference on e-Infrastructure and e-Services for Developing Countries (AFRICOMM 2020) held on December 3–4, 2020. This unique edition was held online due to the ongoing pandemic, but nevertheless the organising committee came up with a very interesting programme that brought together researchers, ICT practitioners, engineers and policy makers to share their experiences and research output during this two-day event.

AFRICOMM 2020 was kickstarted by a pre-event held on December 2, 2020 and organised by AFRINIC and the Internet Society as part of the IETF-Africa initiative. The attendees benefited from a very informative session on how to increase the involvement of academia in Internet Standards development. For the main technical track, AFRICOMM 2020 received a record number of 89 submissions out of which 20 full papers were selected following a very thorough review and shepherding process. The low acceptance rate of 22.4% testifies to the high-quality programme put together by the TPC. The technical talks were grouped in 6 different sessions, namely: Dynamic Spectrum Access and Mesh Networks, Wireless Sensing and 5G Networks, Software-Defined Networking, Internet of Things, e-Services and Big Data, and DNS Resilience and Performance. The papers were pre-recorded and presented during the online session, followed by live Q&A, which allowed participants to actively engage with the authors.

This year's edition also featured three very insightful and enlightening keynote speeches. Prof. Aminata Garba, Assistant Professor at Carnegie Mellon University-Rwanda, talked about Data Infrastructure for Development and the importance for developing nations to harness the power of Big Data. Prof. Thomas Magedanz from Technical University Berlin, Germany presented the Fraunhofer 5G playground, which is one of the most advanced open 5G testbeds for research purposes. Finally, Prof. Nick Feamster from University of Chicago, USA talked about the importance of encrypting DNS traffic and showcased a revolutionary new concept called "Oblivious DNS", designed to keep users' privacy at the centre of everything.

AFRICOMM 2020 would not have been a success without the tireless efforts of the TPC chairs: Ahmed Elmokashfi (Simula Research Lab), Assane Gueye (CMU-Rwanda), Josiah Chavula (University of Cape Town) and Nabil Benamar (Moulay Ismail University of Meknes), together with the 65 reviewers who made sure we had a high-quality programme. Many thanks go to Enrico Calandro (Research ICT Africa) who helped organise 3 different panel sessions on (1) Artificial Intelligence and Social Innovation, (2) Cyber Maturity Assessment and (3) Privacy & Pandemics: Developing privacy laws and policies in a post-COVID Africa.

Congratulations to the best paper "Predictive Policing using Deep Learning: A Community Policing Practical Case Study" by Omowunmi Isafiade, Brian Ndingind-wayo and Antoine Bagula. The paper was selected by a sub-committee based on the quality of writing, the reviews received, its relevance to the conference as well as its potential to solve an African problem.

Our final word of gratitude goes to AFRINIC, the Regional Internet Registry for Africa, who provided tremendous support to the organisation of this conference through its chairmanship and also graciously sponsored the registration fees for all African authors.

December 2020

Amreesh Phokeer
Visham Ramsurrun

The original version of the book was revised: The address of Assane Gueye in the front matter of these proceedings has been updated. The correction to the book is available at https://doi.org/10.1007/978-3-030-70572-5_21

Conference Organization

Steering Committee

Imrich Chlamtac	Bruno Kessler Professor, University of Trento, Italy
Max Agueh	EFREI Paris, France

Organizing Committee

General Chair

Amreesh Phokeer   AFRINIC, Mauritius

General Co-chair

Visham Ramsurrun   Middlesex University Mauritius, Mauritius

TPC Chair and Co-chairs

Josiah Chavula	University of Cape Town, South Africa
Ahmed Elmokashfi	Simula Research Laboratory, Norway
Assane Gueye	CMU-Africa, Rwanda
Nabil Benamar	Moulay Ismail University of Meknes, Morocco

Sponsorship and Exhibit Chair

Aditya Santokhee   Middlesex University Mauritius, Mauritius

Local Organizing Committee

Amreesh Phokeer	AFRINIC, Mauritius
Visham Ramsurrun	Middlesex University Mauritius, Mauritius
Amar Kumar Seeam	Middlesex University Mauritius, Mauritius
Duksh Koonjoobeehary	AFRINIC, Mauritius

Workshops Chair

Enrico Calandro   Research ICT Africa, South Africa

Publicity and Social Media Chair

Senka Hadzic   Research ICT Africa, South Africa

Publications Chair

Rafik Zitouni   ECE Paris, France

Web Chair

Duksh Koonjoobeehary   AFRINIC, Mauritius

Posters and PhD Track Chair

Alemnew Asrese   Ericsson, Finland

Panels Chair

Musab Isah   University of Hafr Al Batin, Saudi Arabia

Technical Program Committee

Abdellah Boulouz	Ibn Zohr University, Morocco
Abdellatif Ezzouhairi	ENSAF, Morocco
Abubakar Elsafi	UJ, Saudi Arabia
Adisorn Lertsinsrubtavee	Asian Institute of Technology, Thailand
Aghiles Djoudi	ESIEE Paris, France
Ahmed Elmokashfi	Simula Research Lab, Norway
Alemnew Sheferaw Asrese	Aalto University, Finland
Alfred Arouna	Simula Research Laboratory, Norway
Ambassa Pacome	University of Cape Town, South Africa
Amreesh Dev Phokeer	AFRINIC, Mauritius
Rafik Zitouni	ECE Paris, France
Anesu Marufu	F-Secure Consultancy Ltd, South Africa
Antoine Bagula	University of the Western Cape, South Africa
Anwaar Ali	University of Cambridge, UK
Assane Gueye	CMU-Africa, Rwanda
Avinash Mungur	University of Mauritius, Mauritius
Christine Wanjiru	University of Cape Town, South Africa
Clarel Catherine	University of Technology of Mauritius, Mauritius
David Johnson	University of Cape Town, South Africa
Elmustafa Sayed Ali Ahmed	Red Sea University, Egypt
Enock Mbewe	University of Cape Town, South Africa
Enrico Calandro	Research ICT Africa, South Africa
Ermias Walelgne	Aalto University, Finland
Fayçal Bensalah	Chouaib Doukkali University, Morocco
Franklin Tchakounté	University of Ngaoundéré, Cameroon
Gerald Nathan Balekaki	Makerere University, Uganda
Gertjan van Stam	SolidarMed, Zimbabwe
Habiba Chaoui	Ecole Nationale des Sciences Appliquées - Kénitra, Morocco
Hafeni Mthoko	University of Cape Town, South Africa
Hanane Lamaazi	Khalifa University, UAE
Heman Mohabeer	BIRGER, Mauritius
Hope Mauwa	University of the Western Cape, South Africa
Ioana Livadariu	SimulaMet, Norway

Isaac Odun-Ayo	Covenant University, Nigeria
Jona Beysens	KU Leuven, Belgium
Josiah Chavula	University of Cape Town, South Africa
Kaleem Ahmed Usmani	CERT-MU, Mauritius
Kamel Boukhalfa	USTHB University, Algeria
Keziah Naggita	Toyota Technological Institute at Chicago, USA
Laureen Akumu Ndeda	Maseno University, Kenya
Lighton Phiri	University of Zambia, Zambia
M. Hammad Mazhar	University of Iowa, USA
Marco Zennaro	ICTP, Italy
Menatalla Abououf	Khalifa University, UAE
Mohammed Fattah	UMI, Morocco
Mukhtar Mahmoud	University of Kassala, Sudan
Musab Isah	University of Hafr Al Batin, Saudi Arabia
Nabil Benamar	Moulay Ismail University, Morocco
Natasha Zlobinsky	University of Cape Town, South Africa
Nawaz Mohamudally	University of Technology of Mauritius, Mauritius
Nii Narku Quaynor	University of Cape Coast, Ghana
Omar Rafik Merad Boudia	University of Oran 1- Ahmed Ben Bella, Algeria
Raj Chaganti	University of Texas at San Antonio, USA
Rajae El Ouazzani	UMI, Morocco
Richard Maliwatu	University of Cape Town, South Africa
Roderick Fanou	CAIDA/UC San Diego, USA
Senka Hadzic	Research ICT Africa, South Africa
Serge Payet	Helix Security, Mauritius
Shree Om	Cape Peninsula University of Technology, South Africa
Umar Sa'ad	Chung-Ang University, South Korea
Visham Ramsurrun	Middlesex University Mauritius, Mauritius
Yahya Slimani	University of Manouba, Tunisia
Younes Balboul	USMBA- ENSA Fez, Morocco
Zeid Kootbally	University of Southern California, USA

Contents

Internet of Things

e-Services and Big Data

DNS Resilience and Performance

Dynamic Spectrum Access and Mesh Networks

TV White Spaces Regulatory Framework for Kenya: An Overview and Comparison with Other Regulations in Africa

Kennedy Ronoh[1(✉)], Leonard Mabele[2], and Dennis Sonoiya[3]

[1] Technical University of Kenya, Nairobi, Kenya
`kennedy.ronoh@tukenya.ac.ke`
[2] Strathmore University, Nairobi, Kenya
`lmabele@strathmore.edu`
[3] University of Strathclyde, Glasgow, UK
`dennis.sonoiya@strath.ac.uk`

Abstract. Dynamic spectrum management is gradually becoming a viable approach for use by national regulatory authorities (NRAs) in administering usage of the radiofrequency spectrum. The concept has proven to be efficient in managing secondary access to television white spaces by permitting white space devices, under the control of geolocation databases. Kenya conducted its first white space trial in 2013 under a static model, which demonstrated the opportunity that could be harnessed in using the lower UHF band to provide broadband internet access in underserved areas, with no harmful interference to the digital terrestrial television service. In the subsequent years, the administration of Kenya permitted multiple trials, of various models, to build a case for adoption of dynamic spectrum access techniques in the UHF band and to drive deployments of white space devices. The Communications Authority of Kenya recently published a framework setting out key aspects for access to white spaces including the algorithms to determine coexistence parameters, that was modified off the dynamic spectrum alliance's model rules. This paper presents an overview of the regulatory framework for use of TV white spaces in Kenya and compares it with other frameworks adopted by African countries and other selected countries globally. The paper further gives recommendations on the path to adoption and implementation of the dynamic spectrum management for national regulatory authorities in Africa.

Keywords: TV White Spaces · Spectrum management · Dynamic Spectrum Access · White Space Devices · Regulations

1 Introduction

The effective management of radiofrequency spectrum requires the active involvement of key stakeholders from standardisation bodies, infrastructure and

R. Zitouni et al. (Eds.): AFRICOMM 2020, LNICST 361, pp. 3–22, 2021.
https://doi.org/10.1007/978-3-030-70572-5_1

service providers, regulatory authorities, equipment manufacturers, spectrum users to academic and industrial researchers [1]. The International Telecommunications Union (ITU) is the specialised United Nations agency for information and communication services, which has a key role in promoting global harmonisation of spectrum allocation. The radiocommunication bureau of the ITU performs activities related to the development of recommendations pertaining to spectrum use by various services as well as periodically updating the radio regulations through regular Radiocommunication Conferences [1]. Regional bodies are also in place to ensure that ITU-R spectrum allocations are adhered to and that there is harmonisation across a specific region. These regional spectrum regulatory groups cover all the continents. At the national level, spectrum management is predominantly under a National Regulatory Authority (NRA), whose role is to regulate spectrum use within their jurisdiction in line with national policies, regional treaties as well as ITU radio regulations and recommendations.

The rise in the demand for wireless broadband services is gradually turning the radiofrequency spectrum into a scarce resource. The fixed spectrum allocation approach traditionally favoured by NRAs leaves portions of spectrum underutilised. Spectrum occupancy evaluations done worldwide show that large portions of spectrum allocated to certain primary users is not activated in many locations within a licensed coverage area [2]. Under a fixed spectrum allocation regime, the primary user has exclusive spectrum rights defined by the provided license on the assigned spectrum. The NRA publishes spectrum assignment plans and issues periodic reports on the usage of frequency bands on the national table of frequency allocations.

Licenses are granted through auction, administrative or incentive pricing schemes [3]. This static licensing regime, hence, limits other users (secondary users) to opportunistically make use of the primary-based assigned frequencies even when they are insufficiently utilised. Secondary access to spectrum is also known as Dynamic Spectrum Access (DSA) or opportunistic spectrum access [4]. The UHF TV (470–694 MHz) spectrum band has been the subject of most research initiatives to develop a dynamic spectrum access (DSA) model that permits secondary users to coexist with primary users through the utilisation of TV White Spaces (TVWS) to provide fixed and mobile Internet access services in underserved areas. This band is particularly prime for rural internet service provision due to its good propagation characteristics over irregular terrain.

TVWS trials have been conducted worldwide to demonstrate and test the use of dynamic spectrum access (DSA) technology, with key trials determining that Digital Terrestrial Transmission (DTT) was not adversely affected by secondary access to the unused TV spectrum. NRAs worldwide have already opened up TVWS for DSA following the success of TVWS trials. Standards have also been developed to make use of this technology. Among the standards are IEEE 802.11af which implements spectrum sensing and IEEE 802.22 which assimilates geolocation database implementation. A number of use cases emanating from the use of TVWS are already gaining ground. Some of them include rural broadband access [4], Internet of Things (IoT) and machine-to-machine communications (M2M) cellular networks and vehicle-to-vehicle communications.

The Communications Authority of Kenya (CA) plans to authorise the commercial deployments for TVWS, for fixed broadband services and for IoT applications, in the 470–694 MHz UHF spectrum band. Currently, the band is allocated to the Digital Terrestrial Television (DTT) broadcasting service on a primary basis as provided in the National Table of Frequency Allocations. To achieve this, a regulatory framework has been developed and is currently under interim approval as at the time of writing this paper. White space devices (WSDs) will operate on non-protected, non-interference and non-exclusive basis. The main aim of developing the regulatory framework is to allow the use of TVWS for rural broadband access.

This paper has three objectives. The first objective is to give an overview of the TVWS regulations for Kenya based on the already developed regulatory framework. The second is to analyse and compare the Kenyan regulations with other regulations in Africa as well as against those of the United States of America, the United Kingdom regulations as well as Singapore and Canada. The final objective is to make recommendations for additional considerations within the regulations.

The rest of the paper is organised as follows. Section 2 discusses the availability of TVWS in Kenya. Section 3 discusses the TVWS trials in Kenya. Section 4 presents an overview of TVWS regulatory framework for Kenya. Section 5 provides an analysis and comparison of TVWS regulatory framework for Kenya with other regulations in Africa and worldwide. Section 6 provides recommendations. Section 7 concludes the paper.

2   Availability of TV White Spaces in Kenya

Kenya completed its digital switchover in June 2015, ushering in an era of DTT in the UHF Band IV (470–694 MHz). A detailed quantitative assessment conducted by the Communications Authority of Kenya (CA) reveals that 28 channels (channel 21 to 48) of 8 MHz bandwidth, assigned for DTT services in Kenya are not fully used at every location and therefore can be opportunistically exploited for TVWS.

Recent measurements conducted in Kisumu, Laikipia and Kitui counties in January and February 2020 by a team of Kenyan researchers working together with CA show that there is plenty of unutilised frequencies in the terrestrial TV broadcasting in Kenya. In Kisumu County, out of the 18 channels assigned for broadcasting, 8 channels were found to be unused or not active. Cumulatively, this demonstrates that 144 MHz is available for TVWS in Kisumu. Figure 1 shows the availability of TVWS in Kisumu county. In both Kitui and Laikipia counties, only four channels have active transmissions out of 9 assigned DTT channels. This means that there are a total of 24 channels available for secondary use (out of a total of 28 channels in the TV spectrum) with a total bandwidth of 192 MHz. This unutilised spectrum can be used for rural broadband access.

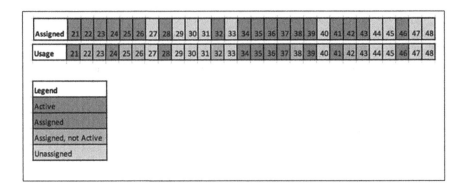

Fig. 1. TV White Spaces availability in Kisumu County, Kenya.

3   TV White Space Trials in Kenya

The CA authorised multiple trials to test the viability of TVWS in Kenya since 2013. The objectives for the trials were to test the capability and viability of the TVWS technology for Kenya as well as undertake the coexistence testing and ensure a low probability of harmful interference to DTT transmissions, which are the incumbent services.

Kenya conducted its first TVWS trial in September 2013, when Microsoft East Africa under the Microsoft 4Afrika initiative was authorised to test the technology with Indigo Telecom for one year. Other partners on the project included Adaptrum and the University of Strathclyde. The trial was conducted in the vicinity of Nanyuki, Laikipia County of Kenya [5]. The trial project was given the name "Mawingu Project".

The execution of this trial did not result in any interference to the existing broadcasting services or assigned services within the bands that were used. Following up to this trial, more trial scenarios were conducted driven by collaborations between – network facilities providers (NFPs) and geolocation database (GDB) providers as well as broadcast signal distributors (BSDs). Table 1 outlines a summary of the trials conducted in Kenya leading to the development of the TVWS regulatory framework.

The findings of these studies were the output of the various TVWS experiments authorised in Kenya as per Table 1. While the initial experiments were conducted without integration to a GDB, the findings still demonstrated no interference to the DTT services. Experiments from 2017 onwards made use of a GDB. The findings of these experiments focused on finding out the available frequencies for TVWS use as measured by CA, operating EIRP, coverage distances and any instances of interference as described in three major trials of 2013, 2018 and 2020 in this paper.

Table 1. TV White Space trials in Kenya.

	Start (and Duration)	Operator	Affiliate NFP	Authorised locations	Database providers and equipment vendor
1	September 2013 (1 year)	Microsoft East Africa	Indigo Telcom	Kajiado and Laikipia	6Harmonics and Adaptrum
2	November 2014 (1 year)	Mawingu Networks	-	Laikipia	6Harmonics, Adaptrum and Nominet
3	November 2016 (1 year)	Pan Africa Network Group Kenya	-	Countrywide	Static Model proposed (No Database)
4	November 2016 (1 year)	Signet Signal Distributor	Mawingu Networks	Countrywide	Static Model proposed (No Database)
5	March 2019 (6 Months)	Mawingu Networks	-	Embu	Adaptrum, Redline and Fairspectrum

3.1   The 2013 TVWS Experiment (Nanyuki)

This was the first Kenyan TVWS experiment. It covered an area of $235\,\mathrm{km}^2$ from three TVWS sectors, each transmitting at 1 W EIRP from 90° 10 dBi UHF sector antennae at heights of 8 to 18 m. The findings provided a throughput of approximately $3 \times 16\,\mathrm{Mbps}$ with no interference experienced to the DTT services. Notably, this experiment leveraged 5.4 GHz microwave backhaul links and the base stations used ran on solar (offgrid) power. Figure 2 shows one of the setups using a 6Harmonics GW 300 base station backhauled by a microwave link at Gakawa Secondary School in Nanyuki, Kenya. This experiment was able to support uninterrupted video conferencing and streaming as well as high speed VPN services.

3.2   The 2018 Experiment (Nanyuki)

This TVWS experiment was conducted with an integration to a geolocation database (GDB) for the first time in Kenya. The database used was from Nominet, a GDB service provider operating in the UK. The base station used was an Adaptrum ACRS 2.0 flushed with the 2018 upgrade of the protocol to access white space databases (PAWS). Manual coordinates were used in this experiment but still demonstrated no interference to the DTT services. No out of band (OOB) emission was experienced as well.

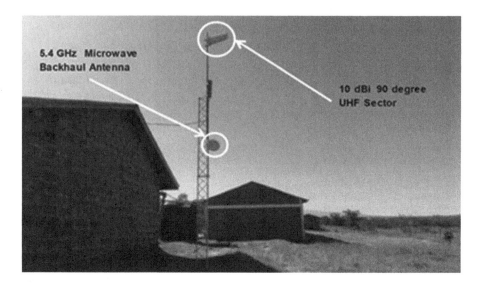

Fig. 2. TVWS Experiment in Nanyuki in 2018.

3.3 The 2020 Experiment (Within Laikipia)

The 2020 experiment was conducted around Nanyuki town using one Adaptrum B1000 base station and four ACRS2 client radios. The client radios were set up in four different locations, each having a directional antenna of 11 dBi gain. The base station transmitted in a 120° sector and the entire links operated in a time-division duplex mode between the base station and the client radios, all in a shared 8 MHz bandwidth channel. During the experiments, no incident of harmful interference was detected

4 Overview of the TVWS Regulatory Framework for Kenya

This section presents an overview of the regulatory framework for TVWS in Kenya. Figure 3 shows the architecture of the TVWS regulatory framework.

4.1 Dynamic Spectrum Access Method

The regulatory framework for TVWS, which is under final review as at the time of writing this paper, evokes that the commercial rollout for TVWS in Kenya will implement the usage of the geolocation databases (GDBs) for spectrum sharing with DTT services as opposed to spectrum sensing. The transmission of White Space Devices (WSDs) will be controlled by a GDB. The GDB providers will have to be qualified by the Communication Authority of Kenya (CA) to ensure that they comply with the procedures for TV White space transmission. Notably,

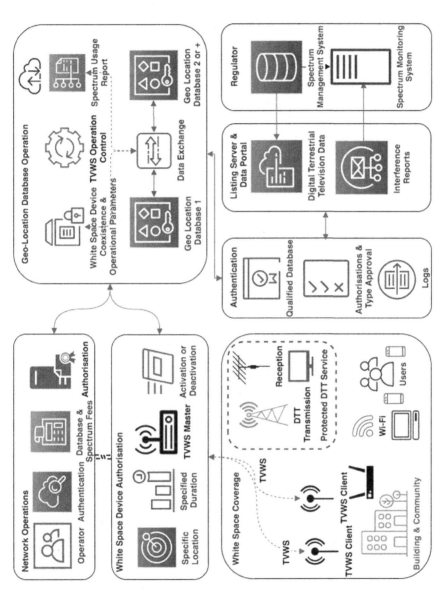

Fig. 3. DSA framework and GDB architecture for TVWS in Kenya.

as part of implementing the TVWS framework, CA has also released the procedure for qualification of the Geolocation Databases (GDBs). The procedures spell a three-phase approval process which involves an application, evaluation and testing and finally qualification. Once a GDB provider has been qualified, the GDB will be listed on the listing server managed by the CA, matching the requirements spelt out in the Protocol to Access of White-Space (PAWS) Databases.

4.2 Licensing Model

Three possible licensing regimes were considered in the regulatory framework; license-exempt, light licensing or full licensing [6]. In a license-exempt regime, no regulatory record is kept of which devices are using RF channels. The disadvantage of this regime is that it poses a risk of interference to broadcasting services if it is to be applied to a TVWS network because it is not possible to identify and locate a device if it causes interference and no protection is provided between TVWS devices.

Full licensing, according to the regulatory framework, means a WSD is charged a fee as a function of the area covered and the duration of usage, the parameters are calculated by a GDB, populated with technical data. In such a model, protection is provided between WSDs. Thus, if one device causes interference to another licensed device, the interfering device may be instructed to change channels or to cease transmission.

In a lightly-licensed model, every master WSD is registered and fully controlled by a GDB. In the event of interference to the primary licensee being detected, the offending devices can be instructed to cease transmission on a particular channel. The network operator requires annual authorisation to operate and pays for the GDB service and a nominal fee for the use of the RF spectrum. CA has adopted a lightly licensing model of service for the implementation of TVWS in Kenya.

4.3 TVWS Spectrum Fees

Under the proposed regulatory framework, TVWS network operation will not be cost-free since the regulator will incur some administrative costs. Some of the costs include the following: update of DTT data portal to enable calculation of TV white spaces, and selection, qualification and regulation of GDBs. Dynamic radio systems such as white space applications are considered to be under non-protected wireless access systems classification in the frequency spectrum fee schedule.

In the regulatory framework, the authority has proposed a fee in line with the frequency spectrum fee schedule and Kenya Information and Communications (Radio Communications and Frequency Spectrum Regulations, 2010). Each authorised WSD will be subjected to an annual fee of KSh. 10,000.00 (approximately $100). This will be reviewed periodically. A potential future costing model being considered by CA is a model that has geographical zones according to population density.

4.4   Geolocation Database Architecture

In order to be qualified to operate, a geolocation database shall be required to have a standard architecture as indicated in Fig. 3. The GDB should be a production-grade, cloud-based system designed to interface with the regulatory authority's spectrum management system in order to determine availability and allow control of secondary access to spectrum white spaces.

The GDB should be compatible with global datasets and be customisable or localised for different regulatory rulesets and models with advanced mapping, planning, and spectrum investigation tools. The GDB should have the computational ability to process algorithms for TVWS coexistence rules based on the Dynamic Spectrum Alliance model; with customisable parameters of a terrain-based radio signal propagation model (including ITU-R 1812).

The GDB should also be able to guarantee the protection of licensed primary services and perform impact analysis of various scenarios based on the rules while adopting advanced planning tools for accurate feasibility studies prior to identification of spectrum for use by the white space devices. It is also mandatory that a GDB should have an interface for DTT transmitter's information update from the regulator's spectrum management database, ideally over SOAP web services. A standard and secure interface should be available on the GDB for certified radios to connect to the database over the protocol to access white spaces (IETF PAWS) [7]. The interface should also have WSD monitoring tools and capability to determine in-channel interference incidents and have a technique to resolve and report to the regulator's spectrum monitoring system. Providers of GDB services should also issue a graphical user interface for monitoring of spectrum utilisation, device management, management of interference and the protected areas as well as a regulator interface that manages and enforces operation of WSDs in accordance with the regulations of TVWS. Moreover, operational logs should periodically be made available to the regulatory authority for every WSD. This should include the initial requests, activation authorisation, aggregate spectrum usage and deactivation incidents. The GDB provider must adhere to the applicable data protection legislation in the country or jurisdiction of operation.

4.5   Eligible Operators

Operators interested in rolling out a TVWS network shall be eligible if they hold a Network Facilities Provider License (Tiers 1, 2 & 3), a Broadcasting Signal Distributor License or a Self-Provisioning Broadcasting License to use TVWS spectrum. Network Facilities Provider Licensee means a licensee authorised by the Authority to build and commercially operate telecommunication or electronic communications systems. Broadcasting Signal Distributor License authorises a licensee to roll out and operate infrastructure for transmission of digital TV and radio broadcasting services. A Self-Provisioning Broadcasting Signal Distribution license is a license that allows an entity to roll out its network or utilise its existing infrastructure network to carry its content. However, the entity will, in addition, be required to have a broadcast content license.

4.6   Maximum Transmit Power

To prevent harmful interference to primary users, maximum power limits shall be specified for each channel at every permitted location. Maximum power limits will also be informed by coexistence calculations. In the regulatory framework, the maximum transmit power has been set to 42 dBm (10 W).

4.7   White Space Devices Coexistence Considerations

DTT broadcast transmissions in the 470–694 MHz are to be protected from harmful interference from secondary transmissions and the adjacent mobile services. To achieve this, the WSD maximum power shall be restricted. Table 1 summarises the coexistence rules for different user types.

Table 2. Coexistence rules for the Kenya DSA framework.

Existing use type	Co-existence solution
Broadcasting service	Maximum power limits to WSDs required protecting DTT broadcasting-service
Broadcasting service (neighbouring countries)	Maximum power limits to constrain interference to neighbouring countries transmissions
Mobile service (450–470 MHz)	Maximum power limits to WSD to limit out of band emissions
Mobile service (700 MHz)	9 MHz guard band to ensure that there is no interference from WSDs

4.8   Device Characteristics and Other Parameters

Under the regulatory framework, manually configured master WSDs will not be allowed to operate. An example is a WSD that requires manual input of geographic coordinates and certain operational parameters. To avoid the risk of harmful interference, the WSDs operation will need to be in line with the minimum technical and operational parameters that are defined in ETSI standards 102, 103 and 301 as well as the DSA model rules and regulations for TV white spaces. All models of WSDs will have to be type-approved by CA before their initial activation for use.

4.9   Exchange of Parameters Between WSD and GDB

After a master WSD establishes communication with a GDB, it will communicate its device parameters. The GDB will then use the device parameters to compute the operational parameters that will be used by the device i.e. the channels available and the maximum transmit power. The master device will then select the operational parameters to use and report as channel usage parameters. If a master device has some client devices under its control, it will obtain generic operational parameters from the GDB, the generic operational parameters are restrictive compared to the normal operational parameters. After the master device receives the generic operational parameters from the GDB, it will broadcast to the client devices under its control. After listening to the master WSD broadcast, the client WSDs will obtain the generic operational parameters which will be used during initial communication with the master WSD. In the initial communication, the client WSDs will send device parameters to the master device. The master WSD will then send the device parameters received from each client to the GDB to compute the operational parameters for each specific client. The master WSD will continuously report the channel usage parameters to the GDB, whether specific or generic operational parameters.

4.10   Interference Management

It is expected that the coexistence rules outlined in the framework will prevent harmful interference to primary DTT service. The following provisions may be used to manage harmful interference that may arise: 1. Broadcasters, consumers, network operators and GDB providers shall report any cases of harmful interference. 2. GDB providers may be ordered to cease providing services. 3. CA may directly blacklist an offending WSD, via a regulator interface made available to the CA by the GDB providers.

5   Analysis and Comparison of Kenya TV White Space Framework with Other Frameworks in Africa

Several countries in Africa have embraced TVWS technology and have already developed frameworks to allow the use of technology. Kenya [4], South Africa [8,9], Ghana [4] and Botswana [10] have also launched trials in the recent past to assess the performance of the technology. Countries in Africa that have already developed TVWS regulatory frameworks include the following: Uganda, Nigeria, South Africa, Malawi and Ghana. Additionally, the Kenyan framework is compared to that of USA and UK. In this section, regulatory frameworks for the mentioned countries are compared and analysed. Recommendations for additional considerations are also made. Tables 3 and 4 shows a comparison of the frameworks.

Table 3. Comparison of TVWS frameworks.

Issue	Kenya [11]	Malawi [12]	South Africa [13]	Uganda [14]	Ghana [15]	Nigeria [16]	USA [17]	UK [18]
Licensing mode	Light licensing	Licence exempt and Licensed	License exempt	Licensed	License exempt	Licensed and license-exempt	License exempt	License exempt
Spectrum band	470–694 MHz	470–694 MHz	470–694 MHz excluding radio astronomy services in 606–614 MHz	470–694 MHz	470–694 MHz	470–694 MHz	Fixed devices only: VHF band (54–72 MHz, 76–78 MHz, 174–216 MHz) Both fixed and portable devices: UHF band (490–698 MHz)	UHF band only (470 to 606 MHz, and 614–782 MHz)
Equipment standards and other reference standards	ETSI EN 301 598 V1.1.1 (2014-04)	FCC standards of 2012	ETSI EN 301 598, PAWS	IEEE 802.11af, IEEE 802.22 and ETSI EN 301 598.	FCC standards	ETSI EN 301 598 V2.1.1 (2018-01)	FCC standards of 2012	ETSI EN 301 598 V1.1.1 (2014-04)
Validity period of parameters	24 h or if the device moves more than100m	Provided by database as part of operational parameters.	24 h for fixed devices, 12 h for portable devices or if it moves 100 m	Database to update master and client when no longer parameters valid.	24 h for fixed devices, 12 h for portable devices or if it moves 100 m	Provided by database as part of operational parameters.	48 h	Provided by the database as part of operational parameters
Channel aggregation	Allowed – up to three	Not specified	Not specified	Allowed	Not specified	Allowed	Allowed for fixed devices	Not specified
Installers	Not specified	Not specified	Accreditation required	Not specified	Not specified	Accreditation required	Accreditation required	Not specified

Table 4. Comparison of TVWS frameworks.

Issue	Kenya [11]	Malawi [12]	South Africa [13]	Uganda [14]	Ghana [15]	Nigeria [16]	USA [17]	UK [18]
DSA method	GDB	GDB	GDB	GDB	GDB and spectrum sensing	GDB	GDB and spectrum sensing	GDB
GDB implementation	Propagation model approach using ITU-R 1812	Propagation model approach	Propagation model approach	Propagation model approach	Protected contour approach	Propagation model approach	Protected contour approach	Location probability
Maximum power	16 W	4 W	10 W for fixed devices, 100 mW for portable devices	4 W for fixed devices, 100 mW for portable devices	10 W in rural areas, 4 W in urban areas	1 W for fixed devices, 50 mW for IoT devices	10 W	10 W
Coexistence considerations	Protection of mobile services and neighbouring countries	Not specified	Protection of astronomy services	Not specified	Not specified	Not specified	Protection of mobile services and neighbouring countries	Protection of mobile services and neighbouring countries
Maximum antenna height	50 m	Not specified	80 m in rural areas, 30 m in urban areas	50 m	30 m	100 m above ground level, 250 m HAAT	30 m	30 m
Fees	Applicable – Same as for ISM	Applicable – as prescribed by the commission	Not specified	Applicable – as prescribed by the commission	Applicable - same as for ISM band	No fees specified	None	None
Approval status	Interim approval	Published	Published	Published	Published	Draft	Published	Published
Types of devices	Master and slave	Master and slave	Master and slave	Master and slave	Fixed, Mode I, Mode II	Master, slave, IoT	Fixed, Mode I, Mode II	Master and slave

5.1   Spectrum Band

The spectrum band that has been set aside for TV White Space network operation in Africa is 470–694 MHz. This is in line with ITU-R regulations. In South Africa, the spectrum band will exclude astronomy services operating in 606–614 MHz band.

To meet the increasing demand for spectrum, there is a need to extend regulatory frameworks to allow dynamic access to other spectrum bands. This is especially useful for upcoming 5G networks [19,20] which has many use cases such as IoT, vehicle to vehicle communications and machine to machine communications. Additional bands that can be considered for DSA are the 1800 MHz mobile band, 700 MHz mobile band, 6 GHz band, lower 26 GHz spectrum band and 3.8–4.2 GHz band.

5.2   Licensing Approach

Most regulations in Africa have adopted the light licensing approach. Although some regulations state "license-exempt" and/or licensed, it implies light licensing because all WSDs have to register with the database and have to pay a nominal fee. Light licensing is appropriate because it will allow ease of control of interference problems that may arise as well as regulation of operation of TVWS network providers.

5.3   WSD Transmit Maximum Power

Fixed, portable and IoT devices maximum transmit power are specified differently. They are discussed separately. For Fixed devices, the maximum transmit power adopted by Kenya is 16 W EIRP. In the South African and Ghanaain regulations, the maximum power is set to 10 W just like in the USA and UK regulations. In the Ghanaain regulations, 10 W is the maximum power for rural areas and for urban areas the maximum power is 4 W. In Nigeria the maximum allowed power is 1 W. For the Portable devices, Only Uganda and South Africa have set maximum power for personal and portable devices at 100 mW EIRP. The IoT devices have an explicit mention in the Nigerian rules which state separate EIRP limits at 50 mW (17 dBm). In the Kenyan regulations, a 42 dBm limit applies to all devices.

The intention of setting maximum power is to protect DTT against harmful interference. In rural areas where there are few DTT services, the maximum power can be increased due to less risk of harmful interference. The regulations that have set their maximum to transmit power to 10 W and 4 W can review their maximum power upwards to 16 W. To limit interference the maximum power for urban areas that are congested can be set to 4 W (36 dBm) and maximum power for rural and less congested areas can be set to 16 W (42 dBm). The increased power for rural areas is especially useful for terrains that pose signal propagation challenges. Recent studies show that 42 dBm (30 dBm conducted power with 12 dBi antenna gain) seems to offer an optimum balance between greater coverage and larger antenna sizes and higher equipment costs, which both also increase with higher gain [21, 22].

Uganda and South Africa have specifically provided that portable devices that will have a maximum power of 100 mW can consider higher maximum power of up to 16 W but under the condition of geofencing and only in less congested rural areas. Geofencing has recently been provided for personal/portable devices under USA regulations [22]. Geofencing means a personal/portable is limited to operate at a certain fixed area with a certain maximum power as provided by the GDB. Examples are the fixed transportable WSD operations such as tractors or other movable machines that are used for farming and that can enable IoT-based agriculture.

5.4   Maximum Antenna Height

Kenya and Ghana have set the maximum antenna height at 50 m and 30 m, respectively. South Africa regulations have set the maximum antenna height at 80 m for rural areas and 30 m for urban areas. Uganda has set a maximum antenna height of 50 m. Nigeria has set the maximum antenna height as 100 m above ground level and 250 m Height Above Average Terrain (HAAT).

To avoid the risk of harmful interference different maximum antenna heights can be set for rural and urban areas like what the South Africa regulations provide. Higher antenna heights can also be considered by other countries especially for rural areas. 250 m HAAT can be considered by other regulations to allow ease of coverage of rural less congested areas with challenging signal propagation environment. Recently, Microsoft proposeda maximum antenna height of 500 m HAAT for rural areas of the USA, that are far off coverage of certain channels of DTT transmitters [22]. This is a proposal that can also be considered by TVWS regulations in Africa.

5.5   Spectrum Sharing Method

The majority of African regulations on the use of TV white spaces adopted the GDB approach, except Ghana which permitted spectrum sensing in addition to the use of GDBs. The GDB approach is considered more reliable than spectrum sensing which is seen to suffer from a hidden node problem [4].

5.6   GDB Implementation

Most regulations make use of a propagation model in the database implementation. Only Ghana makes use of the contour-based approach like the USA regulations. UK regulations have taken the location probability implementation approach. The decision by Ghana to use a contour-based approach is too restrictive and will lead to wastage of TVWS. This is because the approach requires that there be a protection distance between a WSD and the DTT. None of the regulations in Africa has adopted the UK approach, because its location probability approach is computationally intensive and is based on continuously stored UK data.

The geolocation propagation model specified in the Kenya regulations is ITU-R 1812. This is because it is a path-specific propagation prediction method for point-to-area terrestrial services in the VHF and UHF bands, which is more accurate than other models such as Longley Rice. Other regulator frameworks can also consider the ITU-R 1812 propagation model.

5.7   Coexistence Rules

Interference in TVWS networks is the main limiting factor for spectrum re-use. TVWS can be used as long as interference does not exceed a certain threshold beyond which there will be harmful interference. The specified maximum limits are set to ensure co-existence between WSDs and DTT transmission as well as co-existence among WSDs in a TVWS network. In the Kenyan framework, a 9 MHz guard band has been specified to protect mobile services that operate in the 700 MHz band. The Kenyan regulations also specify that the maximum power limits are to limit out of band emissions that may affect the operation of mobile services in the same band. Most regulations under consideration have also specified limits on out band (OOB) emissions. This is necessary to limit adjacent channel interference. Adjacent channel interference refers to interference to a TV receiver from WSDs operating in the adjacent channel. Most regulations have adopted ETSI 301598 standard requirement that specifies maximum out of band emissions for different classes of devices. The out-of-block EIRP spectral density (P_{OOB}), for most regulations, of a WSD has been set to satisfy the following limit:

$$P_{OOB}(dBm)/(100\,\text{kHz}) \leq$$
$$max\{P_{IB}(dBm/(8\,\text{MHz})) - ACLR(dB), \qquad (1)$$
$$-84(dBm/(100\ \text{kHz}))\}$$

where P_{IB} is the measured in-block EIRP spectral density over 8 MHz, and ACLR is the Adjacent Channel Leakage Ratio for different Device Emission Classes outlined in Table 5. Only Uganda regulations have not incorporated this requirement. This can lead to undesired adjacent channel interference.

Concerns have been raised recently over the impact of aggregate interference on DTT transmission and among WSDs [23]. In a TVWS network, interference could be due to either co-channel interference or adjacent channel interference. The given maximum power limits may not be sufficient to protect DTT transmission against the combined effects of aggregate interference especially for TVWS dense scenarios such as cellular access to TV white spaces [24] and IoT [8]. Recent studies have shown that aggregate adjacent channel interference from multiple transmitters has the same effect as co-channel interference [25].

Only the Ghanaain regulatory framework has specifically stated that transmit power control for WSDs is required. This is specified as follows in the Ghana framework: "Transmitted Power Control – A TVWS device shall incorporate transmit power control to limit its operating power to the minimum necessary for successful communication to be completed". This will help limit aggregate interference. This can be considered by other frameworks in Africa.

Optimisation of power and spectrum allocation [26] is another potential solution that can be adopted in the regulatory frameworks to limit the potentially harmful effects of aggregate interference.

Table 5. ACLR for different device emission classes.

Where POOB falls within the nth adjacent DTT channel (based on 8 MHz channels)	ACLR (dB)				
	Class 1	Class 2	Class 3	Class 4	Class 5
$n = \pm 1$	74	74	64	54	43
$n = \pm 2$	74	74	64	54	43
$n = \pm 3$	74	74	64	54	43

5.8   Channel Validity Period

The channel validity period for most of the regulations in Africa is 24 h. In the Malawi and Uganda regulations, it is provided as part of the operational parameters. In Nigeria regulations, devices will operate until they are notified that the parameters are no longer valid.

5.9   Channel Aggregation

Channel aggregation refers to a combination of more than one TVWS channel. In the Africa regulations under consideration, TV channels are 8 MHz. This is beneficial because it will lead to higher throughput. Only Kenya, Uganda and Nigeria regulations have specifically stated that channel aggregation will be allowed. The other countries should consider incorporating the same.

5.10   Border Areas

WSDs must operate in a manner that will not cause harmful interference to broadcast and other services in neighbouring countries. Nigeria and Ghana regulations require that all signals reaching Ghana border must have a noise floor level of −115 dBm. Uganda has not made any provisions for transmissions near border areas. Malawi regulations state, "Where a white space device operates along border areas, a licensee shall ensure that the device does not cause interference to other services from neighbouring countries". Regulations that have no incorporated protection of interference in border areas need to do so to ensure the protection of neighbouring countries DTT transmissions.

5.11 Approval Status of Regulations

Most regulations under consideration have been published. Only Malawi and Nigeria are still having their regulations in the draft stage.

6 Recommended Critical Success Factors for Development of Dynamic Spectrum Management Frameworks

Over the course of the development of Kenya's dynamic spectrum management framework for use of TV white spaces, important lessons were learnt that could be applied by other NRAs that intend to develop similar regulatory frameworks. Several critical success factors were especially important during the process and are recommended for adoption. Firstly, it was learnt leant that it is vital to conduct regular stakeholder engagement and actively involve academic and industrial researchers in the process to incorporate their relevant input. Secondly, fostering an enabling legal and regulatory policy environment to permit alternative approaches to spectrum management was of paramount importance. Thirdly, due diligence assessment on international best practice was a key aspect that enabled the framework to be developed in a relatively short period of time. Lastly, the authorization and monitoring of trial network deployments was a critical factor in determining the technical parameters necessary for effective coexistence of secondary white space devices while protecting the DTT broadcasting service from harmful interference.

7 Conclusion

In this paper, an overview of Kenya's framework for the use of TV White Spaces (TVWS) is presented. TVWS experiments leading to the development of the framework for Kenya are also highlighted focusing on the major lessons learnt particularly inclined to the key requirement of not causing harmful interference to the DTT services. Similarities and variations are noted in the technical and operational requirements of TVWS across different countries as presented in this paper. They clearly point out that the secondary opportunistic utilisation of TVWS depends on the needs and contexts of each country, although guided by international standards.

TVWS is regarded as one of the potential solutions towards bridging the digital divide. However, most of the TVWS networks implemented in Africa as a first step of adopting dynamic spectrum access (DSA) have not been able to move beyond pilot projects. The seven year journey of TVWS studies in Kenya (from the 2013 trial) towards the development of the TVWS framework shows that the TVWS industry is slowly developing and there is a high likelihood of continuous technical and market evolution as DSA grows. This might lead to immediate future regulatory changes even before many commercial deployments of TVWS take off on the African continent. More DSA work based on the TVWS regulations for Kenya will be published in the future studies.

References

1. Matinmikko, M., et al.: Overview and comparison of recent spectrum sharing approaches in regulation and research: from opportunistic unlicensed access towards licensed shared access. In: 2014 IEEE International Symposium on Dynamic Spectrum Access Networks (DYSPAN), pp. 92–102. IEEE, McLean (2014). https://doi.org/10.1109/DySPAN.2014.6817783
2. Patil, K., Prasad, R., Souby, K.: A survey of worldwide spectrum occupancy measurement campaigns for cognitive radio. In: International Conference on Devices and Communications (ICDeCom), pp. 1–5. IEEE, Mesra (2011). https://doi.org/10.1109/ICDECOM.2011.5738472
3. Cristian, G.: TV white spaces: managing spaces or better managing inefficiencies. In: Pietrosemoli, P., Zennaro, M. (eds.) TV White Spaces: A Pragmatic Approach (2013)
4. Kennedy, R., George, K., Vitalice, O., Okello-Odongo, W.: TV white spaces in Africa: trials and role in improving broadband access in Africa. In: AFRICON 2015, pp. 1–5. IEEE, Addis Ababa (2015). https://doi.org/10.1109/AFRCON.2015.7331920
5. Rural Broadband TVWS Trial in Laikipia County Kenya. https://docplayer.net/5987593-Rural-broadband-trials-laikipia-county-kenya-for-the-communications-authority-of-kenya.html. Accessed 20 Oct 2020
6. European Communications Commission (ECC): Light Licensing, Licence-Exempt And Commons. https://docdb.cept.org/download/87ccb237-fa9a/ECCREP132.PDF. Accessed 20 Oct 2020
7. Chen, V., Das, S., Zhu, L., Malyar, J., McCann, P.: Protocol to access white-space (PAWS) databases. https://tools.ietf.org/html/rfc7545. Accessed 20 Oct 2020
8. Steven, S.: Studies on the Use of TV White Spaces in South Africa: recommendations and Learnings. http://www.tenet.ac.za/tvws/recommendations-and-learnings-from-the-cape-town-tv-white-spaces-trialF. Accessed 20 Oct 2020
9. Masonta, M.T., Kola, L.M., Lysko, A.A., Pieterse, L., Velempini, M.: Network performance analysis of the Limpopo TV white space (TVWS) trial network. In: AFRICON 2015, pp. 1–5. IEEE, Addis Ababa (2015). https://doi.org/10.1109/AFRCON.2015.7331923
10. Ndlovu, K., Mbero, Z.A., Kovarik, C.L., Patel, A.: Network performance analysis of the television white space (TVWS) connectivity for telemedicine: a case for Botswana. In: AFRICON 2017, pp. 542–547. IEEE, Cape Town (2017). https://doi.org/10.1109/AFRCON.2017.8095539
11. Communication Authority of Kenya: Authorisation of the Use of TV White Spaces - Kenya. https://ca.go.ke/wp-content/uploads/2020/03/Authorisation-of-the-use-of-TV-White-Spaces-min.pdf. Accessed 20 Oct 2020
12. Nyasulu, T., Crawford, D.H., Mikeka, C.: Malawi's TV white space regulations: a review and comparison with FCC and Ofcom regulations. In: 2018 IEEE Wireless Communications and Networking Conference (WCNC), pp. 1–6. IEEE, Barcelona (2018). https://doi.org/10.1109/WCNC.2018.8377175
13. ICASA: Regulations on the use of TV White Spaces - South Africa. https://www.icasa.org.za/legislation-and-regulations/regulations-on-the-use-of-television-white-spaces-2018. Accessed 20 Oct 2020
14. UCC: TV White Space Guidelines for Uganda. https://www.ucc.co.ug/wp-content/uploads/2017/09/TVWS-Guidelines-for-Consultation-9th-July-2018_v2.pdf. Accessed 20 Oct 2020

15. NCA: Guidelines for the Operation of Data Services using Television White Spaces (TVWS) in Ghana. https://www.nca.org.gh/assets/Uploads/Guidelines-for-TVWS-Data-Services.pdf. Accessed 20 Oct 2020

16. NCC: Draft Guidelines on the use of Television White Space (TVWS) in Nigeria. https://www.ncc.gov.ng/media-centre/public-notices/760-public-notice-draft-guidelines-on-the-use-of-television-white-space-tvws-in-nigeria. Accessed 20 Oct 2020

17. FCC: Amendment of Part 15 Rules for Unlicensed White Spaces Devices. https://docs.fcc.gov/public/attachments/FCC-19-24A1_Rcd.pdf. Accessed 20 Oct 2020

18. OFCOM: TV white spaces - approach to coexistence. https://www.ofcom.org.uk/consultations-and-statements/category-1/white-space-coexistence. Accessed 20 Oct 2020

19. Chávez-Santiago, R., et al.: 5G: the convergence of wireless communications. Wirel. Pers. Commun. **83**(3), 1617–1642 (2015). https://doi.org/10.1007/s11277-015-2467-2

20. Hossain, E., Niyato, D., Han Z.: Dynamic Spectrum Access and Management in Cognitive Radio Networkse. 1st edn. Cambridge University Press, Cambridge (2009). https://doi.org/10.1017/CBO9780511609909

21. DSA Comments ET Docket No. 14–165 Petition for Rulemaking. http://dynamicspectrumalliance.org/wp-content/uploads/2019/06/DSA-Comments-ET-Docket-No.-14-165-Petition-for-Rulemaking-TVWS-Microsoft-Petition-Signed.pdf. Accessed 20 Oct 2020

22. Microsoft TV White Space Proposals to FCC. https://ecfsapi.fcc.gov/file/1050380945109/White%20Spaces%20Petition%20for%20Rulemaking%20(May%203%202019).pdf. Accessed 20 Oct 2020

23. Shi, L., Sung, K.W., Zander, J.: Secondary spectrum access in TV-bands with combined co-channel and adjacent channel interference constraints. In: 2012 IEEE International Symposium on Dynamic Spectrum Access Networks (DYSPAN), pp. 452–460. IEEE, Bellevue (2012). https://doi.org/10.1109/DYSPAN.2012.6478169

24. Ruttik, K., Koufos, K., Jäntti, R.: Model for computing aggregate interference from secondary cellular network in presence of correlated shadow fading. In: 2011 IEEE 22nd International Symposium on Personal Indoor and Mobile Radio Communications (PIMRC), pp. 433–437. IEEE, Toronto (2015). https://doi.org/10.1109/PIMRC.2011.6139998

25. Obregon, E., Shi, L., Ferrer, J., Zander, J.: A model for aggregate adjacent channel interference in TV white space. In: Vehicular Technology Conference (VTC Spring), pp. 1–5. IEEE, Yokohama (2011). https://doi.org/10.1109/VETECS.2011.5956237

26. Ronoh, K.K., Kamucha, G., Omwansa, T.: Improved resource allocation for TV White Space network based on modified firefly algorithm. J. Comput. Inf. Technol. **26**(3), 167–177 (2018). https://doi.org/10.20532/cit.2018.1004074

Filtered Based UFMC Waveform Applied on Joint DVB-T2/NUC System

Anne-Carole Honfoga[1,2]($\boxtimes$), Michel Dossou[2], Péniel Dassi[2],
and Véronique Moeyaert[1]

[1] Electromagnetism and Telecommunications Department, University of Mons,
Mons, Belgium
{anne-carole.honfoga,veronique.moeyaert}@umons.ac.be
[2] LETIA (of Polytechnic School of Abomey-Calavi), University of Abomey-Calavi,
Calavi, Benin
michel.dossou@epac.uac.bj, penieldassi@gmail.com
https://web.umons.ac.be/en/
https://www.uac.bj

Abstract. The Digital Video Broadcasting-Terrestrial, second generation (DVB-T2) system is now mature and being deployed worldwide in direct deployment or in replacement of Digital Video Broadcasting-Terrestrial, first generation (DVB-T). Nevertheless, attempts to improve its performance in terms of distance to Shannon limit, Bit Error Rate (BER), Signal to Noise Ratio (SNR) or coverage are still reported in the literature. On the one hand, the authors of this paper recently reported that Universal Filtered MultiCarrier (UFMC) is, among 5G waveforms, the best compromise in terms of improvement, spectrum efficiency and complexity for the replacement of Cyclic Prefix - Orthogonal Frequency Division Multiplexing (CP-OFDM) in DVB-T2 system. On the other hand, a gain in DVB-T2 performance in Additive White Gaussian Noise and Rayleigh environments was reported in the literature using optimized Non Uniform Constellations (2D-NUCs). This paper first focuses on the maximum obtainable performance improvement of DVB-T2 CP-OFDM with NUCs in Typical Urban 6 (TU6) environment. It concentrates afterwards on the ultimate gain achievable using joint UFMC and NUCs in DVB-T2. TU6 channel is defined in DVB-T2 standard as a generic channel used in simulation to emulate an urban propagation environment. In these conditions, a gain of $0.5\,$dB (for BER $= 3.10^{-3}$) is reported in TU6 using CP-OFDM NUC 32K 256-QAM and Code Rate (CR) $= 1/2$ and $3/5$ in place of sole CP-OFDM. Also, using both technologies in conjunction, namely UFMC NUC 32K 256-QAM CR $= 1/2$ and $3/5$, a gain of $1.2\,$dB (for BER $= 3.10^{-3}$) is achievable which provides a good SNR margin e.g. to increase the emitter's coverage.

Keywords: NUC · UFMC · Urban environment · DVB-T2

This work has been carried out under support from the ARES-CCD within the framework of the PHORAN PFS project. The authors would like to thank François Rottenberg for the implemented channel method in WaveComBox Matlab Toolbox.

© ICST Institute for Computer Sciences, Social Informatics and Telecommunications Engineering 2021
Published by Springer Nature Switzerland AG 2021. All Rights Reserved
R. Zitouni et al. (Eds.): AFRICOMM 2020, LNICST 361, pp. 23–42, 2021.
https://doi.org/10.1007/978-3-030-70572-5_2

1   Introduction

DVB-T2 is the european broadcasting standard second generation which has been adopted or deployed by many countries in Europe and Africa. Due to its high flexibility in the choice of parameters and its performance compared to DVB-T, DVB-T2 has been studied in the scientific literature over the last decade in order to improve its performance and allow the broadcasters to have technical information details for the system implementation.

In this research landscape, many studies have been focused on the field trials, signal robustness (SNR improvement), channel capacity and the spectral efficiency improvement. Indeed, a common method to approach the channel capacity established by Shannon is the application of Bit Interleaved Coding Modulation (BICM) chain when designing a system [1]. This chain consists in the serial concatenation of a Forward Error Correction (FEC) code, a bit interleaver and a constellation mapper. It has namely been adopted in european standards like DVB-T2 [2], Digital Video Broadcasting - Next Generation Handheld (DVBNGH) [3] and also in next-generation terrestrial broadcast american standard Advanced Television Systems Committee, third generation (ATSC 3.0) [4]. The BICM chain firstly designed is that used in DVB-T2 and includes uniform labelled Quadrature Amplitude Modulation (QAM) constellation mapping which induces a noticeable gap between the system capacity and the Shannon limit. Indeed, these constellations approach Shannon limit very closely for low SNR, but the gap becomes more apparent for higher SNR [1].

Despite the fact that both DVB-T2 and ATSC 3.0 standards employ BICM chain, their performance are different. While QAM is used in the BICM chain for DVB-T2, Non Uniform Constellations (NUCs) are used in this chain for ATSC 3.0 system which allows this system to be closer to the Shannon limit. Conventional QAM employed signal points on a regular orthogonal grid whereas NUCs loosened this restriction. The non-uniform concept was first introduced by Foschini [5] which noted the capacity shortfall of uniform QAM and minimized symbol error rates over an Additive White Gaussian Noise (AWGN) channel by providing different constellations which offer a capacity improvement. Indeed, constellation shaping techniques can be separated into two variants: probabilistic shaping and geometrical shaping techniques. While probabilistic shaping addresses the symbol probabilities by using a shaping encoder, the geometrical shaping called NUC, modifies the location of constellation symbols. Two kinds of approaches (1D-NUCs and 2D-NUCs) have been obtained. 1D-NUCs have non-uniform distance between constellation symbols but maintain the square shape which preserves demapping complexity whereas 2D-NUCs increase this complexity by relaxing the square shape constraint. However, 2D-NUCs present better performance than QAM and 1D-NUCs [6]. Several works tackled the demapping complexity reduction of 2D-NUCs [7,8].

On the one hand, BICM brings a capacity gain using the constellation shaping approach. On the other hand, DVB-T2 still uses OFDM which is not optimum in term of spectral efficiency. Indeed, due to the Cyclic Prefix (CP) added to OFDM symbols in order to deal with channel impairment, a spectral efficiency loss is obtained. To overcome this OFDM issue, filter based waveforms proposed for 5G became suitable for DVB-T2. Bank MultiCarrier (FBMC) and UFMC present a filtering characteristic which allows them to deal with channel impairments while avoiding the CP. Thanks to a better spectral behaviour of these waveforms, FBMC has been recently proposed as an alternative to OFDM in DVB-T2 [9]. Moreover, UFMC has been considered more suitable to OFDM in DVB-T2 transmission considering the compromise between respectively their spectral efficiency as it consists in redundant part of data, their SNR gain and their complexity [10]. In comparison with the classical OFDM, UFMC presents a SNR gain of 1.2 dB at a BER of 10^{-3}. On the other hand, the performance gain of 2D-NUCs have been previously highlighted with AWGN and Rayleigh channel models for DVB-T2 [11]. In order to evaluate the maximum reachable gain with constellation shaping technique and multicarrier modulation, the joint use of 2D-NUCs employed in terrestrial broadcasting system ATSC 3.0 and 5G waveform (UFMC) (called DVB-T2/UFMC/NUC) has been proposed for DVB-T2 transmission as the sole use of 2D-NUCs and UFMC respectively allow the increasing of DVB-T2 system performance. DVB-T2/UFMC/NUC has many advantages such as: the increase of the system spectral efficiency due to the CP cancellation and the few guard band of UFMC, the decrease of the bit error probability by reducing the number of constellation points which have the same I (In Phase) or Q (Quadrature) components, the use of Chebyshev filter instead of rectangular filter in OFDM. Also, the characteristic of UFMC waveform makes the system suitable for low capacity applications.

The rest of this paper is structured as follows. Section 2 presents related works about NUCs and UFMC. Section 3 briefly introduces the BICM capacity and the NUCs constellation concept. In Sect. 4, UFMC filtered based waveform is presented. Section 5 presents the lite version of DVB-T2 physical layer and parameters. In Sect. 6, simulation results and performance analysis are presented. Finally, the main findings of the work are summarised in Sect. 7.

2   Related Works

NUCs and 5G waveforms UFMC have been the object of many researches during the last years. NUCs have been proposed in many standards such as: DVB-NGH [3] and ATSC 3.0 [4]. Also, they have been proposed recently for DVB-T2 [11], broadcast/multicast services [12], broadcasting Ultra High Definition (UHD) TeleVision (TV) [13] and converged network of broadcast and broadband [14]. UFMC is a waveform which has been firstly proposed for Long Term Evolution (LTE) [15] and later for 5G system [16,17]. Its low complexity of implementation has been recently demonstrated [18]. In this section, these works are briefly presented.

2.1   NUCs Related Works

– 1D-NUCs have been proposed in DVB-NGH standard in 2012 for Handheld services. The performance obtained is better than DVB-T2 performance [3].

- 1D-NUCs and 2D-NUCs have been compared in DVB-T2 system in 2014 using AWGN and rayleigh channels and the results shown that 2D-NUCs present better performance than 1D-NUCs [11].
- 1D-NUCs and 2D-NUCs of high order constellations have been proposed for UHD TV broadcasting in 2014 to increase the capacity and the performance gain. The results shown that 4096-1D-NUC presents better performance than 4096-QAM and could be used for high data rate transmissions [13].
- An iterative algorithm has been proposed in 2016 to optimize the NUCs for multiple applications like multicast and broadcast services and maximize the gain obtained under different channels [12].
- 2D-NUCs and QAM have been compared in different channel scenarios including Doppler effect. The results show that NUCs can provide a performance gains and induce a high data rate in a converged network [14].

2.2 UFMC Related Works

- Filtered based waveform UFMC has been firstly proposed for LTE communications as an alternative to CP-OFDM [15] in oder to reduce InterCarrier Interference (ICI) and cancel the CP overhead. Due to filtering operation applied on a group of consecutive subcarriers (called sub-band), the out-of-band side lobe levels are reduced which minimizes the ICI.
- Afterwards, UFMC and FBMC have been proposed for 5G system where their performance were compared to CP-OFDM performance. The results shown that UFMC is suitable for 5G communications as it is designed for low latency systems [16,17].
- Furthermore, a low complexity of UFMC hardware implementation has been proposed in 2020. The results shown that UFMC complexity could be comparable to the complexity of OFDM [18].
- UFMC, FBMC and CP-OFDM have been compared in DVB-T2 in terms of spectral efficiency, Power Spectral Density (PSD), performance gain and complexity. The results shown that UFMC is suitable to DVB-T2 transmissions as it outperforms OFDM with a complexity comparable to that for OFDM [10].

3 BICM Capacity and NUC Constellation

The channel capacity is the maximum mutual information between the channel input and the channel output. This capacity has been defined by Shannon as the maximum possible throughput over any given channel [19].

3.1 BICM Capacity

The channel is described by its transition probabilities $p(r_k|s_k = x_l)$ where k denotes the discrete time index, s_k and r_k represent respectively the transmitted and received symbols at time k. The symbol constellation x_l is taken from an alphabet X. When an AWGN channel is used, $p(r_k|s_k = x_l)$ is a gaussian distributed probability density function, centered around the transmitted symbol with a zero mean noise and noise variance according to SNR.

Shannon proved that maximum Mutual Information (MI) can be achieved if the transmitted alphabet (set of constellation points) is Gaussian distributed [12,13]. Then, the theoretical limit expressed in the normalized capacity form is given by $C(bit/s/Hz) = log_2(1 + SNR)$ where SNR is the ratio between the average transmitted power P and the noise power N. However, this limit can never be achieved by any pratical system due to the alphabet X which contains a finite transmitted symbol number. The gaussian distribution is not possible to be achieved in reality. In many communications systems, most pratical finite symbol alphabet inputs are implemented such as QAM. The BICM capacity that characterizes these systems is given by [12]:

$$C = M - \sum_{m=1}^{M} E_{b,y}[log_2 \frac{\sum_{x_l \in X} p(y|x_l)}{\sum_{x_l \in X_b^m} p(y|x_l))}] \tag{1}$$

where M is the number of bits per symbol, y is the received signal, $p(y|x_l)$ is the transition probability density function (p.d.f) of transmitting x_l and receiving y. b can take 0 or 1 values. X_b^m is the subset of the alphabet X (all the possible values x_l ($l = 1, ..., N$) of constellations) for which bit label m is equal to b. $E_{b,y}$ denotes expectation with respect to b and y. If N denotes the number of constellation points, the alphabet of the transmitted symbols needs to be normalized following the power constraint:

$$P_{total} = \frac{1}{N} \sum_{l=1}^{N} |x_l|^2 = 1 \tag{2}$$

The main parameters affecting $p(y|x_l)$ are the SNR and the constellations points position in AWGN channel. The uniform design criteria is the straightforward way to design an alphabet X resulting in uniform constellations.

3.2   Non Uniform Constellations

Uniform constellations are characterized by uniform spacing between constellations points and square shape of the constellations. However, a noticeable gap between BICM capacities with QAM and the Shannon limit is reported [20]. Furthermore, this gap increases with the constellation order [12,13]. At an SNR of 16 dB, the difference with the Shannon limit observed for 256-QAM, 1D-256-NUCs and 2D-256-NUCs are respectively 0.4 dB, 0.15 dB and 0.1 dB [12,13]. In order to reduce the significant gap of uniform QAM constellations, optimal constellation which achieves the smallest gap has been researched. To optimize the uniform constellation, 1D-NUCs have been designed by relaxing the uniformity constraint while keeping the rectangular structure of the constellation. This method confirms the fact that 1D-NUCs can be viewed as a QAM constellation which can be separated into two Pulse Amplitude Modulation (PAM) constellations. Then two PAM demappers are sufficient to demap 1D-NUCs. 2D-NUCs have been designed by relaxing both uniformity and the square or rectangular shape constraints. The constellation values can take any shape inside one quadrant. The other three quadrants are derived from the first quadrant by symmetry. This allows 2D-NUCs to achieve a better performance than 1D-NUCs and the BICM chain capacity to be closer to the Shannon limit with a counterpart in term of increased complexity.

3.3   Relevance of 2D-Demapper for 2D-NUCs

In order to detect the symbol transmitted at the receiver, euclidean distance metric computation is used. The higher the euclidean distance number is, the higher the complexity is. Euclidean distance number computed for 1D-NUCs and 2D-NUCs are respectively $2^{\frac{M}{2}+1}$ and 2^M while one dimensional and two dimensional demappers are respectively used for them. Moreover, the number of parameters to be optimized (called Degrees of Freedom (DOF)) is different for both 1D-NUCs and 2D-NUCs. Equations (3) and (4) are presented in [1,11,12]. In Eq. (3), the term $sqrt(N)$ is due to the rectangular structure of the constellation: the optimal level on the real and imaginary axes are equal. The factor $\frac{1}{2}$ is due to the fact that the optimization is carried out on the positive levels only (the negative levels are identical). In Eq. 4, the factor $\frac{1}{4}$ shows that the four quadrants are symmetric and the factor 2 is due to the fact that the real and imaginary parts of each constellation point are optimized separately. The term -1 in both Eqs. 3 and 4 is due to the power normalization constraint.

$$DOF_{1D-NUCs} = \frac{sqrt(N)}{2} - 1 \tag{3}$$

$$DOF_{2D-NUCs} = 2\frac{N}{4} - 1 \tag{4}$$

Using these equations, we can observe that the higher the constellation size is, the higher the DOF is. In particular, the DOF of 2D-NUCs increases faster with N than in the case of 1D-NUCs. This induces the fast increasing of 2D-NUCs demapper complexity. By this way, one can justify the choice of 2D-NUCs only for constellations of size 16, 64 and 256-QAM and 1D-NUCs for constellations of size 1024 and 4096 in ATSC 3.0. In the following sections, our study is focused on the gain which could be obtained with the use of 2D-NUCs proposed for ATSC 3.0 in DVB-T2. Filter based waveform UFMC will also be applied to 2D-NUCs in DVB-T2 in order to maximize the performance gain. The constellation and capacity optimization algorithm are beyond the scope of this paper. The following section presents the filtered based UFMC waveform.

4 Comparison of CP-OFDM and UFMC

In this section, the main waveforms are briefly introduced and are compared.

4.1 CP-OFDM

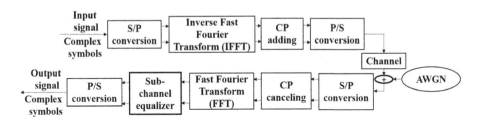

Fig. 1. CP-OFDM block diagram

In CP-OFDM, a set of complex symbols is mapped onto a set of orthogonal carriers (Fig. 1). The symbol mapping method used in DVB-T2 is QAM. Due to the sole use of Inverse Fast Fourier Transform (IFFT) (resp. FFT) process, the complexity of CP-OFDM is very low. The principle of OFDM is to divide the total bandwidth into M subcarriers, so that channel equalization can be reduced as a one tap coefficient per subcarrier. Finally, a CP is added at the beginning of each symbol. It guarantees circularity of the OFDM symbol if the channel delay spread is lower than the CP length [21]. However, CP-OFDM induces high OOB leakage, which requires the need for large guard band and degrades overall spectral efficiency due to the guard band and the CP overhead.

4.2 Filtered Based Waveform: UFMC

OFDM is a multicarrier modulation used in broadband multicarrier communications. However, it presents the shortcoming such as the constraint of Cyclic Prefix (CP) to deal with channel impairment and the high Out Of Band (OOB) emission. UFMC is a waveform for which CP is avoided and induces low OOB emission. The filtering in UFMC is based on a group of subcarriers (sub-band) instead of filtering each subcarrier (FBMC) or filtering together all subcarriers (filtered-OFDM). Dolph-Chebyshev filter for which the Side Lobe Level (SLL) and the filter length can be managed as parameters, has been adopted in order to increase system performance [10,12]. UFMC uses a shorter filter length and in its design, the filter length must be equal to the CP length in order to deal with frequency selective channels. The main parameters of UFMC are L the filter length, SLL, B the sub-band number and B_w the sub-band bandwidth. B_w represents the number of subcarriers used for each sub-band.

Figure 2 presents a UFMC transceiver. Contrary to other waveforms, UFMC uses only the transmit filters. Filters are not applied at the receiver. Indeed,

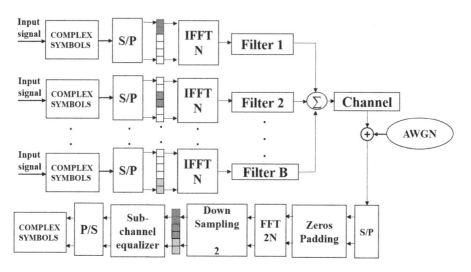

Fig. 2. UFMC block diagram

UFMC employs two NFFT points in the receiver allowing the data symbol recovering without the need of CP. However, the 2 NFFT points cause noise increase problem to the UFMC reception and thus degrade the UFMC performance compared to OFDM when only AWGN is used as channel. Indeed, while the contribution of gaussian noise on the CP is canceled in OFDM at the receiver, in UFMC this contribution is maintained on the filter length used in UFMC. As the 2 NFFT points used in demodulation includes the filter length contribution, this effect is highlighted on UFMC performance when gaussian noise is used. Otherwise, UFMC performance is better than that for OFDM in the presence of frequency selective channels. Furthermore, both OFDM and UFMC use a one tap Zero Forcing equalizer. Deep comparison between OFDM and UFMC in terms of transmitter, receiver and their PSD is presented in [10]. UFMC could substitute CP-OFDM with a high spectral efficiency (128% improvement) due to the CP cancellation and its little guard band (2816 instead of 5503 in OFDM).

5 DVB-T2 Physical Layer

In this section, the DVB-T2 system is briefly presented as well as the modeled channel and simulation parameters.

5.1 Lite Version Including NUCs and UFMC

DVB-T2 is the second generation terrestrial broadcasting system published by European Telecommunications Standards Institute (ETSI) in 2009. It offers a choice of flexibility to broadcasters. Compared to DVB-T, it introduces many innovative features allowing to reach a throughput of 50.32 Mbit/s [22]. The main two parts of this system are the BICM block and the multicarrier modulation block. In the specific way, the first block includes a FEC code Bose-Chaudhuri-Hocquenghem (BCH) and Low Density Parity Check (LDPC), a bit interleaving and a QAM mapping. The second block includes Orthogonal Frequency Division Multiplexing (OFDM)-CP. Indeed, the adoption of a powerful FEC schemes in substitution to combination of a convolutional code with an outer Reed Solomon code results in a larger FEC gain obtained at the price of increased complexity induced by these coders. As known, LDPC is based on a high density parity check matrix with short or long FEC frames and the decoding step is processed using a Belief Propagation (BP) algorithm. Despite the gain provided by FEC scheme, QAM constellations optimization has been studied in the literature. As known, 1D-NUCs with 64 and 256 constellations points have been proposed for DVB-NGH [3] and both 1D and 2D-NUCs have been proposed in ATSC 3.0 in order to increase the BICM capacity. Due to the performance gain obtained with 2D-NUCs in [4,11] and UFMC in [10], we propose in this paper to substitute QAM constellations by 2D-NUCs constellations (like in ATSC 3.0) in DVB-T2, also replacing the OFDM waveform by UFMC. Furthermore, long FEC frame is used at the LDPC coder. Figure 3 presents the implemented system used for simulation.

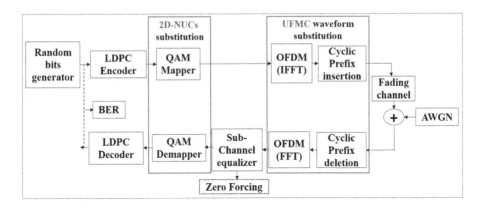

Fig. 3. DVB-T2 model implemented

Due to the fact that LDPC and QAM mapper are in the BICM main blocks which take out the BICM performance, we focus our simulation only on these blocks. As the interleaving block is useful in the presence of impulsive noise, this block is not used in the simulation.

5.2   Channel Used and Parameters

In this subsection, the DVB-T2 system parameters are presented in Table 1.

Table 1. DVB-T2 systems parameters

NFFT	1K, 2K, 4K, ((8, 16, 32)K and ext)
Modulation	4, 16, 64, 256-QAM
FEC frame	long (64800 bits), short (16200 bits)
CR LDPC	1/2, 3/5, 2/3, 3/4, 4/5, 5/6
Bandwidth	1.7, 5, 6, 7, 8, 10 MHz
CP	1/128, 1/32, 1/16, 19/256, 1/8, 19/128, 1/4

Table 2. TU6 channel [22]

PDP description	Path 1	2	3	4	5	6
Delays (ns)	0	200	500	1600	2300	5000
Power (dB)	−3	0	−2	−6	−8	−10

Parameters in red color represent those used in simulation. NFFT is the number of subcarriers used with OFDM. The term *ext* means extended. As 4-QAM constellation has not been optimized for NUCs, the other constellations sizes are used for NUCs simulation. Due to the fact that simulation results given in [11] shown that 2D-NUCs outperform QAM in DVB-T2 system and the gain is highligthed for lower code rates such as 1/2, 3/5 and 2/3, our simulation will be focused on them. UFMC parameters used for simulations are: $L = 32768/128 = 256$, $B = 128$, $B_w = 234$ and $SLL = 60$ dB. Indeed, the maximum gains of NUCs are obtained for CR with high FEC. This means that the number of redundancy bit is high [11] and justifies the choice of these CR. The FFT mode 32K has been chosen as this mode is mainly used by broadcasters for rooftop antenna reception [23]. The constellation size of 256 is used for TU6 channel due to the density of constellation points which performance is normally bad in the worse reception condition. Moreover, the choice of the parameters more suitable for UFMC depends on the CP of the system and the density of the sub-bands. CP=1/128 (low CP of DVB-T2 standard) has been chosen in order to fulfill the UFMC requirements in term of filter length used. Also, it is proven that UFMC performance are better when the number of sub-band increases [10] and the number of bit per symbols increases [24]. The channel bandwidth of 8MHz has been chosen as it is the bandwidth used for network deployment by broadcasters in many European and African countries. In order to evaluate performance in DVB-T2 environment, TU6 channel which models urban environment is used. The Power Delay Profile (PDP) of this channel is presented in Table 2. Method used to implement TU6 channel is based on Tapped Delay Line (TDL) model described in [22]. The Root Mean Square (RMS) delays spread of TU6 is about $1.0616.10^{-7}$ s.

5.3   Non Uniform Constellations Shapes

In this subsection, NUCs used in simulation are presented for each code rate. Figure 4, Fig. 5 and Fig. 6 present 2D-64-NUCs and 2D-256-NUCs respectively for code rate 1/2, 3/5, 2/3.

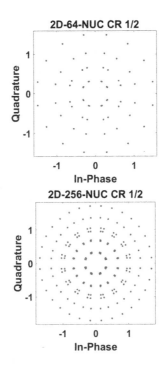

Fig. 4. 2D-64-NUC and 2D-256-NUC constellations for CR 1/2 [4]

As noticeable, these constellations are optimised for each code rate. This means that in comparison with QAM constellations which are designed to work with any code rate, these constellations are designed and optimized for a specific SNR value. This value depends on the FEC frame length, the code rate and the channel distribution. Note that these constellations are already proposed for DVB-T2 system [11].

6   Simulation Results

In order to evaluate the combination of NUCs and UFMC performance in DVB-T2 system, our simulator has been validated (6.A) using AWGN and parameters previously presented. The simulation tool is Matrix Laboratory (MATLAB) version 2016. Simulations have been performed using the Monte-Carlo method. The reception process takes place for each iteration of SNR and the BER is computed

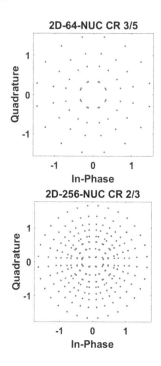

Fig. 5. 2D-64-NUC and 2D-256-NUC constellations for CR 3/5 [4]

between the bits randomly generated and the bits after LDPC decoder. The system has been simulated (6.B) in presence of frequency selective TU6 channel using high order constellations due to the fact that the gain in NUCs and UFMC is maximum with these constellations. Using this channel, 100 different channel realizations have been generated and the performance results presented in this paper are the mean of the computed BER for each realization.

6.1   System and Performance Validation Using AWGN

In order to validate the simulator, OFDM/QAM and OFDM/NUCs simulation results are presented. Results have been compared to simulation results about DVB-T2/OFDM given at 10^{-4} in the implementation guideline of DVB-T2 [22].

Figure 7 presents the simulation results for constellation sizes 16, 64 and 256 and code rates 1/2, 3/5 and 5/6. At a BER of 10^{-4}, the simulation results for DVB-T2/OFDM/QAM and those presented in [22] are comparable. However, when compared to DVB-T2/OFDM/2D-NUCs, there is a noticeable gain for combination of constellations and code rates. The more the constellation size increases, the more the 2D-NUCs gain increases. This confirms the good behaviour of our simulator and the literature trends. Furthermore UFMC/QAM and UFMC/NUCs simulation results are presented on Fig. 9 in order to confirm the fact that NUCs can be used with UFMC waveform.

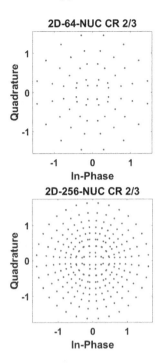

Fig. 6. 2D-64-NUC and 2D-256-NUC constellations for CR 2/3 [4]

Table 3 presents (based on Fig. 3 and Fig. 4) the gains obtained respectively for OFDM and UFMC when NUCs are used. By analysing these gains, we can conclude that the behaviour of NUCs in DVB-T2/OFDM and DVB-T2/UFMC is equivalent at a BER of 10^{-4}: to respectively 1.2 dB and 1.3 dB for $N = 256$ and $CR = 1/2$. Moreover the maximum gain is obtained for constellation $N = 256$ and $CR = 1/2, 3/5, 2/3$. However, UFMC presents a loss when compared to OFDM in presence of gaussian noise. The noise increasing problem in UFMC reception is due to the fact that $2*NFFT$ points are used to achieve efficient demodulation without CP. If UFMC filter impulse response length is L, $(NFFT + L)$ time domain noise samples contribute to the frequency domain noise. As results, the noise power is larger than that for OFDM like presented in [25]. The following part of this section presents simulation results using frequency selective channel which highlights both NUCs and UFMC performance (Fig. 8).

6.2 Simulation Results Using TU6

In order to present UFMC/NUCs performance in DVB-T2 environment, TU6 channel is exploited. Simulation results are obtained using the average of 100 independent channel realisations of a statistical fading generators.

Simulation results are presented on Fig. 9 and Fig. 10 respectively for CR 1/2 and 3/5 and a constellation of size 256. At a BER of 10^{-2}, UFMC/NUCs

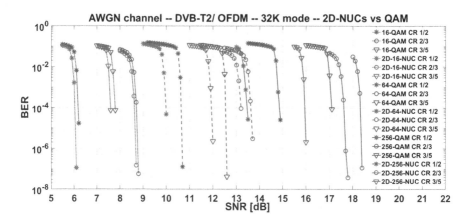

Fig. 7. 2D-NUCs and QAM comparison in DVB-T2/OFDM system

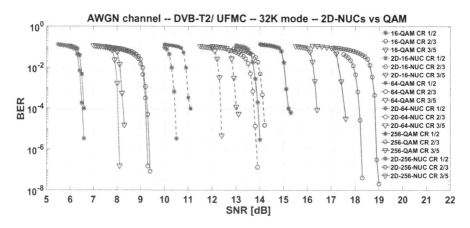

Fig. 8. 2D-NUCs and QAM comparison in DVB-T2/UFMC system

Table 3. Performance gain of NUCs compared with QAM for DVB-T2/OFDM and DVB-T2/UFMC with AWGN (BER = 10^{-4})

Waveforms		OFDM			UFMC		
Mod		QAM	NUC	NUC	QAM	NUC	NUC
CR	N	SNR[dB]		Gain[dB]	SNR[dB]		Gain[dB]
1/2	16	6.2	6	0.2	6.6	6.5	0.1
1/2	64	10.5	10	0.5	11.1	10.4	0.7
1/2	256	14.7	13.4	1.3	15.2	13.9	1.3
3/5	16	7.7	7.5	0.2	8.2	8	0.2
3/5	64	12.5	11.9	0.6	13	12.3	0.7
3/5	256	17	16	1.0	17.5	16.4	1.1
2/3	16	8.7	8.6	0.1	9.3	9.2	0.1
2/3	64	13.6	13.2	0.4	14.2	13.7	0.5
2/3	256	18.3	17.6	0.7	18.8	18.2	0.6

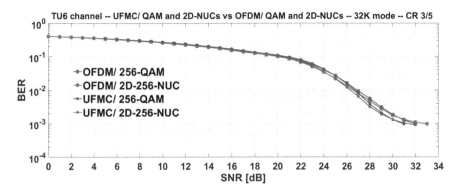

Fig. 9. 2D-NUCs and QAM comparison in DVB-T2/OFDM and DVB-T2/UFMC systems using TU6 channel, constellation size 256 and CR 3/5

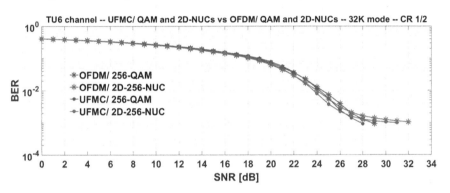

Fig. 10. 2D-NUCs and QAM comparison in DVB-T2/OFDM and DVB-T2/UFMC systems using TU6 channel, constellation size 256 and CR 1/2

Table 4. Performance gain of NUCs compared with QAM for DVB-T2/OFDM and DVB-T2/UFMC using TU6 channel

Waveforms	OFDM			UFMC		
Mod	QAM	NUC	NUC	QAM	NUC	NUC
BER	SNR[dB]		Gain[dB]	SNR[dB]		Gain[dB]
Constellation size 256, CR 1/2						
10^{-2}	24.5	24	0.5	24.3	23.6	0.7
3.10^{-3}	26.5	26	0.5	25.8	25.3	0.5
2.10^{-3}	27	27	0.0	26.4	26.4	0.0
10^{-3}	29	32	-3.0	27.8	30.5	-2.7
Constellation size 256, CR 3/5						
10^{-2}	27	26.6	0.4	26.8	26.3	0.5
3.10^{-3}	29.2	29	0.2	28.4	28	0.4
2.10^{-3}	29.8	29.6	0.2	29	28.8	0.2
10^{-3}	32	32.2	-0.2	30.8	31	-0.2

Table 5. Performance gain of UFMC/NUCs compared with OFDM/QAM in DVB-T2 system using TU6 channel

UFMC/QAM	CR	BER	10^{-2}	3.10^{-3}	2.10^{-3}	10^{-3}
vs	1/2	Gain [dB]	0.2	0.7	0.6	1.2
OFDM/QAM	3/5	Gain [dB]	0.2	0.8	0.8	1.2
UFMC/NUCs	CR	BER	10^{-2}	3.10^{-3}	2.10^{-3}	10^{-3}
vs	1/2	Gain [dB]	0.9	1.2	0.6	-1.5
OFDM/QAM	3/5	Gain [dB]	0.7	1.2	1	1

outperforms UFMC/QAM by 0.7 dB and 0.5 dB and OFDM/QAM by 0.9 dB and 0.7 dB respectively for CR 1/2 and 3/5. At a BER of 3.10^{-3}, UFMC/NUCs outperforms OFDM/QAM by 1.2 dB for CR 1/2 and 3/5 .

Table 4 presents the gain obtained with NUCs using OFDM and UFMC. As presented on the Figs. 9 and 10 and in this table, NUCs outerform QAM for low SNR values. For high SNR values, NUCs present a loss when compared to QAM. The performance gain obtained with the joint usage of UFMC and NUCs are presented on Table 5.

6.3 Analysis

Based on the results presented above, NUCs constellations shaping technique can be jointly used with UFMC in DVB-T2. It presents better performance in AWGN and in TU6 respectively for low SNR values less than 20 dB and 26 dB. For high SNR value, 2D-NUCs performance become worse for both DVB-T2/OFDM/NUCs and DVB-T2/UFMC/NUCs. These results can be explained by three reasons. Firstly, as the aim of this work is to present NUCs in worse reception condition, one hundred independent channel realizations are used for TU6 channel. Due to the averaging of these channel realizations used in simulation, the worse possible realizations of this channel are represented. Secondly, LDPC codes are designed to work in a waterfall region specific for low SNR values. The waterfall region is the SNR region where the BER decreases quickly. This region is followed by the error floor region which starts at a point after which the BER curve does not fall as quickly and a performance flattens [26]. Lastly, NUCs have been designed for specific SNR values. This explains the good behaviour for NUCs in AWGN channel and in low SNR region for TU6 channel. The saturation effect noticed for all the BER curves is due to the first two regions. However, NUCs and UFMC can be jointly used in DVB-T2 and could allow this system to increase its spectral efficiency [10], its performance gain and to be closer to the Shannon limit.

DVB-T2 is already deployed, is ongoing or planned deployments in more than 100 countries corresponding to a real-life implementation in those countries, as shown on the ITU interactive map [27]. The improvements proposed in this work can be considered as principles proposals which can be followed for the next standard revision.

7   Conclusion

In this paper, the impact of BICM/2D-NUCs in DVB-T2/OFDM and DVB-T2/UFMC has been evaluated using constellation shaping proposed for ATSC 3.0. Gaussian noise only and TU6 channel are used to highlight respectively NUCs performance and UFMC/NUCs performance. We evaluated SNR gain of NUCs compared with both DVB-T2/OFDM and DVB-T2/UFMC. Simulation results shown that with 2D-NUCs, 1.3 dB SNR gains can be achieved in DVB-T2 using gaussian noise with both OFDM and UFMC. Furthermore, OFDM has been substituted by UFMC and the gain achieved when compared to OFDM/QAM is about 1.2 dB at a BER of 3.10^{-3} in TU6 channel. These results allow to give some trends about application of 5G waveform UFMC and NUCs jointly in DVB-T2 system. However, the use of this constellation shaping requires the 2D demapper which increases complexity with the constellation order due to the In-phase (I) and Quadrature (Q) component independently optimized.

Nevertheless, many complexity reduction algorithms such as sub-region demapping, sphere demapping proposed in literature can be implemented in the receiver in order to exploit these performance gains. These algorithms are based either on the reduction of the number of Euclidean distance to compute or the number of operators of high complexity of realization used in the reduction.

Future works could be done by exploring topics such as:

– The use of other performance evaluation tools like Modulation Error Ratio (MER) and Error Vector Magnitude (EVM).
– The joint use of NUCs and rotated constellation in order to better improve DVB-T2 BICM capacity.
– The impact of Carrier Frequency Offset (CFO) on UFMC/NUC in DVB-T2.
– The implementation of low complexity demapping algorithm when NUCs and Signal Space Diversity (SSD) technique are used together.
– The complexity evaluation of UFMC/NUC and OFDM/QAM in DVB-T2.

Acronyms list

ATSC 3.0 Advanced Television Systems Committee, third generation. 2
AWGN Additive White Gaussian Noise. 2, 4, 8
BCH Bose-Chaudhuri-Hocquenghem. 9
BER Bit Error Rate. 1
BICM Bit Interleaved Coding Modulation. 2
BP Belief Propagation. 9
CFO Carrier Frequency Offset. 17
CP Cyclic Prefix. 2, 3
CP-OFDM Cyclic Prefix - Orthogonal Frequency Division Multiplexing. 1

CR Code Rate. 1, 10
DVB-NGH Digital Video Broadcasting - Next Generation Handheld. 2, 9
DVB-T Digital Video Broadcasting-Terrestrial, first generation. 1, 2, 8
DVB-T2 Digital Video Broadcasting-Terrestrial, second generation. 1, 2, 10
ETSI European Telecommunications Standards Institute. 8
EVM Error Vector Magnitude. 17
FBMC Filter Bank MultiCarrier. 3
FEC Forward Error Correction. 2, 9, 10
ICI InterCarrier Interference. 4
IFFT Inverse Fast Fourier Transform. 7
LDPC Low Density Parity Check. 9–11
LTE Long Term Evolution. 3
MER Modulation Error Ratio. 17
MI Mutual Information. 5
NUCs Non Uniform Constellations. 2
OFDM Orthogonal Frequency Division Multiplexing. 9, 18
OOB Out Of Band. 7
PAM Pulse Amplitude Modulation. 6
PDP Power Delay Profile. 10
PSD Power Spectral Density. 4, 8
QAM Quadrature Amplitude Modulation. 2, 4, 5
RMS Root Mean Square. 10
SLL Side Lobe Level. 7
SNR Signal to Noise Ratio. 1–3, 5
SSD Signal Space Diversity. 17
TDL Tapped Delay Line. 10
TU6 Typical Urban 6. 1, 10
TV TeleVision. 3
UFMC Universal Filtered MultiCarrier. 1, 3
UHD Ultra High Definition. 3

References

1. Zoellner, J., Loghin, N.: Optimization of high-order non-uniform QAM constellations. In: International Symposium on Broadband Multimedia Systems and Broadcasting (2013). https://doi.org/10.1109/BMSB.2013.6621711
2. European Broadcasting Union: Digital Video Broadcasting (DVB); Frame structure channel coding and modulation for a second generation digital terrestrial television broadcasting systems (DVB-T2). ETSI EN 302 755 V1.4.1 (2015). https://doi.org/10.1109/TCOM.1974.1092061
3. Digital Video Broadcasting (DVB): Next generation broadcasting system to handheld. DVB Document A160 (2012)
4. Advanced Television Systems Committee: ATSC Physical Layer Protocol, Next generation broadcasting system to handheld. Document A/322, Washington, January 2020

5. Foschini, G.J., Gitlin, R.D., Weinstein, S.B.: Optimization of two-dimensional signal-constellations in the presence of Gaussian noise. IEEE Trans. Commun. **22**(1), 28–38 (1974). https://doi.org/10.1109/TCOM.1974.1092061

6. Loghin, N.S., et al.: Non-uniform constellations for ATSC 3.0. IEEE Trans. Broadcast. **62**(1), 197–203 (2016). https://doi.org/10.1109/TBC.2016.2518620

7. Fuentes, M., Vargas, D., Gomez-Barquero, D.: Low-complexity demapping algorithm for two-dimensional non-uniform constellations. IEEE Trans. Broadcast. **62**(2), 375–383 (2016). https://doi.org/10.1109/TBC.2015.2492477

8. Barjau, C., Fuentes, M., Shitomi, T., Gomez-Barquero, D.: MIMO sphere decoder with successive interference cancellation for two-dimensional non-uniform constellations. IEEE Commun. Lett. **21**(5), 1015–1018 (2017). https://doi.org/10.1109/LCOMM.2017.2653775

9. Honfoga, A.C., Nguyen, T.T., Dossou, M., Moeyaert, V.: Application of FBMC to DVB-T2: a comparison vs classical OFDM transmissions. In: IEEE GlobalSIP Conference (2019.) https://doi.org/10.1109/GlobalSIP45357.2019.8969550

10. Honfoga, A.C., Dossou, M., Moeyaert, V.: Performance comparison of new waveforms applied to DVB-T2 transmissions. In: IEEE International Symposium on Broadband Multimedia Systems and Broadcasting (BMSB) (2020, in press)

11. Morgade, J., Ansorregui, D., Mouhouche, B., Jeong, H., Lee, H.: Improving the DVB-T2 BICM performance by newly optimized two-dimensional non-uniform constellations. In: IEEE Fourth International Conference on Consumer Electronics Berlin (ICCE-Berlin) (2014). https://doi.org/10.1109/ICCE-Berlin.2014.7034316

12. Mouhouche, B., Al-Imari, M., Ansorregui, D.: Multichannel design of non uniform constellations for broadcast/multicast services. In: IEEE 84th Vehicular Technology Conference (VTC-Fall) (2016). https://doi.org/10.1109/VTCFall.2016.7881098

13. Mouhouche, B., Ansorregui, D., Mourad, A.: High order non-uniform constellations for broadcasting UHDTV. In: IEEE Wireless Communications and Networking Conference (2014). https://doi.org/10.1109/WCNC.2014.6952116

14. Hong, H., et al.: Evaluation of non-uniform constellations for the converged network of broadcast and broadband. In: IEEE International Symposium on Broadband Multimedia Systems and Broadcasting (BMSB) (2019). https://doi.org/10.1109/BMSB47279.2019.8971876

15. Vakilian, V., Wild, T., Schaich, F., Brink, S.T., Frigon, J.-F.: Universal-filtered multi-carrier technique for wireless systems beyond LTE. In: Globecom Workshop (2013). https://doi.org/10.1109/GLOCOMW.2013.6824990

16. Srikanth, K., Indira, D.S., Kalyan, K.N., Chowdary, R.A.: Characteristic analysis of OFDM, FBMC and UFMC modulation schemes for next generation wireless communication network systems. In: 3rd International conference on Electronics, Communication and Aerospace Technology (ICECA) (2019.) https://doi.org/10.1109/ICECA.2019.8821991

17. AKM, B., Rafee, A.A., Azwad, A.: Novel methods of filtering For FBMC/UFMC based 5G Communication systems. In: 7th International Conference on Smart Computing & Communications (ICSCC) (2019). https://doi.org/10.1109/ICSCC.2019.8843617

18. Guo, Z., Liu, Q., Zhang, W., Wang, S.: Low complexity implementation of universal filtered multi-carrier transmitter. In: IEEE Access (2020). https://doi.org/10.1109/ACCESS.2020.2970727

19. Shannon, C.E.: A mathematical theory of communication, Bell Lab. Syst. J. **27**, 535 (1948)

20. Stott:, J.: CM and BICM limits for rectangular constellations. British Broadcasting Corporation (2013)
21. Nguyen, T.H., Nguyen, D.Q., Thai, L.H., Nguyen, T.K.: Out of band analysis in various 5G-NR downlink waveforms with different numerologies. In: International Conference on Recent Advances in Signal Processing, Telecommunications and Computing (SigTelCom) (2019). https://doi.org/10.1109/SIGTELCOM.2019.8696158
22. European Broadcasting Union: Digital Video Broadcasting (DVB); implementation guidelines for a second generation digital terrestrial television broadcasting system (DVB-T2). ETSI TS 102 831 V1.2.1 (2012)
23. European Broadcasting Union: Frequency and network planning aspects of DVB-T2. TECH 3348 REPORT. VERSION 4.1.2 (2020)
24. Teja, K.R., Raj, C.S., Akhil, G.: Higher order QAM schemes in 5G UFMC system. In: International Conference on Emerging Smart Computing and Informatics (2020). https://doi.org/10.1109/ESCI48226.2020.9167619
25. Liu, Y., et al.: Waveform design for 5G networks: analysis and comparison. In: IEEE Access (2017). https://doi.org/10.1109/ACCESS.2017.2664980
26. Marchand, C.: Implementation of an LDPC decoder for the DVB-S2, -T2 and -C2 standards. Bretagne Sud university Ph.D. thesis, Lab-STICC (2015)
27. International Telecommunication Union: interactive map filter. Status of the transition to Digital Terrestrial Television (2019). https://www.itu.int/net4/ITU-D/CDS/DSO2019/Map_Filter.asp?Country=133&Region=&Status=&Compression=&Standard=2

A Multi-objective Approach for Wireless Heterogeneous Router Placement in Rural Wireless Mesh Networks

Jean Louis Ebongue Kedieng Fendji[1]([✉]) [iD], Christopher Thron[2] [iD], and Anna Förster[3] [iD]

[1] Computer Engineering, UIT University of Ngaoundere, Ngaoundere, Cameroon
`jlfendji@univ-ndere.cm`
[2] Texas A&M University-Central Texas, Killeen, USA
`thron@tamuct.edu`
[3] Sustainable Communication Networks, University of Bremen, Bremen, Germany
`anna.foerster@comnets.uni-bremen.de`

Abstract. The design of a wireless mesh network is usually posed as a multi-objective optimization problem. In this paper, we consider the planning of a wireless mesh network in a rural region where the network coverage and the cost of the architecture must be optimized. In addition, mesh routers are heterogeneous, meaning that they may have different transmission ranges. In the network model, we assume that the region to serve is divided into a set of small zones of various types, including cost-effective locations and zones of interest for which the coverage is mandatory. The objective is then to minimize the number of routers, their types and locations which maximize the coverage percentage of mandatory zones in terms of coverage while minimizing the overall cost of the architecture. To achieve this, we propose three multi-objective approaches. We test the proposed approaches on several random topologies. The min-max regret metric is used to appreciate the quality of solutions of the Pareto front of different approaches.

Keywords: Centre of mass · Simulated annealing · Multi-objective · Mesh router · min-max regret

1 Introduction

Africa is the second-largest continent in size and population in the world after Asia. However, Africa is still experiencing a low percentage of Internet penetration. According to [1], this percentage is barely over half of the rest of the world. In addition, internet use in Africa is mainly restricted to urban or suburban areas, while rural areas lack coverage because of the lack of guarantee of return on investment. However, with the proliferation of wireless technologies, wireless community networks have emerged as a cost-effective alternative for rural coverage. Those networks are usually in form of wireless mesh networks (WMNs)

R. Zitouni et al. (Eds.): AFRICOMM 2020, LNICST 361, pp. 43–55, 2021.
https://doi.org/10.1007/978-3-030-70572-5_3

[2]. WMNs are generally composed of nodes connected in a mesh topology to extend the coverage of standard wireless networks. This type of network makes use of off-the-shelf WiFi technology to provide an attractive approach to reduce the digital gap between rural and urban areas. Several initiatives have emerged, such as Zenzeleni Networks in South Africa or Mesh Bukavu in DR Congo. A map of initiatives throughout the continent can be found in [3].

In rural areas, networks known as rural wireless mesh networks (RWMNs) usually encompass a set of mesh routers (MRs), and a sole gateway connected to Internet via a limited solution such as VSAT [4]. Because of the limited budget during the design phase, the overall cost of the architecture should be minimised. This is achieved by minimizing the number and identifying the locations of router nodes that will maximise the percentage of the region to cover. For this reason, the planning of WMNs in rural areas has been considered as coverage-driven instead of capacity-driven [5], meaning that we have an area to cover rather than a set of users to supply. Pötsch et al. proposed a network planning tool for rural wireless ISPs [6]. In their configuration, they consider a set of points to connect (ISPs) rather than an area to cover. Recently, a new approach based on deep reinforcement learning has been investigated to plan topologies for WMNs [7].

In real-life scenarios, the problem of mesh node placement in WMNs is a NP-hard multi-objective and combinatorial optimization problem, and thus the computational complexity grows exponentially [8]. Therefore, it requires approaches based on meta-heuristics for its resolution.

This paper provides a new formulation of this problem and considers the network model found in [9]. The region of interest is divided into small zones. Each zone is either mandatory (i.e. requires network coverage) or optional (does not require coverage).The model also identifies cost-effective locations for node deployment. In real-life scenarios, network operators are also looking for such locations during the planning stage of the network. Moreover, we consider the fact that heterogeneous routers are used. The objective is then to minimize the overall cost (which depends on the locations and types of mesh routers used) while maximizing the coverage percentage of the zone of interest. To achieve this goal, we propose and compare three multi-objective approaches: Multi-objective Centre of Mass (MCM), Multi-objective Simulated Annealing (MSA) and Multi-objective Simulated Annealing based Centre of Mass (MSAC).

This paper is organized as follows: Section 2 briefly presents related work in WMN planning. Section 3 defines the network model and formulates the placement problem. Section 4 presents the different approaches. Section 5 presents the simulation setup and discusses the results of the different approaches. This paper ends with a conclusion and future work.

2   Related Works

Benyamina et al. [10] provide a comprehensive survey of the planning problem in WMNs. Their work categorizes the design problem in WMNs depending on the flexibility of the network topology, which can be predefined or not. In predefined topologies, each node in the network has a fixed location. The design problem consists into defining new MAC protocols [11,12], optimising channel assignment and efficient routing protocols [13–17] or defining cross layer techniques [18]. In non-predefined topologies, the locations of some nodes must be defined: either the location of the gateway(s) or those of mesh routers, or both. In this case, the problem can be cast as a distribution problem involving facilities and locations, where mesh routers represent facilities and the areas to cover represents locations.

Approaches to solve the placement problem in WMNs are based on different formulations proposed in the literature. Those formulations depend on the type of node considered in the design problem: mesh routers [19,20], gateways(s) [21,22], or both [23]. Earlier approaches for tackling this problem were based on linear programming [24]. However, these solutions were limited to small size networks since this problem is known to be NP-hard. For real size deployments, search techniques and meta-heuristics have been used [9,19,20,25].

Several works formulate the node placement as a multi-objective optimization problem with the aim of minimizing the cost and maximizing the coverage of the quality of service of the network. In [9], authors considered a formulation of mesh routers placement in which a set of clients must be covered in a two-dimensional space. Then they provided a simulated annealing approach to maximize the network connectivity and client coverage. The placement problem of mesh routers in a rural region was introduced in [26]. This work was extended later in [10] and [27], which employed approaches based on the Metropolis algorithm and simulated annealing, respectively.

Most of the works in the literature assumes the routers to be homogeneous, meaning that they have the same transmission range. In addition, the cost of the network is typically assumed to depend only on router cost, which does not take into account the dependence of cost on the installation location.

3   Placement Problem Formulation

We model a given region as a two-dimensional irregular form, and consider the smallest rectangle that can contain this form. We divide the region into squares, which are designated as elementary regions (ERs) as in [27,28]. Each ER can be mandatory in terms of network coverage; or its coverage can be considered as optional when the ER is not of essential interest. An ER can also be considered as forbidden location, meaning it cannot host a node (for instance a lake, river, road...). As in real-life scenarios, an ER can also represent an obstacle that could hinder the connectivity. Moreover, we suppose that the region encompasses cost-effective locations which can contribute to the reduction of cost. In the following for simplicity we employ these abbreviations for the different types of ER: Mandatory ER (MER); Non-line-of-sight ER (NER); Cost-effective ER (CER) or Forbidden ER (FER).

We define a set of matrices to characterize the ERs:

$$Coverage(x, y) = \begin{cases} 1 \text{ mandatory,} \\ 0 \text{ optional.} \end{cases} \tag{1}$$

$$Placement(x, y) = \begin{cases} 1 \text{ authorised,} \\ 0 \text{ forbidden.} \end{cases} \tag{2}$$

$$CoverDepth(x, y) = \begin{cases} 0 & \text{MER not covered,} \\ n & \text{MER covered by n routers.} \end{cases} \tag{3}$$

$$LowCost(x, y) = \begin{cases} 0 & \text{no cost reduction,} \\ c & \text{cost reduction (percentage).} \end{cases} \tag{4}$$

The *Coverage*, *Placement*, and *LowCost* matrices indicate whether or not ERs are mandatory, authorized, or cost effective (as node locations) respectively; while *CoverDepth* specifies the number of number of nodes that cover ERs. Thus, all relevant properties of the ER at (x, y) can be specified by the (x, y) entries of matrices (1–4).

In contrast to previous works, we assume routers to be equipped with omnidirectional antennas having different transmission ranges. The transmission range TR_j of a router R_j is expressed as the number of ERs (i.e. $TR_j = 8$ means that the transmission range of R_j stretches over 8 ERs).

Let p be an ER at position (x, y). If R_j is located in p that means the centre of R_j is $Ctr(j) = (x, y)$, then the set of ERs covered by R_j, CA_j, is given by (5).

$$CA_j = \{(a, b), (x - a)^2 + (y - b)^2 < TR_j^2\} \tag{5}$$

The mesh router node placement problem in rural wireless mesh networks can then be expressed as the determination of a minimum set of routers, their types and locations, which maximizes the coverage of MERs, while minimising the overall cost of the architecture. This cost can be minimised by first minimising the number of routers required to cover the region, then by locating as many routers as possible to cost-effective location. The objective functions are given by (6) and (7).

$$f_1 = \max \frac{sign(\text{CoverDepth} \cdot \text{Coverage})}{\sum \text{Coverage}} \tag{6}$$

$$f_2 = \min \frac{1}{|R|} \sum_{i=1}^{|R|} 1 - \text{LowCost}(\text{Ctr}(i)) \tag{7}$$

f_1 maximises the percentage coverage of MERs, while f_2 minimizes the cost of the architecture. To convert f_1 into a minimisation problem, we only consider the MERs that are uncovered, in other terms with CoverDepth $= 0$. The new objective function f_1' is then given by (8).

$$f_1' = \min \frac{\sum sign((\text{CoverDepth} = 0) \cdot \text{Coverage})}{\sum \text{Coverage}} \tag{8}$$

Since we consider Wi-Fi technology standards, the deployment cost of a router in rural regions is higher than the cost of the router itself since deployment requires a mast and an independent power source. However, this cost can be greatly reduced by using cost-effective locations that may provide a power source, and making the mast unnecessary.

4   Placement Approaches Based on Pareto Front

Two approaches are generally used in multi-objective optimisation: combining objective functions into one by defining weights; or using Pareto front which is composed of non-dominated solutions. Since the determination of weights is usually subjective, the Pareto front approach is preferred.

Usually, objective functions in multi-objective optimization are conflicting. For instance, reducing the number of uncovered MER (f_1) is done at the expense of the cost of the architecture (f_2). Rather than combining objective functions, Pareto optimisation consists of trading-off conflicting objective functions to determine a set of optimal solutions. In a Pareto optimisation, the Optimally is based on the concept of dominance [29].

Definition 1 (Pareto Dominance): Let two solutions (with $x_1 \neq x_2$), x_1 dominates x_2 if x_1 is better than x_2 in at least one objective function and not worse with respect to all other objectives.

Definition 2 (Pareto Optimality): $x^* \in X$ is a Pareto optimum if and only if it is non-dominated by any other element of X. The set of Pareto optima is called Pareto set.

Definition 3 (Pareto Front): The Pareto Front is the set of all Pareto optimal solutions (non-dominated solutions).

An example of Pareto optimization with two functions is given in Fig. 1. Three approaches based on Pareto fronts are proposed: Multi-objective Centre of Mass (MCM), Multi-objective Simulated Annealing (MSA), and Multi-objective Simulated Annealing based Centre of Mass (MSAC).

4.1   Initialisation and Global Parameters of Algorithms

The initial number of routers is unknown at the beginning. A set R of routers with a total coverage RCover = $\gamma \cdot$ TCover (the number of MER which represents the total area to cover) is randomly generated. The multiplicative factor γ is initially set to 1.5, and is gradually decreased to 1. When γ changes, a new R is generated. The initial solution is obtained by placing routers from R randomly in the area to cover. For each router we randomly select an ER until Coverage (ER) = 1 and Placement (ER) = 1 be satisfied. We therefore place the current router in this ER. All the three algorithms are run nRun times. When $\gamma = 1$, the nRun decreases and γ is reset. All the algorithms stop when nRun = 0.

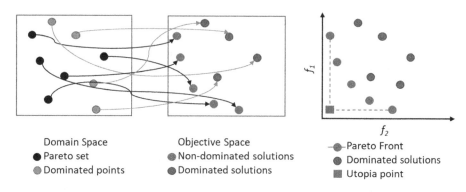

Domain Space   Objective Space
● Pareto set   ◉ Non-dominated solutions
○ Dominated points   ● Dominated solutions

—●—Pareto Front
● Dominated solutions
■ Utopia point

Fig. 1. Example of Pareto optimization

4.2   Multi-objective Centre of Mass (MCM)

Algorithm 1: Multi-Objective Centre of Mass algorithm for single coverage

---

Input   : f_1': First Obj. Funct. (Coverage) f_2: Second Obj. Funct. (Cost)
Output: arch: Pareto Front of non-dominated Solutions
begin
    s:= InitialSolution();
    (cost,cov):= $(f_2(s),f_1'(s))$;
    arch:= createList(1,(cost,cov));
    while *stopping condition not met* **do**
        i := selectARouter();
        if *multiple coverage of i is too large a fraction* **then**
            Search for an ER with CoverDepth = 0, Coverage = 1, and Placement = 1 ;
        else
            Move i to the centre of mass of his single coverage
        end
        s:= NewSolution(i); (cost,cov):= $(f_2(s),f_1'(s))$;
        if *(cost,cov) is non-dominated by any (cost',cov') in arch* **then**
            arch:=updateAndPrune(arch, (cost,cov));
            reset stopping condition;
        end
    end
    return *arch*
end

The MCM algorithm is an enhancement of the Centre of Mass of single coverage (CM) algorithm [30]. It is an attempt to provide CM with features to support multi-objective optimisation problems. The idea behind the MCM approach is to reduce the area covered by multiple nodes by moving each node to the centre of mass of area it is covering alone. The idea is guided by the fact that new uncovered MER can be easily reached in a small number of moves. The MCM basic algorithm is given in Algorithm 1. The following expression is used to check whether multiple coverage is too large a fraction at line 7, as in [30]:

$$(sCov(i) + mCov(i))^2 \cdot rand(x) \leq (mCov(i)))^2 \qquad (9)$$

where sCov(i) and mCov(i) represent respectively single and multiple coverage of router i. rand(x) is used to provide some stochastic properties. More details can be found in [15].

A new solution (line 11) is generated by accepting the new location of router i while maintaining other routers in their current locations. If a non-dominated solution is not found after a certain number of iteration (Stop_MCM), we suppose therefore having reached the optimal and the algorithm stops. updateAndPrune inserts (cost,cov) in arch and removes all dominated solutions from arch.

4.3 Multi-objective Simulated Annealing (MSA)

The MSA algorithm is an enhancement of SA algorithm proposed in [27]. The flowchart of MSA is presented in Fig. 2.

A router is selected and randomly moved, and the coverage change of MER is evaluated. If the change is accepted, we check if the new solution is not dominated by any solution in arch. In this case, the new solution is inserted, updating arch.

The equilibrium state of MSA is controlled by *Stop*, and it is reached when *Stop* = 0. Therefore, the temperature T decreases. MSA stops when $T \leq T_{min}$, the minimal temperature.

4.4 Multi-objective Simulated Annealing Based CM (MSAC)

The MSAC algorithm is a sequential combination of MCM and MSA. At the first stage, the MCM algorithm is used. Then the output serves as the input for MSA. The MCM will provide a rapid initial convergence, and MSA will refine the solution. This can be considered as a multi-objective extension of the Simulated Annealing based Centre of mass introduced in [28]. The flowchart of MSAC is provided in Fig. 3.

5   Simulation Results

To compare the proposed approaches, we randomly generate 12 instances with mandatory areas in terms of network coverage and cost-effective locations. We consider two grids of 50×50 and 100×100, with Stop_MCM = 500, StopEq = 250, nRun = 20. Router transmission range $TR \in [6, 10]$. The unit represents the length of an ER. If size (ER) = 20 m, the radius will be TR $\in [120\,\text{m}, 200\,\text{m}]$, and the grids $1\,\text{km} \cdot 1\,\text{km} = 1\,\text{km}^2$ and $2\,\text{km} \cdot 2\,\text{km} = 4\,\text{km}^2$. This is realistic since 802.11a/b/g/n routers have a theoretical outdoor transmission range ranging 120 m to 250 m. The simulations were conducted using Scilab 5.4.

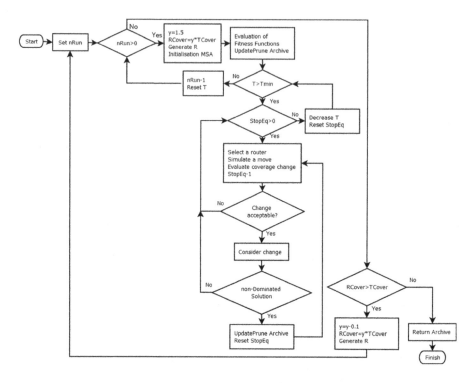

Fig. 2. Flowchart of MSA approach

Although this work is an extension of [9], it cannot be compared directly with the original work because of the multi-objective nature of the new formulation. The work in [9] did not consider the cost and was only focused on the coverage. To evaluate the quality of solutions of the Pareto front of the three approaches the min-max-regret criterion has been used. This metric is suited for non-repetitive decisions, that means the replacement of a solution after its implementation will not be acceptable. Given a solution s ∈ S, its regret value under the scenario x ∈ X is defined by (10).

$$Rg(s,x) = (val(s(1),x) - val_x^*(1))^2 + (val(s(2),x) - val_x^*(2))^2 \quad (10)$$

where $x \in \{1,2,3\}$ represents the different placement approaches, and val_x^* the optimal solution. Since we are in a minimisation problem using non-analytical objective functions, we consider the utopia $val_x^* = (0,0)$, that means the number of MER that are uncovered is zero as well as the cost of the system. The maximum regret value $Rg_{max}(x)$ of solution s is defined as $Rg_{max}(s) = max_{x \in X} Rg(s,x)$. The min-max-regret value is therefore the solution with the minimum maximum regret value. It can be defined by (11).

$$min_{s \in S} Rg_{max}(s) = min_{s \in S} max_{x \in X} (val(s,x) - val_x^*) \quad (11)$$

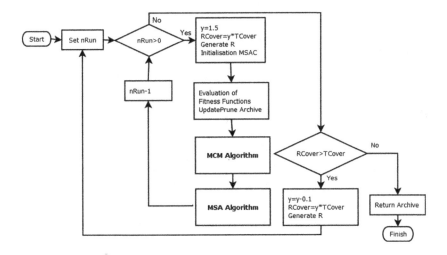

Fig. 3. Flowchart of MSAC Approach

Table 1. max and min-max-regret values.

Instances	1_50	2_50	3_50	4_50	5_50	6_50
MCM	0,925	0,887	0,93	1,001	1,001	0,859
MSA	0,862	0,795	0,703	0,974	0,834	0,716
MSAC	0,78	0,722	0,583	0,922	0,777	0,786
Instances	1_100	2_100	3_100	4_100	5_100	6_100
MCM	0,94	0,94	0,844	0,968	0,928	0,84
MSA	0,867	0,863	0,858	0,932	0,892	0,883
MSAC	0,961	0,884	0,892	0,926	0,916	0,842

Table 1 provides the max-regret value from different approaches for each instance. The min max-regret value is in bold. From Table 1, MSAC provides the min-max-regret value in x_50 instances. However, in larger instances (x_100), MSA dominates the others, apart from instance 5_100 where the MAS value is less than the one of MSAC.

Although the min-max-regret minimizes "the regret" of choosing a solution s, it can sometime skew the result. For instance, Figs. 4 and 5 present the Pareto fronts produced by the different approaches respectively for instances 4_50 and 5_100. In both Figures, MSAC provides the best Pareto front, that means, the Pareto front of MSAC dominated almost all the solutions of the Pareto fronts of other approaches. In other terms, MSAC provides the best trade-offs with the smallest cost percentage and the smallest percentage of uncovered MER. In fact, MSAC is able to relocate as much as possible mesh routers to cost-effective location to reduce the cost of the architecture, according to objective f_2, while maximizing the mandatory region covered by the set of selected routers.

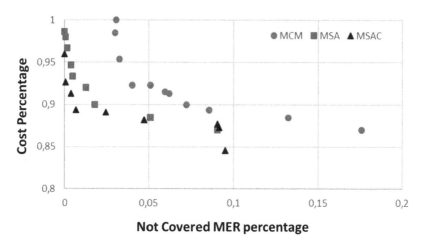

Fig. 4. Pareto fronts in Instance 4_50

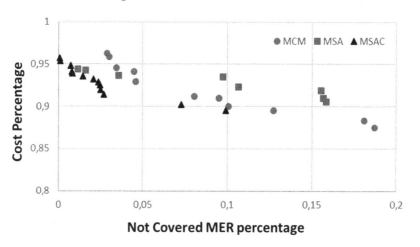

Fig. 5. Pareto fronts in Instance 5_100

6   Conclusion and Future Work

In this paper we introduce a new formulation of the mesh router placement problem in rural areas. Heterogeneous routers have been considered, as well as cost-effective locations that can reduce the cost of the architecture. Three multi-objective approaches have been defined to solve the problem: Multi-objective Centre of Mass (MCM), Multi-Objective Simulated Annealing (MSA), and Multi-Objective Simulated Annealing based Centre of Mass (MSAC). Simulation results have shown a better min-max regret of Pareto front in small instances and large instances respectively for MSAC and MSA. Although MSAC does not provide the min-max regret value in most of large instances, in most of the cases it provides a better Pareto front, meaning a better trade-off between the coverage and the cost of the architecture. Apart from improving MSAC in terms of quality of solution and robustness, future works will integrate suitable empirical path loss models such those defined in [31].

References

1. Africa Internet Users: 2020 Population and Facebook Statistics (2020). https://www.internetworldstats.com/stats1.htm. Accessed 21 July 2020
2. Akyildiz, I.F., Wang, X.: Wireless Mesh Networks. John Wiley & Sons, Chichester (2009)
3. Rey-Moreno, C., Graaf, M.: Map of the community network initiatives in Africa. In: Belli, L. (ed.) Community Connectivity: Build the Internet Scratch, pp. 149–169 (2016)
4. Ebongue, J.L.F.K.: Rethinking Network Connectivity in Rural Communities in Cameroon (2015). arXiv preprint: arXiv:1505.04449. (Lilongwe, M.)
5. Bernardi, G., Marina, M.K., Talamona, F., Rykovanov, D.: IncrEase: a tool for incremental planning of rural fixed Broadband Wireless Access networks. In: 2011 IEEE GLOBECOM Workshops (GC Wkshps), pp. 1013–1018. IEEE (2011)
6. Pötsch, T., Yousaf, S., Raghavan, B., Chen, J.: Zyxt: a network planning tool for rural wireless ISPs. In: Proceedings of the 1st ACM SIGCAS Conference on Computing and Sustainable Societies, pp. 1–11 (2018)
7. Yin, C., Yang, R., Zou, X., Zhu, W.: Research on topology planning for wireless mesh networks based on deep reinforcement learning. In: 2020 2nd International Conference on Computer Communication and the Internet (ICCCI), pp. 6–11. IEEE (2020)
8. Xhafa, F., Barolli, A., Sánchez, C., Barolli, L.: A simulated annealing algorithm for router nodes placement problem in wireless mesh networks. Simul. Model. Pract. Theory **19**, 2276–2284 (2011)
9. Fendji, J.L.E.K., Thron, C., Nlong, J.M.: A metropolis approach for mesh router nodes placement in rural wireless mesh networks (2015). arXiv preprint: arXiv:1504.08212
10. Benyamina, D., Hafid, A., Gendreau, M.: Wireless mesh networks design: a survey. IEEE Commun. Surv. Tutor. **14**, 299–310 (2012). https://doi.org/10.1109/SURV.2011.042711.00007
11. Garces, R., Garcia-Luna-Aceves, J.J.: Collision avoidance and resolution multiple access for multichannel wireless networks. In: Proceedings IEEE INFOCOM 2000. Conference on Computer Communications. Nineteenth Annual Joint Conference of the IEEE Computer and Communications Societies (Cat. No. 00CH37064), pp. 595–602. IEEE (2000)
12. Darties, B., Theoleyre, F., Duda, A.: A divide-and-conquer scheme for assigning roles in multi-channel wireless mesh networks. In: 2009 IEEE 34th Conference on Local Computer Networks, pp. 277–280. IEEE (2009)
13. Chaudhry, A.U., Hafez, R.H., Aboul-Magd, O., Mahmoud, S.A.: Throughput improvement in multi-radio multi-channel 802.11 a-based wireless mesh networks. In: 2010 IEEE Global Telecommunications Conference GLOBECOM 2010, pp. 1–5. IEEE (2010)
14. Ramachandran, K.N., Belding-Royer, E.M., Almeroth, K.C., Buddhikot, M.M.: Interference Aware Channel Assignment in Multi-Radio Wireless Mesh Networks. In: Infocom, pp. 1–12 (2006)

15. Pathak, P.H., Dutta, R.: A survey of network design problems and joint design approaches in wireless mesh networks. IEEE Commun. Surv. Tutor. **13**, 396–428 (2010)
16. Samo, S.D., Fendji, J.L.E.K.: Evaluation of energy consumption of proactive reactive and hybrid routing protocols in wireless mesh networks using 802.11 standards. J. Comput. Commun. **6**, 1–30 (2018). https://doi.org/10.4236/jcc.2018.64001
17. Fendji, J.L.E.K., Samo, S.D.: Energy and Performance Evaluation of Reactive, Proactive, and Hybrid Routing Protocols in Wireless Mesh Network. Social Science Research Net-work, Rochester, NY (2019)
18. Fu, B., Xiao, Y., Deng, H., Zeng, H.: A survey of cross-layer designs in wireless net-works. IEEE Commun. Surv. Tutor. **16**, 110–126 (2013)
19. Xhafa, F., Sánchez, C., Barolli, L.: Genetic algorithms for efficient placement of router nodes in wireless mesh networks. In: 2010 24th IEEE International Conference on Advanced Information Networking and Applications, pp. 465–472. IEEE (2010)
20. Ameen, S.Q., Muniyandi, R.C.: Improvement at network planning using heuristic algorithm to minimize cost of distance between nodes in wireless mesh networks. Int. J. Electr. Comput. Eng. **7**, 309 (2017)
21. Li, F., Wang, Y., Li, X.-Y., Nusairat, A., Wu, Y.: Gateway placement for throughput optimization in wireless mesh networks. Mob. Netw. Appl. **13**, 198–211 (2008)
22. Kemal, M.S., Ceocea, A., Olsen, R.L.: Gateway placement for wireless mesh networks in smart grid network planning. In: 2016 10th International Conference on Compatibility, Power Electronics and Power Engineering (CPE-POWERENG), pp. 144–147. IEEE (2016)
23. De Marco, G.: MOGAMESH: A multi-objective algorithm for node placement in wireless mesh networks based on genetic algorithms. In: 2009 6th International Symposium on Wireless Communication Systems, pp. 388–392. IEEE (2009)
24. Amaldi, E., Capone, A., Cesana, M., Filippini, I., Malucelli, F.: Optimization models and methods for planning wireless mesh networks. Comput. Netw. **52**, 2159–2171 (2008). https://doi.org/10.1016/j.comnet.2008.02.020
25. Wang, J., Xie, B., Cai, K., Agrawal, D.P.: Efficient mesh router placement in wireless mesh networks. In: IEEE Internatonal Conference on Mobile ad-hoc and Sensor Systems, 2007. MASS 2007, pp. 1–9 (2007). https://doi.org/10.1109/MOBHOC.2007.4428616
26. Ebongue, J.L.F.K., Thron, C., Nlong, J.M.: Mesh Router Nodes placement in Rural Wireless Mesh Networks (2015). arXiv preprint: arXiv:1505.03332
27. Fendji, J.L., Thron, C., Nlong, J.M.: Simulated annealing approach for mesh router placement in rural Wireless Mesh Networks. In: 7th International Conference, AFRICOMM, pp. 15–16 (2015)
28. Fendji, J.L.K.E., Thron, C.: A Simulated Annealing Based Centre of Mass (SAC) Approach for Mesh Routers Placement in Rural Areas. www.igi-global.com/article/a-simulated-annealing-based-centre-of-mass-sac-approach-for-mesh-routers-placement-in-rural-areas/243420. Accessed 12 June 2020
29. Ebongue, F.K., Louis, J.: Wireless Mesh Network: a rural community case (2015). http://oatd.org/oatd/record?record=oai%5C%3Aelib.suub.uni-bremen.de%5C%3ADISS%5C%2F00104709

30. Ebongue, J.L.F.K., Thron, C.: Centre of Mass of single coverage: a comparative study with Simulated Annealing for mesh router placement in rural regions. In: Proceedings of CARI, p. 203 (2016)
31. Fendji, J.L.E.K., Mafai, N.M., Nlong, J.M.: Slope-based Empirical Path Loss Prediction Models for rural networks at 2.4 GHz. Trans. Netw. Commun. **7**, 84 (2019). https://doi.org/10.14738/tnc.71.6162

Wireless Sensing and 5G Networks

Indoor Localization with Filtered and Corrected Calibration RSSI

Madikana S. Sediela[1]([✉]), Moses L. Gadebe[1], and Okuthe P. Kogeda[2]

[1] Department of Computer Science, Faculty of ICT, Tshwane University
of Technology, Private Bag X680, Pretoria 0001, South Africa
{sedielaMS,GadebeML}@tut.ac.za
[2] Department of Computer Science and Informatics, Faculty of Natural
and Agricultural Sciences, University of the Free State, P.O. Box 339,
Bloemfontein 9300, South Africa
KogedaPO@ufs.ac.za

Abstract. Nowadays Location-Based Services (LBS) applications are
proposed and presented in literature because of high growth in wireless
sensor networks. The LBS provide useful information about the person
or object's current position. Among these applications, Global Positioning System (GPS)-based positioning and navigation services have been
deployed in an outdoor environment. However, GPS requires being in
sight with satellites due to line of sight challenge. The GPS fails in
an indoor environment because of multipath effects caused by walls or
indoor setup in general. Meanwhile, Wi-Fi-based positioning system are
being proposed in literature and most of them utilizes the fingerprinting
algorithm. Whereby, measurements of Received Signal Strength Indicator (RSSI) are collected during the offline phase for radio map and positioning is performed during the online phase. Similarly, this approach is
faced with signal attenuation challenge caused by walls, desks, moving
people, or just the indoor setup in general. The collection of the signal strengths without correction can affect positioning accuracy. In this
paper, we present a model that utilizes Mean and Standard Deviation
to identify and correct unstable low RSSI outliers during offline phase
of Fingerprinting algorithm. We conducted comparative performance of
Machine learning classification algorithms based on corrected RSSI and
measured RSSI. The simulation results performed in MATLAB, indicates
that correcting the RSSI improves the accuracy, precision, and recall of
Fine Tree, Coarse Decision Tree, and Kernel Naïve Bayes to 95.1%, 94.8%
and 94.5% respectively.

Keywords: Fingerprinting · Mean · Standard deviation · RSSI ·
GPS · Wi-Fi

1 Introduction

Location-Based Services (LBS) applications have recently attracted more attention in the research community. These services are aimed at assisting and

© ICST Institute for Computer Sciences, Social Informatics and Telecommunications Engineering 2021
Published by Springer Nature Switzerland AG 2021. All Rights Reserved
R. Zitouni et al. (Eds.): AFRICOMM 2020, LNICST 361, pp. 59–73, 2021.
https://doi.org/10.1007/978-3-030-70572-5_4

improving customer gratification, thus improved conceptualization and analyses of both staff and customers actions and behaviours [1]. LBS provides useful information about the person's or object's current position. LBS can be categorized into an outdoor and indoor system. Among these applications, GPS-based positioning and navigation services have been deployed in an outdoor environment. However, GPS requires being in sight with GPS satellites. Due to this challenge of a line of sight with GPS satellites, GPS fails in an indoor environment because of multipath effects caused by walls or indoor setup in general [2–4]. Hence, indoor wireless location positioning is gaining momentum to locate objects within close area. Localization techniques such as Wi-Fi [5,6], Bluetooth [7,8], and vision-based techniques [9] are used indoor. Yet again, these techniques come with positioning pros and cons with regards to accuracy, energy consumption, and positioning delay [10].

Positioning are categorized as Trilateration and Fingerprinting methods, the former uses Time of Arrival (TOA), Angle of Arrival (AOA), or Received Signal Strength Indicator (RSSI) and the latter uses RSSI approach to create radio-map and estimates the location by matching RSSI. The fingerprinting method uses a probabilistic matching algorithm such as K-Nearest Neighbour (KNN), Decision Trees, and Naïve Bayes amongst others to estimate and make decisions. Nevertheless, the RSSI fluctuate because of multipath effects, interference, and shadowing effects [11] and without corrections of RSSI the localisation error of the matching algorithm is too high to achieve the needs of indoor LBS.

In this study, we propose a model to correct localisation error based on the fingerprinting algorithm. Our technique computes the mean and standard deviation to correct the measured RSSI values. We provide comparative performance metrics of Machine learning classification algorithms based of corrected RSSI and measured RSSI. Our results show an improvement in localization accuracy, with misclassification of 5.5% and 4.9% from 31.1% and 30.4% in the Kernel Naïve Bayes and Fine Decision Tree, respectively. The result confirms that the proposed model is effective in reducing the localisation error, and that to enhance localization performance we have to employ a filter to reduce RSSI measurements noise during the calibration phase of the fingerprinting algorithm.

The remainder of this paper is structured as follows: In Sect. 2, we present related work. In Sect. 3, we present the methodology followed to improve indoor location estimation. In Sect. 4, we present testing and results. Finally, we provide conclusion and future work in Sect. 5.

2   Related Work

Over the past few years, several models in location tracking and monitoring have been proposed to attempt to reduce the issue of multipath effects, and indeed acceptable results up to a certain extent were achieved. However, more research is explored to attempt to solve the multipath issue that affects localisation accuracy. Researchers in [9], proposed a computer vision application that is used to detect and track any human in the presence of Closed-Circuit Television (CCTV) with face recognition. The study developed a MATLAB 2015b application that focuses on the distance to detect a human being in the presence of camera, the influence of light, and the number of faces that can be detected at the time. The authors in [9] discovered that the application could detect and recognise only one face at a time, in any lighting condition, and up to a distance 300 cm from the CCTV. With limited coverage and effects of shadowing as the number of faces increase, the multipath issue remains a concern, which our research seeks to address.

The authors in [12] used a Wi-Fi integrated Device-free localization (Dfl) system for intrusion detection of the human body. The system relies on RSSI patterns caused when the human body in motion passes through the system. The Dfl system stores the RSSI changes and the raw data of RSSI is filtered using the Alpha Trim Mean Filter. The filter removes both the extreme high and low RSSI values, which are considered as outliers. This approach reduces the noise, however, another study in [13], showed that extremely high RSSI values are much closer to the correct RSSI value. Our proposed model differs with [12] and [13] models, because we do not eliminate nor consider only extreme high RSSI values. We eliminated RSSI values below the mean and standard deviation.

In [14], the authors proposed a Wi-Fi-based location estimation technique based on RSSI measurements from existing access points. They used a fingerprinting algorithm with additional visual access points and also adopted Kalman Filter and Particle Filter to improve localization error accuracy. Their results showed a high occurrence distance error of 4.49 m, because they in [14] focused more on the online phase filtering than the improvement of the calibration phase. A similar technique was proposed in [15], the authors employed Bluetooth technology to estimate the location and to enhance localization accuracy. The authors in [15] proposed propagation model to determine the distance using the RSSI measurements and weighted centroid. The Affinity Propagation Clustering is used to reduce the size of fingerprint by selecting the Required Points (RP) with the largest RSSI, as proposed in [16]. To reduce RSSI noise, authors in [15] used the exponential averaging method, which produced an 1.05 m 1.38 m error on corridor and furnished computer lab respectively. However, the solution is different from our proposed models because the exponential average gives more weight to the recent RSSI, which is filtered in the online phase.

The work presented in [17] differs with the ones in [14] and in [15], they used Artificial Intelligence approaches to improve localization error by deploying the Particle Swamp Optimisation algorithm (PSO). The Fingerprinting algorithm was employed with Wi-Fi RSSI measurements and the Weighted Fuzzy Matching algorithm was used to estimate indoor location. The Weighted Fuzzy Matching algorithm is also used in [18] to compare the effectiveness of Li-Fi compared to Wi-Fi. Besides, in [17], the PSO Algorithm was applied to improve the accuracy. The PSO algorithm reduced the localisation error 2 m to 1.2 m. In Table 1, we present an overview of the various existing localisation techniques and various available gaps to be considered for future work.

Table 1. Indoor localization models.

Author	Proposed model	Technology/Device	Ranging Method/Algorithms	Results	Pros	Cons
[19]	**Bluetooth based indoor location tracking**	– Bluetooth	– RSSI – Fingerprinting – Neural Network	– Using multiple locating modules greatly solved the problem of range	– ILTS is a real-time system that locates and send advert messages	– Bluetooth offers limited coverage – High costs of buying Bluetooth enabled boards and development of an extra program to be used on locating modules
[20]	**Smartphone-based real-time indoor location tracking to monitor the daily activities of the elderly at home**	– Bluetooth – Accelerometer and compass for step detection	– RSSI – Kalman Filter – Triangulation	– 7 out of 24 misestimate steps	– Average location error of 0.47 m	– Tested outdoor – Triangulation is greatly affected by multipath effects
[21]	**RF-based wearable sensor system for locating patients and doctors in a building**	– RF	– RF transceivers	– The receiver should be placed fixed above a certain height to receive a better signal	– Low cost – With better settings and placement of the system parameters, there is a high accuracy rate	– The signal between the transmitter and the receiver may be reflected and/or blocked by the walls – The microcontroller uses high power, which affects the transmitter's battery life
[9]	**Computer vision application which uses the technology of live video to detect and track any human in the presence of the video in CCTV**	– Camera	– Computer vision – Face Recognition	– Detect and recognise faces up to a distance of 300 cm	– Recognise a person in the presence of the camera	– Detects only one face at a time – Limited distance
[22]	**Indoor monitoring system for the elderly**	– Infrared	– ZigBee Network	– 96% detection of patients going out of bed – 95% for patients getting into bed – 97% for patients falling out of bed – 85% for patients entering the washroom	– Low cost	– Low accuracy(at room level) – IR can be harmful to human eyes – IR is meant for short-distance communication

(continued)

Table 1. (*continued*)

Author	Proposed model	Technology/ Device	Ranging Method/ Algorithms	Results	Pros	Cons
[23]	**Bluetooth based positioning**	– Bluetooth	– RSSI – Triangulation – Least Square Estimation	– Could not find the exact coordinates of the reference notes	– Addressed the issue of high infrastructure cost that comes with Wi-Fi AP methods	– Could not find the exact location – Triangulation suffers from multipath effects – Lack of precise time synchronisation in Bluetooth standards
[24]	**An indoor locating system that locates people holding BLE mobile devices**	– Bluetooth – Accelerometer and compass	– Monte Carlo localization algorithm – RSSI	– Computation of MCL was less than the grid-based Markov localisation when the same accuracy level was achieved – High accuracy in the non-LOS environment than triangulation and NB Algorithm – Stability in signal in the LOS environment compared to triangulation and NB Algorithm	– Error less 1 m in a LOS environment – 3 m in a complex non-LOS	– BLE offers limited coverage
[25]	**A system that locates vehicle location indoor**	– Wi-Fi	– RSSI – Fingerprinting – Neural Network	– Has an average error of 2.25 m	– Produced results capable of working as a standard GPS	– Was not tested indoor
[4]	**Three tier Indoor localization to track and locate mobile devices**	– Wi-Fi – Accelerometer, gyroscope and compass	– RSSI – Fingerprinting – K-Nearest Neighbors Algorithm (KNN)	– Accurate in both outdoor and indoor	– Flexible: with few adjustments, can be used in any building.	– Battery consumption

In most of the mentioned models in Table 1, we found that multipath effects and signal strength attenuation caused by the brick walls [26], human beings, and indoor environment setting in general is major concern. These challenges cause a significant error of RSSI measurements classified into [13]:

- **Fading** - which is the error caused by multipath effects of the walls and other indoor structures. Usually, a stronger value of RSSI is only affected by fading indoor.
- **Shadowing** - which is caused by the presence of people. The closer a person is to either a transmitter or a receiver; the more the signal strength will be affected.
- **Interference** - which is caused by the presence of other devices that share radio channels as Wi-Fi such as Bluetooth devices and microwave oven. If these devices co-exist, they will use the same frequency band, and RSSI measurements will be affected.

Therefore, all future location positioning methods must consider all these factors that affects the measure of signals.

3   Methodology

In this Section, we present our proposed model to correct the RSSI measurements. In Fig. 1, our proposed system architecture is represented based on the Fingerprinting algorithm.

Our EMPsys employs the Fingerprinting algorithm, which consist of the offline phase and the online phase. Database generation is performed during the offline phase by scanning for RSSI and populating it in the database from various known required points or points of interest. Our mobile application collects RSSI along with corresponding SSID, MAC address and timestamp from Wi-Fi-Direct-Enabled devices or any other alliance device such as Wi-Fi-Hotspots and sends them to a Firebase real-time database. The RSSI measurements are used to localise the devices, the SSID and MAC address are used to identify the device, and the timestamp is used to specify the time the device information was observed. During the online phase, the smartphone scan for RSSI from unknown location. A machine learning classification algorithm is utilized to estimate the target devices' location by matching with the radio map or database generated during offline.

3.1   Offline Phase RSSI Correction

In this study, we focus only on the offline phase sometimes called calibration phase in order to select a suitable algorithm for our online EMPsys model. We developed our offline proposed EMPsys model on Android Studio and the flow diagram for the offline phase is shown in Fig. 2. The SSID, MAC addresses, RSSI and timestamp at each RP are populated into a database.

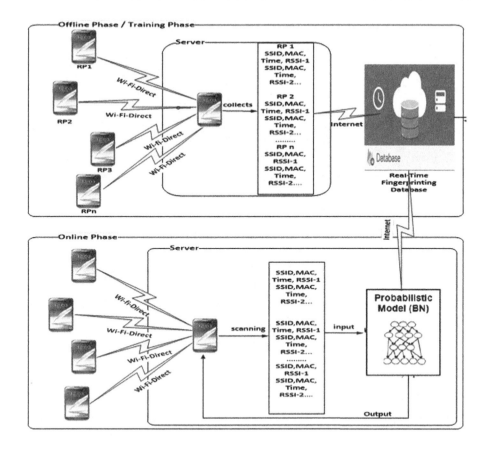

Fig. 1. EMPsys system architecture

The *WifiManager* API was utilized to check whether the Smartphones' WiFi is turned on, If not, the user should press the Calibrate button to turn it On by calling the *setWifiEnabled()* method and start with calibration. The target devices are placed at each Required Points (RP) during the offline phase. A number of N RP_N *(where N* $\epsilon\{1, 2, \ldots, N\}$*)* as represented in Eq. (1), are known locations. At each RP a number of M $RSSI_M$ *(where M* $\epsilon\{1, 2, \ldots, M\}$*)* measurements are collected by calling the *getScanResults()* method. The RSSI measurements are stored in a N × M table as given in Eq. (2).

$$RP_N = \{RP_1, RP_2, \ldots, RP_N\} \tag{1}$$

$$RSSI_{NM} = \begin{bmatrix} RSSI_{11} & RSSI_{12} & \ldots & RSSI_{1M} \\ RSSI_{21} & RSSI_{22} & \ldots & RSSI_{2M} \\ \vdots & \vdots & \ddots & \vdots \\ RSSI_{N1} & RSSI_{N2} & \ldots & RSSI_{NM} \end{bmatrix} \tag{2}$$

The SSID, MAC addresses, RSSI and timestamp at each RP are populated into a database.

Therefore we computed the Mean and the Standard Deviation (SD) on RSSI readings using Eqs. (3) and (5) from each RP to detect outliers. The mean and SD are therefore combined to form Eqs. (4) and (6) respectively

$$mean_{RP_N} = \frac{\sum_{i=1}^{M} RSSI_i}{N} \tag{3}$$

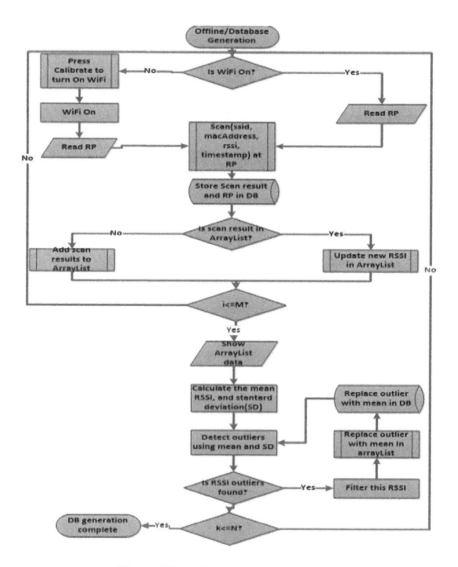

Fig. 2. Offline phase database generation

$$RSSI_{NM} = \begin{bmatrix} \overline{RSSI_1} \\ \overline{RSSI_2} \\ \vdots \\ \overline{RSSI_N} \end{bmatrix} \tag{4}$$

$$SD_{RP_N} = \sqrt{\frac{\sum_{i=1}^{M}(RSSI_i - \overline{RSSI_N})^2}{M}} \tag{5}$$

$$RSSI_{NM} = \begin{bmatrix} SD_1 \\ SD_2 \\ \vdots \\ SD_N \end{bmatrix} \tag{6}$$

For each vector of RSSI measured at RP_N, we apply the mean and standard deviation to filter each vector of RSSI, to correct signal attenuation due to indoor obstacles. All RSSI signals detected to be outliers are filtered and replaced with the mean, to eliminate poor RSSI to only consider stronger signal strengths from the mean.

3.2 Raw Dataset and Properties

The dataset used in our study to simulate the effectiveness of our proposed model is originally collected in the study named SHiB [27] for a smart home environment. The environment in which SHiB dataset was collected is divided into locations named localization, with 10 calibrations. The dataset is published publicly online on GitHub [28]. The values of dataset variables consists of [27,28]:

- Timestamp: The date and time of data which was collected.
- RSSI: Numerical signal strengths from each gateway.
- s1x, s1y, s1z, ..., s5x, s5y, and s5z: Categorical tri-axial accelerometer readings X, Y, and Z, which basically helps to identify activity the user is performing. X-axis is horizontal points right (x+) and left (x−), Y-axis is vertical and points up (y+) and down (y−) and Z-axis points outside (z+) and inside (z−) of the wearable device [29].
- Gateway: Categorical location in which the RSSI signal strength is read, and the Raspberry Pi are installed.
- Localization: Is the Categorical location where the user wrist wearable device is located.
- Activity: Categorical activity is used to determine the localization.

3.3 Classification

We used the SHiB dataset with 10 calibrations collected from 10 users. We combined all 10 calibrations to make as a single dataset with 56099 rows, then we split the dataset as training dataset and testing dataset given as 80% and 20% in MATLAB respectively. We compute the mean and standard deviation from each gateway and filter the RSSI measurements. The RSSI measurements that are considered as outlier are then corrected or replaced with the mean RSSI at each gateway. In the next stage, we simulated the Naïve Bayes, Decision tree, and KNN classification algorithms using the combined dataset as in [28]. Therefore, we compared the performance of each classification algorithms in accuracy, precision, and recall to determine the best performing classifier following a model in Fig. 3, to select a best suitable algorithm for our EMPsys online phase machine learning algorithm.

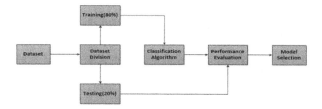

Fig. 3. Localization diagram

4   Testing and Results

The combined dataset with 56099 rows was loaded into MATLAB. The data is split into 80% training and 20% testing. The performance of evaluation on each machine learning algorithms presented in confusion matrix. The metric performance indicators are given by Eqs. (7), (8) and (9).

$$Accuracy = \frac{(TN + TP)}{(TP + TN + FP + FN)} \tag{7}$$

$$Precision = \frac{(TP)}{(TP + FP)} \tag{8}$$

$$Precision = \frac{(TP)}{(TP + FN)} \tag{9}$$

Whereby TN is True Negative, TP is True Positive, FP is False Positive, and FN is False Negative.

4.1   Localization Classification Results

Firstly, we used our combined dataset to predict the location of the user with a wearable device. The predictors used are the accelerometer coordinates, activity, and gateway. The result as summarised in Table 2, shows that the decision tree

Table 2. Localization classification results

Algorithm	Accuracy
Gaussian Naïve Bayes	94.3%
Kernel Naïve Bayes	94.3%
Fine Tree	100%
Medium Tree	100%
Coarse Tree	100%

emerged as the best performing algorithm with 100% accuracy and Naïve Bayes 94.3% accuracy.

Therefore we added unfiltered RSSI readings as another predictor with accelerometer coordinates, activity, and gateway, to check whether it affects the results in Table 2, to predict the location of the user with a wearable device. The results were not affected and remained the same. With good results of over 94% accuracy in all classifiers, we conclude that our combined dataset is effective, and RSSI readings do not affect localization (which is one of the variables in the dataset) prediction at this stage.

4.2   Gateway Classification Results

In the second step, we performed the gateway classification. We split the combined dataset according to each localization. Then, we only used RSSI as a predictor in this stage. We used our algorithm presented in Fig. 2 to compute the mean and standard deviation to filter and correct the RSSI, where all weak signal strength are discarded and replaced by the mean at each gateway. The results of the unfiltered and filtered RSSI are presented in Fig. 4(a) and (b) respectively.

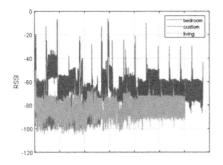
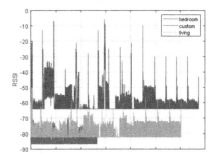

Gateway (Bedroom) Unfiltered RSSI   Gateway (Bedroom) filtered RSSI

Fig. 4. Unfiltered RSSI and filtered RSSI

The comparison results of unfiltered RSSI and filtered RSSI as summarised in Tables 3, 4 and 5. The results show improvements in accuracy, precision, and recall using filtered RSSI feature (Mean and SD). The Kernel Naïve Bayes showed an improved misclassification error from 31.1% to of 5.5% and with the new accuracy of 94.5%. Whereas the Fine Decision Tree showed an improvement from a misclassification error rate of 30.4% to 4.9% and with the new accuracy of 95.1%. In general, we considered the performance metrics and the results shows positive effects on the proposed mean and standard deviation approaches, with Fine Tree, Coarse Decision Tree and Kernel Naïve Bayes showing good results with an overall precision of 95.5%, 95.4%, and 95% respectively and also with the overall recall of 95.1%, 94.8% and 94.5% respectively.

Table 3. Gateway classification accuracy

Algorithm	Accuracy	
	Without filter	With filter
Gaussian Naïve Bayes	65.1%	92.4%
Kernel Naïve Bayes	68.9%	94.5%
Fine KNN	44.3%	80.2%
Medium KNN	47.9%	82.4%
Coarse KNN	55.1%	91.3%
Fine Tree	69.6%	95.1%
Medium Tree	70.1%	95.1%
Coarse Tree	67%	94.8%

Table 4. Gateway classification precision

Algorithm	Precision	
	Without filter	With filter
Gaussian Naïve Bayes	56.6%	93.1%
Kernel Naïve Bayes	72.9%	95%
Fine KNN	27.4%	90.7%
Medium KNN	69.2%	91%
Coarse KNN	61.2%	92.9%
Fine Tree	73.4%	95.3%
Medium Tree	73.8%	95.3%
Coarse Tree	62%	95.4%

Table 5. Gateway classification recall

Algorithm	Recall	
	Without filter	With filter
Gaussian Naïve Bayes	65.1%	92.4%
Kernel Naïve Bayes	68.9%	94.5%
Fine KNN	44%	80.2%
Medium KNN	49%	82.3%
Coarse KNN	55.1%	91.3%
Fine Tree	69.7%	95.1%
Medium Tree	70%	95.1%
Coarse Tree	66.9%	94.8%

The results listed in Tables 3, 4 and 5 show a significant improvement because all lower performing algorithms with unfiltered RSSI reduced misclassification significantly with filtered and corrected RSSI features. Applying our proposed model filter reduced the standard deviation and increased the stability of calibration RSSI measurements from each gateway. In addition, the accuracy of the machine learning algorithms adopted in our study performed better than the model that used the same dataset proposed in [27], which produced 92% accuracy at room level. Thus, we can conclude that our technique is effective and comparative in reducing the location error.

5   Conclusion

In this paper, we presented a model capable of filtering and correcting poorly received signal strength during the calibration phase of the fingerprinting algorithms. We presented challenges that affect RSSI measurements in indoor environment and, proposed a mean and SD RSSI filtering approach and finally compared the unfiltered and filtered RSSI. We selected and combined 10 calibrated SHiB dataset to predict the location of the user with a wearable device in the first stage. We conducted experimentation using several machine learning algorithms with accelerometer coordinates, activity, and gateway variables as our predictors for localization variable classification and all produced over 94% accuracy and shows that our combined dataset is effective. We then added RSSI variable as another predictor and the localization prediction results remained the same, which shows that the RSSI measurements have no effect in the first stage. In the second stage, we applied our proposed model to filter and correct RSSI measurements for gateway classification, and the results show significant improvement in accuracy, precision and recall with filtered RSSI. The results of the experimentation show the need to de-noise RSSI and that mean, and SD filter is important to correct and stabilize RSSI during the calibration phase of the fingerprinting algorithm. The filtering of RSSI approach is effective and comparative in reducing location estimate error with improved classification accuracy. In future, we intend to select a suitable machine learning algorithm for the online phase of our EMPsys and test the system to localize smartphones in real-time.

References

1. Hoshi, H., Ishizuka, H., Kobayashi, A., Minamikawa, A.: An indoor location estimation using BLE beacons considering movable obstructions. In: 2017 Tenth International Conference on Mobile Computing and Ubiquitous Network (ICMU), pp. 1–2 (2017)
2. Ciurana, M., Barceló-Arroyo, F., Cugno, S.: A robust to multi-path ranging technique over IEEE 802.11 networks. Wireless Netw. **16**, 943–953 (2010)
3. Khan, M., Kai, Y.D., Gul, H.U.: Indoor Wi-Fi positioning algorithm based on combination of location fingerprint and unscented Kalman filter. In: 2017 14th International Bhurban Conference on Applied Sciences and Technology (IBCAST), pp. 693–698 (2017)
4. Owuor, D.L., Kogeda, O.P., Agbinya, J.I.: Three tier indoor localization system for digital forensics. Int. J. Electr. Comput. Energ. Electron. Commun. Eng. **11**, 602–610 (2017)

5. Zhou, Z., Yang, Z., Wu, C., Sun, W., Liu, Y.: LiFi: line-of-sight identification with WiFi. In: 2014 Proceedings IEEE INFOCOM, pp. 2688–2696 (2014)
6. Yang, C., Shao, H.-R.: WiFi-based indoor positioning. IEEE Commun. Mag. **53**, 150–157 (2015)
7. Oksar, I.: A Bluetooth signal strength based indoor localization method. In: 2014 International Conference on Systems, Signals and Image Processing (IWSSIP), pp. 251–254 (2014)
8. Huh, J.-H., Seo, K.: An indoor location-based control system using bluetooth beacons for IoT systems. Sensors **17**, 2917 (2017)
9. Saputra, D.I.S., Amin, K.M.: Face detection and tracking using live video acquisition in camera closed circuit television and webcam. In: International Conference on Information Technology, Information Systems and Electrical Engineering (ICITISEE), pp. 154–157 (2016)
10. Luo, J., Zhang, Z., Liu, C., Luo, H.: Reliable and cooperative target tracking based on WSN and WiFi in indoor wireless networks. IEEE Access **6**, 24846–24855 (2018)
11. Li, H., Huang, Z., Sun, H., Wang, X., Qi, J.: A dynamic adaptive indoor ranging model based on RSSI. In: 2020 39th Chinese Control Conference (CCC), pp. 2850–2855 (2020)
12. Pirzada, N., Nayan, M.Y., Hassan, M.F., Subhan, F.: Multipath fading in device-free indoor localization system: measurements and interpretation. Mehran Univ. Res. J. Eng. Technol. **34** (2015)
13. Xue, W., Qiu, W., Hua, X., Yu, K.: Improved Wi-Fi RSSI measurement for indoor localization. IEEE Sens. J. **17**, 2224–2230 (2017)
14. Labinghisa, B., Park, G.S., Lee, D.M.: Improved indoor localization system based on virtual access points in a Wi-Fi environment by filtering schemes. In: 2017 International Conference on Indoor Positioning and Indoor Navigation (IPIN), pp. 1–7 (2017)
15. Subedi, S., Gang, H.-S., Ko, N.Y., Hwang, S.-S., Pyun, J.-Y.: Improving indoor fingerprinting positioning with affinity propagation clustering and weighted centroid fingerprint. IEEE Access **7**, 31738–31750 (2019)
16. Luo, J., Fu, L.: A smartphone indoor localization algorithm based on WLAN location fingerprinting with feature extraction and clustering. Sensors **17**, 1339 (2017)
17. Yu, H.K., Oh, S.H., Kim, J.G.: AI based location tracking in WiFi indoor positioning application. In: 2020 International Conference on Artificial Intelligence in Information and Communication (ICAIIC), pp. 199–202 (2020)
18. Yu, H.K., Kim, J.G.: Indoor positioning by weighted fuzzy matching in Lifi based hospital ward environment. JPhCS **1487**, 012010 (2020)
19. Hassan, A.M.A.: Indoor location tracking system using neural network based on bluetooth. In: International Conference on Electrical, Electronics, and Optimization Techniques (ICEEOT), pp. 73–78 (2016)
20. Liang, P.-C., Krause, P.: Smartphone-based real-time indoor location tracking with 1-m precision. IEEE J. Biomed. Health Inform. **20**, 756–762 (2016)
21. Ouyang, Y., Shan, K., Bui, F.M.: An RF-based wearable sensor system for indoor tracking to facilitate efficient healthcare management. In: 2016 IEEE 38th Annual International Conference of the Engineering in Medicine and Biology Society (EMBC), pp. 4828–4831 (2016)
22. Liu, H., Huang, J., Lu, C., Lan, Z., Wang, Q.: Indoor monitoring system for elderly based on ZigBee network. In: 2016 International Symposium on Micro-NanoMechatronics and Human Science (MHS), pp. 1–7 (2016)

23. Wang, Y., Yang, X., Zhao, Y., Liu, Y., Cuthbert, L.: Bluetooth positioning using RSSI and triangulation methods. In: 2013 IEEE Consumer Communications and Networking Conference (CCNC), pp. 837–842 (2013)
24. Hou, X., Arslan, T.: Monte Carlo localization algorithm for indoor positioning using Bluetooth low energy devices. In: 2017 International Conference on Localization and GNSS (ICL-GNSS), pp. 1–6 (2017)
25. Dinh-Van, N., Nashashibi, F., Thanh-Huong, N., Castelli, E.: Indoor Intelligent Vehicle localization using WiFi received signal strength indicator. In: 2017 IEEE MTT-S International Conference on Microwaves for Intelligent Mobility (ICMIM), pp. 33–36 (2017)
26. Zàruba, G.V., Huber, M., Kamangar, F., Chlamtac, I.: Indoor location tracking using RSSI readings from a single Wi-Fi access point. Wireless Netw. **13**, 221–235 (2007)
27. McConville, R., Byrne, D., Craddock, I., Piechocki, R., Pope, J., Santos-Rodriguez, R.: Understanding the quality of calibrations for indoor localisation. In: 2018 IEEE 4th World Forum on Internet of Things (WF-IoT), pp. 676–681 (2018)
28. GitHub. A dataset for indoor localization using a smart home in a box. https://github.com/rymc/a-dataset-for-indoor-localization-using-a-smart-home-in-a-box. Accessed 08 Jan 2019
29. Gadebe, M.L., Kogeda, O.P., Ojo, S.O.: Personalized real time human activity recognition. In: 2018 5th International Conference on Soft Computing & Machine Intelligence (ISCMI), pp. 147–154 (2018)

A Transmission Power Optimisation Algorithm for Wireless Sensor Networks

Visham Ramsurrun[✉], Panagiota Katsina, Sumit Anantwar, Amar Seeam, and Sheik Muhammad Arshad Mamode Cassim

School of Science and Technology, Middlesex University, Coastal Road, Flic en Flac, Mauritius
{v.ramsurrun,p.katsina,s.anantwar,a.seeam}@mdx.ac.uk,
sm390@live.mdx.ac.uk

Abstract. Wireless sensor networks (WSN) consist of a collection of independent sensor nodes that monitor certain conditions in different locations and transfer data through a network to an endpoint called base station. Because WSN nodes are often deployed outdoors where a direct power outlet may not be available, energy efficiency becomes a key factor in the design of WSNs. This work proposes an antenna transmission power optimisation algorithm (TPOA) which dynamically adjusts the power level of the transmission according to the last received signal strength indicator (RSSI). The mechanism was implemented and tested on an Xbee WSN that uses a modified Mixed Hop and signal Received routing for mobile Wireless Sensor Networks (MHRWSN) protocol. The energy consumption results have shown that the proposed system can save as much as 76% of power in *Tx* operations while maintaining a packet reception rate of above 85% .

Keywords: Wireless sensor networks · Transmission Power Optimisation Algorithm · Received Signal Strength Indicator · Xbee · MHRWSN

1 Introduction

WSN have applications in various fields including environmental monitoring in agriculture, disaster prevention, patient monitoring in healthcare, and machine monitoring in the industrial sector. WSNs are scalable systems that can consist of a few nodes to several thousands. As such, data routing optimisation is key in large systems to save energy, unlike small systems where communication is commonly achieved through flooding. A WSN may consist of any number of nodes scattered in an area that transfer data to a base station (sink node) through a multi-hop network. A node may consist of any number of sensors, a microcontroller, a battery and a radio transceiver that collect and routes data to a sink node [1]. The sink node is where all sensor data is gathered and it may also provide node management, data processing, and visualisation capabilities to end users. Since sensor networks are often deployed in hard-to-reach (for e.g. under a bridge, on a pole) or downright hostile environments (for e.g. underwater monitoring), a node should have long lifetime while being powered solely by batteries that usually cannot be

© ICST Institute for Computer Sciences, Social Informatics and Telecommunications Engineering 2021
Published by Springer Nature Switzerland AG 2021. All Rights Reserved
R. Zitouni et al. (Eds.): AFRICOMM 2020, LNICST 361, pp. 74–85, 2021.
https://doi.org/10.1007/978-3-030-70572-5_5

replaced or recharged. Consequently, power efficiency has always been one of the major design considerations in sensor networks despite major improvements in computation capabilities in the last decade.

Routing algorithms are an essential element in WSNs as they are responsible for the process of selecting best paths for sending packets from one source to a destination. In adhoc networks like WSNs, nodes have to work together in order to determine the best path for the packets. Different categories of WSN routing algorithms have been developed such as active (for e.g. AODV, TORA and SEER), proactive (for e.g. LEACH, GEAR, OLSR, DSDV, RPL and GPS) and hybrid (which works as active and proactive) routing protocols [2, 3]. The aims of these algorithms are to maximize network lifetime, maintain high packet delivery ratio, minimize delay, manage link failures and optimize reliability and overall Quality of Service (QoS). An even more advanced type of routing algorithms that has emerged of the years is the mobility-based routing protocol that can be used in mobile WSNs and Vehicular Ad-hoc Networks (VANETs). One example of such an algorithm is the Mixed Hop and signal Received routing for mobile Wireless Sensor Networks (MHRWSN) [4]. This paper presents an enhanced and energy-efficient version of the MHRWSN algorithm.

1.1 Rationale and Aims

As sensors become cheaper many manufacturers have adopted open source hardware design and standards such as XBee and Zigbee [5]. As a result, transmission power optimisation at the physical layer became viable. Because sensor transceivers share the Industrial, Scientific and Medical (ISM) band with many other devices, signal strength varies widely over time. As a design principle, sensor transceivers are usually set up to transmit at the highest power level to avoid errors and packet loss even when the band is uncongested and irrespective of the distance between nodes. Thus, there is a possibility for power usage optimisation by adjusting power levels based on external network conditions.

The goal of this paper is to implement a dynamically-adjustable power usage mechanism for mobile and static multi-hop networks. The main contributions of our solution are as follows:

- Create a novel RSSI-based transmission power optimisation mechanism that adjusts the transmission power of sensor nodes based on network conditions
- Achieve power savings while maintaining a high packet reception rate and without introducing considerable overhead

The rest of this paper is organized as follows. Section 2 gives a brief review of related works. In Sect. 3, we presents the experimental algorithms and the hardware design that were developed. Section 4 highlights the actual hardware/software implementation setup that was devised. Results and analysis are discussed in Sect. 5. Finally, Sect. 6 provides the conclusion for this paper.

2 Related Work

Ebert et al. [6] studied the relationship between antenna power level and energy consumption of IEEE 802.11 interfaces. They found a strong correlation between RF power levels, energy consumption and data rate while the interface was in transmit mode (Tx). A 1 mW to 50 mW increase in power level increased power consumption by 26% while in Tx mode, thus having a major impact on total energy consumption. Power consumption while in receive mode (Rx) remained unaffected.

Carmona et al. [7] made attempts to optimise power level of sensor nodes based on network conditions. They proposed a power management algorithm that optimised transmission power based on link status indicator (LQI). The algorithm was implemented at the application layer, thus not requiring any change in lower layer protocols. The energy efficiency of the system was estimated by using a mathematical model. A 12% and 22% energy savings have been observed on two different radio modules, with the latter having more varied power levels.

Furthermore, Srinivasan and Levis [8] argued that received signal strength indicator (RSSI) correlates well with packet reception rate (PRR) at high transmission power (Tx) when it is above −87 dBm while LQI of 85 could indicate anything between 10% and a 100% packet reception rate. Thus, LQI does not outperform RSSI in all circumstances as it may have been suggested in other works.

Ferro and Velez [4] proposed a mixed hop count and received signal strength routing protocol (MHRWSN) for mobile wireless sensor networks. They assumed that paths to a sink node are frequently being created and destroyed as nodes may be moving closer or farther from one another. The protocol uses a combination of RSSI and hop count to find the best path for data packets. This approach increases packet reception rate and decreases end to end delay.

Pariselvam et al. [9] developed an RSSI-based low energy utilisation scheme to enhance the network lifetime of the Accidental on Demand Distance Vector (AODV) routing protocol. The RSSI level of every node within the route way was checked to find the optimum path to the target in such a way as to minimize the energy expended during the routing process. This new accidental on Demand Distance Vector with the Low Energy Utilization (LE-AODV) is shown to outperform other protocols, namely AOMDV, AOMR and FF-AOMDV, in terms of packet delivery ratio, highest throughput and lowest energy consumption.

3 Proposed Design

3.1 The Transmission Power Optimisation Algorithm (TPOA)

The algorithm works as follows: when a node R1 transmits a data packet to another node R2 in the network, R2 records the RSSI of the received signal and sends an acknowledgement along with the RSSI value to R1. The RSSI is compared to a threshold and R1 readjusts its power level accordingly. If the node R1 does not receive an acknowledgment after a certain amount of time, it increases its power level to its maximum value and retransmits. This protects R1 from further packet loss due to low power transmission. The system will try to maintain a packet reception rate (PRR) greater than 0.85, the value where energy loss due to retransmission is much greater than transmission at maximum power level (PL). The TPOA assumes that a path to sink is known. It operates in a multi-hop setting on a link by link basis, while the routing algorithm will be tasked to finding a path to the sink node and appropriately assign the next hop address of the remote nodes. In the algorithm, acknowledgement packets are modified to report RSSI value of the packet that is being acknowledged. Since most remote nodes use duty cycling to save energy, this needs to be taken into consideration. Furthermore, because the sink node is assumed to be also connected to a battery, it also goes into an idle mode to save power. However, it always transmits at maximum power level.

```
1   Remote Node
2   upon node R1 goes into an active state
3        if node R1 has data to send
4            transmit data packet to neighbour
5            wait for acknowledge from neighbour
6                if acknowledgement is received
7                    if RSSI value<=upper_threshold and RSSI>=lower_limit
8                        wait x seconds and go back into idle state
9                    else if RSSI value> upper_threshold
10                       if PL < maximum PL
11                           set PL to PL+1
12                           wait x seconds and go back into idle state
13                       else
14                           wait and go back into idle state
15                   else if RSSI value< lower_threshold
16                       if PL < Minimum PL
17                           set PL to PL-1
18                           wait  x seconds and go back into idle state
19                       else
20                           wait x seconds and go back into idle state
21               else
22                   set PL to maximum value
23                   retransmit
24                   wait x seconds and go back into idle state
25       if node R1 receives a data packet from a neighbour
26           record sense data and RSSI R
27           send an acknowledgement with the recorded RSSI value R to neighbour
28           wait x seconds and go back into idle state
29   end upon
```

Fig. 1. Pseudocode of remote node with duty cycling

```
1   Sink Node
2   upon sink node goes into an active state
3        upon base station receives data packet from a remote node R1
4            record sense data and RSSI R
5            send an acknowledgement with the recorded RSSI value R to R1
6        end upon
7   end upon
```

Fig. 2. Pseudocode of sink node

The sink node is similarly tasked to record the RSSI value and report it back in the acknowledgement packet. The pseudocode of the TPOA for the remote node and sink nodes are shown in the Fig. 1 and Fig. 2 respectively.

3.2   The Modified Mixed Hop Count and RSSI Based Routing Algorithm (MHRWSN)

As shown in Fig. 3(a), the idle state of the MHRWSN routing protocol was modified to incorporate the TPOA when transmitting and forwarding data packets. Since it is implemented in the idle state, it will not affect the path selection mechanism of the routing protocol.

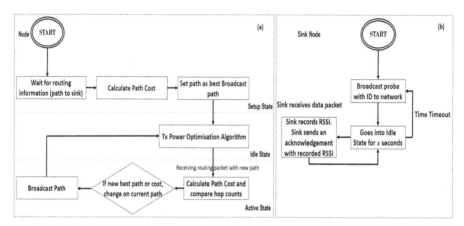

Fig. 3. Flowcharts of MHRWSN with TPOA for (a) Sensor node (b) Sink node

All broadcasts of routing packets are still performed at the maximum Tx power. The TPOA will only try to optimise the Tx power when sensor data is being transmitted. On the other hand, as shown in Fig. 3(b), the sink node will periodically broadcast a packet with its sink ID to the network. This not only permits sensor nodes to initiate their paths, but it causes a periodic refresh of available paths. New paths are identified and installed based on recorded RSSI values, while paths that have ceased to exist are removed.

3.3   Hardware Design

The nodes consist of Xbee Series 1 radio modules that were mounted on Arduino Uno microcontrollers. Even though Arduino microcontroller are not known for their energy efficiency, this setup enabled rapid iterations in both the hardware and software design. The Sparkfun Xbee Shield was used to mount the Xbee radio on the Arduino. The Xbee shield greatly simplified the connection between the radio module and the Arduino radio as it mounted directly onto the microcontroller and did not require any additional connection. A testbed was designed to easily debug and assess the system. The LCD was used to display information such as the current power level, the total number of packets sent since system was started, and a message when a packet was lost (acknowledgement timeout) (Fig. 4).

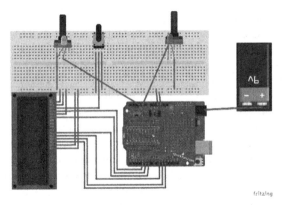

Fig. 4. Testbed with an Arduino UNO, LCD, Xbee radio module, Xbee Shield, a 9V battery and breadboard

4 Implementation

4.1 Software Implementation

The following programming platform, libraries and other software were used during the implementation:

- *Arduino IDE:* The Arduino IDE is an open source programming platform that is used to program Arduino microcontroller in C/C++ languages.
- *Software Serial Library:* This library is used by the Arduino to interface with the Xbee and the LCD. Software serial replicates the functionality of hardware serial.
- *Arduino Xbee Library by Andrewrapp:* The Arduino Xbee library is used by the arduino to communicate with the Xbee. The library supports most Xbee packet types [10].
- *LCD library:* This library allows the Arduino to display information on LCD display with the HD44780 controller [11].
- *XCTU:* XCTU is a software that allows programmers to interact with Xbee RF module. It can interface directly with Xbee radios using AT commands with the AT console GUI. It is also used to configure Xbee radios [12].
- *AT commands:* AT commands are used to send instructions to Xbee Radios like *ATDB*, *ATWR* and *ATPL* [13].

Node Implementation: The TPOA is first implemented in a simple node to node setup. The payload is instantiated as a *unit8_t* that represents the byte type in C. The command *tx.setOption(DISABLE_ACK_OPTION)* disables the acknowledgement of all *Tx* requests that are being made. The acknowledgement packet is modified to include the RSSI value. Thus, we disable the regular acknowledgement of *tx16* packets. The node constantly sends data with the function *xbee.send(tx)* and waits for the modified acknowledgement with the function *rx_packet()*. In the function *rx_packet()*, the node waits for an acknowledgement for 5 s. If it does not receive a packet during that time frame, it assumes the packet was lost. On the other hand, if it receives a packet, it records the RSSI in the packet payload. The algorithm also uses the following two values: *Upper_threshold* is equal to −87 dBm whereas *Lower_threshold* is equal to −80 dbm (A lower RSSI represents a better signal). The algorithm checks the RSSI and compares it to a lower and upper threshold. It then sets the power level accordingly with the *sendAtCommand()* function.

Sink Implementation: The sink does not optimise its transmission power as it may communicate with many remote nodes. It only sends a modified acknowledgment with the RSSI value of any received packet. In this configuration, the sink waits for a packet from a remote sensor node. When a packet is received, it reads the RSSI value from the Xbee radio with the function *getRSSI()*. It then sends a packet with the RSSI as a payload. The sink will not send a regular acknowledgement as the received packet will have the acknowledgement *option(byte)* disabled. The *getRSSI()* function executes the *ATDB* command.

MHRWSN Implementation: The routing algorithm is also implemented using the Arduino IDE according to the specifications given by Ferro and Velez [4].

Xbee Radio Configurations: The Xbee radio settings like *Pan ID, 16-bit source addresses* and *API Enable,* are applied using XCTU.

4.2 Hardware Implementation

Five Xbee modules mounted on Arduino Uno microcontrollers with Sparkfun Xbee shields were made.

Xbee S1 Module with* 1 mW *Wire Antenna: The Xbee Series 1 is one of the most popular 802.15.4 transceivers. Although it is marketed as an 802.15.4 device, it only uses the lower layer of Zigbee and does not support Zigbee routing protocol out of the box. However, the Xbee module can use a serial port to interface with other devices. By using an Arduino to perform network layer operation, we can implement our own routing algorithm [14].

The Sparkfun Xbee Shield: It greatly simplified the communication between the Xbee module and the Arduino. The shield also provides a prototyping area and a serial switch to select between hardware (UART) serial and software (DLine, Arduino Rx and Tx pins) serial. The shield, however, requires headers to be stacked on an Arduino. We therefore soldered the Arduino R3 headers onto the shield with rosin core solder. The headers include a 6-pin, 2 × 8-pin, and 10-pin header [15].

The Arduino Uno Microcontroller: The microcontroller was tasked to run both the transmission optimisation algorithm and the MHRWSN routing algorithm. It communicated with the Xbee with its Tx and Rx pin. The Xbee S1 is just a transceiver, and hence, cannot be programmed to run the algorithm. The microcontroller only interfaced with the Xbee transceiver during these three operations: packet reception, packet reception and AT command.

LCD Screen: The LCD used was a HD44780 standard 2 × 16 lines display with white characters on a blue background. It operates at 5v and both its backlight and contrast can be adjusted. It also support 4 and 8 bit parallel interface.

10 KΩ *Pot, Breadboard and Battery:* The 10 KΩ pots were used to step down the 5V voltage from the digital pins and 5 V pin of the Arduino. They were also used to control the contrast of the LCD screen. A breadboard was used to construct the circuit, together with a 9 V battery with a battery holder for supplying power to the Arduino.

5   Testing, Results and Discussion

To evaluate our TPOA, tests were performed for a multi-hop setup using MHRWSN routing algorithm, with sensor nodes being at two different distance intervals from the sink node, namely 30 m and 70 m. A preliminary pilot test was carried out and it showed distinctly observable and recordable changes in RSSI readings when at 30 m and 70 m respectively. The results were then compared with a setup using fixed power levels. The sink node remained at a fixed location while the location of the other nodes changed after every $n = 50$ packets. The test was performed in an outdoor environment. The packet reception rate (PRR) was recorded after transmitting n packets. A packet is considered lost if the node does not receive an acknowledgment within a limited time frame. The PRR was given by the equation:

$$PRR = 1 - (Total\ Packet\ Loss/Total\ Packet\ Sent) \tag{1}$$

The RSSI value was recorded directly at the sink node. Every change in power level caused by the optimisation algorithm was recorded. The sink node always transmits at the maximum power level. The TPOA was implemented on the other non-sink nodes.

Table 1. Results with nodes at 30 m and 70 m from one another with TPOA

Distance	30 m	70 m
PRR	1	0.98 (1 packet loss)
Average RSSI	−82.36	−83.408
Total packets transmitted while PL = 0	16	5
Total packets transmitted while PL = 1	29	16
Total packets transmitted while PL = 2	3	26
Total packets transmitted while PL = 3	1	2
Total packets transmitted while PL = 4	1	2

As we can see in Table 1, using the TPOA, the setup dynamically adjusted the power levels in order to maintain high packet reception rate. At 30 m, the majority of the packets were delivered using Power Levels 0 and 1, whereas at 70 m, the bulk of the packets

Table 2. Results with nodes at 30 m and 70 m from one another with fixed PL

Distance (30 m)					
Fixed PL	PL = 0	PL = 1	PL = 2	PL = 3	PL = 4
PRR	0.72 (14 packets lost)	0.88 (6 packets lost)	1	1	1
Average RSSI	−89.704	−86.653	−76.793	−69.578	−60.867
Distance (70 m)					
Fixed PL	PL = 0	PL = 1	PL = 2	PL = 3	PL = 4
PRR	0.7 (15 packets lost)	0.78 (11 packets lost)	1	1	1
Average RSSI	−94.790	−90.802	−82.380	−81.591	−79.592

were delivered using Power Levels 1 and 2. From Table 2, we can see that because of the fixed power levels, the setup could not move between power levels to maintain high packet reception rates when needed, thus causing packets to be dropped. As such, we can see the effectiveness of the TPOA in allowing the setup to switch power gears when needed in response to dynamic network conditions so as to maintain high PRR, while using minimum energy.

5.1 Power Consumption

Since only the power level was provided by the manufacturer, the power in milliwatts is calculated with the formula [16]:

$$P(\mathbf{mW}) = 1\,\mathbf{mW} \cdot \mathbf{10}^{(P(\mathbf{dBm})/10)} \tag{2}$$

The manufacturer also mentioned that only the maximum power level is calibrated while the others are only approximations (Table 3).

Table 3. Power level to mW conversions [16]

Power level	Power level (dBm)	Power (milliwatt)
0	−10	0.1
1	−6	0.2512
2	−4	0.3981
3	−2	0.6309
4	0	1

The total power consumed by TPOA was compared to power consumed with fixed transmission power for $n = 50$ packets. A graph of Total power consumption by Tx against total packet number was plotted.

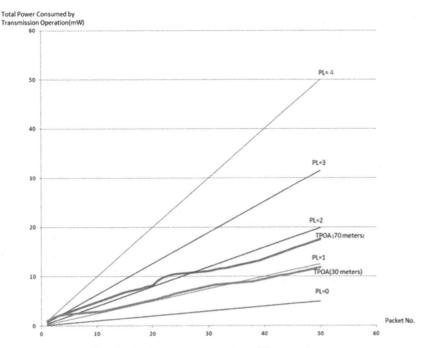

Fig. 5. Total power consumption of *Tx* operations

5.2 Observations

As shown in Fig. 5, TPOA has a total transmitting power consumption of 17.578 mW
at 70 m and 11.8612 mW at 30 m. At 70 m TPOA is comparable to a fixed transmission
power of PL = 2 (20.035 mW consumed). It is about 12% more efficient and it does
so by maintaining a 0.98 packet reception rate. At 30 m TPOA is comparable to PL =
1 (12.203 mW consumed), but TPOA is only about 3% more efficient. However, the
TPOA algorithm has a PRR of 1 while when with fixed transmission power of PL = 1,
the PRR is only 0.88. When compared to a system which only transmits at the highest
power level available, i.e. PL = 4 using a total of 50.012 mW of power, the TPOA is
about 76% and 65% more efficient at 30 and 70 m respectively. Some variations in power
consumption were noticed during transmission of packets 20–25. This may be explained
by the fact that TPOA may have had to jump to a higher power level to transmit some
of the packets because of destructive interference caused by some stray signals in the
testing environment. Thus, we can see that TPOA reduced power consumption while
keeping a high packet reception rate.

6 Conclusion

This paper proposed an effective mechanism to optimise the transmission power of
remote nodes according to actual network conditions using RSSI. The system used two
threshold values to maintain a high packet reception rate of above 85% so as to avoid

loss of energy due to retransmissions. The system was implemented using Xbee module and Arduino microcontroller. The test results showed that the proposed algorithm can save as much a 76% of power in Tx operations. Future works will involve applying the TPOA in other algorithms like AODV.

Acknowledgments. This work was supported by the Mauritius Research and Innovation Council (MRIC) under the URIGS research grant scheme ref. MRC/RUN/1605.

References

1. Gopika, D., Panjanathan, R.: A comprehensive study on various energy conservation mechanisms in wireless sensor networks. In: 2020 International Conference on Emerging Trends in Information Technology and Engineering (ic-ETITE), Vellore, India, pp. 1–5 (2020)
2. Arat, F., Demirci, S.: Energy and QoS aware analysis and classification of routing protocols for IoT and WSN. In: 7th International Conference on Electrical and Electronics Engineering (ICEEE), Antalya, Turkey, pp. 221–225 (2020)
3. Mahakalkar, N., Pethe, R.: Review of routing protocol in a wireless sensor network for an IOT application. In: 3rd International Conference on Communication and Electronics Systems (ICCES), Coimbatore, India, pp. 21–25 (2018)
4. Ferro, J.M., Velez, F.J.: Combined hop count and received signal strength routing protocol for mobility-enabled WSNs. In: IEEE Vehicular Technology Conference (VTC Fall), Quebec City, QC, pp. 1–6 (2012)
5. Orgon, M., Zagajec, L., Schmidt, I.: XBee technology: complex evaluation of radio parameters. In: 11th International Congress on Ultra Modern Telecommunications and Control Systems and Workshops (ICUMT), Dublin, Ireland, pp. 1–6 (2019)
6. Ebert, J.P., Aier, S., Kofahl, G., Becker, A., Burns, B., Wolisz, A.: Measurement and simulation of the energy consumption of a WLAN interface. TKN technical report TKN-02–010, vol. 314. Technical University Berlin, Berlin, Germany (2002)
7. Carmona, C., Alorda, B., Ribot, M.A.: Energy consumption savings in ZigBee-based WSN adjusting power transmission at application layer. In: 24th International Workshop on Power and Timing Modeling, Optimization and Simulation (PATMOS) Palma de Mallorca, pp. 1–6 (2014)
8. Srinivasan, K., Levis, P.: RSSI is under-appreciated. In: Third Workshop on Embedded Networked Sensors (EmNets), Cambridge, MA, USA (2006)
9. Pariselvam, S., Manikandan, M., Praveenkumar, P., Vinothvarma, R.: Energy efficient RSSI based low energy node utilization routing In: MANET. IEEE International Conference on System, Computation, Automation and Networking (ICSCAN), Pondicherry, India, pp. 1–6 (2019)
10. Rapp, A., Kooijman, M.: Arduino library for communicating with XBee radios in API mode. https://github.com/andrewrapp/xbee-arduino. Accessed 02 July 2020
11. Perry, B.: hd44780 - Extensible hd44780 LCD library. https://www.arduinolibraries.info/libraries/hd44780. Accessed 02 July 2020
12. Digi International Inc.: XCTU - Next Generation Configuration Platform for XBee/RF Solutions. https://www.digi.com/products/embedded-systems/digi-xbee/digi-xbee-tools/xctu. Accessed 02 July 2020
13. Digi International Inc.: PL (TX Power Level). https://www.digi.com/resources/documentation/Digidocs/90001506/reference/r_cmd_pl.htm?TocPath=AT%20commands%7CMAC%2FPHY%20commands%7C_____5. Accessed 02 July 2020

14. SparkFun Electronics: XBee 1mW Wire Antenna - Series 1 (802.15.4). https://www.sparkfun. com/products/retired/8665. Accessed 02 July 2020
15. JIMB0: XBee Shield HookupGuide. https://learn.sparkfun.com/tutorials/xbee-shield-hoo kup-guide. Accessed 02 July 2020
16. RapidTables.com: dBm to mW Conversion. https://www.rapidtables.com/convert/power/ dBm_to_mW.html. Accessed 02 July 2020

The Wideband Approach of 5G EMF Monitoring

Nikola Djuric[1(✉)], Nikola Kavecan[2], Nenad Radosavljevic[3], and Snezana Djuric[4]

[1] Faculty of Technical Sciences, University of Novi Sad, Trg D. Obradovica, Novi Sad, Serbia
ndjuric@uns.ac.rs
[2] Falcon-Tech, IT Consulting and Development, Dusana Danilovica 1, Novi Sad, Serbia
[3] Regulatory Agency for Electronic Communications and Postal Services (RATEL),
Palmoticeva 2, Belgrade, Serbia
[4] Institute BioSense, University of Novi Sad, Dr Zorana Djindjica 1, Novi Sad, Serbia

Abstract. The 5G mobile telephony has become one of the worldwide most anticipated technology, which is followed by strong controversy regarding potentially dangerous health effects. This technology relies on electromagnetic field (EMF) emission from its network base stations, increasing the level of existing EMF in the environment. Consequently, this fact has initiated deep concerns of the public, who demanded overall investigation and monitoring of the inevitable 5G EMF exposure. In the last decade, the wireless sensors networks for EMF monitoring emerged as an innovative approach for effective analysis of EMF in the environment. The latest one is the Serbian EMF RATEL network, which offers a sophisticated approach of telecommunication service-based EMF monitoring. This network performs wideband monitoring, counting the EMF contribution of all active EMF sources in a predetermined frequency sub-band. In this paper, the preliminary EMF monitoring of 5G is presented, explaining technical details on the used Narda AMS 8061 sensor, the acquisition process, as well as the analysis and dissemination of the measurement results. The EMF RATEL is envisioned to be a support for the control and management of EMFs in upcoming smart-city ecosystems, in which is expected that will display intensive EMF radiation in living surrounding, regarding various telecommunication services.

Keywords: EMF monitoring · 5G technology · Wireless sensors network

1 Introduction

The latest generation of mobile telephony, named 5G, is rapidly being implemented throughout the world. Following the report of the Global mobile Suppliers Association (GSA), the *"73 operators in 41 countries have launched one or more 3GPP compliant 5G services, the 88 operators have announced that they have deployed the 5G technology in their networks, while 380 operators are investing in 5G networks, in the form of pilots, planned and actual deployments"*, concluding with April 2020 [1].

R. Zitouni et al. (Eds.): AFRICOMM 2020, LNICST 361, pp. 86–98, 2021.
https://doi.org/10.1007/978-3-030-70572-5_6

Even though mobile operators recognize the benefits of 5G deployment, the strong controversy and an unprecedented negative public campaign has been following this technology. The negative campaign is insisting on potentially dangerous health effects of its high-frequency electromagnetic field (EMF), regardless the fact that recent scientific results demonstrate no evidence for such influence [2]. Therefore, it is foreseen that such unwanted shadowing can be one of the key factors for a slow and even delayed establishment of the 5G infrastructure [3]. The true reason lies in the introduction of new 5G base stations, as necessary EMF sources, that need to work in parallel with similar and already existing EMF sources from 2G/3G/4G technologies, raising uneasiness related to potentially exceeding admissible EMF limits [4].

It should be assumed that the public will always insist on lowering the power of the base stations and related EMF strength. Consequently, it would be reflected on dense installation of 5G base stations, as well as increased overall cost of 5G infrastructure. However, a compromise has to be made, highlighting the 5G EMF measurement and monitoring as a greatly important topic. It is to be expected that they have to act as a respectable and trustworthy mediator between public requirements for the safe EMF environment and a necessity of operators to effectively develop 5G infrastructure.

The organization of this paper is the following: Sect. 2 presents standardized approaches for 2G/3G/4G EMF measurement, as well as a proposal for 5G. Section 3 brings details on the EMF RATEL system concept and its 5G EMF monitoring, while Sect. 4 presents some initial results of 5G EMF monitoring by EMF RATEL. Finally, Sect. 5 concludes this paper.

2 Measurement of 5G EMF Level

Regarding the existing base stations in 2G/3G/4G networks, the measurement of emitted EMF level is based on the measurement of a time independent channel and later maximum traffic estimation, as defined in standards EN 50492:2008/A1:2014 [5] and EN 62232:2017 [6], obtaining the worst-case situation and maximum radiated EMF.

Analyzing only one base station, the measurements are performed using frequency-selective equipment, allowing selective EMF measurements in the frequency domain, and enabling the determination of the EMF level per frequency.

The determination of the maximal EMF level in the vicinity of the GSM base station (2G) is based on the *Broadcast Control Channel* (BCCH) signal, which is always broadcasted with constant and maximum power. The BCCH level can be determined after adjusting the measuring equipment to the appropriate GSM carrier frequency, on which this signal is transmitted, in a specific cell sector of the mobile network. The maximum EMF level is determined by measuring electric field level, as:

$$E_{GSM\_BS}^{max} = \sqrt{n_{TRX}} E_{BCCH}, \tag{1}$$

where n_{TRX} denotes the number of transmitters, and E_{BCCH} denotes the measured electric field from one BCCH only [5].

Analogously, the determination of the maximum EMF level, in the vicinity of the UMTS base station (3G), is based on the *Primary Code of the Common Pilot Channel* (P-CPICH) measurement. The measurement equipment has to be tuned to the appropriate

UMTS radio channel center frequency, while decoding P-CPICH signals in the code domain. After decoding, the maximum EMF level can be determined by estimating the maximum traffic load carried by UMTS base station, according to:

$$E_{UMTS\_BS}^{\max} = \sqrt{n_{P-CPICH}} E_{P-CPICH}, \tag{2}$$

where $n_{P-CPICH}$ is the factor defining the ratio of the maximum possible UMTS transmitter power P_{MAX} to the power of P-$CPICH$ signal component $P_{P-CPICH}$. Typically, it is assumed that $n_{P-CPICH} = 10$ [3, 5, 6].

Determination of the maximum EMF level, in the vicinity of the LTE base station (4G), is based on *Cell-specific Reference Signals* (CRS), which are always transmitted in subframes of *Physical Downlink Control Channel* (PDSCH), through one, two or four of LTE base station antenna ports. The CRS level can be determined by adjusting the measurement equipment to the center frequency of LTE radio channel and then decoding the CRS signals in the code domain. After decoding the CRS, the maximum EMF level in a specific LTE cell sector is determined as [3]:

$$E_{LTE\_BS}^{\max} = \sqrt{n_{CSR}} E_{CSR}, \tag{3}$$

where n_{CRS} is the factor that defines the ratio of the total radiated power by all active antenna ports P_{MAX} to the power of the CRS signal component P_{CRS} [3]. The n_{CRS} factor depends on the bandwidth of the LTE channel and it usually is: 300 for the 5 MHz channel, 600 for 10 MHz channel, or 1200 for 20 MHz channel [3].

2.1 Frequency Selective Approach for 5G EMF Measurement

The basic principle to measure EMF level of a pilot signal first, and to apply a proper extrapolation factor afterwards has been standardized for 2G/3G/4G technologies, but it is still under investigation for 5G technology.

There are attempts to develop a methodology for 5G, which will be in-line with this basic principle, utilizing the extrapolation technique and introducing appropriate factors for taking into account a number of 5G features, such as *Time Division Duplexing* (TDD) and sweep beam in the measured level of the 5G signal [7]. Estimation of the maximum 5G EMF level is proposed as following [7]:

$$E_{5G\_BS}^{\max} = \sqrt{N_{sc}(B, \mu) \cdot F_{TDC}} \cdot E_{RE}^{\max}, \tag{4}$$

where $N_{sc}(B, \mu)$ is the total number of subcarriers of 5G carrier, equal to twelve times the total number of *Resource Blocks NRB* (RBs) available for the signal (this parameter depends on bandwidth B and subcarriers numerology μ); the F_{TDC} is a deterministic scaling factor representing the duty cycle of the signal, i.e., the fraction of the signal frame reserved for downlink transmission; E_{RE}^{max} represents the maximum EMF level measured for a single *Resource Element* (RE), i.e. the smallest unit of the resource grid made up of one subcarrier in frequency domain and one *Orthogonal Frequency Division Multiplexing* (OFDM) symbol in time domain [7].

In order to harmonize 4G and 5G extrapolation methods, the proposed pilot channel for 5G is the *Physical Broadcast Channel* (PBCH) *Demodulation Reference Signal*

(PBCH-DMRS). This signal is a part of *Synchronization Signal/Physical Broadcast Channel* (SSB), and its physical location is determined by the Physical Cell ID. According to the proposal and experimental procedure from [7], the maximum EMF level, for a single RE is defined as:

$$E_{RE}^{max} = E_{RE}^{PBCH-DMRS} \sqrt{\frac{F_{beam}}{R}}, \tag{5}$$

where $E_{RE}^{PBCH-DMRS}$ is the average received EMF level for PBCH-DMRS, for a single RE; R is defined as the ratio of the average detected power of all SSBs in a burst to the power of the stronger SSB in the burst (this parameter accounts for the effect of the beam sweeping on the received EMF level of all SSBs in a burst, allowing precise estimation of the maximum received EMF level for PBCH-DMRS, starting from the direct evaluation of $E_{RE}^{PBCH-DMRS}$), while the F_{beam} parameter takes into account the effect of a potential boost of the traffic beams with respect to the maximum level of EMF received from the pilot channel, due to the effect of beamforming produced by the usage of *Multi-User Multiple Input Multiple Output* (MU-MIMO) antennas [7].

However, it can be seen that the estimation of the maximum 5G EMF, using frequency selective measurement, will not be an easy and straightforward task. Thus, some other approaches should be considered, such as the continuous wideband measurement in the dedicated 5G frequency sub-band.

2.2 Continuous Wideband Approach for 5G EMF Measurement

Even though the extrapolation is widely accepted and standardized, it should be indicated that it can result with overestimated EMF levels. In many situations, the base station radiates with lower power than the maximum one and therefore, the present EMF is typically lower than the maximum, considering extrapolation.

In that sense, the continuous EMF monitoring, used in EMF RATEL network [8, 9], can result in a better insight in EMF fluctuation, as shown in Fig. 1.

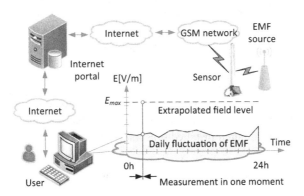

Fig. 1. The extrapolated field level versus continuous monitoring.

The continuous monitoring can be performed over a frequency sub-band, in a way that sums the EMF contribution of all active EMF sources. Such approach is known as wide-band measurement/monitoring and results with one, cumulative field value, regardless the individual contribution of any source.

Such approach cannot distinguish frequencies and thus cannot offer field level per frequency, as the frequency selective measurement does. However, it can be advantageous through its high measurement speed, particularly when cumulative field level is required, as it is the case with investigation over location with unknown EMF sources.

3   The EMF RATEL Monitoring of 5G EMF

The EMF RATEL was launched in 2017, by *Serbian Regulatory Agency for Electronic Communications and Postal Services* (RATEL) [10], as an innovative approach for long-term EMF monitoring. This network is established on spatially distributed wireless monitoring sensors, performing EMF observation over the Republic of Serbia, in order to timely inform the Serbian public on the present level of EMF [8, 9].

3.1   The EMF RATEL Concept

This network uses autonomous EMF monitoring sensors, installed in zones of special interest or zones of high sensitivity. The sensors are joined in a unified EMF wireless sensors network, as shown in Fig. 2.

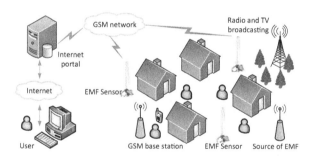

Fig. 2. The concept of EMF RATEL monitoring network.

Those sensors acquire measurement results of daily EMF levels, sending them over the existing mobile telephony network to the centralized database of the EMF RATEL Internet portal. Currently, forty-three sensors are active in major Serbian cities [9], while the goal is to reach one hundred installed sensors till 2021.

3.2   The Service-Based Wideband EMF Monitoring

The EMF RATEL network uses Narda AMS 8061 monitoring sensor [11], for modern EMF monitoring per telecommunication service, i.e. wideband monitoring in service frequency sub-band, known as the service-based monitoring.

The sensor hardware and main features are presented in Fig. 3.

> ITU-T K.83 compliant
> Monitors individually programmable frequency bands
> Internal modem for wireless communication
> USB / Ethernet data transfer
> SD memory card
> Temperature / air humidity sensor
> GPS sensor
> PC software with alarm functions
> Autonomous power supply from solar cells

Fig. 3. Narda AMS 8061 monitoring sensor [11].

Narda AMS 8061 sensor covers a wide frequency range from 100 kHz – 6 GHz, supporting separate and simultaneous monitoring in up to twenty programmable frequency sub-bands, in this main range [11]. Currently, the EMF RATEL is programed to perform service-based monitoring in frequency sub-bands presented in Table 1.

Table 1. The EMF RATEL monitored frequency sub-bands.

No	Frequency sub-band	Telecommunication service
1	87 MHz–108 MHz	FM radio
2	430 MHz–470 MHz	Functional radio links
3	470 MHz–790 MHz	Digital TV (DVB-T2)
4	790 MHz–821 MHz	Mobile 4G download (DL)
5	832 MHz–862 MHz	Mobile 4G upload (UL)
6	880 MHz–915 MHz	Mobile 2G/3G UL
7	925 MHz–960 MHz	Mobile 2G/3G DL
8	1710 MHz–1780 MHz	Mobile 2G/4G UL
9	1800 MHz–1880 MHz	Mobile 2G/3G DL
10	2110 MHz–2170 MHz	Mobile 3G DL
11	2400 MHz–2500 MHz	Wi-Fi
12	2520 MHz–2660 MHz	Mobile 4G – NSA 5G UL/DL
13	3400 MHz–3800 MHz	Mobile 5G DL/UL
14	5200 MHz–5800 MHz	Wi-Fi

Those sub-bands have been defined by RATEL, concerning the existing spectral allocation in the Republic of Serbia. In order to support testing activates on the pilot 5G network, the frequency sub-band from 3400 MHz to 3800 MHz is allocated to 5G.

Furthermore, in order to fully exploit Narda AMS 8061 sensor ability, the frequency sub-bands for 2G/3G/4G technologies have been covered, as well as sub-bands for FM radio, digital TV and Wi-Fi technologies.

The intention was to make a comparison between the EMF level of 2G/3G/4G and 5G technologies, having in mind unreliable information from various social networks, which propagate that 5G EMF level will be drastically higher. Thus, the EMF RATEL feature of the service-based EMF monitoring has been used to help and clarify doubts on the real EMF contribution of existing telecommunication services, while providing authorized measurement results and valid technical information for public debate on EMF levels in environment and their potential influence on health.

3.3 The AMS 8061 Data Transfer in EMF RATEL System

The implemented sensor AMS 8061 is equipped with GSM modem [11], allowing Internet access over the existing mobile telephony network. The sensor measurement results are wirelessly acquired and daily transferred to the centralized database of the EMF RATEL system [12], as depicted in Fig. 4.

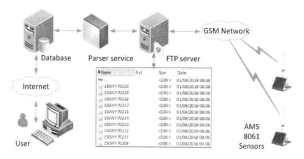

Fig. 4. The AMS 8061 data transfer in the EMF RATEL system [12].

Narda AMS 8061 sensor communicates with the dedicated FTP server, which performs as a centralized data storage hub for all EMF RATEL monitoring sensors. The measurement results are packed into specially formatted ".D61" binary files [11, 12] and transferred with some other data to the FTP personal folder of the sensor [12].

In order to obtain usable data, those ".D61" files are processed with dedicated parser function [12], extracting valuable data from all records and saving them into database. Those data are published and freely offered to interested users.

4   The Initial Results of 5G EMF Monitoring by EMF RATEL

The first 5G testing base station was installed on Science-Technological Park building, in Belgrade, the capitol city of the Republic of Serbia. Therefore, the AMS 8061 sensor was installed in vicinity of this 5G base station, at the distance of 60 m, performing the monitoring of the electric field strength, as shown in Fig. 5.

The EMF RATEL system is intended to transparently and timely inform the Serbian public on daily EMF levels, using a dedicated Internet portal [9]. The measurement data are illustrated by time-line graphs, offering detailed information on EMF fluctuation.

Moreover, several user-friendly features have been implemented in the Internet portal, allowing users to analyze the measurement results per telecommunication service, in the selected time period.

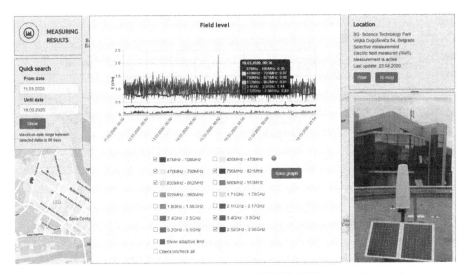

Fig. 5. Dissemination of the service-based EMF RATEL monitoring results.

Regarding handy work, users can select/deselect specific service and can compare its EMF levels with field limits for each service, prescribed by the Serbian legislation for the general population [13], as shown in Fig. 6.

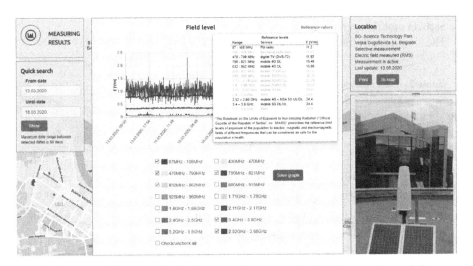

Fig. 6. The Serbian prescribed reference values per service for the general population.

A number of additional features can be found on EMF RATEL Internet portal [9], allowing users to work and analyze measurement results, along with saving and printing. Furthermore, the acquired measurement results are delivered for free use over the national Open Data Portal [14], as shown in Fig. 7, which is the central hub where data of the public interest are gathered, from all Serbian public institutions.

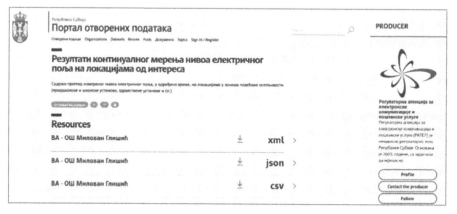

Fig. 7. Part of the Serbian Open Data Portal with results of EMF monitoring.

4.1 Analyses of Measurement Results from Service-Based Monitoring

The AMS 8061 sensor performed EMF monitoring of the 5G EMF strength, every six minutes, as defined by SRPS EN 50413:2010/A1:2014 standard [15], during the fifth month period: from November 1th, 2019 till March 19th 2020, in which 5G network of the Serbian mobile operator Telenor was tested.

The simple analysis of the measurement results is presented in Table 2.

Table 2. Data analyses for EMF RATEL location "BG – Science-Technological Park".

No	Frequency sub-band	Telecommunication service	E [V/m]		
			Max	Average	Limit
1	87 MHz–108 MHz	FM radio	1.65	0.21	11.20
2	430 MHz–470 MHz	Functional radio links	0.61	0.02	11.41
3	470 MHz–790 MHz	Digital TV (DVB-T2)	1.45	0.08	11.92
4	790 MHz–821 MHz	Mobile 4G download (DL)	2.24	0.07	15.46
5	832 MHz–862 MHz	Mobile 4G upload (UL)	0.08	0.01	15.86

(continued)

Table 2. (*continued*)

No	Frequency sub-band	Telecommunication service	E [V/m]		
			Max	Average	Limit
6	880 MHz–915 MHz	Mobile 2G/3G UL	0.10	0.01	16.32
7	925 MHz–960 MHz	Mobile 2G/3G DL	0.18	0.10	16.73
8	1710 MHz–1780 MHz	Mobile 2G/4G UL	0.20	0.01	22.74
9	1800 MHz–1880 MHz	Mobile 2G/3G DL	4.93	1.07	23.33
10	2110 MHz–2170 MHz	Mobile 3G DL	2.00	1.03	24.40
11	2400 MHz–2500 MHz	Wi-Fi	0.21	0.02	24.40
12	2520 MHz–2660 MHz	Mobile 4G–NSA 5G UL/DL	3.28	1.00	24.40
13	3400 MHz–3800 MHz	Mobile 5G DL/UL	4.48	1.02	24.40
14	5200 MHz–5800 MHz	Wi-Fi	0.72	0.45	24.40

The table presents maximal detected values per service, as well as, more importantly, the average electric field value, which reveals that the mobile telephony services dominate the "BG – Science-Technological Park" location, as presented in Fig. 8.

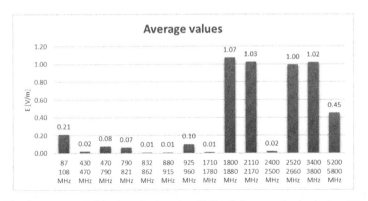

Fig. 8. Average field values for location "BG – Science technological park".

It can be seen that the electric field level of 5G technology is very similar to levels for 2G/3G/4G. Even those values are acquired in testing period it can be presumed that levels will be the same during the full utilization of 5G technology. However, the 5G is to be implemented in the Republic of Serbia during 2021, when additional service-based EMF monitoring campaign will be conducted, in order to obtain real-time EMF levels of fully functional 5G service.

When comparing obtained field levels, it can be noticed that they are far away from the prescribed and allowed Serbian reference levels [13], depicted in Fig. 9.

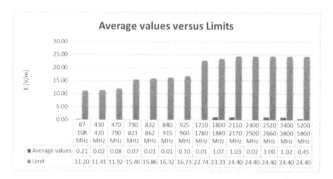

Fig. 9. Averaged field values versus Serbian prescribed reference levels (limit) [13].

It should be emphasized that the Serbian EMF legislation is based on internationally accepted "Guidelines for limiting exposure to time-varying electric, magnetic, and electromagnetic fields (up to 300 GHz)", announced by the *International Commission on Non-Ionizing Radiation Protection* (ICNIRP) in 1998 [16], whose reference levels are additionally reduced by 2.5 times for use in the Republic of Serbia.

Having in mind this fact, the "BG – Science-Technological Park" location, where 5G technology was tested, can be considered as a location with a low level of the high frequency electric field, produced by existing telecommunication services.

However, such conclusion has to be verified by further monitoring campaigns, particularly when 5G is fully deployed in the Republic of Serbia. For such activities, the EMF RATEL feature of service-based EMF monitoring is an excellent base for future comprehensive EMF investigation per telecommunication services.

5　Conclusion

The 5G technology, as natural evolution of mobile telephony, offers a number of features, which will radically improve the technical capability of Internet access and data transfer. However, the 5G has been followed by unprecedented, negative campaign, insisting on irregular levels and unsafe health effects of its high-frequency EMF.

Accordingly, the appropriate methodologies for 5G EMF measurements are being developed, in order to clarify doubts on existing 5G EMF levels. Several techniques have been proposed, where some of them are in-line with standardized EMF measurements for 2G/3G/4G technologies.

However, the Serbian EMF RATEL system offers a different approach, the continuous wideband EMF monitoring per telecommunication services, summing the EMF contribution of all sources per frequency sub-bands. Such service-based approach can be used for 5G, as well as 2G/3G/4G, providing comparison among their EMF levels.

This paper presents the preliminary EMF monitoring results of testing 5G technology in Serbia, exploiting the capability of EMF RATEL system. The early measurements, acquired during the period of five-month-long 5G testing, demonstrate that 5G EMF levels are very similar to the existing 2G/3G/4G EMF levels.

All these levels are far below the Serbian prescribed reference levels. Also, it can be seen that, for some telecommunication services, the acquired EMF levels are twenty and more times lower than the prescribed field limit. However, additional monitoring campaigns are required in future, particularly after the 5G is fully deployed and in the real cases where several base stations cover the same cell.

The service-based EMF monitoring of EMF RATEL intends to improve the quality of human life in approaching modern EMF environment, particularly for developing regions, where social awareness on EMF and environment could be additionally increased. Such approach of EMF monitoring offers daily EMF observation and better knowledge on EMF spatial distribution, as well as demanding feature to timely inform the public on existing EMF levels and their influence on health.

Finally, this system and such feature can serve as an appropriate mediator between normal requests of the general population for the EMF safe living environment and commercial mobile operators that require the installation of additional EMF sources, in order to improve their telecommunication infrastructure.

References

1. Global mobile Suppliers Association (GSA) – April 2020 Report. https://www.ratel.rs/upl oads/documents/empire_plugin/GSA5G.pdf. Accessed 20 May 2020
2. Final Opinion on Potential Health Effects of Exposure to Electromagnetic Fields (EMF) – Scientific Committee on Emerging and Newly Identified Health Risks (SCENIRH) (2015). https://ec.europa.eu/health/scientific_committees/emerging/docs/scenihr_o_041.pdf. Accessed 20 May 2020
3. Pawlak, R., Krawiec, P., Żurek, J.: On measuring electromagnetic fields in 5G technology. IEEE Access 7, 29826–29835 (2019). https://doi.org/10.1109/ACCESS.2019.2902481
4. International Commission on Non-Ionizing Radiation Protection (ICNIRP). Guidelines for Limiting Exposure to Electromagnetic Fields (100 kHz to 300 GHz), Health Physics, vol. 118, no. 5, pp. 483–524, May 2020. https://doi.org/10.1097/HP.0000000000001210.
5. Basic standard for the in-situ measurement of electromagnetic field strength related to human exposure in the vicinity of base stations, EN 50492:2008/A1:2014 (2014)
6. Determination of RF field strength, power density and SAR in the vicinity of radiocommunication base stations for the purpose of evaluating human exposure, EN 62232:2017 (2017)
7. Franci, D., et al.: Experimental procedure for fifth generation (5G) electromagnetic field (EMF) measurement and maximum power extrapolation for human exposure assessment. Environments 7, 22 (2020). https://doi.org/10.3390/environments7030022
8. Djuric, N., Kavecan, N., Mitic, M., Radosavljevic, N., Boric, A.: The concept review of the EMF RATEL monitoring system. In: 22nd International Microwave and Radar Conference – MIKON 2018, 15–17 May 2018, Poznań, Poland, pp. 1–3 (2018)
9. EMF RATEL Internet portal. https://emf.ratel.rs. Accessed 20 May 2020
10. Regulatory Agency for Electronic Communications and Postal Services (RATEL). https://www.ratel.rs/en/. Accessed 20 May 2020
11. User's Manual Narda AMB-8061 Area Monitor Selective (2015). https://www.narda-sts.us/-pdf_files/AMS8061EN-71006-1.22.pdf. Accessed 20 May 2020
12. Djuric, N., Kavecan, N., Kljajic, D., Mijatovic, G., Djuric, S.: Data acquisition in Narda's wireless stations based EMF RATEL. In: International Conference on Sensing and Instrumentation in IoT Era – ISSI 2019, 29–30 August 2019, Lisbon, Portugal, pp. 1–6 (2019)

13. The rulebook on the limits of exposure to non-ionizing radiation, Official gazette of the Republic of Serbia, no. 104/09. https://www.sepa.gov.rs/download/strano/pravilnik5.pdf. Accessed 20 May 2020
14. The Serbian Open Data Portal. https://data.gov.rs/sr/. Accessed 20 May 2020
15. Basic standard on measurement and calculation procedures for human exposure to electric, magnetic and electromagnetic fields (0 Hz–300 GHz), SRPS EN 50413:2010/A1:2014 (2014)
16. Guidelines for limiting exposure to time-varying electric, magnetic, and electromagnetic fields (up to 300 GHz), International Commission on Non-Ionizing Radiation Protection - ICNIRP (1998). https://www.icnirp.org/cms/upload/publications/ICNIRPemfgdl.pdf. Accessed 20 May 2020

ANN-FL Secure Handover Protocol for 5G and Beyond Networks

Vincent O. Nyangaresi[1]([⊠]), Anthony J. Rodrigues[2], and Silvance O. Abeka[2]

[1] Tom Mboya University College, Homabay, Kenya
vincentyoung88@gmail.com
[2] Jaramogi Oginga Odinga University of Science and Technology, Bondo, Kenya
tonyaniceto@gmail.com, silvancea@gmail.com

Abstract. Technical network challenges in 5G relates to handover authentication, user privacy protection and resource management. Due to interoperability requirements among the heterogeneous networks (Hetnets), the security requirements for 5G are high compared to 2G, 3G and 4G. The current 5G handover protocols are based on either fuzzy logic (FL), artificial neural networks (ANN), blockchain, software defined network (SDN), or Multi-layer Feed Forward Network (MFNN). These protocols have either long latencies or focus on either security or quality of services parameters such as user satisfaction. The usage of these inefficient authentication schemes during 5G handovers lead to performance degradation in heterogeneous cells and increases the delay. In addition, 5G networks experience frequent handover failures and increased handover delays. Consequently, the provision of strong security, privacy and low latency handovers is required for the successful deployment of 5G networks such as 5G wireless local area networks (5G-WLAN) heterogeneous networks. These new requirements, coupled with demands for higher scalability, reliability, security, data rates, quality of service (QoS), and support for internet of everything (IoE) have seen the shift from 5G to beyond 5G (B5G). However, 5G and B5G are incapable of providing the complete requirements of IoE such as enhanced security and QoS. This paper sought to develop an ANN-FL protocol that addressed both security and QoS in 5G and B5G networks. The simulation results showed that the developed protocol was robust against attacks such de-synchronization and tracing attacks and yielded a 27.1% increase in handover success rate, a 27.3% reduction in handover failure rate, and a 24.1% reduction in ping pong handovers.

Keywords: 5G · Hetnets · Authentication · Ping pong rate · Handover success rate · Handover failure rates

1 Introduction

Although a number of countries have commenced the deployment of 5G networks, the increased incorporation of automated systems in computer networks and the ever-growing data centric devices may exceed the 5G capabilities. According to researchers

© ICST Institute for Computer Sciences, Social Informatics and Telecommunications Engineering 2021
Published by Springer Nature Switzerland AG 2021. All Rights Reserved
R. Zitouni et al. (Eds.): AFRICOMM 2020, LNICST 361, pp. 99–118, 2021.
https://doi.org/10.1007/978-3-030-70572-5_7

in [1], applications such as virtual reality require a minimum of 10 Gpbs and hence need to shift to beyond 5G (B5G) which promises improved quality of service (QoS), lower latency, higher data rates and system capacity compared to 5G networks. However, authors in [2] explain that 5G and B5G are incapable of providing the complete requirements of the Internet of Everything (IoE) and as such, a high demand for 6G arises. The 6G networks promise ultra massive machine type communications, extreme reliability, low-latency communications, enhanced mobile broadband, large coverage, extremely low-power communications, and support for high mobility [3].

Small cell networks have been introduced to enhance received signal quality and hence improvements in energy, spectral efficiency and throughput of cellular networks [4]. Consequently, 5G, beyond 5G (B5G) and 6G networks are characterized by small sized cells. Ultra densification is another key feature of 6G networks where various access points and nodes have overlapping coverage areas. Consequently, small geographical regions are served by multiple access points with multipoint transmissions. This makes efficient management of interference, frequency allocation, and handoff a necessity [2].

The millimeter (mm) waves utilized in 5G have very high frequencies of above 10 GHz and thus have poor signal propagation characteristics due to channel intermittency [5]. For instance, these mmWave signals are entirely obscured by common building materials such as brick and morta. The human body obstruction causes up to 35 dB of attenuation. Consequently, small obstacle and reflector movements, changes in UE orientation relative to the body or hand, coupled with UE mobility cause rapid signal attenuation. This results into increased number of handovers as the UE looks for a better channel. Since these handovers have to be authenticated, large numbers of handovers result in handover delays, contradicting 5G goals [6, 7].

The security requirements for 5G heterogeneous networks (Hetnets) are high compared to 2G, 3G and 4G due to interoperability requirements among the Hetnets [8]. Unfortunately, the use of inefficient authentication schemes during 5G handovers lead to performance degradation in heterogeneous 5G cells and increases the delay. In addition, authors in [9] explain that apart from increased handover delays, 5G networks experience frequent failures of the handoff process, both of which reduce capacity gains offered by 5G networks.

As pointed out by [7], other 5G network technical challenges relate to handover authentication, user privacy protection and resource management. According to [10], provision of strong security, privacy and low latency handovers is required for the successful deployment of 5G-wireless local area networks (5G-WLAN) heterogeneous networks. As such, a number of authentication schemes have been proposed for networks such as worldwide interoperability for microwave access - local area network (WiMAX-WLAN), UMTS - wireless local area networks (UMTS-WLAN), and LTE- wireless local area networks (LTE-WLAN) have been proposed to boost security and minimize handover delays. However, authentication delays still remain the main challenge in these schemes.

In [11], it is pointed out that 5G networks call for communication processes that exhibit minimal latency. This requirement is cumbersome to achieve especially when combined with needs for security and privacy-preserving strategies. The authors in [12] explain that consistent and effective handover management in 5G Hetnets is a serious challenge. This is because small cells infer frequent handovers, which necessitate frequent UE authentications among cells, leading to heavy signaling overheads among the source gNB, target gNB, UE and the core network, and hence increased handover delays. In [13], the authors pointed out that if the handover procedures are not handled very fast, then the ongoing calls can be terminated, in which case it becomes a dropped call. High call drop probability leads to denial of services (DoS) which deteriorates the network QoS. These are some of the issues that this paper sought to address. Specifically, the contributions of this paper include the following:

I. We deploy ANN and FL to optimize handover initiation and facilitate the selection of the most suitable target gNB respectively.
II. We introduce a multi-factor authentication process for all the handover entities.
III. We demonstrate that (I) and (II) above not only improve the handover efficiency but also secure the handover against attacks.

The rest of this paper is organized as follows: Sect. 2 discusses related work while Sect. 3 outlines the system model. Section 4 presents and discusses the simulation results while Sect. 5 concludes the paper and gives future work.

2   Related Work

The security of 5G and B5G networks handover process has generated a lot of interest, leading to the development or proposals of many authentication schemes. For instance, [7] have developed an authentication scheme using blockchain and SDN to eliminate re-authentication in repeated handovers among heterogeneous cells. This technique exhibited low delay which is applicable in 5G network. A Software-Defined Handover (SDHO) technique has been proposed by [14] to enhance the handover in future ultra-dense 5G networks while [15] have developed a vertical handover framework incorporating IEEE 802.21 Media Independent Handover (MIH) services with OpenFlow protocol (OFP).

To address handover latency problem, authors in [9] proposed an SDN-based mobility and available resource estimation strategy. Here, neighbor gNB transition probabilities of the UE and its available resource probabilities are estimated using Markov chain formulation. On the other hand, researchers in [5] have proposed a 5G handover mutual authentication based on certificates. This requires that users possess certification of other networks in the 5G environment. This method promises privacy, user identity protection and data integrity.

To reduce handover delays, authors in [16] have developed a Heterogeneous Handover Algorithm (HHA) to manage handovers between Wifi, WiMax and LTE networks. This scheme demonstrated better performance in terms of delay, service rate and handover dropping probability in heterogeneous networks.

The authors in [17] employed Fuzzy Logic (FL) to design a vertical handover decision algorithm to facilitate target network selection in 5G IoT networks. To accomplish this, a Multi-layer Feed Forward Network (MFNN) is employed to predict user mobility based on distance, Received Signal Strength (RSS), mobile speed and direction parameters. Regarding target selection, parameters such as traffic load, handover latency, battery power, security and cost are used as inputs to the fuzzy decision model. In addition, researchers in [18] have also proposed a cloud-based machine learning technique to improve QoS by reducing the number of handoffs in networks.

On the other hand, a Simple Password Exponential Key Exchange (SPEKE) efficient authentication to prevent UE disclosures, reduce the size of exchanged messages and make the protocol faster by using a secret key method has been proposed in [19]. In [20], the authors introduce fog computing and radio access network integration based F-RAN architecture for privacy protection in 5G networks. On the other hand, a GPS historical information-based technique using the multilayer perception neural network (MPNN) to reduce handover delays has been developed in [21]. Here, the angle of the target gNB is calculated and the distance to that target is taken into consideration during the handover process, such that some gNBs are skipped based on their angles. Moreover, authors in [16] have also developed a low latency Heterogeneous Handover Algorithm (HHA) to manage hard handovers between Wifi, WiMax and LTE networks.

Authors in [22] have employed the concept of Mobile Relay network (MRN) which uses three Key Distributions Functions (KDFs) and one advanced encryption standard (AES) encryption function for each handover authentication. On the other hand, authors in [23] have employed Certificate Authority (CA) to design a new lightweight intelligent authentication protocol to counter de-synchronization attack, man-in-the-middle (MitM) and attain shorter setup time.

3   System Model

Due to frequent fluctuations in signal quality as a result of multi-path fading, shadowing effects and other environmental conditions, the received carrier power at the user equipment (UE) fluctuates. This may potentially cause ping pong handovers and consequently frequent re-authentications, leading to wastage of network resources. As such, this paper introduced hysteresis margins for all the handover decision parameters. However, the proper determination of these hysteresis margins in highly dynamic 5G networks is a challenging task. This is because small margins lead to surge in ping pong handovers while large margins result in delayed handovers. As such, this paper employed artificial neural network (ANN) for the dynamic determination of ideal hysteresis margins. Further, fuzzy logic (FL) was incorporated into the handover process to facilitate the selection of target cells. The proposed ANN-FL secure handover protocol consisted of three phases: ANN-assisted hysteresis margin optimization, fuzzy logic facilitated handover decision, and handover process security.

3.1   Simulation Environment

In this paper, the simulation environment consisted of seven hexagonal cells with each having its own gNB. The UE moved freely among these cells and when at the hysteresis regions, it could connect to more than one gNB. The decision to handover to any of the target cells was facilitated by ANN-FL based on the six input parameters: received carrier power (P_r), power density (P_D), path loss (P_L), UE velocity (V_{UE}), traffic intensity (A_c) and blocking probability (P_b). The proposed ANN-FL system consisted of two stages as shown in Fig. 1. The first phase was hysteresis margin optimization using ANN while the second phase was fuzzy logic facilitated handover decision.

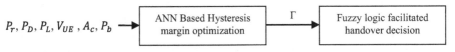

$P_r, P_D, P_L, V_{UE}, A_c, P_b$ →
| ANN Based Hysteresis margin optimization | Γ → | Fuzzy logic facilitated handover decision |

Fig. 1. Proposed ANN-FL system

A typical handover consists of handover initiation, decision and execution. During handover initiation, estimations are made to discern whether a handover is necessary while handover decision involves assessing the set criteria to establish an ideal target cell. On the other hand, handover execution is the actual shifting of the UE to the target cell. As such, the ANN operated in the handover initiation phase, FL operated in the handover decision phase while security aspect of this protocol was employed during the handover execution phase. As shown in Fig. 1, the output parameter of the ANN system is the hysteresis margin.

3.2 Hysteresis Margin Optimization

In this paper, hysteresis was a parameter that examined the differences in the values of the six handover parameters between the source gNB (SgNB) and target gNB (TgNB). This hysteresis was important for the maintenance of minimum difference between SgNB and TgNB handover decision parameter values. For instance, assuming that P_r and P_D decrease exponentially as the UE shifts from either SgNB or TgNB, Fig. 2 shows the hysteresis margin.

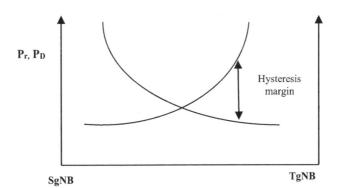

Fig. 2. Handover hysteresis margin

As already alluded, ANN was employed in the determination of the hysteresis margin based on the six input parameters that were measured at both the serving and target cell. Each of these input parameters had threshold values and proper determination of hysteresis margin was crucial in the mitigation of ping pong handovers, and the reduction of handover latencies. On the other hand, its improper determination leads to high number of handover failure rates.

The ANN employed in this paper had intermediary layers (hidden layers with embedded hidden nodes) lying between its input and output layer, and hence was a multilayer neural network (MLNN).The proposed MLNN had several connected processing elements (artificial neurons) whose activation was controlled by the computation of inputs and weights via mathematical equations described below. These neurons comprised of the synaptic weights, activation function and summing function. The nodes in one layer of this MLNN were connected to other nodes in subsequent layer. Figure 3 shows the architecture of this multilayer feed forward neural network where the outputs from the input layers were conveyed to the output layer after processing in the hidden layers.

The training of this MLNN was through the back propagation algorithm. Denoting the input layer, hidden layer and output layer as i, j and n respectively, the following mathematical definitions hold.

Definition 1: Taking f_j as the hidden layer activation function, w_{ji} as the weight associated with the connection link between nodes in input layer i and nodes in hidden layer j, y_i as the input at nodes in the input layer, a_i as the bias associated with each connection link between the input layer and hidden layer, I_j as the summation of weight inputs coupled with bias, and Y_j as the output of the activation function in the hidden layer, the activation process in the hidden nodes is as shown in (1) and (2):

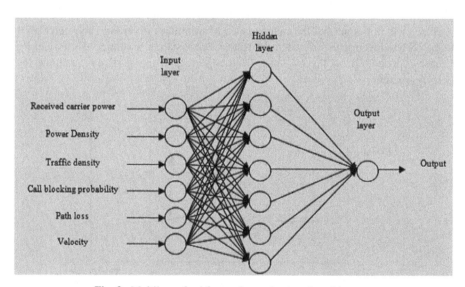

Fig. 3. Multilayer feed forward neural network architecture

$$I_j = \sum_i w_{ji} y_i + a_i \tag{1}$$

$$Y_j = f_j(I_j) \tag{2}$$

Definition 2: Taking h_j as the bias of the hidden node j, φ_j as the adaptive coefficient of the hidden node linear activation function, and $y(n-1), y(n-2)\ldots.y(n-p)$ as the past p figures of merit (FOM) values obtained in the MLNN, the output γ_j of each of the hidden layer neuron is given by (3):

$$\gamma_j = \varphi_j F\left(\sum_{i=1}^{p} w_{ji}y(n-i) + h_j\right) \tag{3}$$

Definition 3: Taking $x_j(j = 1, \ldots.p)$ as the inputs of the neuron, $w_{kj}(j = 1, \ldots.p)$ as the weights of the neuron, ϑ_k as the threshold, $f(.)$ as the activation and y_k as the output of the neuron k, (4) and (5) hold:

$$u_k = \sum_{j=1}^{p} w_{kj}x_j \tag{4}$$

$$y_k = f(u_k - \vartheta_k) \tag{5}$$

Definition 4: Considering the input parameters $(P_r, P_D, P_L, V_{UE}, A_c, P_b)$ and the output of the ANN system (HM^t), the mapping in (6) apply:

$$HM^t = f^t(P_r, P_D, P_L, V_{UE}, A_c, P_b) \tag{6}$$

Where f^t is some non-linear function.

Definition 5: Taking f_n as the output layer activation function, w_{nj} as the weight associated with the connection link between nodes in hidden layer j and nodes in output layer n, y_j as the output in hidden layer nodes, I_n as the summation of weighted outputs in the output layer, Y_n as the final output in the output layer, b_n as the bias associated with each connection link between hidden layer and output layer, the principle of output layer can be expressed as shown in (7) and (8):

$$I_n = \sum_{j} w_{nj}y_j + b_n \tag{7}$$

$$Y_n = f_n(I_n) \tag{8}$$

Definition 6: Owing to 5G's small cells, frequent handovers are exhibited, some of which are ping pongs. As such, adaptive hysteresis margin was employed such that handovers were triggered only when FOMs at TgNB exceeded those at the SgNB with some hysteresis margins. Taking HM_{P_r}, HM_{P_D}, HM_{P_L}, $HM_{V_{UE}}$, HM_{A_c}, and HM_{P_b} as the hysteresis margins for received carrier power, power density, path loss, UE velocity, traffic intensity and blocking probability respectively, a handover was possible when the conditions given in (9) were fulfilled:

$$\left.\begin{array}{l} P_{r_{TgNB}} > P_{r_{SgNB}} + HM_{P_r} \\ P_{D_{TgNB}} > P_{D_{SgNB}} + HM_{P_D} \\ P_{L_{TgNB}} > P_{L_{SgNB}} + HM_{P_L} \\ V_{UE_{TgNB}} > V_{UE_{SgNB}} + HM_{V_{UE}} \\ A_{C_{TgNB}} > A_{C_{SgNB}} + HM_{A_c} \\ P_{b_{TgNB}} > P_{b_{SgNB}} + HM_{P_b} \end{array}\right\} \tag{9}$$

Collectively, these hysteresis margins were represented by an aggregate handover factor Γ. The determination of the right value of the hysteresis margins in (9) being a challenging task, ANN was utilized to dynamically optimize this selection. The optimized Γ was then codified as fuzzy sets and fed into the fuzzy logic controller to facilitate handover decision.

3.3 Fuzzy Logic Facilitated Handover Decision

In the proposed protocol, the fuzzy logic based handover decision consisted of fuzzification, fuzzy inference and defuzzification as shown in Fig. 4. In the fuzzification phase, membership functions for each of the input parameters were defined. To accomplish this, triangular membership function was employed.

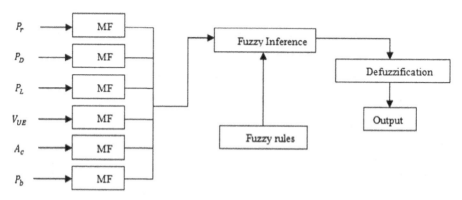

Fig. 4. Fuzzy logic facilitated handover decision

On the other hand, the fuzzy inference employed max-min technique using a number of *IF---THEN* rules. At the output, centroid defuzzification was utilized to arrive at the numerical value of the computed handover decision. In essence, the numerical value of fuzzy deduction was employed to rank each of the candidate target cells. As such, during the defuzzification phase, a decision is made regarding the target network to handover the UE to. For the fuzzy logic system, the following definitions hold:

Definition 7: Taking *L, M* and *H* as logic **L**ow, **M**edium and **H**igh values respectively, the fuzzy sets for each of the six input parameters are given in (10):

$$\left. \begin{array}{l} P_r = \mathrm{F}(L, M, H) \\ P_D = \mathrm{F}(L, M, H) \\ P_L = \mathrm{F}(L, M, H) \\ V_{UE} = \mathrm{F}(L, M, H) \\ A_c = \mathrm{F}(L, M, H) \\ P_b = \mathrm{F}(L, M, H) \end{array} \right\} \quad (10)$$

Definition 8: In the simulated 5G overlay network, let $M_{i \rightarrow i}$, denote handover from one microcell to another microcell, $M_{i \rightarrow a}$ represent microcell to macro-cell handover, $M_{a \rightarrow a}$, denote macro-cell to macro-cell handover, and $M_{a \rightarrow i}$ represent a macro-cell to microcell handover. The output linguistic variable handover decision fuzzy set is given by (11):

$$H_D = F\left(M_{i \rightarrow i}, M_{i \rightarrow a}, \ M_{a \rightarrow a}, M_{a \rightarrow i},\right) \tag{11}$$

Definition 9: Upon satisfaction of (11), a handover time to trigger (HO_{TTT}) timer was activated to check on ping pong rate (PP_{rate}) given by (12):

$$PP_{rate} = \frac{number\ of\ PP\ handovers}{number\ of\ successful\ handovers} \tag{12}$$

This timer was assigned to each handover to check whether the present handover is associated with a previous one. Here, if the HO_{TTT} timer runs out and the FOM_{TgNB} are still satisfactorily above FOM_{SgNB}, a normal handover is assumed and its execution is permitted. On the other hand, if HO_{TTT} timer runs out and FOM_{TgNB} are not still satisfactorily above FOM_{SgNB}, a ping pong handover is assumed and its execution is halted.

3.4 Advance Timing

The simulation process for the ANN-FL commenced by partitioning the tracking area into three regions which correspond to the three fuzzy sets membership functions of Low, Medium and High. These regions were: no handover region (NHR) corresponding to logic Low, low probability handover region (LPHR) corresponding to logic Medium, and high probability handover region (HPHR) corresponding to logic High as shown in Fig. 5. Here, measuring and buffering of FOM was initiated whenever the UE was detected at the LPHR, long before the actual handover initiation at the HPHR. The cellular technology simulated in this research was 5G which has a coverage radius of 248 m. Dividing 248 m by 3 yielded 82.67 m as the radius for NHR, 165.33 m as the radius for LPHR and 248 m as the radius for the HPHR.

As shown in Fig. 5, the NHR lay between the gNB at the origin to a maximum of 82.67 m while the LPHR lay between the 82.67 m and 165.33 m. On the other hand, the HPHR lay between 165.33 m and 248 m. In terms of the handover parameters of received power, power density and path loss, then at the NHR, received power and power density at the UE are strongest while path loss is least compared to both LPHR and HPHR.

On the other hand, at the HPHR, received power and power density at the UE are weakest while the path loss is greatest compared to both LPHR and NHR.

3.5 Parameter Selection and Handover Strategy

Unlike majority of previous FL and ANN based handovers that consider only either the network, user, UE or service requirements for making handover decision, the developed protocol utilized six input parameters that considered all these requirements. Table 1

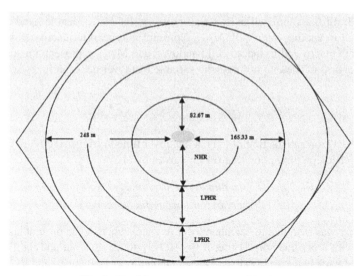

Fig. 5. Tracking coverage area partitioning

gives the justification for the selection of these parameters. As shown in Table 2, these parameters satisfied the necessity for a handover that took into consideration the network, user, UE and service requirements. Another reason for the inclusion of additional parameters is the direct proportion between the number of parameters and the number of rules in the fuzzy logic inference engine. The increment in the number of parameters translate to an increase in the number of rules in the fuzzy logic inference engine, which boosted the performance of the ANN-FL in terms of path loss, ping pong, handover latencies and average number of executed handovers.

Table 1. Parameters selection rationale

Parameter	Rationale
Power density & received carrier power	Guaranteed that the signal levels in the new gNB are strong enough to sustain an ongoing call
Traffic density	Ensured load balancing such that system overloading is mitigated
Call blocking probability	Guaranteed that the handover process does not interfere with new calls being initiated by the UEs
Path loss	Ensured that the new cell does not expose the handed-over calls to major path losses that may lead to packet losses or delays
Velocity	Control handover between macro and micro cells in an overlay network

Here, received carrier power represented network requirements; power density, path loss and velocity represented UE requirements; traffic intensity and blocking probability represented service requirements; while security represented user requirements.

Regarding the handover strategy, this research employed three strategies: fuzzy logic; ANN based; multi-criteria; user centric and function based strategies in form of security,

Table 2. Handover metrics

Handover information gathering phase			
Network based	UE based	User based	Service based
Received carrier power	Velocity Path loss Power density	User preferences User profile Security	Traffic intensity Blocking probability

Handover decision phase	
Criteria	Strategy
Combination of: Network based UE based User based Service based	Function based User centric based Fuzzy logic based ANN based Multi-criteria based

power density and path loss. Multi-criteria approach helped in deciding when the handover should occur, established the target network, and also determined the necessity of the handover. On the other hand, function based strategy was in form of security. The flow chart of the ANN-FL handover decision process is shown in Fig. 6 below.

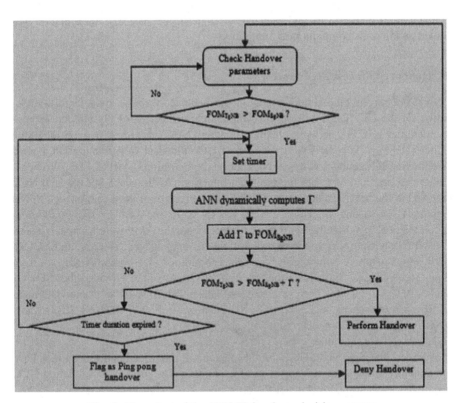

Fig. 6. Flow chart of the ANN-FL handover decision process

As shown here, the first step during the handover decision process was the checking of values of the handover FOMs from both TgNB and SgNB after which these values are compared. If TgNB FOM values are superior to those of SgNB, a timer is set and ANN is activated to dynamically compute aggregate handover margin, Γ which is then added to the SgNB FOM values. On condition that TgNB FOM values are superior to the sum of SgNB FOM values and Γ, an handover is executed. On the other hand, if SgNB FOM values are sufficiently greater than those of TgNB, the timer duration is checked to prevent ping pong handovers as discussed in Sect. 3.3 above. In this protocol, fuzzy inputs variables and three fuzzy sets were designed for each fuzzy variable, hence the maximum possible number of rules in the knowledge base is $3^6 = 729$. For the UE within the micro-cell, the following are examples of these rules:

RULE-1:   *If P_b is low and A_C is low and P_r is low and P_D is low and P_L is low and V_{UE} is low then handover factor is low.*

RULE-729:   *If P_b is high and A_C is high and P_r is high and P_D is high and P_L is high and V_{UE} is high then handover factor is high.*

On its part, the inference engine determined the rules to be triggered and computed the fuzzy values of the output variables using a max-min inference method which tested the magnitudes of each rule and selected the highest one. The max-min method was adopted owing to its computational simplicity.

3.6 Handover Process Security

In this paper, strong mutual authentication was achieved through multi-factor authentication for the UE, SgNB and TgNB using six parameters: Globally Unique Temporary Identifier (GUTI), network chaining counter (NCC), next hop network chaining counter (NH_{NCC}), key derivation function (KDF), Physical Cell Identity (PCI), and Absolute Radio Frequency Channel Number on the Download (ARFCN-DL). To begin with, the Access and Mobility management Function (AMF) sends NH_{NCC} and NCC employed in the previous handover to SgNB. Upon receipt of these parameters, SgNB computes K^*_{gNB} using the received NH_{NCC}, PCI, KDF and ARFCN-DL. In addition, the computed K^*_{gNB} together with NCC received from the AMF were hashed to generate secure hash (SH_{SgNB}). In the next phase, SgNB sends K^*_{gNB}, SH_{SgNB}, and NCC to TgNB, which in turn re-computes K^*_{gNB} value. In addition, it re-computes SH_{TgNB} from K^*_{gNB} and NCC_{SgNB} to validate the received NCC_{SgNB} value. Provided that SH_{TgNB} matches SH_{SgNB}, NCC is now validated and hence TgNB sends an acknowledgment (ACK) together with its NCC_{TgNB} to SgNB as shown in Fig. 7. Next, SgNB forwards its NCC_{SgNB} to the UE together with SH_{SgNB}. The UE re-computes K^*_{gNB} and SH_U to validate the NCC_{SgNB} value.

Provided that SH_U and SH_{SgNB} values match, all the three handover entities have now mutually authenticated themselves to each other. The process of validating NCC prevented de-synchronization attacks.

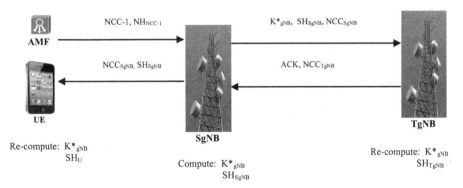

Fig. 7. Handover entities mutual authentication

4 Results and Discussion

To simulate the proposed ANN-FL secure handover for 5G and beyond networks, a number of simulation parameters were employed as inputs. Table 3 shows the values of the parameters that were employed in the developed protocol simulations. As shown in Table 3, a combined random direction (RD) and random waypoint (RWD) were deployed.

Table 3. Simulation parameters

Parameter	Value	Units
Slope correction factor, α	0.88	–
Reference distance for modified SUI, d_0	1	Meters
Reference distance for SUI, d_0	100	Meters
Shadowing correction, S	9.2	dB
Transmission Frequency, f	28	GHz
Maximum gNB-UE distance, d	248	Meters
gNB Transmit power, P_t	20	dBm
Transmitter antenna height, h or h_t	52.5	Meters
Mobility model	RD & RWP	–
Subscriber height, h_0	1.5	Meters
Transmitter antenna gain, G_t	19.2	dBi
Correction for frequency, X_f	−11.5	MHz
Correction for receiving antenna height, X_h	34.1	Meters
Free space path loss, A	41.38	dB
Path loss exponent, y	2	–

As already discussed above, for the ANN-FL handover decision process, six parameters were employed which included received carrier power, blocking probability, UE velocity, power density, path loss and traffic intensity. Table 4 shows the membership functions for the fuzzified input variables.

Table 4. Neuro-fuzzy membership functions

Crisp inputs	Low		Medium		High		Units
	LB	UB	LB	UB	LB	UB	
Received carrier power	−125	−168	−172	−186	−184	−191	dB
Blocking probability	$1.0 * e^{-10}$	$9.0 * e^{-9}$	$8.0 * e^{-9}$	$9.0 * e^{-8}$	$8.0 * e^{-8}$	$9.0 * e^{-7}$	–
Velocity	0	0.9	0.7	2.9	2.5	5	m/s
Power density	−5	−16	−14	−24	−22	−27	dB
Path loss	−9	2	1.8	9	8.8	21	dB
Traffic intensity	0.1	0.2	0.18	0.5	0.48	0.9	Erlang

As shown in Table 4, each of the membership functions of low, medium and high were each decomposed into lower bound (LB) and upper bound (UB) corresponding to the lower and upper concentric circles of the partitioned tracking area. The handover process in the developed protocol encompassed the validation of the UE to the SgNB and TgNB, as well as the authentication between SgNB and TgNB. This mutual authentication served to thwart eavesdropping and de-synchronization attacks common in the standard 5G's improved Authentication and Key Agreement (5G-AKA') protocol. Here, the UE was authenticated at both SgNB and TgNB using its GUTI.

The first step during the handover process was admission control where the TgNB reserved some channels to serve the new UE, which reduced blocking probability. The next phase was that of authentication which involved the usage of previous handover values for NH_{NCC}, together with PCI and ARFCN-DL to derive K^*_{gNB}. In addition, SH was derived for NCC validation using encrypted NCC and the just computed K^*_{gNB} as inputs to the KDF. Figure 8 shows the encrypted present NCC (Pre_NCC), present NH_{NCC} (Pres_NH_NCC), PCI, ARFCN-DL and SH values.

During the handover process, subsequent key derivation through horizontal technique was eliminated and hence although an adversary could have K_{gNB}, Cell Radio Network Temporary Identifier (C-RNTI), NH_{NCC} and NCC, the computation of K^*_{gNB} was infeasible. This is because an attacker now requires K_{AMF} held in either the UE or the AMF. Consequently, the developed protocol assures forward key secrecy. Since the 3GPP specification is that the UE approve any key refresh command once the handover has commenced, any replay attack or malicious key refresh command from the attacker-controlled SgNB was infeasible.

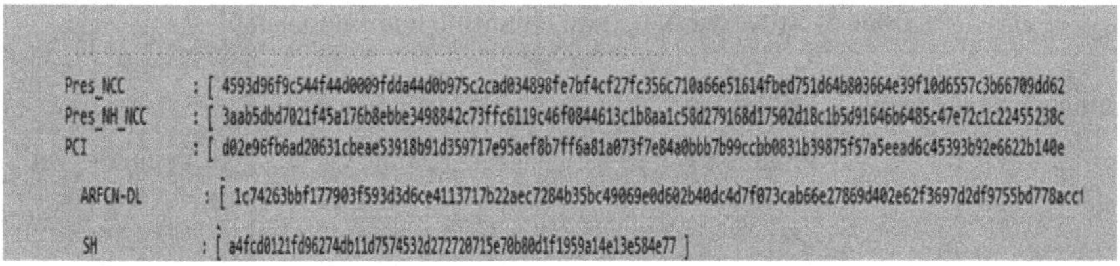

Pres_NCC	: [4593d96f9c544f44d0009fdda44d0b975c2cad034898fe7bf4cf27fc356c710a66e51614fbed751d64b803664e39f10d6557c3b66709dd62
Pres_NH_NCC	: [3aab5dbd7021f45a176b8ebbe3498842c73ffc6119c46f0844613c1b0aa1c58d279168d1750d2d18c1b5d91646b6485c47e72c1c22455238c
PCI	: [d02e96fb6ad20631cbeae53918b91d359717e95aef8b7ff6a81a073f7e84a0bbb7b99ccbb0831b39875f57a5eeead6c45393b92e6622b140e
ARFCN-DL	: [1c74263bbf177903f593d3d6ce4113717b22aec7284b35bc49069e0d602b40dc4d7f073cab66e27869d402e62f3697d2df9755bd778accf
SH	: [a4fcd0121fd96274db11d7574532d272720715e70b80d1f1959a14e13e584e77]

Fig. 8. Encrypted handover parameters

In the proposed protocol, de-synchronization attack is prevented by implementing an NCC validation phase using secure hashes (SH_{SgNB}, SH_{TgNB}, and SH_U). This phase verifies that NCC value sent from SgNB to TgNB is the same one that is sent from the SgNB to the UE. Here, if these NCC values are not similar, handover request is explicitly denied. As such, the developed protocol is robust against session hijacking, replay, DoS, masquerade, eavesdropping, and MitM attacks.

In terms of user untraceability, it was observed that to correctly trace a mobile UE within the tracking area, an adversary needed to correctly determine the UE velocity v_i, waypoint l_i, destination coordinates (x_i, y_i), absolute angle, φ_i, unit vector along this absolute angle $a(\varphi_i)$, and pause time, $t_{p,i}$ shown in Fig. 9.

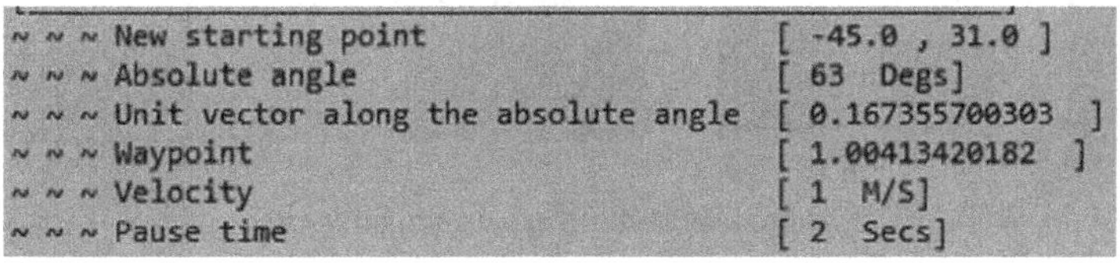

```
~ ~ ~ New starting point                          [ -45.0 , 31.0 ]
~ ~ ~ Absolute angle                              [ 63  Degs]
~ ~ ~ Unit vector along the absolute angle        [ 0.167355700303  ]
~ ~ ~ Waypoint                                    [ 1.00413420182   ]
~ ~ ~ Velocity                                    [ 1  M/S]
~ ~ ~ Pause time                                  [ 2  Secs]
```

Fig. 9. Simulating user untraceability

As such, an adversary required a five tuple non-deterministic finite automaton denoted by M (Q, Σ, δ, q, F) to accurately trace the UE within the tracking area. Table 5 presents details of this automaton.

Given that at every mobility the velocity was randomly selected within the range [v_{min}, v_{max}], pause time was randomly chosen from the range t_{min}, t_{max}], waypoint was stochastically selected from the range [l_{min}, l_{max}], absolute angle was randomly chosen from the range [0, 2Π] and the unit vector along this absolute angle was stochastically selected from the range [$a(\varphi)_{min}$, $a(\varphi)_{max}$], the precise tracing of the UE within the tracking area by an adversary was a non-deterministic polynomial (NP) hard problem.

Regarding computational complexity, time complexity which represented the time it took for the proposed protocol to execute successfully was employed. It was observed that the proposed protocol took an average of 0.0318 s to execute. This time complexity was then compared with those of 5G-AKA', MRN and Certificate based protocols as shown in Fig. 10 below.

As shown in Fig. 10, certificate-based protocol had the largest time complexity of 0.76 s followed by MRN, 5G-AKA' and the proposed protocol with 0.56 s, 0.453 s, 0.0318 s respectively. As such, the proposed protocol had efficient consumption of

Table 5. Adversarial non-deterministic finite automaton

Automaton components	Definition	Values
Q	Finite set whose elements are states	Initial state x_i, y_i, in motion with velocity v_i, pausing for $t_{p,i}$ seconds
Σ	Alphabet	At rest (**R**) or in motion (**M**)
δ	Transition function	$X_{i+1} = X_i + a(\varphi_i).l_i$; $Y_{i+1} = Y_i + a(\varphi_i).l_i$ $t_{i+1} = t_i + t_{p,i} + i_i/v_i$
q	Start state	Initial coordinates x_i, y_i
F	Accept state	Destination coordinates x_f, y_f

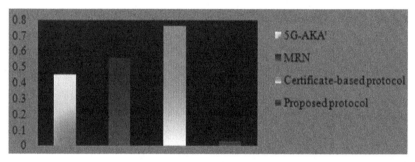

Fig. 10. Time complexity comparisons

the central processing unit (CPU) time. In terms of network resources consumption, signaling overheads were compared among MRN, 5G-AKA', certificate-based protocol and the proposed protocol as shown in Fig. 11. It is evident that MRN and 5G-AKA' both had a signaling cost of 7 messages during the handover process.

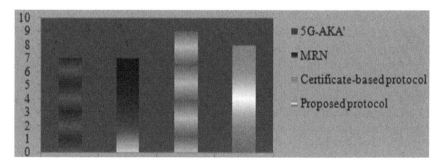

Fig. 11. Network resources consumption comparisons

On the other hand, certificate-based protocol incurred a signaling cost of 9 messages while the proposed protocol had a signaling overhead of 8 messages. Consequently, MRN and 5G-AKA' had the lowest network resource consumption followed by the proposed protocol. On the other hand, the certificate-based protocol had the highest network resource consumption. Although the developed protocol adopted the same architecture as that of 5G-AKA', it incurred one extra signaling overhead that was utilized to validate NCC that served to prevent de-synchronization attack as discussed above. These four protocols were also compared in terms of key complexities as shown in Table 6.

Table 6. Key complexity comparisons

Protocol	Key complexity
5G-AKA'	AKA
MRN	AKA + 3 KDFs
Certificate based	AKA + Symmetric + Asymmetric
Proposed	AKA

It is evident from Table 6 that both 5G-AKA' and the proposed protocol had the same key complexities, which were also the least. This was followed by certificate-based protocol which apart from AKA, it incorporated two additional keys: symmetric and asymmetric. On the other hand, MRN had the highest key complexities which included AKA plus additional 3 KDFs. Concerning handover success rate, handover failure rate and ping pong handover rate, the number of successful, failed and ping pong handovers for the developed protocol were validated against those of the RSSI based protocol. It was observed that within a fixed period of time, these two protocols experienced varied performance. For instance, within a duration of 39 min, the numbers of initiated handovers (I) in the RSSI protocol were 122 while only 31 handovers were initiated in the proposed protocol. This represented a 74.6% reduction in the number of initiated handovers. Out of the 122 RSSI protocol handovers, only 73 were successful (S) while 49 of them failed (F), representing a 59.8% and 40.2% success rate and failure rate respectively, as shown in Fig. 12 and Fig. 13 below. Out of the 73 successful handovers, 23 of them were ping pong (PP) handovers, representing a ping pong rate of 31.5%. On the other hand, in the proposed protocol, a total of 31 were initiated over the same period, out of which 27 were successful (S) while 4 of them failed (F), representing 87.1% and 12.9% success rate and failure rate respectively.

Regarding ping pong (PP) handovers, out of the 27 successful handovers, 2 of them were ping pongs, representing ping pong rate of 7.4% as shown in Fig. 14.

As such, the developed protocol yielded a 27.1% increase in handover success rate, a 27.3% reduction in handover failure rate, and a 24.1% reduction in ping pong handovers.

Fig. 12. Handover success rate

Fig. 13. Handover failure rate

Fig. 14. Ping pong rate

5   Conclusion and Future Work

The goal of this research paper was to develop an efficient and secure handover protocol based on the concepts of fuzzy logic and artificial neuro network. The simulation results have shown that the developed protocol improves the handover success rate, and reduces both the handover failure rate and ping pong handover rates. In terms of time complexity, certificate-based protocol had the largest time complexity followed by MRN, 5G-AKA' and the proposed protocol. Regarding network resource consumption, MRN and 5G-AKA' had the least signaling cost followed by the proposed protocol. On the other hand, certificate-based protocol incurred the highest signaling cost. Concerning key complexities, both 5G-AKA' and the proposed protocol had the same key complexities, which were shown to be the least. This was followed by certificate-based protocol and MRN respectively. In addition, it has been shown that this handover protocol is robust against tracing attacks as an adversary required to correctly determine the UE velocity, way-point, destination coordinates, absolute angle, unit vector along this absolute angle, and pause time, which degenerates to an NP-hard problem. Other attacks thwarted by this protocol were eavesdropping, de-synchronization due to the implementation of strong mutual authentication of all handover entities. Future work in this area involves the validation of the developed protocol against other attack models such as session hijacking, IMSI interception, spoofing, masquerade and packet replay.

References

1. Khan, L.U., Yaqoob, I., Imran, M., Han, Z., Hong, C.S.: 6G wireless systems: a vision, architectural elements, and future directions. IEEE Access **8**, 147029–147044 (2020)
2. Sabuzima, N., Ripon P.: 6G: envisioning the key issues and challenges. arXiv, pp. 1–8 (2020)
3. Zhang, Z., et al.: 6G wireless networks: vision, requirements, architecture, and key technologies. IEEE Veh. Technol. Mag. **14**(3), 28–41 (2019)
4. Mahbas, A.J., Zhu, H., Wang, J.: Impact of small cells overlapping on mobility management. IEEE Trans. Wireless Commun. **18**(2), 1054–1068 (2019)
5. Alican, O., Maode, M.: Secure and efficient vertical handover authentication for 5G Het-Nets. In: 2018 IEEE International Conference on Information Communication and Signal Processing (ICICSP), pp. 27–32. IEEE (2018)
6. Rabe, A., Hesham, E., Sameh, S., Tareq, Y., Mohamed, A.: Handover management in dense cellular networks: a stochastic geometry approach. ArXiv, pp. 1–7 (2016)
7. Yazdinejad, A., Parizi, R.M., Dehghantanha, A., Choo, K.K.R.: Blockchain-enabled authentication handover with efficient privacy protection in SDN-based 5G networks. IEEE Trans. Netw. Sci. Eng. 1–12 (2019)
8. Hu, S., et al.: Non-orthogonal interleave-grid multiple access scheme for industrial Internet of Things in 5G network. IEEE Trans. Industr. Inf. **14**(12), 5436–5446 (2018)
9. Bilen, T., Berk, C., Kaushik, R.C.: Handover management in software-defined ultra-dense 5G networks. IEEE Network **17**, 49–55 (2017)
10. Amit, K., Hari, O.: Design of a USIM and ECC based handover authentication scheme for 5G-WLAN heterogeneous networks. Digit. Commun. Netw. **6**(3), 341–353 (2019)
11. Basaras, P., Belikaidis, I., Maglaras, L., Katsaros, D.: Blocking epidemic propagation in vehicular networks. In: 2016 12th Annual Conference on Wireless On-Demand Network Systems and Services (WONS), pp. 1–8. IEEE (2016)
12. Panwar, N., Sharma, S., Singh, A.: A survey on 5G: the next generation of mobile communication. Phys. Commun. **18**, 64–84 (2016)
13. Babiker, A., Ahmmed, H., Ali, S.: Comparative study 1st, 2nd, 3rd, 4th, generations from handoff aspects. Int. J. Sci. Res. **5**(6), 934–941 (2016)
14. Amina, G., Faouzi, Z., Mahmoud, N.: SDN/NFV-based handover management approach for ultradense 5G mobile networks. Int. J. Commun. Syst. **32**(17), 1–5 (2018)
15. Li, X., Liu, F., Feng, Z., Xu, G., Fu, F.: A novel optimized vertical handover framework for seamless networking integration in cyber-enabled systems. Future Gener. Comput. Syst. **79**(1), 417–430 (2018)
16. Sendhilnathan, S., Phemina, M.: Minimizing handover delay and maximizing throughput by heterogeneous handover algorithm (HHA) in telecommunication networks. Appl. Math. Inf. Sci. **11**(6), 1737–1746 (2017)
17. Azzali, F., Ghazali, O., Omar, M.H.: Fuzzy logic-based intelligent scheme for enhancing QoS of vertical handover decision in vehicular ad-hoc networks. In: IOP Conference Series: Materials Science and Engineering, vol. 226, no.1, pp. 012–081, IOP Publishing (2017)

18. Kene, P., Haridas, S.L.: Reducing ping-pong effect in heterogeneous wireless networks using machine learning. In: Choudhury, S., Mishra, R., Mishra, R.G., Kumar, A. (eds.) Intelligent Communication, Control and Devices. AISC, vol. 989, pp. 697–705. Springer, Singapore (2020). https://doi.org/10.1007/978-981-13-8618-3_71

19. Alezabi, K., Hashim, F., Hashim, S., Ali, B.: An efficient authentication and key agreement protocol for 4G (LTE) networks. In: Region 10 Symposium, pp. 502–507. IEEE (2014)

20. Ku, Y., et al.: 5G radio access network design with the fog paradigm: confluence of communications and computing. IEEE Commun. Mag. **55**(4), 46–52 (2017)

21. Jamal, F.A, Firudin, K.M.: Direction prediction assisted handover using the multilayer perception neural network to reduce the handover time delays in LTE networks. In: 9th International Conference on Theory and Application of Soft Computing, Computing with Words and Perception, vol. 120, pp. 719–727 (2017). Procedia Computer Science

22. Jin, C., Maode, M., Hui, L.: G2RHA: group-to-route handover authentication scheme for 4G LTE-a high speed rail networks. IEEE Trans. Veh. Technol. **66**(11), 9689–9701 (2017)

23. Mahmoud, E.O., Mohamed, H.M., Hassan,, A.: Design and simulation of a new intelligent authentication for handover over 4G (LTE) mobile communication network. In: The International Conference on Electrical Engineering, vol. 11, pp. 1–12. Military Technical College (2018)

Software-Defined Networking

A Middleware for Integrating Legacy Network Devices into Software-Defined Networking (SDN)

Bhargava Sokappadu[(⊠)] and Avinash Mungur

University of Mauritius, Reduit, Mauritius
sokappadu@gmail.com, a.mungur@umail.uom.ac.mu

Abstract. Software Defined Networking (SDN) definitely brings along benefits such as manageability, automation of network and management processes amongst others, however, at the expense of major drawbacks such as huge investment in SDN-capable hardware, vendor lock-in and backward incompatibility with legacy devices. SDN itself being based on a new concept, provides very few aspects in common with traditional networking devices with each SDN vendor usually limiting the SDN capabilities to their own devices only. Even with the introduction of open protocols such as OpenFlow with the aim to provide vendor neutrality, backward compatibility still remains a problem. This paper is geared towards addressing the main issues governing the migration towards SDN and hence provide the desired vendor neutrality, backward compatibility without compromising on networking features, security, ease of deployment and management inter alia. With this concept in mind, an SDN Middleware System has been conceptualized to offer the aforementioned features whereby the backend of the system would be responsible to intercept, inspect and process OpenFlow configurations from the SDN Manager and the SDN Controller and thereafter interpret these commands converting them into the desired configuration in legacy networking terms after which, the legacy nodes are configured with the equivalent of the legacy vendor OS.

Keywords: Software Defined Networking · OpenFlow · Middleware

1 Introduction

Software Defined Networking (SDN) has been one of the major recent changes that has been introduced into the networking era after a long influence of traditional networks. The main key of SDN in tandem with Network Function Virtualization (NFV) is geared to provide automation in the implementation, configuration and operation of networking nodes such as switches, routers, firewalls with minimal manual intervention contrasting against legacy networking principles [1].

Today, key players in the networking ground are massively campaigning software-defined solutions and laying forward advantages to encourage the adoption of SDN.

© ICST Institute for Computer Sciences, Social Informatics and Telecommunications Engineering 2021
Published by Springer Nature Switzerland AG 2021. All Rights Reserved
R. Zitouni et al. (Eds.): AFRICOMM 2020, LNICST 361, pp. 121–139, 2021.
https://doi.org/10.1007/978-3-030-70572-5_8

However, challenges in the migration towards SDN still prove to be undealt with such as huge investments, insufficient multi-vendor interoperability and backward compatibility with legacy systems amongst others [2]. The Open Networking Foundation (ONF) established itself to mitigate the issue of interoperability while providing a unified networking protocol known as the OpenFlow to uniform SDN controller platform. Still, it should be noted that not all network devices are SDN capable and there are yet many legacy network devices in current use.

In this context, this paper aims at assessing the feasibility of optimizing the way SDN works in such a way that legacy networking systems can still make optimal use of software-defined technology irrespective of vendor, hence, addressing the fundamental issues of interoperability and backward compatibility, while reducing the investments involved in the adoption of SDN technology. This would promote the development of a proposed SDN Middleware System that would be able to bridge the gap between SDN standards and legacy networks.

1.1 Problem Statement

The migration towards an SDN platform is highly dependent on the network architecture and inventory which can also imply that SDN adoption requires a major network refresh in order to have SDN capable devices that can support protocols such as OpenFlow. OpenFlow has been established to provide vendor neutrality but however, vendors are putting today their own SDN solutions that are to a major extent, proprietary [3, 4]. These proprietary solutions offer limited interoperability among different vendor devices and the operation is mostly limited to their in-house solutions only.

Hence, SDN is difficult to be deployed in legacy networks that are not SDN-aware such as routers, switches and firewalls which are still very widely in use today. Riverbed Global survey 2017 highlights that 85% of business decision makers claim to be still several years away from digital transformation due to part of their legacy infrastructure [5]. This in turn signifies that a majority of the market is still dependent on their current legacy infrastructure. Migration towards an SDN solution would be more than a paradigm shift and even with open protocols such as OpenFlow, there exists limited documentation for the configuration, implementation and operation of OpenFlow across a multi-vendor network topology and a suitable migration plan. Even Cisco who had once developed the OpenFlow based controller has announced the End of Life [6]. Very little attention is being given to the inclusion of legacy network devices and how they can fit into the SDN scenario.

2   Background Study

In this section, we will provide a brief overview of the SDN concepts and the SDN architecture. An overview of the OpenFlow protocol is also provided.

2.1   Software-Defined Networking Concepts

The SDN Architecture. The basis of SDN Architecture can be summarized into 3 principles:

1. Decoupling of controller and data planes.
2. Logically centralized control.
3. Exposure of abstract network resources and state to external applications [11].

Traditional routers and switches incorporate a strong amalgam between the control and data planes. This tandem rendered management operation such as configuration and troubleshooting very challenging. In order to alleviate these issues, traffic engineering approaches to separate control and data plane was a must. Over time, equipment vendors implemented packet forwarding logic directly into the hardware, separate from the control plane software. In addition, another issue that needs to be addressed with isolation of the control plane is to have a single management platform (later defined as the SDN controller) which would act as the "brain" of the network architecture. As compared to local control in conventional networks, the centralized SDN controller would therefore be responsible to provide control traffic to the network equipment via programmability in the control plane through the SDN controller and since a uniform control platform is maintained, a network-wide visibility, scalability and decision-making could be achieved [11].

Having key roles, SDN controllers are designed to provide better adaptive network path selection, while minimizing outages during network changes such as routing and providing enhanced security such as blocking suspected attack traffic. The SDN controllers assume the role of logically centralizing control procedures while providing standardized communication protocols – which is possible with the use of OpenFlow as open routing software. This would imply that a single server (the SDN controller) can store all the routing, switching rules and contain all the decisions while the networking devices being controlled would in turn rely on the intelligence of the SDN controller [7, 12–14]. Figure 1 depicts the typical SDN Architecture that has been devised and which is used by most SDN platforms including OpenFlow.

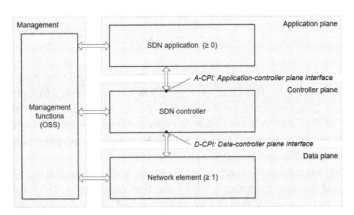

Fig. 1. SDN architecture overview [11]

The OpenFlow Protocol. The OpenFlow Protocol aka OpenFlow Switch Protocol set up by the ONF is the medium that defines how the OpenFlow controller communicates with the OpenFlow switches. Similar to a traditional switch, the OpenFlow switch relies on basics such as routing and switching but with certainly a major variety of features. However, one major difference in the configuration between these two is that OpenFlow switches need to be managed by an OpenFlow controller which can configure the switch through the OpenFlow switch's tables. This is equally applicable to OpenFlow and OpenFlow-hybrid switches, where the latter can perform both traditional networking and SDN capabilities at the same time but would still require an OpenFlow controller for the OpenFlow segment to be operational.

1. Flow table.
2. Group table.

Figure 2 shows the SDN architecture within an OpenFlow switch and the main components of the OpenFlow switch and its interaction with the OpenFlow controller.

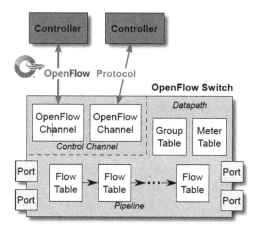

Fig. 2. Main components of an OpenFlow switch [15]

Each of the above tables may contain individually a set of different flow entries and group entries respectively. Therefore, the OpenFlow controller can add, update, delete, flow entries and group entries using the OpenFlow Switch protocol. A flow table would contain a set of flow entries where each entry would define parameters similar to the policy, condition and action triad but specific to the OpenFlow protocol such as match fields, actions on traffic, and instructions among others.

Within the flow table, the matching sequence of traffic compared against the flow entry starts in a top-down approach where the first matching entry in each table is executed first and if a policy and condition is matched, the corresponding actions as defined in the flow table entry are applied. Otherwise, if there is no suitable match, the result is based on the Table-miss flow entry parameters that define what action to take when no match has been found, for example this can be allow/drop on no match.

Traffic matching a flow entry can be as an action, forwarded to either a physical or virtual port and actions can be set to redirect traffic to a group that can provide additional processing. In this case, a group entry would therefore contain a set of actions determined by the group type itself [15].

2.2 Current Research Developments

Currently, there exists very limited research material regarding the compatibility of legacy devices with OpenFlow controllers or other SDN venues. Most of these researches are geared towards the performance analysis of OpenFlow controllers in a lab network with limited deployment in practical network setups [16–18]. The issue of legacy device support is addressed partly by [19] where the use of home gateways to be integrated in an OpenFlow-based SDN network while at the same time exploiting the hardware available to accelerate traffic and its processes. However, it can be inferred that home gateways (CPEs) are not suitable to fit into an SDN topology since they lack advanced functionalities and granular access to physical registers which are usually vendor-locked. The "HARMLESS" approach as depicted in [20] is among the few that partially addresses the research problem concerns and the strategy here is to add a SDN switch that can add SDN capability to legacy network systems by including a layer of virtualization based on Tagging and Hairpinning. Among the few papers, [20] focusses on operability and cost of legacy networks in SDN networks but yet, we consider the approach to technically insufficient since HARMLESS would require additional hardware such as server for spine topology where the use of 10G switches are solicited with overwhelming port capacities and additional CPU which is at the expense of providing a low-cost solution. The research from [21] provides a good basis to use the OpenFlow configurations but provides very limited information on how the interpretation and conversion is realized from the OpenFlow, how the administration is handled and how it can be used for various configurations. The research lacks qualitative evaluation and test cases that would suit more than the TCMA performance. The incremental deployment of SDN as mentioned in [22] provides a limited practical approach on how SDN can be implemented into hybrid networks. Following the critical review of several papers [16–20, 23, 24] it is with concern that we conclude that limited importance is being given to the main aspects of SDN adoption which we believe to be primordial and hence form the very basis of this research which is geared towards support for legacy devices, multi-vendor support, device discovery, ability for multiple configurations, minimal required resources, ease of implementation and management, cost effectiveness, security, scalability and performance.

3 Proposed SDN Middleware System

Typically, a basic SDN topology would require the SDN controller in the Control Plane, the OpenFlow switch in the Data Plane with the network elements associated to the switch and the OpenFlow Manager in the Management/Application Plane that would be used to manage the configuration of the SDN controller. The functionalities of a practical SDN environment would be as per Fig. 3.

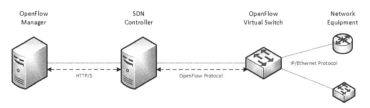

Fig. 3. Practical SDN setup

During the end-to-end network configuration of the switch to allow data plane process the traffic of the network elements, several protocols are used. First, the configurations executed in the OpenFlow Manager are triggered via the HTTP/s to the SDN controller. The SDN controller sends its configuration (flows) up to the OpenFlow switch via Open-Flow protocol while for the Data plane layer on the OpenFlow switches, it is the usual TCP/IP stack protocol that is preserved.

However, in order to have the control of non-SDN compliant devices, there is the need to have the middleware that would bridge the gap between the configuration of SDN and legacy devices and hence, through a single management console as well. This can be achieved by having terminal direct access to the manageable legacy switches via remote management protocols such as SSH. In this light, the approach of the proposed middleware is to be able relay the information input into the OpenFlow Manager which would be the management console, to both the SDN controller and the configuration of legacy devices. In this project, the middleware is highly leveraging on the fact that the configurations "pushed" from the OpenFlow Manager are in HTTP requests and responses while the parameters are most commonly sent via JSON scripts.

In the proposed solution, the middleware should therefore be able to effectively "tap" into the path across the flow sequence from source (OpenFlow Manager) to sink (Network Devices) and interpret the HTTP/S/JSON messages from the OpenFlow Manager parsing them into the proprietary language based on the operating system of the legacy switch. The middleware would therefore fit into the topology as proposed in Fig. 4.

The SDN Middleware System proposed will have several uses one of which is fundamentally to be able to gain management of a "hybrid" architecture – containing both SDN-capable and legacy network nodes. This is typically the observed scenario in practice where either campus or data center networks even though have part of their network SDN-ready, still retain some of the legacy networking devices such as routers and switches especially those that offer compatibility with older protocols/services.

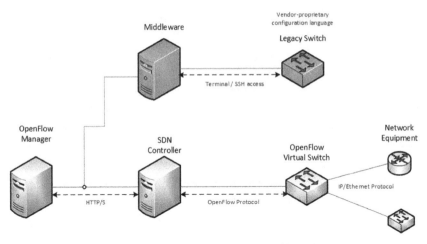

Fig. 4. SDN middleware in practical hybrid architecture

4 Design

In this section, the detailed design of the SDN Middleware System is provided comprising of its architecture and software component.

4.1 General Architecture

Figure 5 outlines the overview of the proposed architecture for the SDN Middleware System depicting the primary components within the architecture. The Middleware server would logically sit in between the path from the SDN Manager towards the network nodes while passing through the SDN controller for configurations. The first aim is that the Middleware server should be able to familiarize with the network by identifying the different legacy nodes that are connected. Next, it should be able to intercept and inspect the SDN messages that are being configured from the SDN manager along the path towards the sink (legacy nodes). The Middleware server would then process these SDN/OpenFlow messages into appropriate interpretation that would be then used as configuration parameters to be deployed to the legacy nodes.

4.2 Software Design

Initialization of the Middleware. As a basic requirement of the Middleware service, it should be able to connect and manage legacy network nodes in the first instance making this feature the very basis of the Middleware solution. This pre-requisite would involve the Middleware to have the ability to keep a known repository of the legacy device nodes and their respective Cookie mapping such that each device connected can be uniquely represented (to be discussed in the later section) that are connected and further details such as Management IP, Vendor are highly desirable. This would be similar to a topology inventory map closely related to a sort of a neighbor/discovery table of the

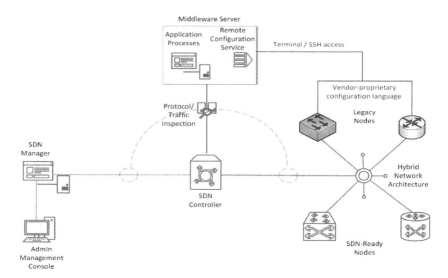

Fig. 5. SDN middleware general architecture

architecture. In order to address this issue, the use of device discovery is highly solicited – this includes the use of protocols such as LLDP for devices directly connected to the Middleware while SNMP for those that are remotely connected.

Interception of SDN Messages. Whenever a flow deployment is executed from. OFM, the OpenFlow Manager calls a corresponding RESTCONF API from the OpenDaylight controller which is specific to the configuration deployed. Further to this, the command is executed through a HTTP PUT request which embeds a set of parameters corresponding to the RESTCONF API in a sequence of JSON parameters. It is much easier to capture and decipher the HTTP commands rather than intercepting the OpenFlow protocol messages between the controller and the OpenFlow switches the former being more structured (JSON as compared to OpenFlow messages that are more complex to interpret). Therefore, the flow of the command is from the SDN manager towards the SDN controller and the PUT request is executed at the SDN controller.

The interception of these messages can either be done at port or service level or by tapping from the interface itself but at the expense of careful filtration and inspection of only related information using packet-capture and packet-inspection tools. The SDN Middleware System shall therefore leverage on intercepting these HTTP commands and strip the different parameter values which will be further processed to generate relevant configurations in the proprietary script of the legacy devices.

Inspection of SDN Messages. Following the interception of messages, the gathered raw data would have to be further filtered to obtain the desired parameters through the process of inspection. Deep-packet inspection would be used to further drill down into the details following the HTTP messages. The parameters that interest the most are the JSON objects with their member key and values that are located inside the HTTP PUT requests. These parameters will be the variables to be interpreted to build the commands for the legacy nodes.

Processing the SDN/OpenFlow Messages. OpenFlow configurations are sent from the SDN controller to the OpenFlow switch by making use of flow entries within flow tables as viewed in Sect. 2. The parameters that are used within the definition of flow entries are those that are actually embedded within the JSON and have been inspected earlier. The summary of operation of each of these fields are as per below:

- Match Fields – contain the parameters to be used to determine a match in ingress and egress port headers. For example, match source IP address or MAC address.
- Priority – contain the precedence of the flow entry.
- Counters – contain the hit count whenever packets match the parameters set.
- Instructions – set the action to be taken for e.g. drop, output port-no. etc.
- Timeouts – the maximum amount of time before the flow is disregarded by the switch.
- Cookie – denotes an opaque data value that maybe used to filter flow entries following flow modification or flow statistics but is not used for packet processing.
- Flags – Modify the way flow entries are managed.

One way the SDN controller can determine to which switch the configuration is sent is usually through the OpenFlow Device ID which should be unique throughout the SDN domain. Since the OFM/SDN controller can see only the switches connected via OpenFlow but does not show any visibility on legacy nodes, the SDN Middleware System shall itself run on OpenFlow as the back-end connector with the OFM and thus, the SDN Middleware will also be managed and configured using the OFM itself. Therefore, extrapolating this in practical scenario, there will be a single SDN Middleware System to control various legacy nodes and given that the SDN Middleware System runs on OpenFlow, the OFM will be showing only one OpenFlow switch which is the Middleware itself but there would be no way to select the specific legacy node. So therefore, there should be at least one unique identifier value that can be used to determine the specificity of each of the legacy device. In order to address this issue, given that the Cookie (this Cookie value is restricted to OpenFlow and not in reference to the HTTP cookies) value in a flow entry is an opaque value that is not used in decision making, the Middleware can make use of the Cookie value in order to determine the identity of the switch to which the configuration is to be sent. A different parameter could also be used as unique identifier for the legacy switches as well. The decision-making process in terms of OpenFlow Device ID and Cookie value is demonstrated as per Fig. 6.

Referring to Fig. 6, each legacy switch has been assigned a specific Cookie value (in hexadecimal) of 0x001 and 0x002 respectively. In this specific SDN domain, the OpenFlow Manager will be able to see two OpenFlow switches connected and active with the SDN controller. The SDN controller will still be differentiating among the different OpenFlow switches using the device ID (here ID = 1234 for the OpenFlow switch and ID = 1001 for the OVS underlay within the Middleware). Therefore, to send a configuration to OpenFlow switch, the Device ID is directly selected while to send configurations to legacy nodes, specifically to the Middleware, the Device ID of the latter (1001) would be selected. The Middleware will in turn pass the JSON parameters and the legacy node is determined by the Cookie value, for example, if a flow entry with Cookie value with 0x001 is encountered, the Middleware would know that this configuration is

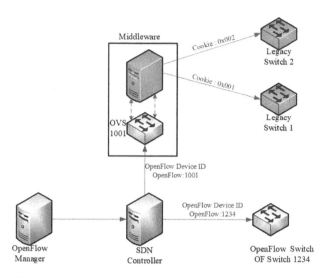

Fig. 6. Decision-making of the SDN controller and middleware

meant for Legacy Switch 1. This also means that a table of values of Cookie v/s Switch needs to be populated and maintained as a legacy node is added to the Middleware.

OpenFlow messages sent between the controller to the OpenFlow switch are characterized by their OpenFlow command message. For example, insertion of a flow entry into a table, it would correspond to an OFPFC_ADD message and a modification of an existing flow would be an OFPT_FLOW_MOD request. The different types of request provide information regarding the nature of the configuration is to be done on the Open-Flow switch i.e. whether it is an add request, delete request among others. This information in the OpenFlow header is also parsed by the Middleware to interpret into the type of command to be executed on the legacy node.

Preparation of the Command Block. The parameters that have been processed from the JSON into OpenFlow protocol will be stored in variables within a local repository of the Middleware. These variables will then be used in the command execution process in sending the configuration to the legacy nodes. Prior to that, it would be important to known how each of the different OpenFlow commands will be "converted" into the legacy command. For example, assuming the case where a command from the SDN manager is sent to the SDN controller to create an Access Control List (ACL) between two hosts, the Middleware should be able to interpret and parse the parameters into an ACL entry that can then be applied to different legacy nodes. However, the main issue is that OpenFlow messages are more elusive compared to legacy network configurations that are more easily interpretable in terms of keywords that can be found within the configuration lines. This is a major "limitation" of OpenFlow since OpenFlow messages are difficult to be interpreted, however the easiest approach is to program the Middleware such that based on the correlation of the retrieved parameters, it can interpret the logic behind the OpenFlow command. Below is a sample flow entry within an OpenFlow-based OVS.

```
cookie=0x777, duration=189.072s, table=200, n_packets=0,
n_bytes=0, priori-
ty=2,ip,nw_src=192.168.100.100,nw_dst=192.168.100.200 ac-
tions=drop
```

From the above, example of OpenFlow command, the following can be extracted:

- Cookie = 0x777
- Table ID, Priority = 200,2
- Network Source = 192.168.100.100
- Network Destination = 192.168.100.200
- Actions = Drop

The parameters of this flow entry within the flow table relates to the an OpenFlow entry to block traffic from source network 192.168.100.100 and destination network 192.168.100.200. Since the source and destination networks are of /32 subnet mask, this means that this corresponds to a host-to-host deny ACL entry when mapped to legacy network configuration. As shown in Fig. 7, the matched flow-entry components are mapped to the respective variables within the Middleware which will be used for the command execution process.

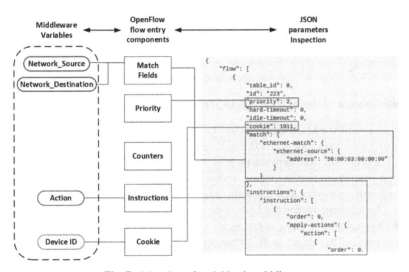

Fig. 7. Mapping of variables in middleware

Command Execution. Each different legacy device coming from a different vendor, OS/Firmware version or capability is most likely to have its own language set in terms of command configuration and this entails to exquisite command execution on per-device basis and a generic command set might not be applicable for all legacy nodes. Command execution implies pushing of the desired configuration into the legacy device for which, other than the command itself, the privilege to apply the configuration is required. Thus, in this design, the command execution would be done by performing an SSH to the legacy device and executing the commands through a preconfigured script and scripting techniques which will contain the instructions based on the OS/Firmware and variables that have been stored previously. Along with the instructions and parameters, remote device access credentials are fundamental to be able to have the privilege to perform the configuration. Therefore, it will also be required that these credentials to be input and stored into a repository via the management console. This will be parsed through the Device Registration process.

5 Implementation

The implementation of the SDN Middleware System has been made using open-source based solutions as far as possible mostly to provide scalability for adjustments and limit the cost of development. The SDN Middleware System architecture is loosely based on a Linux platform atop having the following running features of:

- OpenFlow vSwitch to interface with the SDN Controller/Manager.
- Node-Red on Linux (Ubuntu) Platform which retains the backbone of the Middleware engine based on JavaScript.
- TShark component to provide packet-capture features.
- MySQL Database to provide repository.
- Apache HTTP server with PHP (LAMP) and JavaScript for providing Middleware GUI features.

5.1 Initialization of the SDN Middleware System

The first action of the Middleware would be to be able to perform neighbor discovery in order to gather information on the different legacy nodes that have been connected thereto. The protocols used depends on how the devices are connected to the Middleware and in this case, given that the legacy nodes are directly connected, LLDP protocol for neighbor discovery has been used, another major reason being LLDP support by multiple vendors. The implementation has been done as the LLDP service installed on the Linux and a Shell script polling devices at specific intervals of 30 s which is the default LLDP frequency timer. The output of this repeated process is then processed to extract the required parameters such as Vendor, System Name, and others which are then used to update the table "Inventory" within the database and this acts as the node inventory for listing the connected devices and also updating the entries for changes.

5.2 Interception of SDN Messages

The interception of messages involves the deep packet inspection of the egress traffic of the SDN Manager towards the SDN controller and for this purpose, TShark variant of Wireshark has been used to effectively sniff the traffic on the interface that is being used to tap the traffic (in this scenario). In order to simplify the sniffing process, filters for TCP protocol ports at Transport layer and HTTP PUT requests at the level of the Application layer have been used to increase efficiency. These packets specifically would contain the parameters being sent to the SDN controller. Given the bulky output during HTTP/S inspection, the output following the inspection is first written in a file locally on the Middleware before further processing/inspection of SDN messages can begin. However, the payload of this HTTP request contains the actual data elements that are required for the Inspection part. This payload would be in raw HEX format.

5.3 Inspection of SDN Messages

The output of the Inspection is in raw format and embeds several other HTML codes along with the HTTP PUT request. The purpose of the Inspection layer is to strip the required information only, to have it handy in a format that would be suitable for further processing of the SDN messages. In this context, since the intercepted output is raw, unparsed format, the inspection would result in extraction of the payload in JSON format that would ease the processing steps. The content of the stored file will have its data payload extracted and the HEX converted to string format following which, with the help of indexing methods, only the required payload in the JSON format is extracted. This JSON script is then used for further processing and at the same time, logged to the Middleware database for logging and auditing purposes. This format serves as the base material that would be used in the building of the command blocks for code execution. The output of the Inspection process would give an output in a readable structure that contains specifically the parameters that will be used for further processing.

5.4 Processing of SDN Messages

This segment of the implementation will deal with the extraction of required parameters from the extracted JSON format into a set of variables that will thereby be used for command execution part. Thus, this involves deeper analysis of the inspected data to match against the components of Flow Entries within a flow table. This has been conceived in practice by the indexing of the keyword components of the JSON and storing each component and its respective defined parameter into a well-structured table within the Middleware's internal database. Similarly, this algorithm for parameter extraction has been developed using JavaScript in Node-Red with the output of this process used for storage and triggering for command preparation.

5.5 Command Preparation and Execution

This part of the implementation process is the most fundamental since it deals with the final aspect of the Middleware's process which is to successfully be able to send the configuration to the legacy device based on the language the configurations on the legacy device is based on. During the implementation, the language that has been tried to abide to is the Cisco IOS. As depicted in the earlier sections, the components being analyzed compose of an OpenFlow entry that is complementary to the Cisco IOS Access

Control List. Similarly, each vendor would have its own language set for configuration but yet, the parameters to be used within the configuration remain the same variables throughout the different vendors. Hence, this segment would interpret these parameter options as variables from the Middleware's database and embed them appropriately as per the language set of the vendor (in this case Cisco IOS) and send this configuration to be executed at the legacy device. When it comes to execution, it is primordial to have the privilege to be able to configure the device for which credentials such as Username and Password would be required. To address this issue, the implementation also involves a Device Registration process that would allow the entry of the device's credentials that are bound to the Cookie which form the device's identity and until the device has not been registered, no command execution will take place.

The command execution is invoked upon the value of the Cookie ID and the configuration has been implemented through a Shell Script that based on the Cookie ID would fetch the corresponding device details from the Middleware's database, such as, IP address, Username and Password. After gaining SSH access, the Shell Script pertaining to the device configuration itself is then executed into the device and the appropriate logs such as time and command execution are stored back into the database for logging and auditing purposes. Based on the value of the Cookie following the inspection process, the configuration values are extracted from the database and a Shell script is generated in an executable format.

6   Test Results

The test bench used has been in a scenario with OpenDaylight OpenFlow controller, OpenDaylight OpenFlow Manager, and legacy devices based on Cisco IOS and HP ProCurve switches. For test input data at the SDN Manager, the equivalent of Access Control List as an OpenFlow Flow entry has been configured and deployed on both the Cisco IOS and HP ProCurve switches and the same OpenFlow configuration has been extrapolated using a Flow entry to perform static NAT (SNAT). This has produced successful results in converting these commands to their legacy counterparts in Cisco IOS and HP ProCurve for the ACL part while the SNAT was successfully tested on a Cisco router. The SDN Middleware System has been implemented on a Virtual Machine with 4 vCPU, 8 GB RAM and 50 GB disk space. Figure 8 and 9 provide the timeline since the command is executed at the SDN Manager up to the configuration of the legacy node.

Fig. 8. Timeline of events for configuration size of 1.2 KB for an ACL

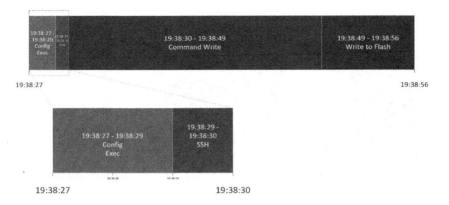

Fig. 9. Timeline of events for configuration size of 4.5 KB for an ACL

It can be inferred that the average of the process duration from the time the command has been executed from the SDN Manager until the configuration is saved is 12 s where the majority of this time is consumed by the legacy node to save the configurations to the flash (8 s) as compared to the performing the configuration onto the device itself (Command Write) takes only 2 s. SSH and Configuration Execution processes take only 1 s each which also means that the SDN Middleware System itself performs the Interception of the SDN messages, Inspection of the SDN messages, Processing of the OpenFlow commands and Preparation of command block processes in only 1 s altogether demonstrating a highly time-efficient system. The long time for writing the configuration to the flash is considered normal since these devices need to copy the configuration from the running memory to the flash and storing as the startup configuration file and by default these legacy nodes have limited resources as well and these results are therefore deemed acceptable since the Command Write process takes only 2 s relatively and this is where the configuration gets added onto the device but onto the volatile memory and it is normal that command execution onto volatile memory takes less time than saving the configuration.

From the above, it can be inferred that for a configuration file size of 4.5 KB, the mean end-to-end process is completed within 31 s where the majority of this time is consumed in writing the command to the device (19 s) while the least time is taken to establish the SSH session (1 s). A long time of 19 s for the command write is expected since the configuration 4.5 KB would contain bulkier configurations of more lines of command. The results for the time duration for the configuration script sizes of 1.2 KB and 4.5 KB are compared side-by-side as per Fig. 10 to give a comparison of the different times taken by each process with increase in configuration size.

The statistical summary in Fig. 10 gives a much more in-depth comparison of the different process times. It can be deduced that despite the variation in configuration size, there are two processes namely SSH establishment and Writing to Flash that have remained constant at 1 s and 8 s respectively for both configuration sizes. This would mean that SSH and Writing to Flash are independent of configuration size and this is theoretically correct since firstly, SSH establishment occurs before the Command

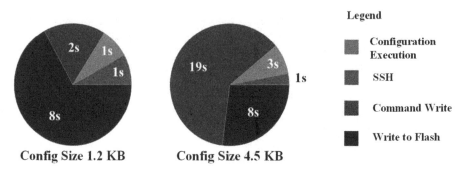

Fig. 10. Comparison of time duration for configuration sizes of 1.2 KB and 4.5 KB

Writing process and simple consists of key exchange and authentication. Next, writing to flash is dependent on the hardware resources in copying the running configuration into the startup configuration making these two processes as independent variables. However, executing the configuration onto the legacy device definitely depends on the configuration size as depicted by Fig. 10 where there is in an increase of 2 s is noted for a configuration increase from 1.2 KB to 4.5 KB which is deemed normal since a larger SDN command execution would imply more processing involved at the level of the Middleware in terms of packet interception, processing of SDN messages and extraction of the parameters in building the command block.

On a final note, it can be said that the SDN Middleware System metrics comply to the requirements in terms of performance metrics especially when comparing to the time involved in the configuration when manual intervention is required to configure the legacy device.

7   Evaluation of the SDN Middleware System

This section provides a cost and performance evaluation of the proposed SDN Middleware System.

7.1   Novelty and Contribution

Our paradigm approach compared to previous research works aims at providing a Middleware that can inspect, interpret, convert and execute the SDN functions while providing the dashboard for Device registration, selection, auditing among others altogether within a single solution. This method has been clearly shown to perform conversion of OpenFlow commands without the use of APIs and amidst a practical test case scenario of a hybrid network architecture where the SDN controller manages the SDN-ready switches while the SDN Middleware manages the legacy nodes while providing higher granularity of configuration.

7.2 Cost Evaluation

Throughout the design and implementation of this project, cost aspects have been given great considerations and as far as possible, any expense or purchase of software or hardware resources have been overridden at its best. For this purpose, a maximum number of open-source products have been solicited to establish the minimal cost target. For the implementation, there has been only EVE-NG and VMware Workstation Pro that are licensed products that have been used. Again, these can also be considered to be void as inclusion for the costs since EVE-NG has only been used to emulated the Cisco IOS virtual platform and same configuration has been tested on a hardware Cisco device as well while VMWare Workstation Pro has been used to host the Ubuntu Linux Kernel for the different services. Hardware requirements being minimum, our hosting environment has been a laptop and undoubtedly, the OVF could be deployed in any virtualized environment and no specific hardware are required as such. The requirements would be specific to a basic Virtual Machine resource provisioning. As mentioned during our choice of the following components, Ubuntu Server Platform, Node-Red, OpenDaylight Open Flow Manager, OpenDaylight SDN Controller, LAMP architecture, LLDP services among others, all of these have been built using open-source solutions rendering the SDN Middleware Architecture free from any CAPEX and OPEX.

7.3 SDN Middleware System Performance

This aspect covers the overall performance of the SDN Middleware System in terms of processing, memory and disk usage while in use. It is to be also noted that during the implementation, the SDN Manager, the SDN Controller, Open vSwitch and the Middleware components have been installed on the same virtual machine for ease of testing. The performance metrics of the system have been monitored and recorded over a period of approximately 10 h of intermittent usage. It can be inferred that the system uses a maximum of 17% of the provided resources. It can be deduced that the virtual machine, again encompassing all components utilizes an average of 5.4 GB of RAM (with an idle RAM usage, unused memory of 2.65 GB) which is reasonable for a system running the SDN Manager, SDN controller, LAMP, Node-Red and Open vSwitch in addition to normal Linux processes.

8 Conclusion

The prime motive behind this paper lies today's inevitable problem of the amalgam of operations between Software Defined Networking and legacy networking devices which pose not only a disparity in the technological timeline but also broaden the financial gap whilst leaving the network industry, the only choice of fully migrating to SDN in one go. This major hurdle remains among the primordial reasons of the reluctance or repulsion towards SDN today. For this reason, this paper has as main objective to the bridge gap between SDN and traditional networking devices by the deployment of a proposed SDN Middleware System capable of providing interoperability between OpenFlow-based SDN and legacy protocols and vendor neutrality without compromising the financial aspect. In this paper, it has been shown how the SDN Middleware System has been devised to perform packet inspection to capture, inspect and understand the SDN messages into a meaningful form from where the required parameters are used to produce the equivalent legacy OS configuration. In addition, the legacy configuration can also be varied to suit the OS depending on the legacy device to provide compatibility across multiple vendors. The functionalities of the SDN Middleware System have been put to test to achieve an execution time of the automatic process of deployment from the SDN Manager up to the device configuration to be achieved within approximately 12 s which is undoubtedly much lower than that of a human-intervened manual process. At the same time, it has been illustrated how multiple configurations can also be executed through the SDN Middleware System and how it also provides the GUI platform for ease of management while interconnecting the different segments. It should be highlighted that all the implementation of the SDN Middleware System has been designed based on an open-source platform to render the Middleware to zero cost of software operation where only hardware resources are required. Taking all these aspects into consideration, it can definitely be concluded that the devised SDN Middleware System complies to the aims of this paper and based on the results, it can be classified as a major contribution in this field of research to establish the basis towards vendor neutrality and interoperability in the adoption of SDN.

References

1. Santana, G.A.A.: VMware NSX Network Virtualization Fundamentals. VMware Press, Palo Alto (2017)
2. Sokappadu, B., Hardin, A., Mungur, A., Armoogum, S.: Software defined networks: issues and challenges. In: Conference on Next Generation Computing Applications (NextComp), Mauritius (2019)
3. Open Networking Foundation: ONF Strategic Plan, ONF Board, Menlo Park, California, March 2018
4. Cisco: Cisco Application Policy Infrastructure Controller Data Sheet. Cisco Inc., San Francisco (2018)
5. Riverbed: Riverbed Future of Networking Survey Finds Legacy Networks Holding Back Cloud and Digital Transformation. Riverbed, San Francisco (2017)
6. Cisco Inc: End-of-Sale and End-of-Life Announcement for the Cisco Open SDN Controller 1.x. Cisco Inc. (2016)
7. Feamster, N., Rexford, J., Zegura, E.: The road to SDN: an intellectual history of programmable networks. ACM: Association for Computing Machinery (2013)
8. Open Networking Foundation: Open Networking Foundation Press Release. Open Networking Foundation, Oregon (2011)
9. Gartner: Gartner Identifies the Top 10 Strategic Technology Trends for 2014. Gartner Inc., Orlando (2013)
10. Fortinet: The Fortinet SDN Security Framework. Fortinet Inc, Sunnyvale (2016)
11. Open Networking Foundation: SDN Architecture Overview. Open Networking Foundation, Palo Alto (2014)
12. Caesar, M., Feamster, N., Rexford, J., Shaikh, A., van der Merwe, J.: Design and implementation of a routing control platform. In: Proceedings of the 2nd USENIX Symposium on Networked Systems Design and Implementation (NSDI) (2005)

13. Lakshman, T.V., Nandagopal, T., Ramjee, R., Sabnani, K., Woo, T.: The SoftRouter architecture. In: Proceedings of the 3rd ACM Workshop on Hot Topics in Networks (HotNets) (2004)
14. van der Merwe, J., Cepleanu, A., D'Souz, K., Freeman, B., Greenberg, A., et al.: Dynamic connectivity management with an intelligent route service control point. In: ACM SIGCOMM Workshop on Internet Network Management (2006)
15. Open Networking Foundation: OpenFlow Switch Specification Version 1.5.1. Open Networking Foundation, March 2015
16. Shamim, S., Shisir, S., Hasan, A., Hasan, M.: Performance analysis of different open flow based controller over software defined networking. Glob. J. Comput. Sci. Technol. **18**(1), 11–16 (2018)
17. Umenne, P., Lindinkosi, Z., Kingsley, A.O.: Emulating software defined network using Mininet and OpenDaylight controller hosted on Amazon web services cloud platform to demonstrate a realistic programmable network. In: Easychair (2018)
18. Kim, H., Kim, J., Ko, Y.-B.: Developing a cost-effective OpenFlow testbed for small-scale software defined networking. In: 16th International Conference on Advanced Communication Technology, Pyeongchang, South Korea (2014)
19. Miano, S., Risso, F.: Transforming a traditional home gateway into a hardware-accelerated SDN switch. Int. J. Electr. Comput. Eng. (IJECE) **10**(3), 2668–2681 (2020)
20. Csikor, L., Szalay, M., Retvari, G., Pongracz, G., Pezaros, D.P., Toka, L.: Transition to SDN is HARMLESS: hybrid architecture for migrating legacy ethernet switches to SDN. IEEE/ACM Trans. Netw. **28**(1), 275–288 (2020)
21. Hand, R., Keller, E.: ClosedFlow: OpenFlow-like control over proprietary devices. ACM (2014)
22. Hong,D.K., Ma, Y., Banerjee, S., Mao, Z.: Incremental deployment of SDN in hybrid enterprise and ISP networks. ACM (2016)
23. Franciscus, X.A.W., Gregory, M.A., Khandakar, A., Gomez, K.M.: Multi-domain software defined networking: research status and challenges. J. Netw. Comput. Appl. **87**, 32–45 (2017)
24. Sonchack, J., Adam, J.A., Keller, E., Jonathan, M.S.: Enabling practical software-defined networking security applications with OFX. In: Network and Distributed System Security Symposium (2016).

Rate of Network Convergence Determination Using Deterministic Adaptive Rendering Technique

Ayotuyi T. Akinola$^{(\boxtimes)}$ (ID), Matthew O. Adigun (ID), and Pragasen Mudali (ID)

University of Zululand, KwaDlangezwa, RSA
ruthertosin@gmail.com

Abstract. Software-Defined Networking (SDN) has become a popular paradigm for modern day optimal performance of the network system as a result of the separation of the control component from other network elements. This enables the maintenance of the flow table structure on these devices while optimal forwarding of packets is enhanced via the central controller. Being a growing network architecture which is supposed to be able to meet up with increasing traffic demands in the future, it becomes apparently important that the mechanism that takes care of the QoS of the network demands is put in place. Such demands include the smooth running of big data transmission, D2D video exchange, Voice over IP and real-time multimedia applications which needed certain QoS requirements for optimal service delivery. However, fewer research articles have reported on the improvement on the QoS routing especially in connection with the SDN paradigm. We propose a multi-criteria routing algorithm that is based on deterministic Adaptive rendering technique called DART_MCP. Our DART_MCP QoS routing algorithm deployed Dijkstra's algorithm to simplify the topology of the network before using multiple-criteria energy function to address the QoS requirements. We recorded a relatively stable bandwidth and user experience maximization under a low rate of network convergence in comparison with other approaches.

Keywords: SDN · Protocol · Multi-criteria · ART · SDN · DART_MCP

1 Introduction

The Software Defined Networking has recently been a popularly recognised approach in the networking field as a better platform for a fast and easily deplorable networking system that addresses most common challenges encountered in the networking field today [1, 2]. Due to the spurious increase in the number of devices that access the internet especially the mobile devices, the act of ubiquitous computing had been a common practise nowadays. Many real time applications are commonly seen running concurrently which are highly resource consuming applications such as real-time multimedia, device to device video chat and Voice over Internet Protocol applications [3]. Several existing Internet transmission approaches are still deploying Best-Effort single service which is

R. Zitouni et al. (Eds.): AFRICOMM 2020, LNICST 361, pp. 140–150, 2021.
https://doi.org/10.1007/978-3-030-70572-5_9

not good enough or perhaps practically impossible to enhance the smooth running of the applications aforementioned. In a similar manner, the OpenFlow has evolved as a core technology and a robust enabling approach for realizing a flexible control of network traffic in SDN thus, proven to be a reliable solution for the future Internet technology [1, 4].

The marriage of the novel SDN architecture and OpenFlow have given an optimistic platform for a tailored networking service provisioning that is expected to meet up the need of the future demands in terms of Quality of Service (QoS) requirements. By QoS, we mean the provisioning of several network QoS based on the best network state requirements for optimal performance of each application. Hence, QoS routing entails the consideration of both the network optimal path selection as well as the quality of the network based on the available resources to be able to make an appropriate decision for user demands [5]. This implies that the QoS routing for an SDN based network environment needs to speak to both network extension as well as the efficiency of the network flows in such a manner that the stability of the network is guaranteed over a specified range of time. Moreover, as the future network demands are gradually ascending its peak, the quest' for fast deployable and efficient utilization of network resources becomes a challenge [6].

As several applications evolve and many are still yet to be released, it becomes more paramount that the QoS routing algorithm needs to be more equipped to be able to meet up with the needs of network users. Asides, the need to maintain good network qualities, several network traffic flow challenges also forestall the drop in the network qualities which can be check through the routing algorithms. An example includes traffic flow interference which often results in network instability [7–9]. Furthermore, several literature have proposed various QoS routing algorithms which among which include HAS_MCP, H_MCOP and SA_MCP but most of these approaches are confined to a speculative framework with the evaluations restricted only to algorithm evaluation with respect to memory consumption and complexity computation [4, 10]. Moreover, none of these algorithms has featured the concern for network instability that arises from traffic flow interference within the networking environment [10]. It is easier to include several constraints into a routing algorithm however, the daunting task lies on how the bunches of network constraints (such as "k"), is able to relate to network stability.

The challenge of flow interference is divided into two types which are intra or inter traffic interferences [11]. Intra occurs within switches in the same slots while Inter is experienced in different slots on the network. These interferences are caused by the sharing of the same network channels and or control flow paths. Thus, the QoS routing algorithm needs to be robust to be able to prevent the occurrence of network interferences thereby ensuring that the users' network optimal performance are guaranteed. This paper thus creatively introduces the adaptive rendering technique (ART)-enabled algorithm which is typically a computer graphics rendering approach coupled with deterministic multi-criteria energy function to enhance optimal QoS routing performance. This approach was typically deployed to be able to address the interference in network flow which impedes the network stability. Thus, this serves as one major contribution that our proposed QoS routing algorithm is unravelling to the body of knowledge in Software Defined Networking field.

The remainder of this article is organized as follows. Section 2 gives some brief explanation of the related works on the previous routing algorithms attempts while Sect. 3 provides the proposed algorithm model. Section 4 discusses a short preliminary result of the experimentation while Sect. 5 concludes the paper alongside with its future works.

2 Related Works

SDN is one of the latest approaches for an optimal network performance most especially with increasing demands in network performance to meet up with the users' device requirements. Several attempts have been carried out by the scholars to bring about the improvement in network users' experience. The work of Hilmi Enes Egilmez produces the LARAC algorithm [12]. The algorithm introduced a multiplier that represented two major concerned parameters being cost and delay to video streaming service. The algorithm was able to use the iterative method similar to Lagrange relaxation to select the optimal path for the network packets. It is one of the effective algorithms that address the constrained shortest path problem. In [13], the authors propose an algorithm that uses Multi-constrained approach to find the shortest path for routing in a network. However, the work does not discuss any optimization techniques to improve the proposed algorithm. The work presents three path computation algorithms and further opened up future works such as integrating the algorithm to address admission control and resource setup. The convergence speed after failure is also proposed to verify the degree of stability of the proposed algorithms.

The work of Chen and others in [14] proposes Interference azimuth spectrum (IAS) and geometry based stochastic models (GBSMs) as an important mechanism of an analytic framework which measures the network interference performances. Several numerical examples were depicted to demonstrate the usefulness of the mechanism though the work proposes that other effects of interferences can result from specific multiple access and adaptive transmission schemes. The survey article in [15] provides various routing algorithms varying from approximate to exact solutions. These algorithms derived their solutions using Multi-constrained optimal path problem (MCOP) that includes several metrics such as packet delay, available bandwidth, packet loss and buffer overflow. Most of the review algorithms in the survey are restricted to a speculative framework and take little or no cognisance to the memory requirement or computational complexity of the proposed algorithms. Among such works include the work of Lee and others in [16] that propose a Fallback algorithm of one main constrain. This algorithm serially considers other constrains if it meets the requirement else it continues the search. The major issue with this approach is that it does not guarantee the optimal routing path and also, it cannot be used for an autonomous network environment where attaining an optimal solution becomes non-negotiable.

Moreover, a novel QoS provisioning architecture called PRICER was developed to enhance QoS routing update (ROSE) as well as promoting effective pricing incentive for routing algorithm (PIRA) [17]. This proper incentive was carried out through integrating efficient pricing function into the QoS routing algorithm. Extensive simulations as well as the conducted theoretical analysis proved the better performance of the proposed architecture over the existing state of the art approaches with an added contribution in terms of evaluating the staleness of the network link-state information.

Gang Liu and K. Ramakrishnan propose a heuristic algorithm called Heuristic Multi-constrained optimal path problem (H_MCOP) [18]. This algorithm provided a cost function that helps to prune up the paths that violate the candidate path list thus achieving an optimal path solution. The algorithm also uses the Dijkstra's shortest path approach to predict the pruning and ordering process thus making the algorithm somehow intelligent towards arriving at a precise solution. The enhancement of the prune algorithm with any of the established ϵ-approximate algorithm to achieve BA*Prune, therefore made this approach to be a comparable solution to some of the best know polynomial-time ϵ-approximate algorithms. However, the proposed algorithm is regarded as being classical and needed more improvements to achieve an optimal performance.

Several other similar QoS routing solutions have left out the information of the link state in the process of deriving an optimal network path by assuming the state is accurate and readily available. Examples of these algorithms include the general simulated annealing multi constrained path problem (SA_MCP) which happens to be an expansion of local search algorithm [10] as well as the upgraded version of it called Heuristic simulated annealing multi constrained path problem (HSA_MCP). The upgraded version was able to enhance better optimization process to be executed faster than the former but however not tailored to enhance a stable network [10]. The work of Apostolopoulos and others in [19] incorporate different update policies to check the link state such as equal class, threshold and exponential class policies. It was derived that with a given threshold value (τ), the update link signal is triggered under the threshold policy used such that when $|l_c - l_o|/l_o > \tau$, with the l_o being the least advertised value among the available latency and l_c appears to be the current latency of the link.

However, among all the highlighted literature, none of them had address the impact of network interference within a network hence there is a need to establish stability in a network that is designed to meet up the varying users' network requirement. Considering various approaches that try to optimize the network requirements that are needed by users, we extended the knowledge body along network routing through integrating the network stability measures into the routing technique that we propose to optimise the QoS routing algorithm. In order to achieve this, we deploy the Dijkstra's algorithm to simplify the network topology for easy analysis and then make use of the multi-criteria energy function to deploy the network requirement constraints while the stability evaluation in relation to interference was implemented into the Adaptive Rendering Technique approach to optimise the users' need.

3 Proposed Algorithm Model

There are three SDN network flows that were considered within the network environment which are transferred between the data plane elements and the network controllers. These are majorly symmetric messages, asynchronous messages and controller-to-switch messages [20]. The symmetric messages are typically the echo and hello messages which do not need any solicitation from a controller. The Asynchronous messages are typical messages that are sent to the controller in response to the reception of packets by the switches such as flow_removed and packet_in messages. The last and commonest type of message is the controller-to-switch messages which are responsible for delivering messages to the switches without any necessary acknowledgement.

The development of deterministic Adaptive Rendering Technique (DART_MCP) algorithm contains the Monte-Carlo (ZZ) buffer which supposedly assists in establishing the stability of the network performance in relation to the effect of network interferences. The buffer approaches the versatility of distributed networks as it can render wide influx of transferred packets while maintaining the QoS of varying network users.

One major goal of proposing the DART_MCP algorithm among the various available ones in the networking environment is its ability to enhance an optimal performance in terms of rate of network stability when tailored user requirements are to be harnessed. In this section, we deploy a mechanism similar to the ticket based probing TBP used in [21] however we deploy network interference alleviation scheme to enhance network stability while meeting up with user requirement. This network interference alleviation was modelled into the rendering equation to input network stability. Since the rendering equation is already established as proven by the published works in [23] and [24]. The modelled equation is written in Eq. 1 thus:

$$L_o(x, w_o, \lambda, t) = L_e(X, w_o, \lambda, t) + \int_\Omega^1 f_r(x, w_i, w_o, \lambda, t) L_i(x, w_i, \lambda, t)(w_i.n)dw_i \quad (1)$$

Where $L_o(x, w_o, \lambda, t)$ equals to the total outgoing packets from various network hosts with bandwidth "λ" directed in a poisson distribution manner of "w_o" through time "t" on a path distance of "x" away.

λ represents the bandwidth.

w_o represents the poisson distribution value.

t represents the time for packet delivery.

$L_e(X, w_o, \lambda, t)$ represents outward packet distribution.

Ω represents units of packets transmitted through mean network n containing all possible values of w_o.

$\int_\Omega^1 ....dw_o$ is an integral value over Ω.

$f_r(x, w_i, w_o, \lambda, t)$ is the bidirectional poisson distribution of packets whose proportion varied from w_i to w_o over distance.

x, time t and bandwidth λ.

w_i is the inverse packet flow from controllers to hosts.

n is the mean controller equidistance apart.

$w_i.n$ is the weakening interference factor of packets as it transverse the network.

Hence, Eq. 1 expresses the solution to the DART_MCP algorithm model whose analysis enhances network stability through elimination of network interference. Our idea is that once the solution to a single interference is determined, it is sufficient enough to address similar multi-objective optimization problem efficiently, then the summation of such singular solution gives the aggregate of the larger network interference problem, hence, the stability of such network can be guaranteed based on the aggregate solution.

We formulate the users' requests as a poisson distribution requesting for network resources and we considered this as an optimization problem that needed to find a balance between the network resources and user requirement. We look at a poisson cluster process which is motion-invariant requests, thus from a single user point process. For practical illustration, assuming a request is sent from the source to the sink, however the best route at any point in time is required which meet the user requirements. The throughput, latency and bandwidth of the routes were specified on the routes connecting one node to the other thus depicting the state of network routes at timeslot t.

4 Result and Discussions

4.1 Performance Tests

We first deployed an OMNeT++ network simulator aided by a real word traces to a certain the performance of adaptive rendering algorithm. Recall the proposed rendering equation that was proposed in Sect. 3 to address the flow interference that brings about instability in networks performance. We simulated a network provider which enables the operation of four data center with each having 50 controllers each. Four different instances of application were hosted on each data centre and the Wikipedia request traces [25] which happen to be a real word traces was used to represent the network traffic arising from the requests. We first test the rate of congestions for the traffic flows through the request for the running applications. This was ranged for an interval of 50 h which is approximately two days' duration. We divided the whole traffic flow among the users to attain normal distribution state (even).

We set the controllers to have a fixed bandwidth capacity with the running applications instances consuming relatively same amount of bandwidth. We briefly access the level of bandwidth consumption and the nature of user experience in the course of affirming the level of stability of the network performance. We intend to find out the average bandwidth utilization over a duration of 50 h as discussed earlier when the capacity of each controllers were set to 1000 units. The first inference we are interested in was the rate of consumption of the bandwidth on arrival of several requests as shown in Fig. 1. One important deduction from the experiment is the maximization of the bandwidth cost. We inferred from the experiment that the rate of average bandwidth consumption barely exceeds 1.80, thus providing a benefits to the service provider in terms of bandwidth maximization.

The service providers do not unnecessarily incur more expenses and cost on extending insufficient bandwidth. The experiment in this section is therefore very useful in maintaining a fairly stable network provisioning, considering the limited size of bandwidth at hand.

Furthermore, the Fig. 2 showed us more information about the optimization of the bandwidth for network stability on the part of user experience. The Fig. 2 depicted a relatively stable experience over a range of 0.50 irrespective of the fluctuations in the average requests that was incurred. The red line which showed the fluctuating requests with the least at around 2200 and highest of almost 3500 requests was optimized to maintain a stable average user experience of 0.50. The figure also depicted the impact of time function on the network when it was almost tending toward 50 h. A tilt was experienced which could be attributed to the accumulated network flows which was probably meant to initiate the attainment of a new stability level for the network user experience. Thus, the AUE is maintained under a stable rate below 0.75 stability level.

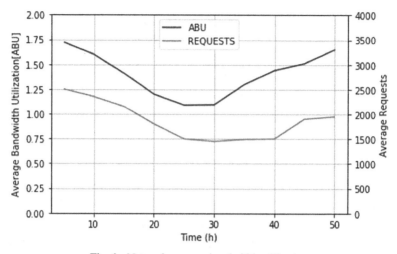

Fig. 1. Network average bandwidth utilization

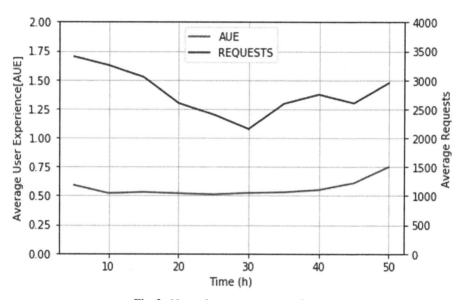

Fig. 2. Network average user experience.

4.2 Convergence Rate

The need to deploy this work on a new platform to test the rate of it convergence is buttress on the fact that we used a separate script to aid the determination of the rate of convergence. We deployed the gt-itm application that was used in [22] so as to produce the required network topology. The performance was tested using the number of success rate achieved and the duration of time at which the algorithm performs the simulation (running time). We considered the performance of the DART_MCP with one competitive algorithm from the earlier mentioned algorithms which is HAS_MCP.

We also evaluate the performances of the algorithm when there is an increasing number of packet transfer and the packet size was kept constant as well as when the packet size was varied with constant packet transfer rate within the network. The diagram in Fig. 1 and 2 compare the performance of both HAS_MCP and DART_MCP algorithms especially in terms of the duration of delays before a stable state is reached by the algorithms. We selected only these two among others for this test because only HSA_MCP can be seen to perform at least in a comparable manner to our proposed algorithm. A total of 10 controllers and 1500 switches were used to investigate the impact of network interference on the stability that was attained in the course of packet routing. The delays were measured in milliseconds while the progressive results were derived in the course of sending packets. The three dimensional representation was depicted in Fig. 3 and Fig. 4 for HSA_MCP and DART_MCP respectively.

Table 1. The analysis representations. Comparison of network stability delays.

SDN resources		Algorithm delays			
Switches	*Controllers*	*H_MCOP*	*SA_MCP*	*HSA_MCP*	*DART_MCP*
300	2	128	88	47	26
600	4	255	176	96	55
900	6	388	267	145	83
1200	8	518	356	194	111
1500	10	650	450	245	140

The figures clearly showed that for network nodes of 1500 running with 10 controllers, it took HAS_MCP approximately 245 ms to attain network stability while on the other hand, DART_MCP in Fig. 4 only used 140 ms instead. The differences between these two values occurred as a result of network interferences as earlier highlighted. Under this experimental design, there are some cases in which an appropriate number of controllers would have enabled total avoidance of network interferences however, this was designed to see how much of the effects could be reduced by the deployed algorithms.

Thus, a vast difference of 105 ms existed in the performance of the two algorithms when compared. It is noteworthy to understand that at each interval, the amount of delays could be calculated to determine the corresponding values under similar conditions. However, to avoid unnecessary replication of graphs, we just selected the same number of network setup but running on different algorithms to compare the performances. The remaining results were depicted in Table 1. Hence, in a case where we are short of network resources especially controllers and at the same time we are trying to accommodate more network hosts, a high stability routing protocol will be of importance which can help to reduce if not totally alleviating the effect of network interferences. Based on these four tested algorithms, DART_MCP provides us with the best network stability,

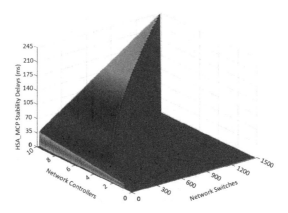

Fig. 3. HAS_MCP Delay before attaining network stability

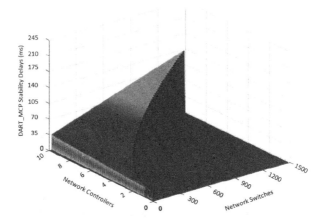

Fig. 4. DART_MCP's Delay before attaining network stability

causing a reduction in the network delays with the percentage of 42.9 as depicted by our experiments.

5   Conclusion and Future Works

This work was motivated by the need for an improved routing network in SDN that focus on a stable network performance when larger network nodes were associated. We identified basically the impact of network interference on affecting the combination of user requirements which invariably reduces the success rate and the running time of the network. The success rate and running time directly speaks to the throughput and the latency experienced in the course of the network operations therefore necessitating the need for their optimisation. We address these basic challenges through deploying a deterministic adaptive rendering technique (algorithm) called DART_MCP. The tests on the efficiency of our proposed approach was first carried out to determine the stability in rate of bandwidth consumption as well as the stability in the user experience that is deciphered. The DART_MCP algorithm contains the Monte-Carlo (ZZ) buffer which supposedly assists in establishing the stability of the network performance in relation to the effect of network interferences. The buffer approaches the versatility of distributed networks as it can render wide influx of transferred packets while maintaining the QoS of varying network users.

Hence, the proposed algorithm was able to optimize the network metrics requirements to a level that is optimal on the basics of this work in the domain of SDN. The evaluation of the algorithm against others showed that our proposed algorithm was able to maintain lower network running time and higher success ratio to provoke low latency and higher throughput respectively. Further experiments also showed a faster convergence (with a reduction of 42.9% in network delays) in attaining the network stability state for DART_MCP than the existing algorithms even though for the kind of design, interference could not be totally eradicated meaning that our proposed algorithms could assist in managing the network resources especially in a situation where the number of controllers available is fewer than what is required. We were also able to reduce the key inhibitors to network stability which is predominantly the control flow path issues and the co-channel interferences. The future work that we envisaged in this work is to introduce the deployment of machine learning algorithms or some AI mechanisms thereby introducing some level of intelligence to enhance the performance of the SDN system in terms of stability.

Acknowledgment. The authors acknowledge the funds received from the industry partners: Telkom SA Ltd., South Africa in support of this research.

References

1. Zhu, M., Cao, J., Pang, D., He, Z., Xu, M.: SDN-based routing for efficient message propagation in VANET. In: Xu, K., Zhu, H. (eds.) WASA 2015. LNCS, vol. 9204, pp. 788–797. Springer, Cham (2015). https://doi.org/10.1007/978-3-319-21837-3_77
2. Zhu, W., Song, M., Olariu, S.: Integrating stability estimation into quality of service routing in mobile ad-hoc networks, pp. 122–129. IEEE (2006)
3. Akinola, A.T., Adigun, M.O., Mudali, P.: Effects of scalability measures on control plane architectural designs in different data centre architectures. In: Southern African Telecommunication and Network Applications Conference, Arabella, Hermanus, Western Cape, South Africa, pp. 198–203 (2018)
4. Nguyen, V.D., Begin, T., Guérin-Lassous, I.: Multi-constrained routing algorithm: a networking evaluation. In: IEEE 37th Annual Computer Software and Applications Conference Workshops (COMPSACW), pp. 719–723 (2013)
5. Akinola, A.T., Adigun, M.O., Akingbesote, A.O., Mba, I.N.: Optimal route service selection in ad-hoc mobile E-marketplaces with dynamic programming algorithm using TSP approach. In: International Conference on E-Learning Engineering and Computer Software, pp. 74–81 (2015)
6. Zhang, S.Q., Zhang, Q., Bannazadeh, H., Leon-Garcia, A.: Routing algorithms for network function virtualization enabled multicast topology on SDN. IEEE Trans. Netw. Serv. Manage. **12**(4), 580–594 (2015)

7. Yeganeh, S.H., Tootoonchian, A., Ganjali, Y.: On scalability of software-defined networking. IEEE Commun. Mag. **51**(2), 136–141 (2013)
8. Song, P., Liu, Y., Liu, T., Qian, D.: Controller-proxy: scaling network management for large-scale SDN networks. Comput. Commun. **108**(1), 52–63 (2017)
9. He, M., Basta, A., Blenk, A., Kellerer, W.: Modeling flow setup time for controller placement in SDN: evaluation for dynamic flows. In: IEEE International Conference on Communications (ICC) (2017)
10. Sheng, L., Song, Z., Yang, J.: A multi-constrained routing algorithm for software defined network based on nonlinear annealing. J. Networks **10**(6), 376–385 (2015)
11. Sridharan, V., Gurusamy, M., Truong-Huu, T.: On multiple controller mapping in software defined networks with resilience constraints. IEEE Commun. Lett. **21**(8), 1763–1766 (2017)
12. Egilmez, H.E.: Adaptive video streaming over openflow networks with quality of service. Citeseer (2012)
13. Wang, Z., Crowcroft, J.: Quality-of-service routing for supporting multimedia applications. IEEE J. Sel. Areas Commun. **14**(7), 1228–1234 (1996)
14. Chen, Y., Mucchi, L., Wang, R., Huang, K.: Modeling network interference in the angular domain: interference Azimuth spectrum. IEEE Trans. Commun. **62**(6), 2107–2120 (2014)
15. Garroppo, R.G., Giordano, S., Tavanti, L.: A survey on multi-constrained optimal path computation: exact and approximate algorithms. Comput. Netw. **54**(17), 3081–3107 (2010)
16. Lee, W.C., Hluchyi, M.G., Humblet, P.A.: Routing subject to quality of service constraints in integrated communication networks. IEEE Network **9**(4), 46–55 (1995)
17. Cheng, G., Ansari, N., Papavassiliou, S.: Adaptive QoS provisioning by pricing incentive QoS routing for next generation networks. Comput. Commun. **31**(10), 2308–2318 (2008)
18. Liu, G., Ramakrishnan, K.: A* Prune: an algorithm for finding K shortest paths subject to multiple constraints. In: Twentieth Annual Joint Conference of the IEEE Computer and Communications Societies, pp. 743–749. IEEE (2001)
19. Apostolopoulos, G., Guérin, R., Kamat, S., Tripathi, S.K.: Quality of service based routing: a performance perspective. SIGCOMM Comput. Commun. Rev. **28**(4), 17–28. ACM (1998)
20. Karakus, M., Durresi, A.: A scalability metric for control planes in software defined networks (SDNs). In: 30th International Conference on Advanced Information Networking and Applications (AINA), pp. 282–289. IEEE (2016)
21. Chen, S., Nahrstedt, K.: Distributed quality-of-service routing in ad hoc networks. IEEE J. Sel. Areas Commun. **17**(8), 1488–1505 (1999)
22. Modeling Topology of Large internetworks. https://www.cc.gatech.edu/projects/gtitm/2014, https://www.cc.gatech.edu/projects/gtitm/
23. Kajiya, J.T.: The rendering equation. In: Proceedings of the 13th Annual Conference on Computer Graphics and Interactive Techniques, pp. 143–150, August 1986
24. Ng, T.T., Pahwa, R.S., Bai, J., Tan, K.H., Ramamoorthi, R.: From the rendering equation to stratified light transport inversion. Int. J. Comput. Vis. **96**(2), 235–251 (2012)
25. Wikipedia Request Traces. https://www.wikibench.eu/

An Enhanced Flow-Based QoS Management Within Edge Layer for SDN-Based IoT Networking

Avewe Bassene[(✉)] and Bamba Gueye

Université Cheikh Anta Diop, Dakar, Senegal
{avewe.bassene,bamba.gueye}@ucad.edu.sn

Abstract. IoT infrastructure makes great demands on network control methods for an efficient management of massive amounts of nodes and data. This network requires fine traffic control management to ensure an adequate QoS for data transmission process, especially in a low-cost network that covers smart territories deployed in so-called "technological lag" areas. Software-Defined Networking (SDN) enables to handle dynamically network traffic as well as flexible traffic control on real-time. However, SDN technology exhibits several issues with regard to additional processing time or loss that are associated to control plan. These factors can lead to performance degradation of the SDN control traffic flows within data plane which is not tolerated in medium/low capacity IoT environment.

This paper proposes an Enhanced Flow-based QoS Management approach, called $EFQM$, that reduces spent time within control plane as well as uses SDN controller either to reduce loss or to optimize bandwidth according to flows latency and bandwidth requirement. Our experimental results show that $EFQM$ outperforms $AQRA$ in terms of response time and packet loss rate. Furthermore, by considering a default routing and delay as metrics, $EFQM$ improves the average end-to-end flow performance by 7.92% compared to $AQRA$. In addition, $EFQM$ enhances end-to-end flow performance by 21.23% and 23.52% compared to $AQRA$ respectively according to delay and packet loss rate. The measured $EFQM$ runtime is 23.29% shorter than $AQRA$.

Keywords: Edge computing · Internet of Things · Quality of Service · Software-Defined Networking · Performance

1 Introduction

Recent years, Africa has registered many IoT environment projects that plane to develop by rapidly reducing the technological divide that affects the continent. This environment is well known according to the huge and various volumes of

R. Zitouni et al. (Eds.): AFRICOMM 2020, LNICST 361, pp. 151–167, 2021.
https://doi.org/10.1007/978-3-030-70572-5_10

generated traffic. IoT networks are equipped by a large number of sensors, and thus, they should be managed efficiently by network operators [1,2].

Software Defined Networking (SDN) is a constantly progressive technology that offers more flexible programmability support for network control functions and protocols [3]. SDN provides logical central control model for implementation and maintenance of programmable networks. SDN decouples data and control plane over a well-marked and comprehensible controlling protocol like "$OpenFlow$" [4]. $OpenFlow$ acts as de facto signaling protocol between control and data planes that are used to program SDN switches. By decoupling control and data planes, SDN technology enable to monitor network conditions and network resource allocation on the fly. Therefore, SDN is amongst the key enabling technology for new generation networks.

Congestion is often the most used criterion to improve network performance in IoT environments. Indeed, from SDN control plane, congestion management makes it possible to improve the network Quality of Service (QoS) by optimizing traffic important factors such as delay, loss, bandwidth, etc. In addition, IoT networks are reputed for their non-compliance according to fixed standards (for instance, protocols and ports used). As consequence, it is not just sufficient to give a good QoS-aware approach by just reading such an instable traffic characteristics. Furthermore, with respect to a real-time QoS-aware study that incorporating SDN technology, it is mandatory to take into account traffic characteristics. In fact, selected parameters include both information coming from external entity to which device is connected (IoT server) and current traffic data QoS requirements in terms of delay, bandwidth and loss recorded from different architecture layers.

Previous work like $AQRA$ [5] aims to guarantee adaptive multiple QoS requirements of high-priority IoT applications by dropping low/medium priority flows that seize the network resource of high-priority flows until the QoS requirements can be guaranteed. However, this removing operation is not trivial since it leads to longer transmission delay and processing overhead at the SDN switches. Furthermore, the end-to-end traffic QoS management as described in [5] can be improved by reducing packets disruption at the edge layer and transposing the optimization factors lower in network architecture. Indeed, this improvement can decrease loss rate, avoid congestion and consequently increase the network scalability to adapt it to different environment devices ability.

Therefore, this paper aims to reduce processing latency due to SDN switches transmission disruption, which leads to packets lost and a delay extension. In fact, the obtained network degradation is caused by "$Flow\_mod$" rules sent from the SDN controller [6] and can lead to mighty waste time (up to 64 ms in normal operation, when changing paths occurs). Starvation problem is considered.

In addition, according to 3GPP $Long$ $Term$ $Evolution$ (LTE), each bearer has a corresponding QoS class identifier (QCI), and each QoS is categorized by service type, priority, packet error rate (PER) and packet delay budget (PDB) [7]. Some flows have $QCIs$ vector that allow a low PDB values. Avoiding the transfer of such packets to the control layer could considerably reduce latency or otherwise (allowing them) can be effective for bandwidth and loss sensitive flows.

The rest of the paper is organized as follows. Section 2 reviews related works. Processing delays, bandwidth and loss impact in SDN switches and the multi-layer traffic flow operations are discussed in Sect. 3. Our $EFQM$ SDN-based framework from perception to network layers is described in Sect. 4. Section 5 evaluates $EFQM$ overall performance. Finally, Sect. 6 concludes this paper.

2   Related Work

Various motivations have led to numerous proposals on IoT networking QoS improvements in SDN-based network architecture. Most of related work particularly focus on algorithmic optimization which can give an effective approach to overcome QoS problem in IoT environment.

Deng et al. [5] propose $AQRA$ for SDN-based IoT network to fulfill a multi-QoS requirement of high-priority IoT application. The key idea is to remove low or medium priority flows in favor of high priority flows until QoS requirements can be guaranteed. However, frequent deletion of flow causes traffic loss in current SDN hardware switches when currently active traffic flow is modified during ongoing traffic transmission. The deletion operation adversely impacts in the end-to-end transmission delay performance and packet loss rate. This action requires processing overhead at the hardware switch ($i.e.$ $TCAM$ reordering [8]) and it is new type of traffic disruption that is not currently handled by SDN switches [6].

X. Guo et al. [9] present $DQSP$ an efficient QoS-aware routing protocol with low latency and high security. $DQSP$ is one of the widely-used deep reinforcement learning method that combines $DDPG$ algorithm and centralized control characteristics of SDN-based IoT network. $DQSP$ outperforms the traditional $OSPF$ routing protocol in term of delay especially when network is under attack.

Authors in [10] propose SDN-based framework to fulfill IoT service QoS requirements. It consists of finding shortest path with minimum-delay and maximum-bandwidth for delay/bandwidth-centric traffic. It decomposed problems into server selection problem and path selection problem which are implemented in controller as QoS-aware route and least-load IoT server modules. The proposed framework achieves high throughput and low delay. Nevertheless, the authors just considered two metrics which are not discriminator.

According to $PFIM$ [7], the authors proposed a pre-emptive flow installation mechanism for IoT devices. It can learn the transmission intervals of periodic network flows and install the suited flow entry into SDN switches before packets arrival. However, they considered only delay metric.

The authors of [11] describes an admission control approach called $REAC$ which can control traffic flows. Indeed, the edge router monitors the delay performance to admit flows to the network that guarantees good quality for high-priority flows. However, we only considered a single QoS requirement based on delay. In addition, the same authors do not consider the starvation problem of low priority flows.

Deep packet Inspection (DPI) is use in [12] to improve QoS for certain network traffic. DPI-based traffic classification is used with current port and queue capacity from utilization monitor for a network flow routing decision based on *DiffServ* for *QoS* and *multi-path* for load balancing. However, the proposed model increases runtime delay due several initial packets traffic duplication from the ingress port. In addition, it needs additional data plane entities and only treat two metrics (delay and throughput).

Finally, a fog computing with heuristic algorithm of lower complexity is proposed in [13] in order to provide a low cost and QoS-aware *IoT* infrastructure. However, *IoT* end devices must support a specific functions, for instance, act as gateway.

In contrast, to previous studies, *EFQM* promotes several metrics in order to cover a wide performance of *IoT* traffic characteristics as well as limits flow deletion process by fixing different sorting levels.

3   Brief Overview on Considered SDN-Based QoS Problem

LTE is an end-to-end *IP* network that provides *IP* connections from the terminal to the core network. *QoS* implies services to be differentiated based on the *QCI* which determines the priority level of each service class and specifies the maximum one way allowed values in terms of *delay*, *jitter*, and *packet loss* [14]. Nevertheless, complexity residing in such data leads to increased processing operation. This cause disruption in network traffic that directly affect bandwidth, delay and loss sensitive services due to networks bottleneck.

According to hierarchical network, the backhaul portion of the network comprises the intermediate links between the core network and the small sub-networks at the edge of the network. Since *LTE* architecture is designed to support high data traffic and a guaranteed *QoS* to end-to-end *IP* based service [15], we believe that network degradation can be considerably limited with fine grained low levels traffic managing, *i.e.* portion between network and perception layer which is often subject to local control. In addition, a local performance management adapted to the quality of the network, to the cost of equipment and to local available resources would give more scalability and cost adaptability to the proposed model. Thus, a fine grained *QoS* management at edge and control layers is proposed to effectively improve end-to-end transmission performance.

In Sect. 4, we describe SDN-based *EFQM* framework and its operation in these specific network areas. Let's first exploit the SDN-based *IoT* network architecture and explain the current state of addressed problem.

3.1   SDN-Based IoT Network Architecture

The SDN-based *IoT* network architecture is composed by five layers. Each layer, according to specific embedded components, ensures communication with adjacent levels components (highest, lowest and centralized control equipment).

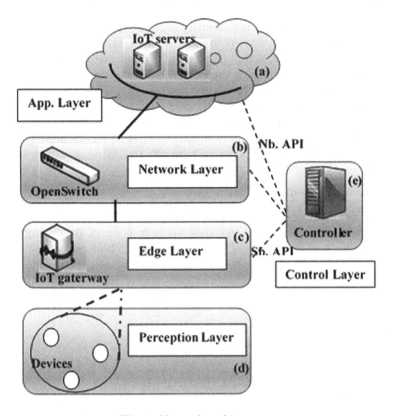

Fig. 1. Network architecture

Figure 1 presents our architecture where the network layer consists of a set of programmable devices that perform packets forwarding towards data plane.

The control plane (*Controller*) is the component that caries communication between other equipment via a dynamic routing protocol. The main goal of the controller is to tell to the second major component (*dataplane*) of the network how to process each incoming frame/packet/dataset using "*OpenSwitches*".

The hierarchical network architecture as illustrated in Fig. 1 is formed by:

1. "(a)" *Application layer*: contains *IoT* applications or services;
2. "(b)" *Network layer*: consists of set of *SDN OpenFlow* switches;
3. "(c)" *Edge layer*: consists of set of edge equipment (*APs*);
4. "(d)" *Perception layer*: *IoT* devices belong to this layer;
5. "(e)" *Control layer*: the control plane consists of the *SDN* controller which communicates with "(a)" through Northbound *API* (Nb. *API*) and with "(b)" and "(c)" through Southbound (Sb. API).

The edge equipment is *OpenFlow-enabled* so they can be controlled by the SDN controller using the *OpenFlow* protocol. This layer connects to "(d)" via wireless communication technologies. Devices in "(d)" forward/receive data to/from "(a)" by accessing layers "(c)" and "(b)".

The controller contains module named "topology discovery" which discovers all network elements in the data plane and builds real time network topology. Another module ("network status monitoring") monitors and collects the network condition periodically. The communication between the data plane and the controller uses a standardized *OpenFlow* protocol.

Furthermore, *EFQM* Framework is able to manage the behavior of both *Open − switches* and *IoT* gateway via southbound *API*. It can also receives messages from *IoT* servers via northbound *API*. However, a gateway has the possibility to decide whether it must route traffic to control plane or not.

3.2   Problem Statement

When the *IoT* devices transfer the message from "*Perception layer*" to "*Application layer*", *Packet_In* message undergo a set of processing in each intermediate node before reaching their destination. These processes to ensure the optimal management of traffic for high performance level. Indeed, with advanced communication emergence devices, current networks should support several services such as video streaming, web browsing, online gaming, etc. These services that have different delay constraints, bandwidth and *QoS* requirements can cause network processing problems.

These problems often create network performance degradation which results in congestion at data plane equipment. Our aim is to overcome these constraints by ensuring that each packet fulfills all its *QoS* requirements from source to destination nodes. Therefore, a controller with a global and centralized network programmability view can give dynamic control flows and flexible network resource management which avoid *IoT* network contention and anomalies. In fact, most transport protocols only consider network congestion as a factor of traffic degradation, when adjusting end-to-end traffic behavior towards improving flow reliability.

However, it has been shown that traffic loss can occur in current *SDN* hardware switches when the forwarding rule being applied to a current active traffic flow is modified during ongoing traffic transmission [6]. It is attributed to the processing latency, which is the amount time we need in order to modify forwarding rule within a hardware switch. The obtained latency can cause transmission disruption that leads to packet loss for a transient period of time, as well as congestion due to the frequent recovery caused by these losses.

Relative to this last case, authors in [5] propose an approach that considers *SDN* controller *Flow_mod* message to remove low or medium priority flows which use network resource of high priority flows up to that the *QoS* requirements can be guaranteed. We think that, avoiding intentional flow deletion and reducing the controller computational overhead can improve existing approach. Indeed, Sect. 3.3 highlights a couple of issues according to *AQRA*.

The use of *SDN* technology could lengthen the processing delay for latency-sensitive packets or could be an improving factor for metrics such as loss or bandwidth. Otherwise, these metrics also is related to the *QCI* vector parameters assigned to each flow. Therefore, a suitable QoS-aware proposal must be approached from two main point of view: technological adhesion and real time traffic requirement. It is worth noticing that good performance could be achieved both in terms of end-to-end delay and runtime when a QoS-aware decision includes flow QCI vector parameters specification and overhead related to SDN technology adhesion.

3.3 $AQRA$ Drawbacks

The basic idea of $AQRA$ [5] in QoS-aware admission control is to remove low or medium priority flows which use network resources in favor of high priority flows until QoS requirements are guaranteed. This operation is not trivial since it causes both processing overhead with respect to SDN switches and delayed transmission. Indeed, when $Flow\_Mod$ messages are sent from controller to switches, a delete command for current flow rule F_c arrives to a switch. Afterwards, selected switch removes F_c and applies the next matching flow rule (F_{next}) to the current traffic. Subsequently, F_{next} aims to replace F_c to serve the current traffic after F_c deletion.

In fact, the operation consists of: *(i)* remove the current flow rule; *(ii)* replace current flow rule with respect to the next flow rule that fulfills the same criteria as the deleted one in order to preserve the current traffic which should not be used otherwise. Therefore, during the time between the corresponding flow rule searching and its application to current traffic, any other packet arriving at the current switch will be lost since the previously matching flow rule has already been deactivated.

In addition, the path change events are applied to all switches along dedicated path. In fact, the total flow transmission time grows with increases in the number of path change events which varies between 1 and 8. In regard to normal operation, path change causes disruption time for approximately 64 ms [6]. This leads to both a substantial transmission delay and congestion that overload the network traffic. This phenomenon can be even worse during a repetitive flow deletion as observed in [5]. The disruption time is also related to total transmission delay and runtime.

To overcome this problem, we directly send, according to the default algorithm, the high priority, loss-sensitive (to avoid traffic jams in the edge gateway) and delay-sensitive packets according to QCI values. Only medium and low priority packets will be transferred to $EFQM$ to ensure traffic QoS requirements. By so doing, we reduce network contention as much as possible for loss-sensitive and delay-sensitive flows that were directly sent.

4 $EFQM$ SDN-Based Framework

4.1 $EFQM$ Background

In contrast to previous studies like [5,12,16], $EFQM$ involves two major steps: a *simulated annealing* (SA)-based QoS routing and *Admission Control* (AC).

The general idea is to compute a QoS-aware best routing paths for each flow and then to control its admission by choosing path that fulfills traffic QoS requirement in a dynamic way at the controller. To reduce the controller workflow and improving delay, traffic classification is performed at the edge layer.

In fact, the edge layer is the first level of sieving in relation to our model. A classifier is used at IoT gateway. Therefore, a "$(classScpt)$" script, based on QCI vector parameters of each flow, figures out whether data packets should be rerouted under controller advices or not ($i.e.$ default routing).

Table 1. Different classified classes in EFQM.

Classes	QCI values
Prioritized	1, 2, 4, 5, 6
Non-prioritized	3, 7, 8, 9

It is worth noticing that the shortest path routing (default forwarding) is a simple and fast packet forwarding protocol that always routes every traffic via shortest path, but lacks the sense of load balancing [17]. However, our traffic classification class takes into account this issue. Table 1 defines the classification model used by $classScpt$ for each incoming flow. Two classes are defined: "$prioritized$" and "$non\text{-}prioritized$" classes.

The $classScpt$ algorithm ensures that bandwidth sensitive flows does not compete bandwidth utilization and buffer resources with the small flows ($prioritized$) which can lead to loss. It ensures faster completion times and lower latency for time sensitive traffic while minimally impacting throughput. It is worth noticing that $classScpt$ algorithm will be explained in Sect. 4.3.

Note that the scheduling scheme presented here is a bearer class QoS control scheme. A bearer is a logical channel which establishes a connection between IoT server and $enodeB$. IoT devices may request many services having diverse QoS requirements according to a given time. Therefore, to distinguish between these different services, $3GPP$ defined the set of characteristics for 9 $QCIs$ as presented in [18].

Table 1 is specifically based on this standard. QoS requirements vector consists of different flow specification like QCI value (integer), priority, service type, PDB (ms), PER (between $10^{(-2)}$ to $10^{(-6)}$). QCI vector can be obtained from the $sFlow$ protocol [19] which provides the consumable resources statistics of IoT servers for the controller using the $sFlow$ Agent and the $sFlow$ Collector.

Unlike [5,19], Table 1 is performed by taking into account values mentioned above since few applications can be delay-sensitive while having non-bandwidth guaranteed (service type = non-GBR). Previous works present acceptable loss rates ($PER = 10^{(-2)}$) and guaranteed bandwidth (service type = non-GBR). Since the default routing is moderately sensitive to load balancing, then the later type of traffic, in case of low PDB value, can be directly sent in order to avoid delay.

With respect to controller, we consider the following classifier classes according to a fine QoS-aware control admission. Therefore, *IoT* traffic can be grouped into 3 classes:

1. *Delay-centric* (D-centric): mission-critical or event-driven applications.
2. *Bandwidth-centric* (B-centric): associated with continuous traffic, (query-driven and real-time monitoring).
3. *Best-effort* (Be-centric): which consists of general applications such as non-real time monitoring.

According to this second class values and packets specification, chosen path, from all recorded ones must satisfy the traffic needs. Thus, this fine grained path selection also reduces harmful congestion within switches for flows directly sent (default route) from the *IoT* gateway. The overall system design and proposed controller architecture are illustrated respectively in Figs. 2 and 3.

Figure 2 depicts 3 separate components distributed on two layers (edge and control layers). A heuristic algorithm called *"Simulated Annealing"* (*SA*) is used to find the approximate optimal solutions. According to edge layer, an *IoT* gateway is used to perform *classScpt* classification algorithm based on Table 1 entries. In regard to control plane, a *SA-based QoS* routing algorithm performs candidate paths selection with *QoS* constraints such as delay, bandwidth and packet loss rate. The appropriate path is finally chosen by an admission control algorithm according to current traffic load. In fact, path selection with multiple constraints in an *IoT* network communication is an *NP-complete* problem [10].

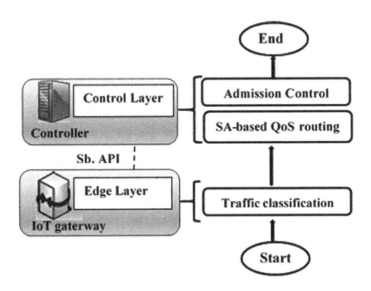

Fig. 2. *EFQM* at a nutshell.

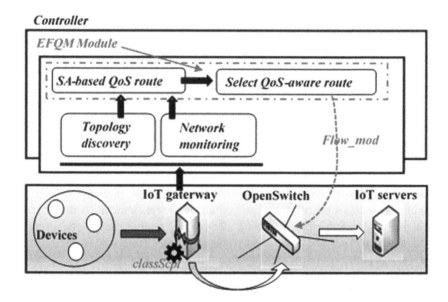

Fig. 3. $EFQM$ controller architecture.

4.2 $EFQM$ Architecture

The proposed controller architecture in Fig. 3 shows the different components in detail with traffic flows processing from $Perception\ layer$ to $Application\ layer$. The $classScpt$ script gives the classification level allowing to ensure both, a good completion time for high latency packets and prevent controller overloading. The $classScpt$ can send packets directly to the network layer (white arrows) or ask the controller for adequate QoS fulfillment (black arrows). It should be noted that when candidate paths are obtained from SA-based QoS routing algorithm, the best path is selected by an admission control component. Afterwards, the suited $Flow\_mod$ message (rule) is sent by controller to switches for processing packets of concerned flows.

Therefore, we avoid intentional flows deletion in order to limit unnecessary losses while respecting the flows deadlines. A detailed $classScpt$ algorithm processing is proposed in the next section. This algorithm gives a basic flows classification in edge layer, according to Table 1 class model. For instance, **Algorithm** 1 depicted in Fig. 4 illustrates packets dispatching steps from the time they attempt IoT gateway in edge layer.

Note that IoT gateway is SDN-$enable$ therefore it can communicate with the controller via southbound API. Once the traffic reaches this level, two choices are possible: either route the traffic directly to the $OpenFlow$ switches, or, contact the controller for adequate routing rules ($Flow\_mod$ message).

Algorithm 1: Classification with *classScpt*
1:      t_{init} = time() = 0
2:      current_flow = [[qci_values], flow_timestamp]
3:      prioritized = [1, 2, 4, 5, 6]
4:      non_prioritized = [3, 7, 8, 9]
5:      function: dispatcher(current_flow):
6:          if (flow_timestamp > t_{init})
7:              if (current_flow = prioritized)
8:                  then *default_route* (current_flow)
9:              end if
10:              if (current_flow = non_prioritized)
11:                  then *send_to_ctrl* (current_flow)
12:              end if
13:          end if
14:      end function

Fig. 4. Traffic classification algorithm

4.3   Traffic Classification

Upon receiving message from perception layer, whatever the traffic class, the *IoT* gateway, with *classScpt*, looks for the traffic corresponding class *QCI* values (*"prioritized"* or *"non-prioritized"*). The timestamp is used to ensure dissimilarity between flows. If the flow is *prioritized* (*QCI* value belong to 1, 2, 4, 5, 6) then the message is sent to next corresponding switch through the shortest path (*default_route* algorithm), else, the message is encapsulates within a *Packet_In* message and sent to the controller (*send_to_ctrl*) for appropriate path computation.

A controller by having a global view of network statistics information (topology and measurement), *SA*-based *QoS* routing algorithm and *EFQM* module, computes and selects the path that is most suited with respect to packet requirement. Afterwards, *EFQM* installs the response with the *Flow_mod* message on track switches along choosing path. Finally, effective traffic routing is performed without any intentional flow deletion.

A couple of functions that are used by *SA*-based routing algorithm and *EFQM QoS*-aware admission control are illustrated from Eqs. 1 to 5. Furthermore, Table 2 describes the meanings of different parameters that are used in Eqs. 1, 2, 3, 4, and 5.

Table 2. Key nomenclatures.

C_p	Cost of path P
W_x	Weight for x QoS requirement
MR_p	Miss Rate for metric x
$p(C_p, C_x, t)$	Probability to accept new path x
ABW_p	Available bandwidth according to fixed routing path P
e_i	i^{th} link in the routing path P
c_i	e_i link capacity
b_i	Current bandwidth load on e_i
a_i	Available bandwidth on e_i

$$C_P = W_d \frac{(P_d - R_d)}{R_d} + W_j \frac{(P_j - R_j)}{R_j} + W_l \frac{(P_l - R_l)}{R_l}. \tag{1}$$

$$W_x = \frac{MR_x}{MR_d + RM_j + RM_l}. \tag{2}$$

$$MR_x = \frac{(flows\ that\ can\ not\ meet\ requirement\ x)}{(flows\ in\ pList)} \tag{3}$$

$$p(C_P, C_X, t) = \begin{cases} 1 & C_X < C_p \\ e^{\frac{-c|C_X - C_P|}{t}} & C_X \geq C_p \end{cases} \tag{4}$$

$$ABW_P = \min_{e_i \in P} a^i \ ; \ a_i = c_i - b_i \tag{5}$$

EFQM QoS-aware routing flowchart is illustrated in Fig. 5. It combines *SA*-based *QoS* routing algorithm and an admission control function. According to flow *QoS* requirement and source/destination IP addresses, *EFQM* uses Dijkstra's algorithm to compute the shortest path P_s then the cost of P_s named C_{ps} using Eq. 1.

The used metrics are *delay* (d), *jitter* (j) and *loss rate* (l). Path P_s is stored in a list named *pList*. P_s consists of an initial solution of *SA*. An iteration value t is set and decreases whenever t is not null. The cost function computing needs the weights W_x of each metric x (Eq. 2). If t is canceled and no path is accepted, a new neighbor N is determined and the process is repeated. Path acceptance probability is determined by Eq. 4. If it exists a path X which cost improves the cost of P_s, then X replaces P_s. This process is the basis of this algorithm and it is repeated until t is equal to 0. So each time an improved path is found, it is appended to *pList*.

Finally, *pList* is built based on potential candidate paths. In fact, *SA* algorithm avoids being trapped in local optima but does not eliminate the possibility of oscillating indefinitely by returning to previous visited paths. The list *pList* is consequently defined to avoid this paths revisited. *SA* can be replaced by the *tabu search* algorithm if the state space was larger. *tabu search* can also minimize the size of *pList* with an automatic memory-based reaction mechanism.

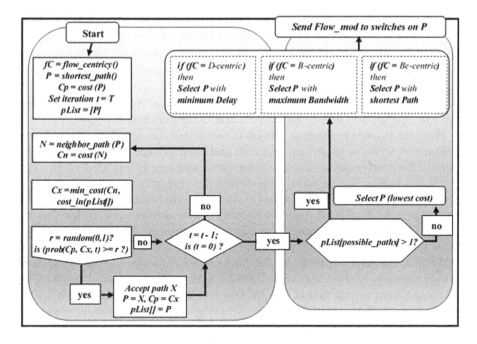

Fig. 5. Flowchart of proposed EFQM

In fact, a suitable path is chosen among candidate paths within *pList*. This choice is crucial since all paths are improving paths. Therefore, the best one that meets the needs of the current centric traffic will be the selected path.

Therefore, according to $EFQM$, each packet is optimally forwarded in order either to minimize end-to-end delay, or increase bandwidth, or reduce contention to satisfy resource limits of IoT server. This is suitable specifically for network with limited resources.

The implementation setup and $EFQM$ performance evaluation is presented in the Sect. 5. $EFQM$ is compared to $AQRA$ [5] according to overall flow end-to-end performance and system runtime evaluation. MR_x consists of miss rates for metric x requirement, as shown in (Eq. 3). For any given link e in path P with capacity c and available bandwidth a, the "*Available Bandwidth*" (ABW) of a routing path P is computed by (Eq. 5).

5 $EFQM$ Evaluation

Our experimental testbed is based on "Ryu" SDN controller [20] and "$Mininet$-$Wifi$" [21]. Ryu is an $OpenFlow$ based controller which provides python language based application development. According to topology discovery, we use a Ryu module/library called *topology*. A *python* graph library $networkX$ is used for network view. The proposed system is simulated within $Ubuntu$ 18.04.1 LTS.

The deployed testbed network consists of three *OpenFlow* core switches, two *OpenFlow* edge switches, 15 *OpenFlow-enabled* access points connected to 20 end devices accessing the network via WiFi (*IEEE* 802.11n). Three stations included in network act as application servers with different services requirements. We used *iPerf* an active measurement tool [22] in order to generate test traffic and measure the performance of the network. *iPerf* enables to get, for each test, the reports of loss, bandwidth and other parameters.

The performance evaluation is done in two steps: the overall end-to-end performance in terms of delay and loss rate and total system runtime. Firstly, we evaluate the transmission time for *prioritized* and *non-prioritized* traffic. For *prioritized* traffic, the measurement is the total transmission delay for packets sent with *default_route* function of *classScpt*. In contrast, for *non-prioritized* flow delay consists of time required to route a flow using the controller specifications. Secondly, we assessed the runtime estimation in *EFQM* process from source to servers.

EFQM is compared with *AQRA* [5] in relation to overall end-to-end flow performance and system runtime. Table 3 shows the experimental result. The end-to-end flow performance of *EFQM* by considering the default route is 7.92% better than *AQRA* in terms of *delay*. Nevertheless, *AQRA* gives an enhanced packet loss rate (reduced by 8%) than *EFQM*.

The end-to-end flow performance of *EFQM* with history reduces that of *AQRA* with history by 21.23% and 23.52% in terms of *delay* and *packet loss* rate, respectively. This is due to the fact that, in *AQRA* [5], sending packets with very high priority is affected not only by the waiting time for routing decision coming from the controller but also by the network degradation comes from frequent low priority packets deletion.

Regarding to default route, even if it does not guarantee all *QoS* requirements, it fulfills *delay* and better escapes bottlenecks given the limited size of low-priority data. In addition, elephant flows that are more suitable to overload the network are optimally managed in terms of *QoS* by *EFQM*, therefore less interference by sending priority flows are noticed. This situation explains losses reduction as illustrated in Table 3 by *EFQM* with history.

Table 3. End-to-end flow performance.

Overall end-to-end performance	Delay (ms)	Packet loss rate (%)
AQRA (with history)	89.10	0.051
EFQM (default route)	82.04	0.056
EFQM (with history)	70.18	0.039

The total runtime of *EFQM* is computed by subtracting from the end-to-end delay, the time between the gateway and the controller (T_{gc}) plus time between controller and the servers (T_{cs}) as described in equation (Eq. (6)).

$$T_{runtime} = T_{end\_to\_end} - (T_{gc} + T_{cs}) \tag{6}$$

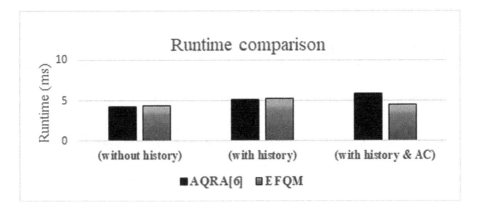

Fig. 6. Runtime comparison

Figure 6 illustrates the runtime comparison of proposed $EFQM$ and $AQRA$ [5] according to use or not of $pList$ (history), of admission control algorithm (AC) or none of them. Compared to $EFQM$, $AQRA$ [5] proposes best runtime in two scenarios: reduce runtime by 0.96% with history and 1.38% without history. This is due to $classScpt$ processing time which exists in any of these scenarios. However, $EFQM$ decrease $AQRA$ [5] runtime by 23.29% when we consider history and AC. Indeed, time used by the $AQRA$ controller model to drop packets at edge level increases it processing time due to the waiting of next flow receive for applying the new control rules and path change processing.

In addition, The AC processing latency increases this runtime delay due to packets deletion in edge layer. This situation occurs when there are multiple successive low-priority flows or multiple flows with the same priority coming at the same time to edge equipment. It should be noted that $EFQM$ does not control incoming flow as long as it arrives at the controller. Note that by sending directly packets, $EFQM$ avoids overloading the controller as well as considerably reduces local buffer (gateway) utilization rate.

To the best of our knowledge, $EFQM$ gives a good QoS-aware approach that outperforms previous studies. Indeed, it takes into account 3 metrics to cover a wide performance aspect of IoT traffic, in contrast to former works such as [7,9,11] that consider just 1 metric like delay; or 2 metrics like [10].

6   Conclusion

This paper illustrates a new flow QoS management mechanism for SDN-based IoT network. $EFQM$ proposes a framework which aims to reduce flow processing delay and congestion caused by frequent packets deletion. Therefore, it limits flow deletion process by fixing two sorting levels for better performance.

Firstly, $EFQM$ separates vulnerable latency, loss sensitive and very high priority flows to others. These flows are sent directly to avoid delay constraints.

The remaining traffic flows are sent to a fixed controller. A second level of sorting based on flows specific requirements is applied after the computation of the overall enhanced paths. Our evaluation results have shown that, $EFQM$ (default route) outperforms $AQRA$ with history in terms of end-to-end delay performance.

Furthermore, the end-to-end flow performance of $EFQM$ with history reduces $AQRA$ with history by 21.23% and 23.52% according to delay and packet loss rate, respectively. Finally, by considering history approach and AC, $EFQM$ runtime decreases by 23.29% compared to $AQRA$ runtime. However, $AQRA$ gives best packet loss rate (reduced by 8%) than $EFQM$ (default route) and decreases $EFQM$ runtime in two scenarios: 0.96% with history and 1.38% without history.

We plan to compare $EFQM$ and $AQRA$ under different conditions and scenarios, for instance, when the topology is highly dynamic with more or less switches in the data plane.

References

1. Pham, C., Rahim, A., Cousin, P.: Low-cost, long-range open IoT for smarter rural African villages. In: Proceedings of IEEE ISC2, Trento, pp. 1–6 (2016)
2. Seye, M.R., Diallo, M., Gueye, B., Cambier, C.: COWShED: communication within white spots for breeders. In: Proceedings of IEEE ICIN, France, pp. 236–238 (2019)
3. Haleplidis, E., Pentikousis, K., Denazis, S., Salim, J.H., Meyer, D., Koufopavlou, O.: Software-defined networking (SDN): layers and architecture terminology. IRTF, ISSN 2070–1721, RFC 7426, pp. 1–35, January 2015
4. McKeown, N., et al.: OpenFlow: enabling innovation in campus networks. SIG-COMM Comput. Commun. Rev. **38**(2), 69–74 (2008)
5. Deng, G., Wang, K.: An application-aware QoS routing algorithm for SDN-based IoT networking. In: Proceedings of 2018 IEEE ISCC, Natal, pp. 186–191 (2018)
6. Oh, B., Vural, S., Wang, N., Tafazolli, R.: Priority-based flow control for dynamic and reliable flow management in SDN. IEEE Trans. Netw. Serv. Manag. **15**(4), 1720–1732 (2018)
7. Sulthana, S.F., Nakkeeran, R.: Performance analysis of service based scheduler in LTE OFDMA system. Wireless Pers. Commun. **83**(2), 841–854 (2015)
8. He, K., et al.: Measuring control plane latency in SDN-enabled switches. In: Proceedings of ACM SIGCOMM SOSR, USA, pp. 1–25 (2015)
9. Guo, X., Lin, H., Li, Z., Peng, M.: Deep reinforcement learning based QoS-aware secure routing for SDN-IoT. IEEE Internet Things J. **7**, 6242–6251 (2019)
10. Montazerolghaem, A., Yaghmaee, M.H.: Load-balanced and QoS-aware software-defined internet of things. IEEE Internet Things J. **7**(4), 3323–3337 (2020)
11. Jutila, M.: An adaptive edge router enabling internet of things. IEEE Internet Things J. **3**(6), 1061–1069 (2016)
12. Jeong, S., Lee, D., Hyun, J., Li, J., Hong, J.W.: Application-aware traffic engineering in software-defined network. In: 19th APNOMS, Seoul, pp. 315–318 (2017)
13. Gravalos, I., Makris, P., Christodoulopoulos, K., Varvarigos, E.A.: Efficient network planning for internet of things with QoS constraints. IEEE Internet Things J. **5**(5), 3823–3836 (2018)

14. 3GPP: Quality of service (QoS) concept and architecture. TS 23.107. Accessed 29 May 2020
15. Mesbahi, N., Dahmouni, H.: Delay and jitter analysis in LTE networks. In: Proceedings of WINCOM, Fev, pp. 122–126 (2016)
16. Qin, Z., Denker, G., Giannelli, C., Bellavista, P., Venkatasubramanian, N.: A software defined networking architecture for the internet-of-things. In: Proceedings of IEEE NOMS, Krakow, pp. 1–9 (2014)
17. Amira, H., Mahmoud, B., Hesham, A.: Towards internet QoS provisioning based on generic distributed QoS adaptive routing engine. Sci. World J. **2014**, 1–29 (2014)
18. Maharazu, M., Hanapi, Z.M., Abdullah, A., Muhammed, A.: Quality of service class identifier (QCI) radio resource allocation algorithm for LTE downlink. PLOS ONE J. **14**(1), 1–22 (2019)
19. sFlow.org: www.sflow.org
20. Ryu: Component-based software defined networking framework. https://github.com/faucetsdn/ryu
21. Mininet-wifi: Emulator for software-defined wireless networks. https://github.com/intrig-unicamp/mininet-wifi
22. iPerf: The ultimate speed test tool for TCP, UDP and SCTP. www.iperf.fr

Internet of Things

IoT Sensing Box to Support Small-Scale Farming in Africa

Antonio Oliveira-Jr[1,2]([envelope]) [iD], Carlos Resende[1] [iD], André Pereira[1],
Pedro Madureira[1] [iD], João Gonçalves[1] [iD], Ruben Moutinho[1] [iD], Filipe Soares[1] [iD],
and Waldir Moreira[1] [iD]

[1] Fraunhofer Portugal AICOS, 4200-135 Porto, Portugal
{antonio.junior,carlos.resende,andre.pereira,pedro.madureira,
joao.goncalves,ruben.moutinho,filipe.soares,waldir.junior}@fraunhofer.pt
[2] Institute of Informatics (INF) - Federal University of Goiás (UFG), Goiânia-GO
74690-900, Brazil
antoniojr@ufg.br

Abstract. Small-scale farming has an important role in agriculture. Driven by the popularization of the Internet of things (IoT), this paper presents an IoT sensing box prototype coupled with soil analysis through computer vision to help small-scale farmer improve their yields. The idea of combining image-based soil classification with regular soil sensors is to improve the reliability of the sensed data, by minimizing the occurrence of incorrect estimates for specific soil types. The prototype follows a Do-It-Yourself (DIY) approach, and is based on commercial off-the-shelf (COTS) hardware and open source software. Additionally, the prototype includes a casing to house all the hardware which was designed considering standard 3D printing to be easily replicated. As the presented solution is currently on a prototype stage, the validations carried out in a controlled, in-lab environment include guaranteeing the proper process for image acquisition and data quality of the computer vision component (images collected from sensor camera, and their quality), suitable data exchange over the sockets, and the sensing box's ability to gather data.

Keywords: Internet of Things · Sensing box · Computer vision · Soil analysis · Small-scale farmers · Rural Africa

1 Introduction

One can see the impact and importance of Information and communication technology (ICT) for agriculture given the incentives for rural digital transformation and market value of digital farming for upcoming years [9,11]. Given the importance of the small-scale farming for food production worldwide [10,18], it makes sense to also provide access to ICT solutions for the small producers.

© ICST Institute for Computer Sciences, Social Informatics and Telecommunications Engineering 2021
Published by Springer Nature Switzerland AG 2021. All Rights Reserved
R. Zitouni et al. (Eds.): AFRICOMM 2020, LNICST 361, pp. 171–184, 2021.
https://doi.org/10.1007/978-3-030-70572-5_11

Moreover, IoT adoption in Africa is of interest for while now [14,15,17] and even with its still low penetration, one can find different efforts to provide access to ICT, for instance, Gichamba et al. [16], Sousa et al. [24] and Oliveira et al. [19] focus on the provision of mobile aplications and communication infrastructure to reduce digital divide and improve the quality of life of people in rural areas of Kenya and Mozambique.

Motivated by that, we have proposed an IoT sensing platform [20,21] to popularize digital farming in rural Africa, helping farmers better understand their soil condition. Following this work, this paper presents the IoT sensing box development which is composed of sensors that provide pH, moisture, air temperature, and light readings. These readings are to keep small farmers and soil experts aware of the soil current status. The IoT sensing box also includes an image acquisition module for computer vision-based soil classification related with texture and colour information.

The sensing box component follows a Do-It-Yourself (DIY), and integrates single-board computer, microcontroller, sensors, Wi-Fi communication module, LEDs and LED driver with extensible software that implements sensor reading modules, and communication sockets (for data exchange and sensor configuration). The hardware and software architectures of the sensing box not only ease further developments on top of the solution, but also facilitate the assembly of the solution based on hardware easily found in local markets.

Moreover, the IoT sensing box presents the design details of the casing proposed to accommodate all its hardware (i.e., sensors, micro-controller, SBC, illumination, mounting parts). The casing was thought to allow ease assembly of the components as well as providing protection while the solution is being used for data collection or being transported. Additionally, the design considered standard 3D printing dimensions, so the casing can be easily printed and replicated elsewhere.

It is worth mentioning that the proposed IoT sensing box integrates the Project AFRICA [22] that aims at developing a green-energy driven technology solution to support the on-site, cost-affordable fertiliser production to small-scale farmers in Africa.

In order to provide a better understanding of the proposed IoT sensing box, this paper is organized as follow. Section 2 details the IoT sensing box architecture focusing on the considered hardware. Then, Sect. 3 goes through the image acquisition setup needed for the computer vision-based soil analysis. Section 4 summarizes the casing design and assembly based on specific requirements, while Sect. 5 describes the final IoT sensing box prototype and software architecture. Section 6 concludes the paper.

2 IoT Sensing Box Architecture

The actual version of the IoT sensing box considers the Wi-Fi interface to function as an access point to which the user equipment (e.g., smartphone, tablet, laptop) connects serving as relay to send the data to the backend server. It is important to mention that the IoT sensing box is built in modular way to allow the inclusion of other wireless communications technologies (such as LoRa, BLE) as well as other sensors and probes. Figure 1 presents the hardware architecture of the IoT sensing box, showcasing its sensors, interfaces, and radio communication.

As the IoT sensing box is meant to be easy replicated, we followed a DIY approach considering components that i) can be easily found in local markets; and ii) can be easily connected without the hardware complex tasks. The hardware architecture can be seen as having three main parts as follows.

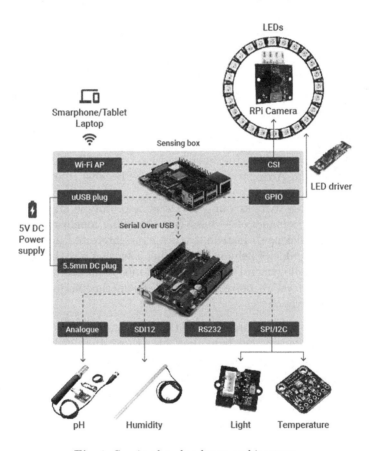

Fig. 1. Sensing box hardware architecture.

Single-Board Computers (SBC) - The IoT sensing box has two SBCs, a Raspberry Pi which is the brain of the solution, and an Arduino that interfaces with all soil and environment sensors. Our choice for these SBCs come from project AFRICA's requirement for considering low-cost, off-the-shelf hardware. Both SBCs are regularly used in DIY projects as they are cheap and with enough features to allow fast development and prototyping as desired by the project's consortium.

Moreover, the Raspberry Pi has been chosen as it offers i) a built-in Wi-Fi communication interface that can be configured in access point (AP) mode, and through which the User Equipment (UE) will connect to get sensor data; and ii) an interface with the camera module through its Camera Serial Interface (CSI) port using a ribbon cable, and control the LED driver activation through its General-Purpose Input/Output) GPIO interface for the image acquisition process.

It is important to mention that the use of Wi-Fi is also a project requirement since the sensing box is to provide a communication means over this wireless technology. This also explains why we have not considered other technologies such as Global System for Mobile Communications (GSM) or Low Power Wide Area Network (LPWAN), as the box is meant to connect to another device (i.e., smartphone) and not a network.

The Arduino, through a header with screw connectors and protoboard space [1], offer different interfaces, such as SDI12, SPI/I2C, RS232 and analogue. The reason we considered Arduino as interface to sensors is due to i) lack of support to SDI12 protocol by the Raspberry Pi [12]; and ii) Arduino allows a low-level control of the microcontroller, its timers and interrupts. The interface between the Raspberry Pi and Arduino uses a common USB cable through serial communication.

It is worth noting that, as our work is at a prototype stage, we are not interested in the performance of Arduino (e.g., handling concurrent sensors) and RPi (e.g., energy efficiency). Instead, we are more interested in understanding whether they are capable of helping us building a sensing box that is cheap and easy to implement following a DIY approach. A more complete set of validation tests and results are yet to be realized through experiments in near future as project AFRICA advances.

Sensors - Different sensors are used in the IoT sensing box to measure pH, moisture, air temperature and light, and also to capture images of the soil. These sensors are cheap, easy to find and are based on well-known interfaces (i.e., SDI12, SPI/I2C, RS232 and analogue).

The pH sensor for semisolid material with an analogue interface is a DFRobot SEN0249 [4]. It is connected to the Arduino through the screw connectors on the Arduino header.

We also use a multi-depth industrial grade soil monitoring probe that communicates through SDI. This is the Sentek drill & drop soil moisture, salinity and temperature probe [7]. If cost or market availability may be an issue, a low-cost alternative should be a Seeed studio 314010012 moisture and temperature sensor [8].

An Adafruit 2652 BME280 I2C/SPI temperature sensor [2] is connected to the sensing box by soldering its pins into the protoboard space of the Arduino header.

The SeeedStudio (101020030) digital light sensor [6] is connected through the I2C interface available in the sensing box (Arduino header).

The Pi NoIR Camera V2 [5], capable of 1080p video and still images, connects to Raspberry Pi through CSI port.

Power Supply - In order to power all the hardware present in the IoT sensing box, we considered the situation when access to power grid is available, or the use of alternative supply in the case remote sensing is being done.

A 5V DC power supply is considered to feed the system. Such supply can be composed of standard AC/DC power adaptors that are compatible with Raspberry Pi and Arduino, or a power bank compatible with Arduino and Raspberry Pi requirements.

3   Image Acquisition Module for Computer Vision

Capacitance sensors have long been suspected of sensitivity to variations in temperature. This can be corrected if the soil type or soil texture are known. Dalton et al. [13] found that correction protocols have improved the variation of water content, previously overestimated due to diurnal fluctuation only. Therefore, we raised the hypothesis of using computer vision to classify the type of soil so that it can be later crossed with the remaining data of the sensor probes, in multiple soils to be tested in the future.

The computer vision component [21] classifies soils according to the Food and Agriculture Organization (FAO) World Reference Base soil groups (WRB), and USDA Soil Taxonomy suborders [25]. Deep Learning [23] approaches have recently had a great impact in image analysis. Due to the large variability of soil characteristics in the world, in [21] we have studied machine learning approaches with Convolutional Neural Networks to the context of soil images. In the current IoT sensing platform it is envisioned that 2D images of the soil are collected together with the other sensor readings in the same locations.

In order to work properly, the camera and light system that integrate the image acquisition module were calibrated to provide high image quality for the computer vision-based soil classification to work properly. The following main tasks were performed to allow the IoT sensing box prototype to satisfactorily capture high quality soil images.

Focus Adjustment: We started the calibration process by evaluating the sharpness variation while manually adjusting the camera focus to around 30 cm. The target used was a printed version of the ISO 12233:2000 test chart, over a light absorbing black-out material. The actual distance between the camera and the target is 33 cm, but we must leave some tolerance because soil matter can be irregular after mixing. The photo in Fig. 2a was obtained directly from the camera without post-processing. We could observe that the edge-to-edge sharpness is not totally constant, however this is not an issue as some irregularity of the soil is also expected in real world.

Colour Assessment and Camera Parameters Adjustment: Figure 2b shows a capture of a real ColorChecker® Digital SG by x-rite [3], covering a good range of colour space. To avoid hotspots, the ISO and shutter speed of the

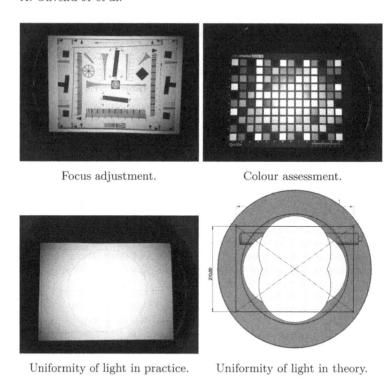

Focus adjustment.   Colour assessment.

Uniformity of light in practice.   Uniformity of light in theory.

Fig. 2. Camera and light calibration.

camera had to be adjusted. ISO went down to 100 to preserve detail and reduce noise as much as possible, and the shutter was set to 1/30 s. Due to the weight of the whole IoT sensing box, the camera should not shake and create motion blur in normal wind speeds in the crop fields. This can be confirmed in field tests and some fixes are possible.

Centrality and Uniformity of Light: To measure the area covered by the illumination system, a target composed by a A4 paper with a circle corresponding to the real diameter (180 mm) of the sensing box was used to make the photo in Fig. 2c. Our soil classifier only requires squared images, so the goal was to obtain a 200 × 200 mm image with uniform light. By comparing Fig. 2c with Fig. 2d where the dimensions of the A4 rectangle (297 × 210 mm) are shown, it can be observed that the theoretical FOV of the LED set was mostly achieved.

Region Selection Based on Entropy Levels: It is of utmost importance that the square region selected contains homogeneous levels of pixel intensity. To assess that, entropy levels were calculated for different crops sizes in the LUV colour space. L stands for luminance, whereas U and V represent chromaticity values of colour images. According to Table 1, 0.94 of entropy is reached with image crops below 87%. In this case, an image up to 1700 × 1700 pixels can be taken and delivered to the artificial intelligence model that classifies the type of soil.

Table 1. Entropy measurements.

Histogram Entropy Luminance	0.09	0.94	1.00
Histogram Entropy U	0.06	0.29	0.32
Histogram Entropy V	0.09	0.17	0.20

4 Casing Design and Assembly

The protective casing for the IoT sensing box was designed in order to prevent moisture and dust from reaching the hardware, robust outdoor use, compact, easy assembly (i.e., few elements, large parts, simple mounting), based on locally available resources, easy usability, safe transport and simple maintenance.

As presented in Fig. 3, to provide a better handling of the IoT sensing box, the sensing box casing includes a handle element (1 and 2) to allow for easy to transport as well as quick assembly into the cabinet. Different spaces are moulded with the shape of the electronic components to allow assembly through the upper part of the casing (3). One side of the casing (4) exhibits all the input and output interfaces of the sensing box, allowing quick access without mounting or dismounting the casing. Between the cabinet and sensing box, there is a small thin layer of foam (5) to absorb shocks and minimize the entry of dust and moisture.

Fig. 3. Detailed view of the casing: 1,2) Sensing box handles; 3) Electronic components; 4) Input and output interfaces; 5) Foam shock-absorption.

The exposed elements are built with edges and grooves so that, when the pieces are put together, there is an extra layer of protection between the electronic components. This concept looks at the case from three relevant perspectives, namely protection, simplicity and usability, in order to guarantee proper shelting of the inner components of the proposed IoT sensing box, and allows its easy replication anywhere else in the world.

Figure 4 highlights all external components, along with the areas that the user may or not interact or block. The design focuses on resulting casing that provides an intuitive and natural interaction with the user. The buttons, sensors and interfaces are appropriately identified and resort to different interruption symbols and information that indicate where the user should not place objects or interact (i.e., to refrain from blocking the light sensor).

The design has slots to facilitate the accommodation of the humidity and pH probes so that they seamless integrate into the IoT sensing box when it is being transported or not used. The position of the slots took into account the internal space to ensure the proper positioning of all parts, to result on a robust structure, and to provide all mechanical properties for intense outdoor use and shock absorption.

5   IoT Sensing Box Prototype

Initial validations have shown that the sensing box and the cabinet interact perfectly. The fitting between them, made by the union of the end of the sensing box with the concavity of the cabinet, results in a quick adjustment and alignment and easy to process in any situation. Figure 5 shows the outside view of the sensing box prototype and the cabinet responsible for blocking the external

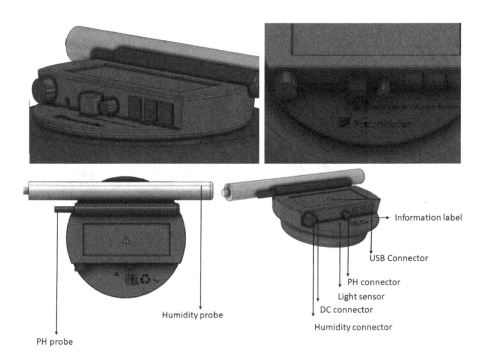

Fig. 4. Sensing box - exterior components.

Fig. 5. Prototype and validation of the cabinet for controlled light.

light. The projected views of the expected FOV of each LED are shown in the transparent drawings.

The two elements, when assembled, transform into a single one and create a field with absence of exterior light fulfilling the computer vision requirement for non-existence of light to allow better image acquisition. The weight of the sensing box combined with the weight of the internal components make the box maintain pressure in the cabinet and the structure set is kept stable for field use. The sensing box fulfills the expectations of housing all components in a robust way and ensuring that they are protected. The interaction area (i.e., power button, plugging slots, warnings) with the user is functional as it also offers the slots for the placing the external probes (i.e., moisture and pH).

5.1   IoT Sensing Box Software

The Sensing Box Software is composed of three software modules, with two running in the Raspberry Pi (Camera Reading SW Module and Arduino Readings SW Module) and one running in the Arduino (Multi Sensor SW Module). These SW modules communicate between each other via three sockets, with two for the communications between the Raspberry and the user equipment connected to it through the provided Wi-Fi access point (configuration sockets and ZeroMQ sensor data), and one for the communication between the Raspberry Pi and the Arduino by serial socket.

The sensing box software architecture, as shown in Fig. 6 contains two types of sockets, a TCP-based one and a serial one. Each socket implements its own protocol based on the particularities of their type, as detailed next.

The **ZeroMQ sockets** are used for the communication between the Raspberry Pi and the UE connected to the sensing box. These sockets are implemented based on a publish/subscribe paradigm. These roles are changed for the Sensor Data Socket, here the software modules in the Raspberry Pi open the socket in publisher mode and publish the sensor data message, while the software running on the UE opens the socket in subscriber mode and consumes the sensed data.

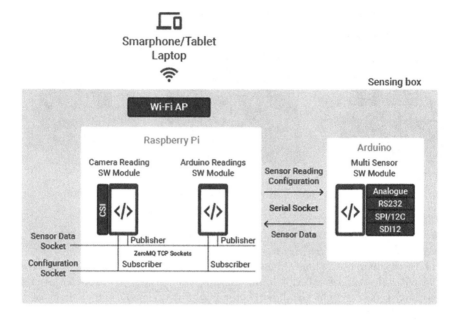

Fig. 6. Sensing box software architecture.

```
{                                              {
 "configurations": [                            "data": [
  {"device_id": "1",                             {"device_id": "1",
   "device_config": [                             "device_data": [
    {"config_id": "1", "config_value": "XYZ"},     {"sensor_id": "1", "sensor_value": ["ABC", "GHI", "XYZ"]},
    {"config_id": "2", "config_value": "XYZ"},     {"sensor_id": "2", "sensor_value": ["XYZ"]},
    ...                                            ...
    {"config_id": "n", "config_value": "XYZ"}      {"sensor_id": "n", "sensor_value": ["ABC", "XYZ"]}
   ]                                             ] },
  },                                             ...
  ...                                           {"device_id": "n",
  {"device_id": "n",                             "device_data": [
   "device_config": [                             {"sensor_id": "1", "sensor_value": ["XYZ"]},
    {"config_id": "1", "config_value": "XYZ"},     {"sensor_id": "2", "sensor_value": ["XYZ", "GHI"]},
    {"config_id": "2", "config_value": "XYZ"},     ...
    ...                                            {"sensor_id": "n", "sensor_value": ["XYZ"]}
    {"config_id": "n", "config_value": "XYZ"}     ]
   ]                                            }
  }                                            ],
 ]                                             "timestamp": "XYZ",
}                                              "message_id": "XYZ",
                                   (a)         "sensingbox_id": "XYZ"
                                              }
                                                                          (b)
```

Fig. 7. (a) Configuration and (b) Sensor data messages.

The information exchanged in these sockets follows a well-defined structure based on JSON (JavaScript Object Notation) data-interchange format. Figure 7 outlines this structure. The configuration message (Fig. 7a) is composed of an array of devices, identified by their unique id (device_id), which also have a set of configurations (device_config) properly identified by an ID that is unique to that device context (config_id) and composed of the respective configuration value (config_value). A device on this context represents a sensor with one or multiple sensing capabilities (for example the Sentek drill & drop soil sensor is capable of sensing moisture, salinity and temperature, so it is a device with multiple sensors, or sensing capabilities).

Following this structure, new devices and device configurations can be added to the configuration message simply by adding new elements to the array. The socket and the Arduino Readings SW Module are agnostic in what regards the information present inside this structure, so to add new devices and device configurations to the configuration message, the developer only needs to update the software running on the UE and the Multi Sensor Software Module running on the Arduino to correctly create and interpret the new devices and configurations.

The sensor data message (Fig. 7b) is composed of an array of devices, identified by their unique id (device_id), having a set of data values (device_data), also identified by an ID that is unique to that sensor context (sensor_id) and respective data value (sensor_value). As in the configuration message, a device on this context represents a sensor with one or multiple sensing capabilities, and each sensor inside the data array represents the various sensors in the device (considering again the Sentek drill & drop soil sensor, it is a device with multiple sensors - the moisture, salinity and temperature).

Based on this structure, new devices and/or sensors and their sensed data can be added to the sensor data message simply by adding new elements to the arrays. The socket and the Arduino Readings SW Module are again agnostic in what regards the information present in this structure, so to add new devices and/or sensors and their sensed data to the sensor data message changes are only required in the software running on the UE and the Multi Sensor Software Module running on the Arduino to suitably create and interpret the new sensor data. The **Serial Socket** is just a relay for the data available on the ZeroMQ socket that allows configuration and sensor data to reach and leave the Arduino, respectively.

The presented software architecture is easily integrated in the sensing box hardware and, straightforwardly, communicates with its default sensors, while providing a communication interface for the UE. In addition to this, the software architecture allows for an easy integration of new sensors just by including the sensor driver on the Arduino Multi Sensor SW Module, and its configuration and sensing data in the configuration and sensor data messages. With this, the addition of new sensors in the sensing box is limited to modifications on Arduino software, which is by design thought for low to medium level technical users.

6   Conclusions

This paper presents the recent developments of an IoT sensing box for collecting data on the soil and surrounding environment. The box is coupled with soil image analysis through computer vision to improve the reliability of the sensed data, and to ultimately help small-scale farmers by improving their yields and income. The selection of the hardware to build the sensing box was performed having in mind a DIY approach, and aligned with the box's requirements of familiarity, low-cost, simplicity and market availability on the target deployment countries. The software was developed to allow an extension by low to medium level technical users, and can be easily adapted to new application scenarios and use cases. The image acquisition module was designed and configured to answer the requirements of the computer vision for soil classification. The design details of the protective casing to house all the hardware (i.e., SBC, microcontroller, sensors, illumination, mounting parts) that compose the IoT sensing box were presented in detail.

As the proposed sensing box is currently at prototype stage, we have validated a few aspects in a controlled, in-lab environment, namely i) the software architecture and socket communication were tested with sensor data being collected and made available in the sockets; ii) the image acquisition module was finetuned to guarantee high quality images for the soil image analysis; and iii) the protective casing was validated concerning the fitting between of the sensing box into the cabinet, assembly of all components and cabling, and interaction of the user with the sensing box.

The next steps in the research path are to deploy the prototype in real rural environment and to validate the technology in such scenarios. The deployment fields are those of the Project AFRICA's partner countries, namely Ghana, Uganda, and South Africa. The field tests will be carried out with farmers and soil experts of each country, and shall help improving the prototype towards its final version.

Such field tests shall include the validation of the set of chosen hardware (i.e., boards and sensors), the ability to provide accurate readings on the target parameter (i.e., pH, moisture, air temperature, and light), the communication between the sensing box and user equipment, energy consumption tests, tests with green-energy solutions to power the sensing box, and usability tests.

Additionally, to correctly apply the computer vision study, camera parameters may have to be recalibrated during tests in the real crop fields. Factors like wind conditions and temperature, may affect camera and LED behavior, as creating motion blur or variate field-of-view in the images. In addition, more wavelengths of light should be tested besides the current white LEDs. We started with white light because our soil classifier with artificial intelligence models were trained with this type of images. However, we expect that the estimation of soil type can be obtained from the colour information presented in those alternative images to predict and complement the texture information

Finally, we expect to have image datasets collected with the prototype that will allow us to assess some challenges of applying transfer learning, from 2D profiles of soil samples cut in depth to 2D soil samples of the surface acquired by our camera system.

Acknowledgement. This work was funded under the scope of Project AFRICA: On-site air-to-fertilizer mini-plants relegated by sensor-based ICT technology to foster African agriculture (LEAP-Agri-146) co-funded by the European Union's Horizon 2020 research and innovation programme under grant agreement Number 727715 and Fundação para a Ciência e a Tecnologia (FCT) under reference LEAP-Agri/0004/2017.

References

1. Adafruit - proto-screwshield (wingshield) r3 kit for arduino. https://www.adafruit.com/product/196. Accessed 04 April 2020
2. Adafruit bme280 i2c or SPI temperature humidity pressure sensor. https://www.adafruit.com/product/2652. Accessed 04 April 2020
3. Colorchecker® digital sg. https://www.xrite.com/categories/calibration-profiling/colorchecker-digital-sg. Accessed 01 May 2020
4. Dfrobot - gravity: Analog spear tip ph sensor / meter kit. https://www.dfrobot.com/product-1668.html. Accessed 04 April 2020
5. Pi noir camera v2. https://www.raspberrypi.org/products/pi-noir-camera-v2/. Accessed 04 April 2020
6. Seeed technology co., Ltd., grove - digital light sensor - tsl2561. https://www.seeedstudio.com/Grove-Digital-Light-Sensor-TSL2561.html. Accessed 04 April 2020
7. Sentek - drill & drop sensor technology. https://sentektechnologies.com/product-range/soil-data-probes/drill-and-drop/. Accessed 04 April 2020
8. Sentek - soil moisture & temperature sensor. https://www.seeedstudio.com/Soil-Moisture-Temperature-Sensor-p-1356.html. Accessed 04 April 2020
9. AgriResearch: digital transformation in agriculture and rural areas under horizon 2020 societal challenge 2 (sc2). EU Report June 2019 Update
10. Biénabe, E., Sautier, D.: The role of small scale producers organizations to address market access (2005)
11. BlueWeaveConsulting: global digital farming market by component (hardware, software, others), by application (precision farming, live stock monitoring, green house farming, others), by region, global forecast to 2025. Report BWC19388. https://www.blueweaveconsulting.com/global-digital-farming-market-bwc19388. Accessed 04 April 2020
12. Coppock, J.: Development of a raspberry pi based, SDI-12 sensor environmental data logger (2015)
13. Dalton, M., Buss, P., Treijs, A., Portmann, M.: Correction for temperature variation in sentek drill & drop^{TM} soil water capacitance probes
14. Dlodlo, N., Kalezhi, J.: The internet of things in agriculture for sustainable rural development. In: 2015 International Conference on Emerging Trends in Networks and Computer Communications (ETNCC), pp. 13–18 (2015)
15. Dupont, C., Sheikhalishahi, M., Biswas, A.R., Bures, T.: IoT, big data, and cloud platform for rural African needs. In: 2017 IST-Africa Week Conference (IST-Africa), pp. 1–7 (2017)

16. Gichamba, A., Waiganjo, P., Orwa, D., Wario, R., Ngari, B.: Prototyping magriculture applications among smallholder farmers. In: 2016 IST-Africa Week Conference, pp. 1–7 (2016)

17. Masinde, M.: IoT applications that work for the African continent: innovation or adoption? In: 2014 12th IEEE International Conference on Industrial Informatics (INDIN), pp. 633–638 (2014)

18. McDonagh, J., Farrell, M., Conway, S.: The Role of Small-scale Farms and Food Security, chap. 2, pp. 33–47. John Wiley & Sons, Ltd. (2017). https://doi.org/10.1002/9781119072737.ch2. https://onlinelibrary.wiley.com/doi/abs/10.1002/9781119072737.ch2

19. Oliveira-Jr, E., Pereira, E., Madureira, P., Almeida, P., Moreira, W.: Community tools for digital inclusion. In: Mendy, G., Ouya, S., Dioum, I., Thiaré, O. (eds.) AFRICOMM 2018. LNICST, vol. 275, pp. 265–274. Springer, Cham (2019). https://doi.org/10.1007/978-3-030-16042-5_23

20. Oliveira-Jr, A., Resende, C., Gonçalves, J., Soares, F., Moreira, W.: IoT sensing platform for e-agriculture in Africa. In: 2020 IST-Africa Week Conference (IST-Africa) (2020)

21. Oliveira-Jr, A., et al.: IoT sensing platform as a driver for digital farming in rural Africa. Sensors **20**(12), 3511 (2020). https://doi.org/10.3390/s20123511

22. Project-AFRICA: On-site air-to-fertilizer mini-plants relegated by sensor-based ICT technology to foster African agriculture. https://www.project-africa.info. Accessed 12 Jan 2020

23. Sandler, M., Howard, A., Zhu, M., Zhmoginov, A., Chen, L.C.: MobileNetv2: inverted residuals and linear bottlenecks. In: Proceedings of the IEEE Conference on Computer Vision and Pattern Recognition, pp. 4510–4520 (2018)

24. Sousa, A., Resende, C., Pereira, A., Moreira, W.: Comm4Dev: communication infrastructure for development, March 2019

25. IUSS Working Group Wrb: World reference base for soil resources 2014, update 2015: International soil classification system for naming soils and creating legends for soil maps (2015)

A Group-Based IoT Devices Classification Through Network Traffic Analysis Based on Machine Learning Approach

Avewe Bassene$^{(\boxtimes)}$ and Bamba Gueye

Université Cheikh Anta Diop, Dakar, Senegal
{avewe.bassene,bamba.gueye}@ucad.edu.sn

Abstract. With the rapid growth of the Internet of Things (IoT), the deployment, management, and identification of IoT devices that are connected to networks become a big concern. Consequently, they emerge as a prominent challenge either for mobile network operators who try to offer cost-effective services tailored to IoT market, or for network administrators who aim to identify as well reduce costs processing and optimize traffic management of connected environments. In order to achieve high accuracy in terms of reliability, loss and response time, new devices real time discovery techniques based on traffic characteristics are mandatory in favor of the identification of IoT connected devices.

Therefore, we design GBC_IoT, a group-based machine learning approach that enables to identify connected IoT devices through network traffic analysis. By leveraging well-known machine learning algorithms, GBC_IoT framework identifies and categorizes IoT devices into three classes with an overall accuracy equals to roughly 99.98%. Therefore, GBC_IoT can efficiently identify IoT devices with less processing overhead compared to previous studies.

Keywords: Internet of Things · Network traffic characteristics · Machine learning algorithms

1 Introduction

Recent long range radio transmissions enable affordable IoT solutions for underserved areas [1,2]. According to Africa, smart cities and/or smart territory enable new opportunities for tackling urban explosion challenge.

Smart cities were originally designed to solve urban planning and sustainable development problems according to northern countries cities. Leveraging IoT networks in Africa can facilitate transport mobility, reduce energy consumption and offer optimal and innovative solutions for waste management and sanitation. Recently, Africa has registered many smart city projects that plan to develop by rapidly reducing the technological divide that affects the continent [3]. Recent works center on the deployment of IoT communication solutions for low-income developing countries [1,2,4].

© ICST Institute for Computer Sciences, Social Informatics and Telecommunications Engineering 2021
Published by Springer Nature Switzerland AG 2021. All Rights Reserved
R. Zitouni et al. (Eds.): AFRICOMM 2020, LNICST 361, pp. 185–202, 2021.
https://doi.org/10.1007/978-3-030-70572-5_12

Former works have mainly focused to deploy low cost networks which are mandatory within these under-served countries. Therefore, smart cities or territories are equipped by a lot of devices that need to be deployed and managed efficiently. Thus, it is useful to monitor IoT traffic characteristics in order to propose performance levels that meet current realities requirement. For instance, realities regarding to Quality of Service (QoS).

To meet this challenge, connected network devices type should be known. It is worth noticing that existing identification and classification proposals are based on unitary approaches and these methods are not suitable for wider IoT network such as smart cities or territories, which support an important number of devices. Consequently, approaches that are suitable for selected agglomerations that host heterogeneous IoT devices should be defined.

In fact, devices categorization can provide an adequate level of QoS by containing multicast traffic (unnecessary broadcasting) and reducing their impact on other applications. It also allows administrators to scale their networks according to appropriate performance levels in terms of reliability, loss and latency necessary for environmental, health or security applications. Furthermore, it can avoid congestion by adapting traffic load according to each devices category requirement.

In order to provide an efficient classification model, we seek to monitor either traffic features that as substantive as possible within network topology (physical or logical), or features which have already shown their effectiveness in previous works [5,8,9,12].

Therefore, the GBC_IoT framework contributions are as follows:

- According to traffic generated by devices, it enables to accurately classify devices with respect to their behavior
- It takes into account the presence of a huge and heterogeneous IoT smart-Network devices
- It avoids classification based on no reliable traffic features often done by previous works such as DNS queries [5], TCP sessions length [6,7] and traffic Active volume [8].

The rest of this paper is organized as follows: Sect. 2 reviews the related work on this field. We present in Sect. refsec:expSetup our experimental setup. A grouped-based device classification approach with Machine Learning techniques is performed in Sect. 4. Section 5 discusses our contributions according to previous works. Finally, Sect. 6 concludes our paper.

2   Related Works

Former works like [8,9,12,13] propose methods to identify IoT device based on various features embedded in generated traffic. Nevertheless, they have not take into account the impact of existing uncertainties linked to traffic: from features selection to end user behaviour.

Authors in [6,7] use *ML* approaches to identify *IoT* devices from network traffic analyzing. They aim to decide device reliability to join a secure network. The targeted features are optimal length of *TCP* sessions. We do not consider this approach, since features such as session length and intersession duration are strongly dependent on fixed timeout value which can be arbitrarily assigned to individual schemes. In addition, obtaining complete *TCP* flow requires waiting for the end of the session to be able to extract all the functionalities from flow. Devices such as *Nest security camera TCP* sessions can sometimes last several hours or days [5].

Motivated by privacy concerns, Apthorpe et al., illustrated how an Internet service provider (*ISP*) can infer the type of connected *IoT* device by traffic analysis [11]. Nevertheless, they only use a limited, stable and rather "predictable" number of device in terms of traffic (hub, camera and sleep monitor). Proposed approach also depends on a single feature: domain of *DNS* queries. Nevertheless, devices such as *Amazon Echo* and *Triby Speaker* deal with several home automation devices and this diversity gives them strong dynamic network behavior. These devices can communicate with an increasing number of Internet nodes which the designer cannot define in advance [15].

Miettinen et al. present a method to identify connected *IoT* device type in order to constrain vulnerable devices communications [12]. They use a wide variety of features extracted during configuration phase. However, this approach can not be used if device configuration phase is missed.

An identification based on *MAC* addresses is not efficient since potential attacker can usurp *MAC* addresses of compromised *IoT* device [16]. Indeed, although *MAC* addresses can be used to identify the manufacturer of a particular device, to our knowledge, there is no established standard for identifying the brand or type of a device based on its *MAC* address. Some approaches focus on identifying specific hardware characteristics or drivers (e.g. [17]) to recognize *IoT* device. Notwithstanding, such approaches are not efficient, since the same hardware or driver components can be deployed in wide variety of devices.

The authors of [5,15] proposed a mixed characteristics in order to identify *IoT* devices. According to performance concern, *ML* approach is used to find the minimum number of packets necessary for early identification of Internet traffic in [18].

Nevertheless, previous works with respect to overall accuracy (99.9% in [5], 99% in [9,12], 95% in [8]), do not carry out fine *IoT* devices characterization that takes into account error related to the choice of features and the unpredictability linked to different factors such as applications, materials and traffic load [19]. In fact, according to working days and hours, autonomous communication protocols, devices add/remove or frequent firmware updating are other factors that alter network behavior. The entire dataset needs to be trained each time these last two cases (add/remove or update) occur in the environment in order to take account these changes.

The work done in [10] is one of the first large-scale study to explore the nature of *M2M* traffic. It compares *M2M* and traditional smartphone traffic from different perspectives: time variations, mobility, network performance, generated traffic volume, etc. The authors of [10] do not take into account the complexity (huge quantity of data) of the "new" *IoT* devices existing on the market today.

The works in [8,9] use *ML* techniques to characterize *IoT* devices within a smart network. However, they consider more features and they do not take into account privacy concerns. Traffic active volume is used in [8] to cluster *IoT* attributes and it cooperates in *IoT* devices classification. However, for device such as "*Netatmo Welcome*", we see that traffic Active volume feature is dependent on working days/times and used protocols, therefore, this attribute cannot be considered as a reliable classification indicator.

3   Experimental Setup

3.1   Dataset Description

The used datasets come from daily traffic captured in a campus network set up as a "Smart environment". These traces are proposed by A. Sivanathan et al., [9] and are formed by a set of 28 *IoT* devices. Traffic is captured and stored on the Internet via "*TP Link Archer C7*" Gateway flashing with the "*OpenWrt*" firmware.

Table 1. Iot devices composing overall traces classified by types.

Devices	Types
HP Printer, PIX-STAR Photo-frame, Hello Barbie	**Others**
Chromecast, Triby Speaker	**Multimedia**
Smart Things, Amazon Echo	**Hub**
Belkin Wemo switch, TP-Link Smart plug, iHome, Belkin wemo motion sensor	**Switches & Triggers**
Withings Smart scale, Blipcare Blood Pressure meter, Withings Aura smart sleep sensor	**Healthcare**
NEST Protect smoke alarm, Netatmo weather station	**Air quality sensors**
LiFX Smart Bulb, Philips Hue lightbulb	**Bulbs**
Belkin NetCam, Ring doorbell, August doorbell camera, Canary camera, TP-Link Day Night Cloud camera, Samsung SmartCam, Dropcam, Insteon Camera, Withings Smart Baby Monitor, Netatmo Welcome	**Cameras**

Devices that make up this environment and on which our study will focus are presented in Table 1. On this day, traces are available for free download at *http://149.171.189.1*. A more detailed explanation of the environment configuration and the data collection method is presented in [12].

3.2   Dataset Preprocessing

A first approach is to use the *PCAP* files of daily captured traces of September 27th called *Dataset*-1, September 30th called *Dataset*-2, and October 2nd 2016 called *Dataset*-3. We then made an analysis at two levels: Packet levels with the *"tShark"* utility and *"CICFLOWMETER"* [18] for flow level. *"CICFLOWME-TER"* is a bidirectional network traffic flow generator tool written in *Java*. It offers more flexibility in the choice of studied features, add of new features and increased control of the flow delay time. It is free and public accessible, it analyses *PCAP* files larger than 100 *MB* and provides a *CSV* file with visual analysis report of 84 network traffic features. Here is what motivates his choice.

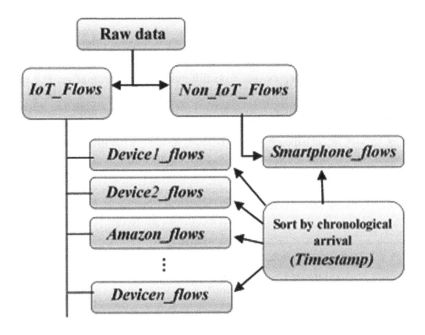

Fig. 1. Datasets preprocessing steps.

Raw network traffic is preprocessed to extract bidirectional flows. Flows is described by set of features such as *flow duration, total size of packets* (bidirectional), *active/idle time, source/destination IP*, packets *inter-arrival time, protocol* and *ports*, etc. It gives an overview of a coexistence of two types of devices (*"IoT/non IoT"*) in the same environment.

We define *"IoT"* device as being a device intended to perform a specific task, unlike *"non IoT"* device such as: laptops, desktops or smartphones. With the help of *MAC* addresses, we split traffic by type of devices and by entity (unique device). We then separate each portion of obtained traffic. It facilitates labelling both unique and groups of devices data. For instance, label

"*IoT_Flows*" groups together $PCAP/CSV$ files containing traces coming from the network traffic generated only by IoT devices. While "*Amazon_Flows*" consists of $PCAP/CSV$ files with flows coming from the network traffic generated by the *Amazon Echo* device. Finally, we used the *Timestamp* feature to order flows in chronological arrival. Figure 1 illustrates the different steps it order to extract flows. For the rest of our work, data analysis and visualization are performed using the "*PYTHON*" scikit-learn libraries in *Jupyter* Notebook and *t-SNE*.

We propose a classification approach which studies bidirectional flows characteristics for each of the 28 testbed devices. For this end, 6 *ML* algorithms are used (*ANN*, *k-NN*, *DT*, *GBN*, *RF*, *SVM*). It aims to classifying devices according to category to which their behaviors are closest. Finally, algorithms that reach the greatest precision are those chosen as best suited to our model.

Figure 2 describes our approach. The choice of these 6 algorithms is motivated by the fact that it is significant to have an overview of all aspects of the studied datasets. Indeed, in a test environment, each of these algorithms has these strengths and weaknesses based on different types of scenarios: For example, *DT* is too sensitive to small changes in the training dataset [20], while *SVM* and *RF* are insensitive to noise or overtraining, and thus, has ability to deal with unbalanced data. This is a good choice when different datasets are processing. According to *k-NN* classifier, while it is less sensitive with imbalanced training sample data, the training sample size had a strong impact on the accuracy of classification [21]. Moreover, the choice of a good value of k can be beneficial. All these above factors mentioned (including parameters choice) must be take into account to hope for a good performance level in various processed datasets.

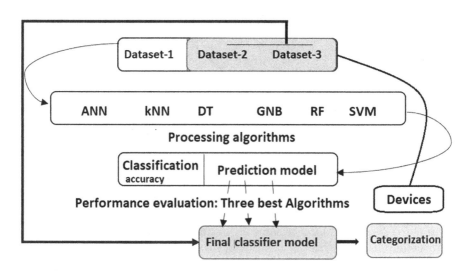

Fig. 2. Experimental processing approach.

3.3   Testbed Architecture

We use *Dataset*-1 to train a classifier with algorithms above. It is the one that present less missing values which can affect the training process. We then randomly splits it into training (90% of total instances) and validation (10%) sets.

Our model is obtained by considering reached accuracies values. The classification process is repeated 10 times to tuned hyper parameters for most of the 6 algorithms. Afterwards, we considered *ANN*, *RF*, *SVM* algorithms that best perform. Finally, independent new test datasets are collected (*Dataset*-2, *Dataset*-3) from spanning days (October 27th & October 30th), that have not been seen before. These datasets are used for devices categorization purposes. Devices are categorized two times from each dataset to get their final class. The best classification accuracy value is adapted. This value depends on both the combined results of algorithms and on the best reached performance according to the final datasets (*Dataset*-2 and *Dataset*-3).

4   Experimental Results

4.1   Leveraging Hybrids Features

Generally, two features combined are able to carry more traffic identification information than a single one [22]. The term "hybrid features" refers to a group of two or more traffic features in the hope of obtaining high precision in traffic identification. Features such as *packet size* and *inter-arrival times* have proven to be effective in many *IoT* devices or applications identification works [5,22,23].

A proposed model is based on hybrid features. As seen above, a precise identification of *IoT* device based on only one feature is difficult if not impossible because of traffic's various interfering factors. Hybridization lets us show specific shared behaviors in group of given devices. Table 2 illustrates an overview of the list of devices that share common characteristics.

According to Table 2, each index *G*1, *G*2 and *G*3 constitutes a particular group based on exposed fingerprints. Firstly, we observe that some devices share

Table 2. List of devices sharing common characteristics.

Index	Devices
G1	Smart Things, Withings Smart Baby Monitor, Netatmo weather station, Withings Smart scale, Withings Aura smart sleep sensor, HP Printer
G2	Netatmo Welcome, TP-Link Day Night Cloud camera, Samsung SmartCam, Drop-cam, Insteon Camera, Belkin Wemo switch, TP-Link Smart plug, iHome, Belkin wemo motion sensor, NEST Protect smoke alarm, Blipcare Blood Pressure meter, Lightbulbs, LiFX Smart Bulb, PIX-STAR Photo-frame, Nest Dropcam
G3	Triby Speaker, Amazon Echo

functionalities that we characterize as stationary; These devices use a local gateway as a DNS resolver and communicate with a single DNS server throughout their activities (network lifetime). In fact, considering factors can distinguish their traffic. Most of these devices communicate with their associated DNS server via a range of source ports. In fact, only 20% of them use specific source ports number. For instance, "*Netatmo weather station*" uses local gateway address as a resolver and communicates with a single DNS server "*netcom.netatmo.net*" with destination port 25587. "*Withings Smart scale*" receives DNS responses from the server "*scalews.withings.net*" through the local gateway. This group of devices with similar behavior is listed as index $G1$ in Table 2.

The index $G2$ group devices class displaying behaviors depending on generated traffic destination; external (destination outside the local network (internet)) or internal (see Table 2). It constitutes our second observation. Externally, these devices communicate with their $STUN$ servers via arbitrary IP addresses and a range of port numbers between TCP 3205 and TCP 4603. Internally, they use $mDNS$ as name resolution protocol through UDP port 5353. The $mDNS$ protocol is intended to resolve host names to IP addresses in small networks with no local DNS server.

According to second observation, the fingerprints exposed by the external communications protocols ($STUN$) and local $mDNS$ allows to determine this second group of devices. Due to the instability of this devices, it cannot be precisely defined because, device such as *Amazon Echo* deals with several home automation devices (*Belkin Wemo, SmartThings, Insteon*, etc.). This gives them a dynamic network behavior. [15] shows that these devices can communicate with an increasing number of internet nodes which the designer cannot define in advance. Indeed, $G3$ index with respect to Table 2 illustrates such situation.

Furthermore, thanks to a careful observation of traffic, we were able to obtain a first distinction object for studied IoT devices. This distinction is based on the use of a hybrid model and allows us to define the presence of three categories of device in our traces. However, this is far from sufficient since, despite observations on which Table 2 is based, we find factors that remain similar between devices of different groups. For instance, a couple of devices, tagged by index $G1$ and $G2$ in Table 2, use the source port 49153 in their external $HTTP$ communications (*iHome, Withings Smart scale, Samsung SmartCam*), while others use it to communicate internally (*Belkin Wemo switch, Belkin wemo motion sensor*). *Amazon Echo* distinctly shares the same NTP server with *LiFX Smart Bulb* and *Insteon Camera*. An invariant port number is used in $XMPP$ communications (TCP 5222) for *Withings Aura smart sleep sensor*, *HP Printer* and *Samsung SmartCam*.

This similarity calls for a better refinement of our model in order to dispel the confusion between devices. For that, focus on characteristics more suitable to the devices traffic footprint, thus important traffic features are extracted first to avoid overfitting in data as described in next section.

Table 3. Best selected features and its weight.

Features	Weight
Bwd Pkt Len Max	0.01165
Bwd Pkt Len Std	0.00036
Flow Byts/s	0.00056
Flow Pkts/s	0.00648
Flow IAT Mean	0.00879
Flow IAT Max	0.00827
Flow IAT Min	0.00321
Fwd Header Len	0.00539
Bwd Header Len	8e−05
Fwd Pkts/s	0.01853
Pkt Len Max	0.00195
Pkt Len Mean	0.01459
Pkt Len Std	0.02289
Pkt Len Var	0.02309
Pkt Size Avg	0.05113
Init Bwd Win Byts	0.08353

Since sensors behavior is very application specific, we therefore believe that total size of sent or received packets (*TotLen_Pkts*) is a common communication feature that can be assigned to any device with a sensor. In addition, *TotLen_Pkts* and *inter-arrival times* (*IAT*) have proven their effectiveness in numerous works and specifically in [24], authors have shown that packets from an early stage of Internet flow can contain enough information for traffic classification.

4.2 Traffic Features Selection

We maintain total packet size (*TotLenBwdPkts*) and inter-arrival time (*FwdI-ATMean*) features and apply dimensionality reduction techniques to the rest of traffic. It aims to find not only the most important features after those already chosen but also to exclude redundancies into the data and classifiers overtraining. This makes data easily interpretable and increases computational performance. These techniques also avoid an arbitrarily revoking of features which may prove to be relevant in the definition of a specific group of devices. We use the *"RandomForestRegressor"* class of scikit-learn to get 16 from 80 features extracted before. Table 3 illustrates the obtained set of features as well as associated weight.

In fact, results presented in Table 3 illustrate that the total number of received bytes within an initial time window (*Init Bwd Win Byt*), as well average packets size (*AvgPacketSize*), variance packet length (*Pkt Len Var*), and standard deviation packet length (*Pkt Len Std*) are the most suitable features according to device category detection. According to the remainder of our analysis, we have grouped these 4 best features above to those already maintained (*TotLen-BwdPkts FwdIATMean*) and then we empirically reduce this number in order to obtain better performance with a minimum number of features, i.e. we repeated testbed processing by reducing the number of features and writing down the observed classification accuracy values.

Our experimental results reach overall accuracy of 99.98% with a minimum of 3 features (*TotLen Bwd Pkts, Fwd IAT Mean, Init Bwd Win Byts*). The final features that best describing traffic behavior are then used to form six different *ML* classifiers in order to predict group (class) to which each *IoT* device in the dataset belongs (strongly close). Three classes are defined; C_{WMS}, C_{AEC} and C_{SSC} to represent devices whose traffic behavior is closest to that of the following *IoT* devices traffic in the respective order: *Wemo motion sensor (WMS)*, *Amazon Echo (AEC)* and *Samsung SmartCam (SSC)*. The choice of these classes is based on the similarity observed in Table 2 and on the fact that these devices traffic admit features of almost all the environment equipment.

Belkin Wemo Motion Sensor (WMS) is a motion detector that combines traffic with that of several devices; switches, bulbs and multimedia (Belkin wemo switch, switching on and off a television, a bulb, a hi-fi system, a radiator, a fan, etc.). *Amazon Echo (AEC)* is a connected speaker working with home automation equipment; *i.e.* Air quality sensors (Temperature display, temperature regulator), heater, WiFi IP Surveillance camera, LED bulb, Healthcare: Omron connected blood pressure monitor (Monitoring of morning hypertension, Detection of irregular heartbeats, Detection of body movement, visceral fat, *BMI* and metabolism rest). *Samsung SmartCam (SSC)*: HD video camera, two-way talk feature, motion and audio detection, night vision, etc.

In addition, these devices traffic admit less missing data (verify by chronological timestamp values and Pandas *"isna()"* method) among devices in the same index. Artificial Neural Networks (*ANN*), k-Nearest Neighbors (*k-NN*), Decision Tree (*DT*), Naive Bayes (*GNB*), Random Forests (*RF*), Support Vector Machine (*SVM*) classifiers are used in our simulations.

We then assess the effectiveness of our classifiers by applying them to an independent new test datasets. We repeat this experiment on new datasets in order to consolidate ours results.

4.3 Data Visualization

This section studies *IoT* devices activity defined by the 18 traffic features previously obtained. For each devices category, we extract these features in a new dataset. Differentiation can be noticed by visualizing the proximity between our data points. It enables to get an insight of their reconciliation and to assess the discriminating aspect of proposed model. We want to visualize the role played by selected features and their effectiveness to differentiate traffic generated by each class of devices.

Figure 3 describes data visualization results using t-Distributed Stochastic Neighbor Embedding (*t-SNE*) algorithm. It should be noted that according to

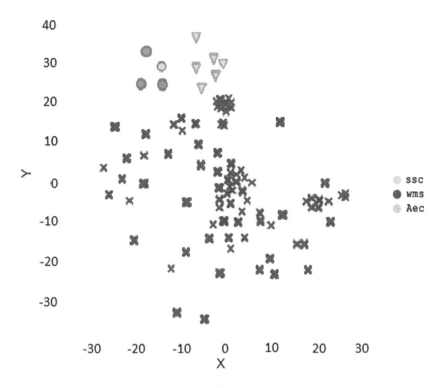

Fig. 3. Data visualization with t-SNE.

tags illustrated in Fig. 3, "*SSC*" means *Samsung SmartCam*, "*WMS*" means *Wemo motion Sensor*, and "*Aec*" means *Amazon Echo*.

t-SNE is a non-linear dimension reduction technique which is particularly well suited to visualize large datasets. It is widely applied in image processing, NLP, genomics data and speech processing. *t-SNE* is an unsupervised machine learning algorithm that attempts to represent similar data points next to each other while preserving the overall structure of the dataset.

We can note that Fig. 3 depicted data points form visual clusters corresponding to network traffic generated by different categories of IoT devices. Indeed, most data points for same IoT device are close to each other, while data points for different IoT devices are far apart. Our findings exhibit that selected features are effective enough to discern these three devices classes.

4.4 Classification

Classification Results. For classes C_{WMS}, C_{AEC} and C_{SSC}, devices are classified using following metrics:

Accuracy: means the proportion of correctly classified flows.

Precision: exhibits the ratio $TP/(TP + FP)$; (i) where TP and FP express the number of true positives and false positives.

Recall: illustrates the ratio $TP/(TP+FN)$; (ii) where FN means the number of false negatives. Furthermore, TP/TN are outcomes where the model correctly predicts positive/negative class. Similarly, FP/FN are outcomes where positive/negative class is incorrectly predicted by the model. A weighted harmonic mean of precision and recall is **F1-Score**.

F1-Score: reaches its best score at 1 and the worst at 0. The obtained formula expressed as follows by Eq. 1:

$$F1 - Score = 2 * (Precision * Recall)/(Precision + Recall). \tag{1}$$

Since test datasets varies in size, micro-average is used to computes different metrics in order to assess the overall *precision, recall* and $F1 - score$ (Table 4). The macro-average method can be used when you want to know how the system works globally across all datasets. It computes metric independently for each class, then takes the average (so all classes are treated equally), while a micro-average aggregates the contributions of all classes to calculate the average metric. Classifiers that reach the best overall performance are chosen by vote.

Table 4 shows that Artificial Neural Network (ANN), Decision Tree (DT), Random Forest and SVM reach the highest overall precision rate close to 99.9%. The k-Nearest Neighbors $(k\text{-}NN)$ algorithm then comes with an overall accuracy of 98.4%. This means that these algorithms are able to uniquely identify a category of IoT device with very high probability. These results once again demonstrate the skill of proposed features to accurately identify devices categories. ANN improvement requires to encode categorical variables label to numerical ones. In addition, we have enough data collected to reach a high precision, which was a limit with work in [5].

Similarly, for each category, we estimate the precision, recall and F1-score individually to show the ability of classifiers to identify each of them (binary decision). Table 5 illustrates obtained results. For each class taken individually, it can be seen that ANN, DT, RF and SVM algorithms are able to positively verify a class of devices with a high precision (between 89.9% and 100% for

Table 4. Overall performance on the test set of the different classifiers.

Algorithms	Accuracy	Micro-avg precision	Micro-avg recall	Micro-avg F1 score
ANN	0.999	0.999	0.999	0.999
k-NN	0.984	0.984	0.984	0.984
DT	0.999	0.999	0.999	0.999
GNB	0.649	0.649	0.649	0.649
RF	0.999	0.999	0.999	0.999
SVM	0.999	0.999	0.999	0.999

Table 5. Precision, Recall and F1-score on the test set for different classifiers.

Algorithms	Precision			Recall			F1-score		
	C_{SSC}	C_{WMS}	C_{AEC}	C_{SSC}	C_{WMS}	C_{AEC}	C_{SSC}	C_{WMS}	C_{AEC}
ANN	1.	1.	1.	1.	1.	.998	1.	1.	1.
k-NN	.797	.974	.984	.708	.998	.957	.935	.989	.968
DT	1.	1.	1.	.996	1.	1.	.999	.997	1.
GNB	.785	.958	.715	1	.605	.767	.553	.749	.737
RF	1.	1.	1.	.898	1.	1.	.999	1.	1.
SVM	.809	1.	1.	.807	1.	1.	.809	1.	1.

ANN, *DT*, *RF*; and between 70.8% and 100% when *k-NN* is included. *GNB* is amongst algorithms that be downgraded because of his worst performance (overall near 76.3%).

Afterwards, we classify the rest of testbed devices by group. The three best algorithms which offer the high precision are chosen by vote. We then submit samples of each of these 26 devices to our prediction models obtained above from *MLPC.predict()*, *SVC.predict()* and *RFC.predict()* classes. These classes are those used in the prediction phase for respectively *ANN*, *SVM* and *RF* algorithms. Table 6 shows classification results. It is worth noticing that:

1. Any device classified as belonging to a single class X by the three algorithms with an accuracy greater than 75% is retained as belonging to X.
2. Device belongs to a class X if predicted by at least two out of three algorithms as being similar to X with overall accuracy greater than or equal to 80%.
3. Any device classified as belonging to the three classes by the three algorithms with any accuracy rate is downgraded.
4. Any classification giving an overall accuracy between 85% and 100% obtained by two out of three algorithms, for device classified twice, the classification of the two algorithms prevails over the remaining one.
5. Any other classification obtained is rejected and the equipment is considered unrecognized.

Case (3) is observed for two devices; *NEST Protect smoke alarm* and Hello Barbie in Table 6. These devices are downgraded and considered as unrecognized. This is due to a lack of collected data. Indeed, over a 24-h observation period, few data is captured for these devices in the smart environment. Device such as "*Netatmo Welcome*", "*Triby Speaker*" and "*TP-Link Day Night Cloud camera*" belong to case (2). *Netatmo Welcome* is accurately classifier as C_{AEC} with 99.98% by *SVM* and 86.93% by *RF*.

Regarding to *Triby Speaker*, it is mapped as C_{WMS} with accuracies of 88% by *SVM*, 95.41% by *ANN* and 47.8% as C_{AEC} by *RF*. *TP-Link Day Night Cloud camera* is identified with accuracy near 90.88% as C_{AEC} by *RF*, 99.95% by *SVM* and as C_{WMS} with 88.18% of precision. "*August Doorbell Cam*" and "*Ring Door Bell*" are also downgraded, because no traffic instance of this devices

Table 6. Group-based Iot devices classification.

Devices	C_{CSS}	C_{WMS}	C_{AEC}
Dropcam	⊗	✓	⊗
Netatmo weather station	✓	⊗	⊗
LiFX Smart Bulb	⊗	✓	⊗
Triby Speaker	⊗	✓	⊗
TP-Link Day Night camera	⊗	⊗	✓
Withings Aura smart sleep sensor	⊗	✓	⊗
iHome	⊗	✓	⊗
Withings Smart Baby Monitor	⊗	⊗	✓
NEST Protect smoke alarm	⊘	⊘	⊘
PIX-STAR Photo-frame	✓	⊗	⊗
Insteon Camera (Wifi & Lan)	⊗	⊗	✓
Belkin wemo motion sensor	⊗	✓	⊗
Smart Things	⊗	⊗	✓
Belkin Wemo switch	⊗	✓	⊗
TP-Link Smart plug	⊗	✓	⊗
HP Printer	⊗	✓	⊗
Nest Dropcam	⊗	✓	⊗
Amazon Echo	⊗	⊗	✓
Netatmo Welcome	⊗	⊗	✓
Samsung SmartCam	✓	⊗	⊗
Blipcare Blood Pressure meter	⊗	✓	⊗
August Doorbell Cam	—	—	—
Awair air quality monitor	✓	⊗	⊗
Canary Camera	✓	⊗	⊗
Google Chromecast	⊗	⊗	✓
Hello Barbie	⊘	⊘	⊘
Phillip Hue Lightbulb	⊗	✓	⊗
Ring Door Bell	—	—	—

is observed in dataset. This probably due to their absence (out of service) during the capture phase. Overall, only around 3% devices is not classified for reasons mentioned above. Any other device in Table 6 belongs to case (1).

Performance Evaluation. In order to assess overall performance of our model, we focus on the total number of packets (*Tot Fwd/Bwd Pkts* columns) contained in the first flows generated by each device. We attempt to find optimal number of packets needed to accurately recognize a device. Let p the number of packets sent and received by each device in chronological order, we rearrange the testbed by varying the value of p from 2 to 10. The Random Forest classifier is used in this empirical qualifier experiment. Indeed, RF is one of the trio of algorithms that reaches best accuracy values and is suited for models performance comparison with work in [5].

A small value of p (e.g. $p = 1$) seems insufficient to ensure a certain verdict. Figure 4 illustrates the obtained results. We observe that the overall accuracy rate increases according to the number of packets. For $2 \leq p \leq 10$, the accuracy rate goes from 98.81% to 99.98%. It increases by 1.4% between 2 and 3 and by only 0.3% between 3 and 10, 10 maximizes the value of p since no variation is noted next. The accuracy reaches its best rate for $p = 4$ and does not vary regardless to p. We already obtained a suitable precision of 98.81% with only 2 packets received ($p = 2$). However we do not adapt this value since *NEST Protect smoke alarm* and *"Hello Barbie"* are downgraded (Table 6). In fact, flow observed for each of these devices consists of only 2 packets and we see above that the identification of these devices by the three classifiers was uncertain.

Based on obtained results, we reach overall accuracy value near 99.98% with RF for an optimal value of 4 packets. The limited number of devices representative classes explains this high rate because although the number of devices is relatively large, they are finally grouped into only few classes (3). Furthermore, our model offers better performance and less overhead compared to previous work [5]; GBC_IoT reaches 99.98% with $p = 4$ while 6 packets are necessary in Shahid et al. model to achieve relatively the same accuracy, Fig. 4.

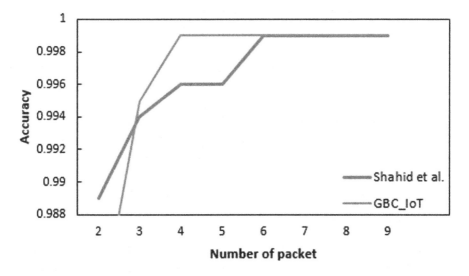

Fig. 4. Overall performance comparison according to number of packet sent and received.

5   Discussion

An unitary classification technique using four features is proposed by Shahid et al. [5] to distinguish traffic from four IoT devices. GBC_IoT approach is better since it uses fewer features and addresses more IoT devices (28 vs. 4). In addition, it gives less computational overhead with an optimal number of packets for device recognition. There is lack of traditional devices (Smartphone, Tablet, PC, etc.) in traffic traces studied in [5], which is not the case in a real IoT environment. Thus, a question is: what would be the performance of their model in a real environment which exhibits the behavior of traditional equipment on studied datasets?

Furthermore, in front of huge amount of available IoT devices, it becomes difficult to deal with a single classifier for each device as performed in [5]. The same is true for works in [8,9,22]. Thus, we propose an optimal and less computational model that train classifiers for groups of devices sharing similar behaviors. The authors in [18] evaluated the effective number of packets in early stage Internet traffic identification. They show this value between 5 and 7. GBC_IoT require just 4 packets to accurately identify IoT device class studied here. A common limitation of works related to IoT (including ours) is the limited number of devices studied due to the lack of publicly available data. However, to deal with a single classifier for every device does not seem to be a good approach. GBC_IoT is more suitable for managing a smart territories scale environment which hosts a large number of devices, since it proposes to classify any device among three instead of 28 or probably more.

GBC_IoT is limited by active classification, it cannot classify additional device that be added to network until it has enough traffic data. It would be interesting to adapt it to a real-time classification model, thereby, it might be adequate for fine group-based traffic QoS management. As solution, we propose an IoT environment based on Software-Defined Network (SDN).

According to this context, the controller with a global view of the network will detect any new added device $app\_profile$ and its GBC_IoT-based class. Thus, data forwarding decision rules will arise from both device application QCI requirements vector and GBC_IoT classification result. Thereby, GBC_IoT should be implemented as a module in the SDN controller. A better alternative approach is to implement it in a hybrid SDN-based IoT network architecture, which is easier to deploy in current networks. However, studies based on our approach must be carried out, trying above all to choose features that are more independent of network structure. A set of features such that there is none that depends on the physical structure of the network would give more scalability to our model.

As summary, the proposed model does not use any of the features mentioned in Sect. 2; TCP $session$ $length$ [5], $traffic$ $volume$ [10], domain of DNS $queries$ [11], MAC addresses or NIC. In addition, GBC_IoT uses less features for a better precision then literature [5,15]. According to performance concern, GBC_IoT framework gives less computational overhead with a minimum of 4 packets for traffic identification as illustrated by obtained results in Fig. 4. This number is between 5 and 7 in [18] and equals to 6 in [5].

To the best of our knowledge, this is the first work that uses ML approach to deal with classification problem relating to both the increasing number and diversity of connected IoT devices and that avoids the use of features that more likely to affect traffic behavior. Indeed, it becomes difficult and resources intensive to deal with a single classifier for every device among thousands of different types of available devices in the market. Thus, a classifier that deals with groups of devices that share similar behaviors is more suitable for this wide variety of equipment in IoT worlds.

6 Conclusion

Nowadays, recognition as well devices integration become a challenging research field with respect to IoT networks. Therefore, we proposed a group-based IoT devices classification using network traffic characteristics. Visualization using t-SNE highlighted the effectiveness of selected features. According different used ML algorithms, we achieve an overall accuracy of 99.98%. Furthermore, our model classifies 26 amongst the 28 devices provided by traces collected in [9].

Based on our experimental results, we can conclude that Group-Based IoT devices Classification related to passive network traffic analysis can offer great accuracy in devices behavior recognition and is more suitable for smart territories environment that host thousands of different types of devices.

We believe that a group-based classification (active/passive) of IoT device according to their traffic characteristic is the more suitable approach. However, continuously update the proposed model is necessary due to regularly network behavior changes over time for different reasons. The integration of SDN concepts would be an asset and a good prospect for improving our model, since an instant and adequate model can be implemented according to network real-time state.

References

1. Pham, C., Rahim, A., Cousin, P.: Low-cost, long-range open IoT for smarter rural African villages. In: Proceedings of IEEE ISC2, pp. 1–6, Trento (2016)
2. Seye, M.R., Diallo, M., Gueye, B., Cambier, C.: COWShED: communication within white spots for breeders. In: Proceedings of IEEE ICIN, pp. 236–238, France (2019)
3. Agence Française de Développement (AFD), ASTON. https://www.afd.fr/fr/actualites/aston-transition-numerique-villes-africaines
4. Muthoni, M.: IoT applications that work for the African continent: innovation or adoption? In: Proceedings of IEEE ICII, pp. 633–638, Porto Alegre, Brazil (2014)
5. Shahid, M.R., Blanc, G., Zhang, Z., Debar, H.: IoT devices recognition through network traffic analysis. In: Proceedings of IEEE ICBD, pp. 5187–5192, USA (2018)
6. Meidan, Y., et al.: ProfilIoT: a machine learning approach for IoT device identification based on network traffic analysis. In: Proceedings of SAC, pp. 506–509, Morocco (2017)
7. Meidan, Y., et al.: Detection of unauthorized IoT devices using machine learning techniques (2017). arXiv:1709.04647
8. Sivanathan, A., et al.: Characterizing and classifying IoT traffic in smart cities and campuses. In: Proceedings of IEEE INFOCOM WKSHPS, pp. 559–564, Atlanta, GA (2017)
9. Sivanathan, A., et al.: Classifying IoT devices in smart environments using network traffic characteristics. In: Proceedings of IEEE Transactions on Mobile Computing, vol. 18, no. 8, pp. 1745–1759, 1 August 2019

10. Shafiq, M.Z., Ji, L., Liu, A.X., Pang, J., Wang, J.: Large-scale measurement and characterization of cellular machine-to-machine traffic. In: Proceedings of IEEE/ACM Transactions on Networking, vol. 21, no. 6, pp. 1960–1973, December 2013

11. Apthorpe, N., Reisman, D., Feamster, N.: A smart home is no castle: privacy vulnerabilities of encrypted IoT traffic (2017). arXiv:1705.06805

12. Miettinen, M., et al.: IoT sentinel: automated device-type identification for security enforcement in IoT. In: Proceedings of ICDCS, pp. 2177–2184, Atlanta, GA (2017)

13. Blake, A., David, M.: Identifying encrypted malware traffic with contextual flow data. In: Proceedings of AISec, pp. 35–46 (2016)

14. Sivanathan, A., Sherratt, D., Gharakheili, H.H., Sivaraman, V., Vishwanath, A.: Low-cost flow-based security solutions for smart-home IoT devices. In: Proceedings of IEEE (ANTS), pp. 1–6, Bangalore (2016)

15. Ayyoob, H., et al.: Verifying and monitoring IoTs network behavior using MUD profiles. In: Proceedings of IEEE Transactions on Dependable and Secure Computing (2020)

16. Tang, Y., Zhang, Y.-Q., Huang, Z.: FCM-SVM-RFE gene feature selection algorithm for leukemia classification from microarray gene expression data. In: Proceedings of FUZZ, pp. 97–101, Reno, NV (2005)

17. Weiss, M., et al.: Time-aware applications, computers, and communication systems. Technical Note (NIST TN) - 1867 (2015)

18. Peng, L., Yang, B., Chen, Y.: Effective packet number for early stage internet traffic identification. Neurocomput. J. **156**(25), 252–267 (2015)

19. Li, Y., Noseworthy, B., Laird, J., Winters, T., Carlin, T.: A study of precision of hardware time stamping packet traces. In: Proceedings of IEEE ISPCS, pp. 102–107, Austin, TX (2014)

20. Prasad, A., Iverson, L., Liaw, A.: Newer classification and regression tree techniques: bagging and random forests for ecological prediction. Ecosyst. J. **9**, 181–199 (2006)

21. Thanh Noi, P., Kappas, M.: Comparison of random forest, k-nearest neighbor, and support vector machine classifiers for land cover classification using sentinel-2 imagery. Sens. J. **18**(1), 18 (2017)

22. Linlin, W., Peng, L., Su, M., Yang, B., Zhou, X.: On the impact of packet inter arrival time for early stage traffic identification. In: Proceedings of IEEE iThings and IEEE GreenCom and IEEE CPSCom and IEEE SmartData, pp. 510–515, Chengdu, China (2016)

23. Qazi, Z.A., et al.: Application-awareness in SDN. In: Proceedings of ACM SIGCOMM, pp. 487–488, NY, USA (2013)

24. Este, A., Gringoli, F., Salgar elli, L.: On the stability of the information carried by traffic flow features at the packet level. Comput. Commun. Rev. J. **39**, 13–18 (2009)

Performance Evaluation of Spreading Factors in LoRa Networks

Smangaliso Mnguni[1]([✉]), Pragasen Mudali[1], Adnan M. Abu-Mahfouz[2], and Matthew Adigun[1]

[1] University of Zululand, Richards Bay, South Africa
mngunismangaa@gmail.com
[2] Council for Scientific and Industrial Research, Pretoria, South Africa

Abstract. LoRa Networks is one of the fast-growing and promising technologies to enable communications for the Internet of Things (IoT) devices on a large scale or long-range communication. Spreading Factors (SF) plays a significant role in enabling multiple long-range receptions of packets with every packet assigned a different spreading factor. Therefore, a change in SF is necessary for improving the data rate for transmission where the link is better and allow LoRa networks to adapt the range trade-off. This work uses FLoRa open source framework for carrying out end-to-end LoRa simulations network in the OMNET++ simulator. In this paper, we investigated the Adaptive Data Rate (ADR) and provided the behaviour of SF and data rate in LoRa wide Are network (LoRaWAN). Some of the findings includes the ability of transmitting data very fast possessed by the low SF no matter the size of the network and high amount of energy consumed by the high SF.

Keywords: Spreading factors · LoRa networks · IoT · Gateway · Simulation

1 Introduction

Recently Internet of Things (IoT) has gained momentum and opened up new challenges in the establishment of efficient networks. The establishment includes low energy consumption of IoT devices and transmitting a large amount of data through wireless communication. These IoT/smart devices can be deployed using short-range technologies such as Bluetooth, infrared and ZigBee, or long-range technologies such as Sigfox, NB-fi and LoRa. In addition, IoT devices have the capability of being located inside buildings, underwater or underground. A Low

Supported by organization x.
Smangaliso Mnguni is a Masters student in the Department of Computer Science at the University of Zululand. His research interest is under LoRa gateway placement in the Internet of Things (IoT) and Low Power Wide Area Networks (LPWAN).

R. Zitouni et al. (Eds.): AFRICOMM 2020, LNICST 361, pp. 203–215, 2021.
https://doi.org/10.1007/978-3-030-70572-5_13

Power Wide Area (LPWAN) usually provides a long-range transmission, wireless connectivity (using a star topology) and increased power efficiency [10,13]. LoRaWAN is one of the technologies provided by LPWAN which has a lot of capabilities and promising features. LoRa devices use LoRaWAN standards for communication, and it can improve power efficiency. The choice of parameters used for radio resources and the number of gateways deployed such as transmission power, coding, spreading factors and bandwidth impacts the LoRaWAN network performance in terms of latency, robustness, and coverage. In the Chirp Spread Spectrum (CSS) wherein physical layer, a based ALOHA method consists of several SFs to pick from, in order to trade data rate for a long-range [5]. Therefore, higher SF allows more extended range at the expense of lower data rate, and vice versa. In different channels the transceivers can take control of receiving different data rates where the data rate is defined as time-on-air of the data transmitted [18].

A high packet error rate may occur as a result of letting nodes choose their power control and SFs, which cause an unfair network performance [17]. In this equation, for LoRa modulation BW as a parameter play a significant role such that a doubling of it automatically doubles the transmission rate. Furthermore, at a given SF the bit rate and symbol rate are directly proportional to the frequency bandwidth, SF bits of information can effectively be encoded by a symbol since there are chirps in a symbol [1]. Many studies have been trying to solve the gateway placement in LoRa networks by introducing different algorithms to achieve maximum coverage. However, many algorithms were a none success and the impact of SFs and data rate in the algorithms were not considered to improve them. This paper is solving the problem of SFs and data rate in LoRaWAN networks for the gateway to be optimally placed.

The rest of this paper is organized as follows. Section 2 provides an overview of LoRa/LoRaWAN. Section 3 provides the relevant and related work for the study, and Sect. 4 discusses the approached used in the study. Section 5 describes the framework for LoRa simulations, and Sect. 6 discusses the evaluation of performance in LoRa networks. Finally, Sect. 7 provides concluding remarks.

2   Overview of LoRa/LoRaWAN

There are two components a LoRa network relies on, namely LoRa and LoRaWAN. In a protocol stack, each of these components corresponds with a different layer. The LoRa Alliance, on the other hand, describe LoRaWAN as an open standard, Semtech developed the LoRa physical layer, which however remains the sole LoRa integrated circuit producer [11]. The relation between the spreading factor (SF), bandwidth (BW), bit rate (R_b) and symbol rate (R_s) is summarized in the form of Eq. (1) [18].

$$R_b = \frac{BW \times SF}{2^{SF}} = (SF)R_s \tag{1}$$

LoRaWAN is the system architecture and ALOHA based communication protocol for a network using the LoRa physical layer. LoRa wireless, with the option for different bandwidth and spreading factor (SF) uses CSS modulation for optimization of modulation to meet data and the long-range requirements. LoRaWAN can communicate over the air with a gateway and involves protocol stack with LoRa wireless; usually, network servers communicate with the gateways, and LoRa Physical layer creates communication between LoRa nodes and the gateway [21]. Chirp modulator passes through the data for binary chirp modulation in a waveform:

$$s(t) = \sqrt{\tfrac{2E_s}{T_s}} \cos\left[2\pi f_c t \pm \pi \left(u\left(\tfrac{t}{T_s}\right) - w\left(\tfrac{t}{T_s}\right)^2\right)\right] \tag{2}$$

where $s(t)$ is function respect to time, E_s represents the energy of $s(t)$ in the symbol duration T_s. Carrier frequency is denoted by f_c, the sweep width and peak-to-peak frequency deviation are presented by constant w and u respectively, both normalized by symbol rate. Adaptive Data Rate (ADR) enables the tradeoff between energy consumption, robustness, and network throughput through the support of LoRa while the bandwidth is fixed.

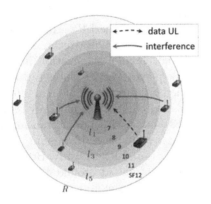

Fig. 1. Uplink (UL) system architecture consisting of several LoRa nodes and one gateway located uniformly in a certain R km radius [7].

In Fig. 1. ALOHA is used by the LoRa devices for a random transmission in the UL and satisfy an additional maximum $p0 = 1\%$ duty cycling policy. According to this cycling policy, LoRa nodes with higher SFs transmit less often as compared to those with lower SFs, for a simplicity BW = 125 kHz is kept constant for every transmission. However, packet loss may still occur if concurrently received signal of the same SF and frequency interfere at the same gateway regardless of simplification. Furthermore, $l_1, l_2..., l_n$ denotes Euclidean range between gateway and LoRa nodes [7,8]. Finally, for a system model or settings a cell of radius R was considered with one or two gateways centered for a different scenarios and LoRa nodes were randomly distributed within the cell, another factor for data transmission is the distance which determines which SF and channel a packet to be transmitted into.

3   Related Work

Since LoRaWAN is an actively studied protocol, other researchers have been working around this area. In [12] authors evaluated the LoRaWAN based protocol using the permanent outdoor testbed, In their evaluation metrics like packet delivery ratio, payload length and link checks were taken into consideration focusing on Adaptive Data Rate (ADR) impact. They revealed that regardless of distance, the ADR schemes assign either the slowest data rate (SF12: BW125) or the fastest (SF7: BW250) primarily.

Another author in [2] evaluated the LoRa transmission parameter selection to ensure reliable and efficient communication amongst the Low Power Wide Area Network (LPWAN) devices. Communication reliability and energy consumption matrices were included in the study, and it was observed that more than 6720 possible settings are available for LoRa device configuration with the use of bandwidth setting, transmission powers, code rate and spreading factors. However, it is still a challenge to determine the required communication performance with minimal energy transmission cost.

The researchers in [14, 15] studied the LPWANs coverage in channel attenuation model and range evaluation for LoRa technology. The intention was to see the impact of distance and channel attenuation in IoT networks, and the nodes were placed in different places such as water (attached in the radio mast of a boat) or ground (attached on a roof rack of a car) for measurements in different scenarios in an area called Oulu, Finland. They reported that for a node operating in the 868 MHz ISM band with power transmission of 14 dBm and a maximum of spreading factor resulted in a maximum communication range of 30 km and 15 km on water and ground respectively. However, the model was not tested in bidirectional communication. At around 40 km/h speed they revealed, because of the duration of the LoRa-modulated communication performance get worse. The extensive research around ADR scheme has resulted in authors to propose another algorithm for modification and addition in order to extend LoRa performance by a suitable allocation of spreading factors. Through the simulation results, EXPLoRa showed much-improved performance compared to the ADR scheme. However, the algorithm selects the spreading factor based on the number of devices deployed in a network [6].

However, it is still necessary to conduct more experiments in a different environment such as testbed to verify the results and find different aspect as to how the SFs and data rate impacts the LoRa networks.

4   Simulation Setup

Network deployment plays a significant role in network throughput, an impact of range on performance can be provided by deploying gateways at a fixed distance without even a need for that gateway(s) to be continuously relocated. Furthermore, simultaneous data collection is possible through permanently deploying nodes at a fixed range. We used an end-to-end simulation-based to test the algorithm enhanced with the support of FLoRa which allows bi-directional communication.

4.1 Design and Layout

The LoRa simulation consists of two network scenarios, one with 100 nodes and the other with 20 nodes, in both scenarios gateway(s) were varied from one to two. All experiments were simulation-based which runs on virtual machine ubuntu 18.10 environment, the simulator integrated inet-4.1.1 with omnetpp v5.5.1. The simulator is written in C++ programming language. The gateway(s) in both network scenarios were placed central in the simulation area and LoRa devices distributed around them, as shown in Fig. 2 and Fig. 3. The gateway is responsible for facilitating communication in the network, and it is connected to a network server.

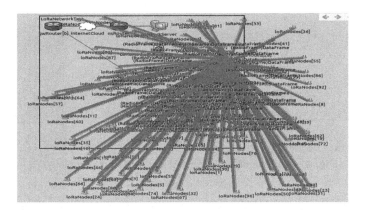

Fig. 2. Example of the first scenario with 100 nodes.

4.2 Topology and LoRa Devices

A star-of-stars topology approach was followed in this study, in which LoRa devices send/receive packets through the channel to/from one or more gateway. The gateway act as a middle man between the LoRa devices and network server by forwarding packets via high throughput and reliable link. It is assumed that at least one gateway will receive the packet and forward them to the network server after end devices have sent them as illustrated in Fig. 4.

4.3 LoRa Simulations a Framework

This section discusses LoRa simulations in details, including the configuration of LoRa devices deployed and together with their parameters. Framework for

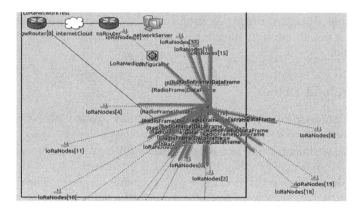

Fig. 3. Example of the second scenario with 20 nodes.

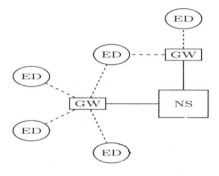

Fig. 4. Example of LoRa network star-of-stars topology.

LoRa (FLoRa) carries out end-to-end simulations for LoRa network. The framework is based on a simulator called OMNET++ and takes advantage of INET framework components, with modules from a network server, gateway(s) and LoRa nodes FloRa allows the creation of LoRa networks. Adaptive Data Rate (ADR) helps in dynamic management of parameters configuration with the support of LoRa nodes and network server. Finally, for every LoRa node present in the network energy consumption statistic is collected, and LoRa physical layer characterization is described [20].

4.4 LoRa Links

In the LoRa physical layer transmission parameters are configured through the support of FLoRa such parameters include transmission power, code rate, bandwidth, center frequency and spreading factor. These parameters influence the occurrence of collision and transmission range. In example, suppose the receiver sensitivity is less than received power the LoRa transmission is successful. The long-distance path loss equation below was used to model the transmission range, received power and receiver sensitivity by determining path loss based on a distance between receiver and transmitter:

$$PL(d) = \overline{PL}(d_0) + 10n \log(\tfrac{d}{d_0}) + X_\sigma \qquad (3)$$

Where the mean path loss for distance d_0 is denoted by $\overline{PL}(d_0)$, $X\sigma$ and n represents zero-mean Gaussian distributed random variable and path loss exponent respectively. A transmission is regarded as successful if no interference occurred during LoRa transmission of packets. Furthermore, the assumption is made two transmissions in an orthogonal channel (meaning transmission of different SFs) do not collide not unless otherwise. Lastly, the transmission power is calculated as: TP = 2 dBm + 3 dBm ×intuniform (0,4) and communication model was validated against the results [19].

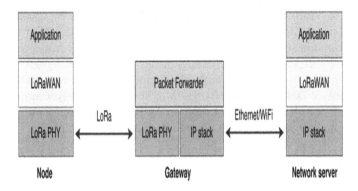

Fig. 5. Corresponding protocol stack and available FLoRa modules [19].

The protocol stack of nodes, gateways and network server is shown in Fig. 5. Gateway is responsible for forwarding messages between the nodes and network server, whereas nodes and network server have an application layer.

4.5   Energy Consumption Module

In a particular state, the amount of time spent by LoRa radio determines the energy consumed. State-based energy consumer module is used to model energy expenditure. Sleep, receive and transmit all form three primary state of LoRa radio after receiving or transmitting a frame the radio is switched to sleep mode. Level of transmission power always controls the energy consumed in the transmit state [3, 4, 9].

5   Evaluation of Performance

Initially, the adaptive communication is evaluated in LoRa networks through simulations. Firstly, the simulation setup is described, followed by obtained results. Finally, the experimental simulation is the summary of findings.

5.1 Parameters of the Simulation

The performance of LoRa networks was evaluated with the help of FloRa. Two simulation experiments conducted, in the first one, a network of 100 nodes was created varied from 100 to 700 in steps of 100. For both experiments, the number of LoRa gateway(s) varied from one to two, and for LoRa physical layer European environmental parameters were used as explained in Table 1. The second simulation consists of a 20 nodes network with different gateways, where every LoRa node deployed pick an arbitrary transmission power and spreading factor distributed within a permissible range.

INET framework played a significant role in modelling the backhaul network with a transmission power of 10 ms and no packet loss. In the simulation, a typical sensing application was considered. After distribution time, each LoRa nodes sent a 20-byte packet with a mean of 1,000 s. The size of the deployment area was set to 500 m by 500 m for the first scenario, 10000 m by 10000 m for the second scenario. All the deployed LoRa devices were located within the square region to communicate with the gateway(s), and nodes were randomly placed. The simulated time for both experiments lasted one day, and ten iterations run for accuracy of the results. LoRa networks performance was evaluated with and without Adaptive Data Rate (ADR). Both at the network server and the nodes mechanisms is disabled in networks with no ADR, ADR-node ran on all variants of ADR and nodes at the network server when ADR was enabled.

Table 1. Parameters for simulation

Parameters	Value(s)
Transmission power	2 dBm to 14 dBm
Spreading factor	7 to 12
Code rate	4/8
Bandwidth	125 kHz
Carrier frequency	868 MHz

Performance of the network evaluated with LoRa devices of different densities, in the deployment area, the number of nodes were varied from 100 to 700 with the steps of 100. Lastly, below performance matrices were considered in the simulation process:

- Energy consumption per successful transmission, LoRa nodes total energy divided by the total number of messages received by the network server.
- Delivery ratio, as the number of messages correctly received by the network server divided by the total number of messages sent by the end nodes.

6   Simulation Results

Initially, the performance of networks with ADR was evaluated than followed by the analysis impact of the algorithm implemented for spreading factor allocation. Next, we compare the performance of the algorithm if the network has one gateway or two gateways. Finally, the evaluation of energy efficiency in the algorithm.

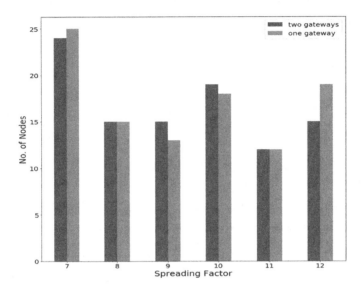

Fig. 6. Comparison of the number of nodes of each spreading factor.

Figure 6 shows the average number of nodes for both scenarios allocated to each spreading factors in different networks, and Each network consists of 100 nodes with one and two gateway(s) respectively. It is observed that most nodes were assigned to the lowest spreading factor number 7 in both scenarios, meaning most nodes were close to the gateway(s). A spreading factor of 7 allows nodes to take as less as possible to communicate with the gateway(s). However, the possibility of collision between the packets is more likely to increase when the number of nodes with the same spreading factor increases drastically. The same number of nodes were observed in spreading factors of 8 and 11 for both scenarios, respectively. The transmission power was kept constant throughout the simulation. However, in certain areas, it is observed that gateway and nodes can only communicate if transmission occurs at a high spreading factor and high transmission power.

Figure 7 shows the energy consumed by nodes transmitting data in different spreading factors. As expected, the spreading factor of 12 has the highest amount of energy consumption in both cases. Bandwidth channel was set to 125 kHz throughout the simulation, nodes assigned to spreading factor of 12

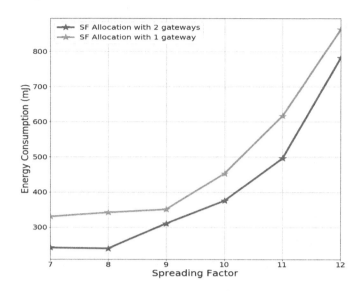

Fig. 7. Energy consumed by nodes in each spreading factors.

consumed a high amount of energy due to transmission distance the higher the spreading factor, the more time taken to transmit a packet which results to high energy consumption during the process. The increase of packet transmission is influenced by the increasing number of encoding bits, which allows radio module to consume more power. The spreading factor with one gateway consumed more energy compare to spreading factor with two gateways, energy consumed in both scenarios increased as the spreading factor increases. It is due to the lack of available gateways to transmit in a network with one gateway.

Figure 8 represents the energy consumed at different spreading factors as a function of the payload useful bits. It is observed that with the increase of useful bits in the network the energy consumption decreases, the energy consumed depends on the number of spreading factor, i.e. if a node uses a spreading factor of 12 to transmit packets the time-on-air will increase since the longer the distance, the more time it takes to transmit which results to the increase of energy consumption. If the node is closer to the gateway spreading factor of 7 will be picked for packet transmission depending on how near it is, in that case, less time will be taken on air due to short distance to travel which decreases the energy consumption as the useful payload bits increases. It is noted that energy consumed and the time-on-air increased with the decrease of the coding rate, where the code rate denotes a useful number of bits or transmission bits.

Figure 9 shows how time-on-air, payload and spreading factors have strongly impacted the packet transmission from nodes to the gateway(s). It is observed that time-on-air increases as the number of spreading factor increase, spreading factor of 12 have the highest amount of time-on-air due to distance between nodes and the gateways. There was a minor difference time-on-air between the

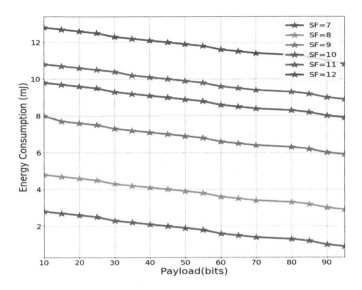

Fig. 8. Energy consumed per payload bits at different spreading factors.

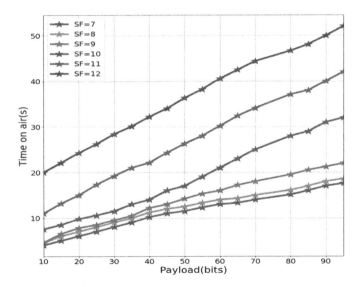

Fig. 9. Time on air vs payload at a different spreading factor.

nodes used a spreading factor of 7 and 8 which means the distance between those two spreading factors to the gateway was almost equal for every channel picked up. For every step up in spreading factor doubles the time-on-air for the same amount of data to be transmitted, the longer the time-on-air results in fewer data transmitted per unit of time with the same bandwidth [16].

7   Discussion

Whist the simulation results showed some key findings, solutions for the challenges in LoRa networks are highlighted and discussed. According to the algorithm implemented transmission power can increase the spreading factor until the packets from nodes are successfully transmitted to the network server via link budget. However, Adaptive Data Rate of nodes can only allow the increase of spreading factor while transmission power remains constant. From the observation of the results, it is not deniable that in some cases, nodes can be a secure link with the gateway if it transmits at a high spreading factor and high transmission power.

8   Conclusion

In this paper, the evaluation of LoRa network performance has been conducted with the use of adaptive communications. FLoRa was used to carry out end-to-end simulations which were integrated to OMNet++ and INET framework. Our results showed that most nodes picked up a spreading factor of 7 in both scenarios as the results of most nodes in the network not being far away from the gateway(s). If nodes are closer to the gateway, less energy consumed for packet transmission. However, there are high chances of packet collision due to congestion in the channels. The spreading factor has an enormous impact on network coverage, energy consumption and latency, as does the data rate. Appropriate choosing the transmission power and spreading factor automatically improves the link budget.

Acknowledgment. The authors wish to express their appreciation to the Department of Computer Science at the University of Zululand. This research was supported by the Council for Scientific and Industrial Research, Pretoria, South Africa, through the Smart Networks collaboration initiative and IoT-Factory Program (Funded by the Department of Science and Innovation (DSI), South Africa).

References

1. Augustin, A., Yi, J., Clausen, T., Townsley, W.M.: A study of LoRa: long range & low power networks for the Internet of Things. Sensors **16**(9), 1466 (2016)
2. Bor, M., Roedig, U.: LoRa transmission parameter selection. In: 2017 13th International Conference on Distributed Computing in Sensor Systems (DCOSS), pp. 27–34. IEEE (2017)
3. Bor, M.C., Roedig, U., Voigt, T., Alonso, J.M.: Do LoRa low-power wide-area networks scale? In: Proceedings of the 19th ACM International Conference on Modeling, Analysis and Simulation of Wireless and Mobile Systems, pp. 59–67 (2016)
4. Bouguera, T., Diouris, J.F., Chaillout, J.J., Jaouadi, R., Andrieux, G.: Energy consumption model for sensor nodes based on LoRa and LoRaWAN. Sensors **18**(7), 2104 (2018)

5. Caillouet, C., Heusse, M., Rousseau, F.: Optimal SF allocation in LoRaWAN considering physical capture and imperfect orthogonality. In: 2019 IEEE Global Communications Conference (GLOBECOM), pp. 1–6. IEEE (2019)
6. Cuomo, F., et al.: Explora: extending the performance of lora by suitable spreading factor allocations. In: 2017 IEEE 13th International Conference on Wireless and Mobile Computing, Networking and Communications (WiMob), pp. 1–8. IEEE (2017)
7. Georgiou, O., Raza, U.: Low power wide area network analysis: can LoRa scale? IEEE Wirel. Commun. Lett. **6**(2), 162–165 (2017)
8. Khutsoane, O., Isong, B., Abu-Mahfouz, A.M.: IoT devices and applications based on LoRa/LoRaWAN. In: IECON 2017–43rd Annual Conference of the IEEE Industrial Electronics Society, pp. 6107–6112. IEEE (2017)
9. Kim, D.H., Lim, J.Y., Kim, J.D.: Low-power, long-range, high-data transmission using Wi-Fi and LoRa. In: 2016 6th International Conference on IT Convergence and Security (ICITCS), pp. 1–3. IEEE (2016)
10. Magrin, D., Centenaro, M., Vangelista, L.: Performance evaluation of LoRa networks in a smart city scenario. In: 2017 IEEE International Conference on communications (ICC), pp. 1–7. IEEE (2017)
11. Marais, J.M., Malekian, R., Abu-Mahfouz, A.M.: LoRa and LoRaWAN testbeds: a review. In: 2017 IEEE Africon, pp. 1496–1501. IEEE (2017)
12. Marais, J.M., Malekian, R., Abu-Mahfouz, A.M.: Evaluating the LoRaWAN protocol using a permanent outdoor testbed. IEEE Sens. J. **19**(12), 4726–4733 (2019)
13. Mnguni, S., Abu-Mahfouz, A.M., Mudali, P., Adigun, M.O.: A review of gateway placement algorithms on Internet of Things. In: 2019 International Conference on Advances in Big Data, Computing and Data Communication Systems (icABCD), pp. 1–6. IEEE (2019)
14. Petäjäjärvi, J., Mikhaylov, K., Pettissalo, M., Janhunen, J., Iinatti, J.: Performance of a low-power wide-area network based on LoRa technology: doppler robustness, scalability, and coverage. Int. J. Distrib. Sens. Netw. **13**(3), 1550147717699412 (2017)
15. Petajajarvi, J., Mikhaylov, K., Roivainen, A., Hanninen, T., Pettissalo, M.: On the coverage of LPWANs: range evaluation and channel attenuation model for LoRa technology. In: 2015 14th International Conference on ITS Telecommunications (ITST), pp. 55–59. IEEE (2015)
16. Potéreau, M., Veyrac, Y., Ferre, G.: Leveraging LoRa spreading factor detection to enhance transmission efficiency. In: 2018 IEEE International Symposium on Circuits and Systems (ISCAS), pp. 1–5. IEEE (2018)
17. Reynders, B., Meert, W., Pollin, S.: Range and coexistence analysis of long range unlicensed communication. In: 2016 23rd International Conference on Telecommunications (ICT), pp. 1–6. IEEE (2016)
18. Reynders, B., Meert, W., Pollin, S.: Power and spreading factor control in low power wide area networks. In: 2017 IEEE International Conference on Communications (ICC), pp. 1–6. IEEE (2017)
19. Slabicki, M., Premsankar, G., Di Francesco, M.: Adaptive configuration of LoRa networks for dense IoT deployments. In: NOMS 2018–2018 IEEE/IFIP Network Operations and Management Symposium, pp. 1–9. IEEE (2018)
20. Sommer, C., German, R., Dressler, F.: Bidirectionally coupled network and road traffic simulation for improved IVC analysis. IEEE Trans. Mob. Comput. **10**(1), 3–15 (2010)
21. Wixted, A.J., et al.: Evaluation of LoRa and LoRaWAN for wireless sensor networks. In: 2016 IEEE SENSORS, pp. 1–3. IEEE (2016)

e-Services and Big Data

Least Cost Remote Learning for Under-Served Communities

Olasupo Ajayi$^{(\boxtimes)}$, Hloniphani Maluleke , and Antoine Bagula

Department of Computer Science, University of the Western Cape,
Cape Town, South Africa
olasupoajayi@gmail.com

Abstract. Remote teaching and learning (RTL) is a system of education, wherein teachers and learners are not in the same location but separated by time and space. Global pandemics such as the COVID-19, necessitate social distance, thereby rendering traditional "contact" based classroom learning unfeasible. e-Learning which is a viable alternative often depends on reliable Internet. Unfortunately, Internet penetration in many areas of the world is still abysmally low. RTL in these under-served regions of the world is thus a major challenge. In this paper, we review the state of RTL and consider feasible options for under-served communities. Requirement for RTL, including data and associated cost of attending classes online are also considered. Finally, recommendations for achieving least cost RTL for under-served communities are given.

Keywords: e-Learning · Remote teaching · Distant learning · Rural development · Network connectivity

1 Introduction

Remote teaching can implicitly be defined as teaching from a distance or one in which the teacher and students are not physically in the same location. There are a number of formalized definition for remote teaching, among which are "a setting where the learners and teachers (or information source) are separated by time and distance and therefore cannot meet in a traditional classroom setting" [1]. The Merriam-Webster dictionary defines it as a means of education where teachers and students meet outside the conventional classroom environment, but rather use electronic means to have classes [2]. A common thing among the numerous definitions is the partial or complete absence of a formalized physical teaching and learning environment such as a physical classroom. This instead is mostly replaced with electronic alternatives such as emails, videos, voice recordings, lecture slides or presentations and virtual classrooms.

Remote Teaching and Learning (RTL) up until now might have remained a luxury rather than a necessity; however in times of epidemic outbreaks such as the recent COVID-19 pandemic caused by a type of Coronavirus and transmitted via interpersonal contacts [3], the world has had to adopt it. A fundamental requirement for live and interactive RTL is the Internet. In many developed

© ICST Institute for Computer Sciences, Social Informatics and Telecommunications Engineering 2021
Published by Springer Nature Switzerland AG 2021. All Rights Reserved
R. Zitouni et al. (Eds.): AFRICOMM 2020, LNICST 361, pp. 219–233, 2021.
https://doi.org/10.1007/978-3-030-70572-5_14

countries of the world, Internet access is common place, however, this is not the case globally especially in Africa and parts of Asia. A report by the International Telecommunication Union (ITU) shows that in 2019, less than 30% of Africans had access to Internet. Similarly in the same period only 48% of Asians could access the Internet. These figures are in sharp contrast to those of Europe (83%) and the United States (77%) [4]. Figure 1 shows the global Internet penetration rate according to the ITU.

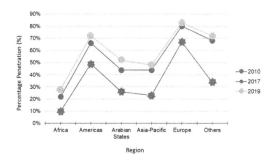

Fig. 1. Global internet penetration rate [4]

In a similar report by the Internet World Stats [5], 500 million users accessed the Internet in Africa as at end of 2019. This number represents less than 40% of the entire African population and only 11% of the total number of global Internet users. This low Internet penetration rate can be attributed to a number of factors many of which are not unrelated to poverty and under development. We refer to these areas as under-served communities.

In this paper, we perform a survey of RTL in under-served areas of the world, such as Africa and parts of Asia. We consider a number of RTL options and their viability in these parts of the world. We perform a systematic analysis, taking into consideration the amount of data required and the cost of accessing the Internet in these under-served communities. From these we make suggestions on the best ways to achieve low cost RTL in these communities.

The rest of the paper is arranged as follows: a review of RTL options is done in Sect. 2, followed by a data requirement to cost mapping in Sect. 3. These are followed by our recommendations for under-served communities in Sect. 4, while Sect. 5 concludes the paper.

2   Review of Literature

2.1   Learning Platforms

Television: The Television (TV) has for a long time played a vital role in education. The term educational or instructional TV refers to the utilization of television and/or television programs to argument learning [6]. Though particularly useful in teaching younger children (in pre- and elementary school), it has also found useful application in high school and tertiary institution. It is thus a very useful RTL tool [7]. Educational TV is often applied in a number of ways, such as: i.) One-way broadcast: wherein student viewers simply watch live or pre-recorded lesson(s) via the TV. Communication here is purely unidirectional, from the teacher to the student(s). ii.) Pseudo-Interactive broadcast: a model similar to the direct broadcast, however, a moderator can pause the playback to allow for audience engagement in form of questions or to emphasize certain concepts. iii.) Two-way Interactive broadcast: wherein teaching is augmented with telecommunication, thereby allowing for a two-way communication between the teacher (who is live) and the student(s). Asides from the traditional teacher-student learning, the TV also plays a prominent role in indirect teaching. This, often referred to as "edutainment", is one in which educational contents are infused into entertainment programmes. This indirect learning is targeted at all ages, and includes TV stations such as: Nickelodeon with programmes primarily designed for children and teenagers, to National Geographic and Discovery World targeting a wider and older age bracket. In [8], the authors did a comprehensive survey of the role of TVs in education in Kenya. They considered different types of TVs and their functions as it relates to education. A similar work was done in [9], but targeted at teachers' view and use of TVs as a learning tool in a city in Nigeria.

Radio: Radio has long since been a tool of mass media. Its relative affordability and easy of understanding has helped its wide spread global adoption. With respect to RTL, radios have played a pivotal role, especially in under-served communities. They have been used as a medium: to reach/inform local farmers, for spiritual guidance by religious leaders and for formal teaching and learning as is the case with RTL. The authors in [10], surveyed various ways radios have been used in RTL in developing countries. Some of these include: literacy and language training, family planning and farming best practices. In [11], the authors discussed open challenges to effective learning using radios; while in [12], initiatives for radio-based learning in under-served communities are discussed.

Podcasts: A Podcast is akin to a radio programme, albeit one that is available on-demand and accessible through the Internet. It is a digital audio file shared among listeners through the Internet [13]. Podcasts unlike regular audio streaming are episodically and uses RSS (Really Simple Syndicate). This provides automatic notification and the ability to download new content [15]. Podcasts have in recent times gained widespread popularity with about 1 million active podcasts and over 50 billion streams till date [14]. Among the numerous advantages of podcasts, the two most important for education are: on-demand listening, such that listeners can listen to whatever they want, from wherever they are and at any time they want [17] and replay value or replayability. As an educational tool, [13,15,16], have surveyed the applications of podcasts as an excellent tool for RTL new languages. Salas and Moller [18] have also shown the advantages podcasts and other multimedia platforms have on learners when used in tandem with traditional learning techniques. The authors in [17] and [19], extensively surveyed the impact of podcasts in education and gave numerous examples to justify their usefulness educational tools.

Despite the advantages of podcasts, some of its inherent disadvantages are its inability to hold students' attention, which might be a major challenge. Similarly, if not well managed Podcasts, might end up being distractions to students. There is also the risk of teachers becoming complacent, replacing actual teaching with podcasts. Students might also abandon actually studying/reading books in favour of podcasts. Finally, podcasts might be restrictive if used alone, rather than as a tool to augment traditional teaching [16,18].

Webinars: Webinar or Web-seminar are presentations (usually video), workshops or lectures delivered in a virtual room through the Internet [20]. UNICEF defines it as an online learning event, meant to impact knowledge or skills using audio-visuals [21]. Two major reasons behind the widespread global adoption of webinars are the relative ease of setting them and limited resources (financial) requirement. Costs of auditoria, accommodation, security, flight and other logistics often associated with physical conferences/seminars are eliminated with Webinars. These are traded for Internet access.

Webinars have found applications as marketing and sales tool [23], as conference/business collaboration tool [22] and for RTL [21,22]. Unlike webcasts (such as Podcasts) which are often uni-directional broadcast, Webinars allow for interaction between the audience and presenter(s). Webinars are excellent tool for RTL in under-served communities because they are cheap to setup, can be recorded and distributed to students/participants, can be assessed through multiple platforms (mobile, web, computers etc.); and allow for interactivity through audio Q&As, opinion polls, direct messages and text-based chats. For bandwidth conservation, webinars can also be audio only, with accompanying slides distributed afterwards. Of these factors, perhaps the most important advantage of webinars is their ability to be recorded and distributed to participant, to be replayed (repeatedly) at convenient times. Specifically because in most rural/developing communities, stable Internet connectivity (if in existence) is a luxury not many can afford.

Zoom [22], Skype [24], Google Meet [25], BigBlueButton [26] are some of the common platforms for hosting webinars. Skype and Zoom both offer features tailored to education such as: whiteboards, annotation and integrated into Learning Management Systems (LMS). Google Meet is a part of the Google Ecosystem and has excellent integration with Google Classroom. BigBlueButton (BBB) unlike the platforms (which only incorporate educational features as add-ons) was designed ground up for education and online learning. It features include: webcam integration, private/public chat, polling, breakout rooms, single and multi-whiteboards etc.

Massive Open Online Course (MOOC): Massive Open Online Course (MOOC) as the name connotes are courses availed to a large number of learners, freely through the Internet [43, 51]. Initially provided and managed by Universities, MOOC became popular in the early 2010s and were popularized by MOOC providers such as edX (2012) [32], Coursera (2012) [33] and Udemy (2010) [34]. Though MOOCs are in themselves free, providers often require learners to pay to access courses with edX being an exception to this. Born from a collaborative effort of a number of Universities (MIT, Harvard, University of California, etc.), edX offers its courses as truly open (and free) to learners.

Despite their numerous advantages and being around for close to a decade, MOOCs are only just beginning to be appreciated in developing countries of Africa and Asia [52]. This poor penetration can be attributed to two factors: i.) their complete reliance on stable Internet connectivity, as the Internet is a major requirement for accessing MOOCs [53]; ii.) lack of accreditation of MOOCs as suitable substitutes to traditional class-taught courses by education authorities [54, 55]. However, in recent times, there has been a steady increase in MOOCs in a number of third world countries. Adham surveyed a number of MOOC platforms in Arab countries with SkillAcademy and Edraak being the prominent ones [42]. In Africa, with the exception of a few instances, the closest semblance to MOOCs is the University correspondence learning. Correspondence learning is a form of education where students and teachers are not in the same physical location. Unlike e-Learning or MOOC, there are few or no actual classes in correspondence learning; rather the exchange of assignments, projects and study materials between lecturers and students is done through announcement boards, posts and/or "pigeon holes" [41]. The African Council for Distance Education (ACDE) serves as a unifying body for open and distance education providers in Africa. Some of its members include the National Open University of Nigeria [38], University of South Africa (UNISA) [39] and Zimbabwe Open University [40] etc. Outside the ACDE, African Universities either provide online courses to students directly (such as the UCT Online short courses [37] and the Distance Learning Institute of the University of Lagos (Unilag) [36]), or through MOOC providers (such as those on edX and FutureLearn [35]).

Notwithstanding the technological and infrastructural limitations, efforts are been made to improve MOOCs in Africa. The Rwandan Kepler project is one such example and is one in which students are camped together in IT-enabled camps and taught using MOOC platforms [44]. The "MOOCs for Africa and future emerging countries" of the Swiss Agency for Development and the "New Economy Skills for Africa Program ICT" are other examples [48]. To narrow the digital divide and provided necessary infrastructure, a number of global trust funds in collaboration with the World Bank have incorporated projects targeted at improving economies and education in Africa through digitization. Notable examples of these are the New Economy Skills for Africa Program (NESAP) [45, 48], Africa Centres of Excellence [46] and Digital Economy for Africa (DE4A) [47] projects.

2.2 Educational Learning Management Systems

According to the World Bank, "the world is facing a learning crisis" and if unchecked, 56% of children would be half as productive as they should be when they reach adulthood [58]. The UNESCO provides a list of Learning Management Systems (LMS), which includes: ClassDojo, Edraak, Moodle, and Google Classroom [49]. Beyond these, there are a plethora of alternatives including Sakai, Blackboard, PowerSchool, etc. These systems provide resources and tools for managing virtual classrooms and/or remote learners. They incorporate features such as: assignment management, automated marking and grading, whiteboards, chat rooms and resource sharing.

However, despite their rich features sets, many do not address the peculiar nature of under-served areas. For instance, in many parts of Africa, electricity is a still a challenge as many communities are either not connected to the electric grid or where connectivity exists, the supply is irregular and often times completely unavailable for days. Network connectivity is also a challenge in these areas. It is therefore pertinent that LMS support asynchronous and offline functionalities. Only a few solutions support these, notably Kolibri, Paradiso and Moodle. In Kolibri, only one device needs to connect to the Internet and once connected, contents are downloaded to it. Upon returning to the community, the downloaded content are distributed to other devices via local networks [50]. This is a very viable option for remote locations in Africa. Paradiso operates in a similar manner but targets single individual without the re-distribution feature.

Prices of smart phones are dropping and are now more readily accessible to learners in under-served areas. Though, many African dwellers still use feature phones, the mobile operating system KaiOS [59] brings "smartness" to such phones, thereby allowing users run advanced applications on low end devices. With such OS, mobile based LMS could therefore be a suitable platform for learning management in low income areas. Tools such as Cell-Ed and Ustad Mobile are viable options that fit the bill. Cell-Ed, is a mobile based LMS that incorporates micro-lessons, assessments and customized certifications. It also works offline and does not require persistent Internet connection [60]. Like Cell-Ed, Ustad Mobile offers similar features but in a more robust and holistic manner. With features such as virtual classrooms, course work and assignment submission, it is a complete LMS squeezed into a phone. Though it can be used offline, users need to occasionally connect to the Internet to synchronize and update learning contents [61]. Apart from Cell-Ed and Ustad Mobile, other LMS providers also have mobile versions of the systems on both Android and Apple IOS. Though these systems provide similar functionalities as Ustad, they often require persistent Internet connection.

3 Data Requirements and Costing

In this section an analysis of the cost of accessing the Internet vis-à-vis RTL alongside the quantity and accessibility to data required are considered.

3.1 Data Cost

The Internet is a fundamental requirement for RTL. Accessing the Internet can be achieved wired or wirelessly. The proliferation of mobile devices including phones, laptops and tablets have in recent times heightened the adaptation of wireless networks. This is specifically the case, when access is required by anyone and from anywhere. Despite the widespread global adaptation, there are many areas of the world where people have limited wireless network coverage and when available, are often barely affordable. Accessing the Internet for RTL in under-served communities is thus a challenge.

In order to effectively mimic real/physical classroom based teaching, RTL require live two-way video streaming, virtual whiteboards and interactive forums for questions and answers. These require large volume of data, which in most times is outside the reach of learners in these low income areas of the world. Figure 2 shows a comparison of 1 GB data bundle prices for a number of African countries. Data prices were cheapest in Egypt at US$1.13 and most expensive in South Africa at $8.28. The average price of 1 GB data bundle is approximately $2.60 [64].

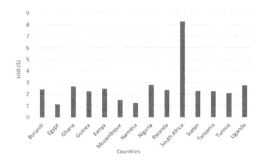

Fig. 2. Comparison of 1 GB data cost across select African nations

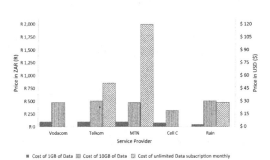

Fig. 3. Cost of data bundles in South Africa

A number of option do exists, including the use of night or off-peak data bundles. These are often times relatively free or significantly cheaper than their peak/day-time counterpart. Survey reports, have shown that it is imperative that learners be on a data bundle, as off bundle prices are exorbitant. In South Africa for instance, in an article published by Fin24 [56], it was reported that telecommunication services providers MTN and Vodacom charged up to 2,100% more for out-of-bundle data. It was also reported that while on contract, a 20 GB data bundles from Vodacom cost ZAR329 ($20) or ZAR0.02 ($1.2$E10^{-3}$) per megabyte, while the out-of-bundles rate was ZAR0.44 (2.6E10^{-2}$) per megabyte. This is an estimate of about 2,100% higher for out-bundle than in-bundle. Similarly, MTN's 25 GB data bundle costs ZAR1,250 ($75), equating to about ZAR0.05 (3.0E10^{-3}$) per megabyte while out-of-bundle costs 6.0E10^{-2}$ per megabyte. This represents a 1,880% difference between in and out-bundle charges.

Data bundle prices for major operators in South Africa are compared in Fig. 3. Cell C and Vodacom as at the time of writing, did not have unlimited data bundles for wireless network but Cell C offered unlimited plan through fibre to home connections. For month-on-month unlimited plan, Rain offered the best price at ZAR479 ($29), while MTN was the most expensive at ZAR1,999.00 ($120).

3.2 E-Learning Data Requirements

On the average a typical University lecture includes 5 min for introduction to a lesson, 40 min of lesson and about 15 min of questions and answers. Table 1 shows a comparison of e-Learning related components, their respective data demand and corresponding costs. On the table we assumed an average uncompressed data size and a cost of ZAR120 ($7.2) per Gigabyte of data. Average file sizes and content counts per Gigabyte were obtained from [65,66] and WhatsApp mobile application.

On Table 1, a sixty minute live online lecture, viewed at 720p (1280×720 resolution) would cost the learner at least ZAR144 ($8) to attend. This is excluding the cost of downloading study materials in pdf or pptx format. If these were included the price could rise to about ZAR150 ($9). However, if the same lecture was audio based only, the cost would drop to about ZAR10 ($0.6) – study materials inclusive. These could be supported with instant messages (chats), which are relatively cheap. On the table, we included the cost of chat using an over-estimated rate of 1 message per minute. Using WhatsApp's data consumption per message as a yardstick, the cost of an hour of interactive chat session cost a negligible fraction of a Cent.

4 Recommendations for Under-Served Communities

As defined in the introductory section, under-developed or under-served communities are remote locations such as villages and townships with limited electricity

Table 1. Mapping of data requirement and cost for e-Learning

Method	Format	Comment	Avg. usage/session	Avg. quantity/GB	Cost (US$)
Document	PowerPoint		30–40 Slides	2,860 Slides	0.1
	Word	Word document in "docx" with basic fonts	12 Pages	18,874 pages	$4.8E10^{-3}$
	PDF		12 Pages	3,146	$2.8E10^{-2}$
	Excel		2 Pages	166 pages	$8.7E10^{-2}$
Interactive	Image	We assume a single Powerpoint slide to contain at least one image, however uncompressed (1.5 MB/image) in JPEG format	30–40	588	0.49
	Audio	MP3 file with 44.1 kHz sample rate and 16 bits depth	60 min	2000 min	0.22
Presentation	Video	720p HD video at 30 frames per second and bitrate of 1.5 Mbps	60 min	60 min (1.2 GB)	8.65
	Podcast	MP3 audio file with 128 kb/s bit rate	60 min	18:12:16 Duration	0.39
Webinar/Virtual classroom	Video	720p HD video at 30 frames per second and bitrate of 1.5 Mbps	60 min	60 min (1.2 GB)	8.65
	Audio	MP3 audio file with 128 kb/s bit rate	60 min	18:12:16 Duration	0.39
	Chats	Text only at an over-estimated rate of 1 message/minute	60 messages	13.5 * 106 messages	$3.0E10^{-5}$
	Whiteboard	Predominantly white image at 1.5 MB per image	30–40	588	0.49
Assessment sheets	Excel		2 Pages	166 Pages	$8.7E10^{-2}$

supply and Internet access. This section focuses on options for RTL for such communities.

4.1 Television

The advantages of educational TV are numerous, including but not limited to higher retention rates, improved grades and enhancement of story-telling and narrative skills [27,28]. Educational Television utilizes cheap and widely available technology (TV and playback device), thereby making it suitable for applications in remote/distant learning in rural and lower socio-economic communities [27,29].

4.2 Podcasts

For developing countries with limited Internet connectivity and network bandwidth, podcasts can make for an excellent choice in delivering RTL. With regards duration, a study carried out by Misener [31] showed, that the median duration of language learning podcasts was about 20 min for children educational podcasts and about 45 min for high school and college content. By recording podcasts in mono rather than stereo and at a bit rates of 64 kbps or 96 kbps, the podcast's file size can be made smaller; as both of these would result in about 0.5 MB and 0.75 MB of file size per minute respectively. Therefore, a 45 min lecture, recorded at 64 kbps would be approximately 21.6 MB in size. These can be made even smaller by compression or using a different file format such as the open source Ogg vorbis audio format [30].

4.3 Webinars

Despite the advantages webinars have, Internet remains a major concern especially in under-served communities. An hour long lecture on BBB can consume as much as a Gigabyte of data when streamed live or downloaded afterwards. A Gigabyte of data on the average costs about ZAR121 ($8.53) in South Africa [56] and NGN1,000 ($2.56) in Nigeria. While these might not seem cheap for an hour of learning, these rates are extremely expensive for communities where a large percentage of the citizenry survive on less than $2 a day [57].

4.4 Low Cost Options

- **Asynchronous lectures:** wherein lectures are pre-recorded and distributed to learners. This is recommended because the recordings would be available for learners to download at their most convenient times. This might for instance be at night for learners on cheaper night data plans or during the weekends when data traffic might be less.

- **Compression:** Video resolutions play an important role in determining size. Larger dimensions (in pixels) translate to larger video sizes and by extension bit rate required to download or stream the video. Using YouTube as a reference, video files are available in the following resolutions: 1920 × 1080 (1080p), 1280 × 720 (720p), 640 × 480 (480p), 480 × 360 (360p), 426 × 240 (240p) and 256 × 144 (144p). From [63], a 30 min video at 360p would have an average size of 375MB, while the same video at 1080p would average 3.3 GB in size. The importance of Video resolution can therefore not be overemphasized. Beyond resolution, frame count is an equally vital factor to consider. Frame per second (FPS), represents the number of image frames to be displayed every second; and can range from 12 to 60. When considering the educational space, a typical lecture comprises of a white board with texts. The content on the screen (white board and texts) do not change very often, hence, a low FPS of between 15–30 could suffice. This could further reduce the size of video recordings.
- **File Format:** Saving documents as certain file types could also significantly reduce their size, while retaining the same information. For instance, the pdf format is a globally accepted file format, that is smaller and non-editable (by default) compared to Microsoft Word or Powerpoint file format. Saving Lecture notes and presentations in pdf format can thus be highly beneficial. LATEX offers an even smaller footprint, but requires the file to be recompiled by the recipient. These text files (in pdf or LATEX) can be accompanied with audio recordings of associated lecture. Like with text documents, audio files can also be saved in formats that utilize smaller disk space. Compared to the Microsoft wav file format, mp3, m4a and ogg offer smaller file footprint, yet maintain the audio quality. A combination of lecture notes/slides in pdf or LATEX format and embedded or accompanying audio recording of lectures could be a light weight alternative to live or pre-recorded lectures. These low profile documents can be sent as emails or distributed to students using social media platforms such as WhatsApp and WeChat.

4.5   Hardware

Though the focus of this paper is not on hardware, it is worth mentioning required hardware necessary to access the various e-Learning channels. Most e-Learning platform are deployed in a form of client-server architecture, where both the learners and teachers are clients and the learning platform (LMS, service applications) is the servers. For Moodle, a popular open source LMS, the minimum requirement for the clients is any device with a web browser. The underlying operating system is insignificant, however, read/write support is required [67]. For live interactive online learning, both teachers and learners would need additional hardware, including a web camera, speaker and microphone. A comprehensive hardware requirement specification is given in [62]; including a system with at least 1 GHz processor, at least 16 GB of storage space, 1 GB RAM, sound card with microphone & speakers, video adapter & monitor and network interface card (wired or wireless). For software, the general requirements are any operating system, modern browser and audio codecs. With most of the processing being done remotely, light weight and comparatively inexpensive devices can be used. This is particularly advantageous for under-served communities, as basic laptops, Chromebooks, cheap android tablets and even single board computers (such as the Raspberry Pi, Tinker Board and Odroid) would suffice.

4.6   Corporate and Governmental Participation

Participation of corporate organizations and government can go a long way in improving RTL in under-served communities. Efforts could be in terms of infrastructure support, such as the INITIC Raspberry Pi labs projects in Togo [68], Kepler project in Rwanda [44], the MTN digital libraries in Nigeria and South Africa, and Samsung Digital Transformation centre in Cape Town. Support can also be in form of direct funding as with the Global Partnership for Education (GPE), Africa Centres of Excellence [46], Digital Economy for Africa (DE4A) [47] projects

Governments can also play key roles in enabling RTL. These can be in form of policies and/or direct intervention. Some notable governmental efforts include: enacting policies that ensure access to educational websites are zero-rated, as is the case in South Africa and Zambia; providing infrastructure for 4G coverage, as done in Kenya [69]; and running educational programmes on dedicated government owned TV and Radio stations. The latter has been implemented in a number of countries in Africa [70].

5   Conclusion

Remote Teaching and Learning (RTL) has never been more relevant as it is today. As at the time of writing, the ravaging global pandemic and consequent national lock downs have forced a global review of our ways of life. With respect to teaching and learning, schools and various educational institutions have now turned to RTL and e-Learning models. However, a fundamental requirement for RTL is the Internet, which Unfortunately is not readily available in remote and low-income (under-served) areas. In this paper, we have reviewed the state-of-the-art with regards RTL and considered options that are feasible in these under-served communities. We identified the requirement for remote learning, in terms of data and the associated cost. Finally we made some recommendations on how to achieve least cost RTL for under-served communities. For low income areas Radios & TVs are the best RTL tools, as they are comparatively cheaper than most of the other options. For Internet-based learning, the global drop in price of Internet and smart phones has helped increase Internet accessibility in Africa to about 28.2%. With this development, learning options such as podcasts, asynchronous and self-paced MOOCs might now be considerable. However, widespread live online classes and webinars might still be some years away.

It is important to note that the approaches discussed in this work are not exhaustive, as there are others not covered, such as distribution of educational content on CDs and USB drives, augmented reality, Text-based RTL using social media tools. This work also did not consider infrastructural requirements that need to be in place for RTL nor were actual examples of live online lectures used. Furthermore, only high level details of data compression techniques and options were given. These could be avenues for extending this work in the future.

References

1. TYWLS Queens. www.tywlsqueens.org/. Accessed 01 Oct 2020
2. Merriam-Webster: Distance learning. www.merriam-webster.com/dictionary/distancelearning. Accessed 27 Mar 2020
3. WHO: Coronavirus. www.who.int/health-topics/coronavirus. Accessed 27 Mar 2020
4. ITU: Measuring digital development: facts and figures 2019. Telecommunication Development Bureau, International Telecommunication Union (ITU)
5. InternetWorldStat.com: World internet usage and population statistics 2019 year-end estimates. www.internetworldstats.com/stats.html. Accessed 27 Mar 2020
6. Guba, E., Snyder, C.: Instructional television and the classroom teacher. AV Commun. Rev. **13**(1), 5–27 (1965)
7. Shabiralyani, G., Hasan, K., Hamad, N., Iqbal, N.: Impact of visual aids in enhancing the learning process case research: district Dera Ghazi Khan. J. Educ. Prac. **6**(19), 226–33 (2015)
8. Munene, T., Mutsotso, S.: Kibabii Uni. Use Television in Promoting Teaching and Learning in Schools
9. Benwari, N.: Television as an instructional tool for concept analysis. World J. Educ. **5**(1), 124–30 (2015)
10. Sarmah, B., Lama, S.: Radio as an educational tool in developing countries: its evolution and current usages. In: International Conference on Developmental Interventions and Open Learning for Empowering and Transforming Society, p. 14 (2017)
11. Chandar, U., Sharma, R.: Bridges to effective learning through radio. Intl. Rev. Res. Open Distrib. Learn. **4**(1), (n.p.). www.irrodl.org/index.php/irrodl/article/view/118/198. Accessed 02 Oct 2020
12. Berman, S.: The return of educational radio? Intl. Rev. Res. Open Distrib. Learn. **9**(2) (n.p.). www.irrodl.org/index.php/irrodl/article/view/563/1038. Accessed 02 Oct 2020. National Geography Channel. www.nationalgeographic.com
13. Phillips, B.: Student-produced podcasts in language learning-exploring student perceptions of podcast activities. IAFOR J. Educ. **5**(3), 157–171 (2017)
14. Adgate, B.: Podcasting is going mainstream. https://forbes.com/sites/bradadgate/2019/11/18/podcasting-is-going-mainstream/4d18f6c01699. Accessed 15 Apr 2020
15. Rosell-Aguilar, F.: Podcasting as a language teaching and learning tool. Case Stud. Good Pract. **10**(3), 31–39 (2015)
16. Yaman, I.: The potential benefits of podcasts for language learning. J. Educ. Instr. Stud. World **6**(1), 60–66 (2016)
17. Goldman, T.: The Impact of Podcasts in Education. Santa Clara University. www.scholarcommons.scu.edu. Accessed 15 Apr 2020

18. Salas, A., Moller, L.: The value of voice thread in online learning: faculty perceptions of usefulness. Q. Rev. Distance Educ. **16**(1), 11–24 (2015)
19. Kay, R.: Exploring the use of video podcasts in education: a comprehensive review of the literature. Comput. Hum. Behav. **28**(3), 820–831 (2012)
20. Lande, L.: Webinar best practices: from invitation to evaluation. www2.uwstout.edu/content/lib/thesis/2011/2011landel.pdf. Accessed 19 Apr 2020
21. Arivananthan, M.: Webinar - efficient and effective live learning events. www.unicef.org/knowledge-exchange/. Accessed 19 Apr 2020
22. Zoom. www.zoom.us/education. Accessed 19 Apr 2020
23. Voskamp, M.: Webinars as an effective marketing and sales tool. Master's thesis, Department of Behavioural Sciences, University of Twente (2012)
24. Skype. www.education.skype.com/. Accessed 19 Apr 2020
25. Afrianto, D.: Using Google Hangout for teaching English online. In: Proceedings of the 4th International Seminar on English Language and Teaching (ISELT-4), pp. 89–96 (2016)
26. BigBlueButton. www.bigbluebutton.org/teachers/. Accessed 19 Apr 2020
27. Linebarger, D., Piotrowski, J.: TV as storyteller: how exposure to television narratives impacts at-risk preschoolers' story knowledge and narrative skills. Br. J. Dev. Psychol. **27**(1), 47–69 (2009)
28. Anderson, D., Lavigne, H., Hanson, K.: The educational impact of television: understanding television's potential and limitations. Intl. Encycl. Media Stud. (2012)
29. Oliver, R., McLoughlin, C.: An investigation of the nature and form of interactions in live interactive television (1996)
30. Moffitt, J.: Ogg Vorbis–Open, free audio–set your media free. Linux J. **2001**(81), 9 (2001)
31. Misener, D.: I analyzed 10 million podcast episodes to find the average length. https://blog.pacific-content.com/how-long-is-the-average-podcast-episode-81cd5f8dff47. Accessed 15 Apr 2020
32. EDX. www.edx.org. Accessed 15 Apr 2020
33. Coursera. www.coursera.org. Accessed 15 Apr 2020
34. Udemy. www.udemy.org. Accessed 15 Apr 2020
35. Future Learn. www.futurelearn.com. Accessed 15 Apr 2020
36. UNILAG DLI. http://dli.unilag.edu.ng/. Accessed 20 Apr 2020
37. UCT. www.uct.ac.za. Accessed 20 Apr 2020
38. NOUN. www.nou.edu.ng. Accessed 20 Apr 2020
39. UNISA. www.unisa.ac.za. Accessed 20 Apr 2020
40. ZOU. www.zou.ac.zw. Accessed 20 Apr 2020
41. U.S. Department of Education: Higher Education Opportunity Act - 2008. www2.ed.gov/policy/highered/leg/hea08/index.html. Accessed 22 Apr 2020
42. Adham, R., Lundqvist, K.: MOOCs as a method of distance education in the Arab world - a review paper. Eur. J. Open Distance e-Learning **18**(1), 123–139 (2015)
43. Masters, K.: A brief guide to understanding MOOCs. Internet J. Med. Educ. **1**(2), 2 (2011)
44. Kepler project. www.kepler.org/. Accessed 21 Apr 2020
45. NESAP-ICT.   https://siteresources.worldbank.org/Education/Resources/.../brochure.pdf. Accessed 22 Apr 2020
46. Africa centres of excellence project. www.aau.org/current-projects/africa-centers-of-excellence-project/. Accessed 22 Apr 2020
47. Digital economy for Africa. https://olc.worldbank.org/content/digital-economy-africa. Accessed 22 Apr 2020

48. Boga, S., McGreal, R.: Introducing MOOCs to Africa: new economy skills for Africa program (2014)
49. UNESCO: Distance learning solutions. https://en.unesco.org/covid19/educationresponse/solutions. Accessed 20 Apr 2020
50. Kolibri: The Offline App for universal education. https://learningequality.org/kolibri/. Accessed 21 Apr 2020
51. Liyanagunawardena, T.: Massive open online courses. Humanities **4**, 35–41 (2015)
52. Liyanagunawardena, T., Williams, S., Adams, A.: The impact and reach of MOOCs: a developing countries' perspective. eLearning Pap. **33**, 38–46 (2014)
53. Warschauer, M.: Technology and Social Inclusion: Rethinking the Digital Divide. MIT Press, Cambridge (2004)
54. Hood, N., Littlejohn, A.: MOOC quality: the need for new measures. J. Learn. Dev. **3**(3), 28–42 (2016)
55. Pietkiewicz, K., Driha, O.: Issues for MOOC recognition/certification/accreditation. In: MOOC Book, pp. 4–23 (2016)
56. Fin24 news. www.fin24.com
57. The World Bank: Understanding poverty. www.worldbank.org/en/topic/poverty/overview. Accessed 22 Apr 2020
58. The World Bank: The education crisis: being in school is not the same as learning. http://worldbank.org/en/news/immersive-story/2019/01/22/pass-or-fail-how-can-the-world-do-its-homework. Accessed 13 May 2020
59. Kai OS. https://kaiostech.com/. Accessed 13 May 2020
60. Cell-ED. https://cell-ed.com/. Accessed 13 May 2020
61. USTAD mobile. https://ustadmobile.com/lms/. Accessed 13 May 2020
62. Hussain, S., Wang, Z., Rahim, S.: E-learning services for rural communities. Intl. J. Comput. Appl. **68**(5), 15–20 (2013). (0975–8887)
63. Hindy, J.: How much data does YouTube actually use? www.androidauthority.com/how-much-data-does-youtube-use-964560/amp/. Accessed 18 May 2020
64. Research ICT Africa dominant operators' data prices remain static while SA struggles to get and stay online. https://researchictafrica.net/wp/wp-content/uploads/...South-Africa-.pdf. Accessed 24 May 2020
65. Anon. (n.d.) How Big is a Gig? www.iclick.com/pdf/howbigisagig.pdf. Accessed 18 May 2020
66. SDS: Data volume estimates and conversions. www.sdsdiscovery.com/resources/data-conversions/. Accessed 25 May 2020
67. Moodle: Installing moodle. https://doc.moodle.org. Accessed 24 May 2020
68. INITIC. www.initic.be/p/kuma-project.html. Accessed 24 May 2020
69. Feleke, B.: Google launches balloon-powered internet service in Kenya, CNN News. www.cnn.com/2020/07/08/africa/google-kenya-balloons/index.html. Accessed 02 Oct 2020
70. World Bank: How countries are using edtech (including online learning, radio, television, texting) to support access to remote learning during the COVID-19 pandemic. www.worldbank.org/en/topic/edutech/brief/how-countries-are-using-edtech-to-support-remote-learning-during-the-covid-19-pandemic. Accessed 02 Oct 2020

Digitizing Physical Assets on Blockchain 2.0: A Smart Contract Approach to Land Transfer and Registry

Isaac Coffie[1] and Martin Saint[1,2(✉)]

[1] Department of Information and Communications Technology,
Carnegie Mellon University Africa, Kigali, Rwanda
`coffie@andrew.cmu.edu, msaint@cmu.edu`
[2] Kigali Collaborative Research Centre, Kigali, Rwanda
`https://www.africa.engineering.cmu.edu, https://www.kcrc.rw`

Abstract. The real estate market in many African countries reflects inefficiency, indiscipline, suspicion, and fraudulent activity. Beyond the direct personal and financial costs, the friction of the existing property transfer process prevents assets from being utilized and valued at their maximum utility. The frustrations and lack of trust affect most real estate markets across Africa, including Ghana, where we will focus the investigation and examples in this paper. Remarkably, the existing Ethereum blockchain platform and smart contract capabilities can be used to bring efficiency, accuracy, trust, and value to the property transfer and registration process without a significant investment in new infrastructure.

We develop a blockchain smart contract appropriate for the continent that provides transparency and traceability of digital assets from initial registration through all subsequent transfers. While blockchain-based land registration systems have been proposed and even implemented in other contexts, they are primarily for land title and deed registration. The system proposed in this paper performs these functions while also allowing the owners to trade in the tokenized assets. While we focus on the technical contribution, we also consider the infrastructure, legal, financial, and cultural factors relevant to designing a land registry solution for a developing country.

While we focus on the case of Ghana, our solution is applicable anywhere and is particularly appropriate for Africa because it does not require any new infrastructure. A similar approach may be taken for a variety of e-government services such as digital identity management and online certificate management.

Keywords: Blockchain 2.0 · Smart contract · Ethereum · Digital assets · e-infrastructure · e-government · Land title · Land registry

---

© ICST Institute for Computer Sciences, Social Informatics and Telecommunications Engineering 2021
Published by Springer Nature Switzerland AG 2021. All Rights Reserved
R. Zitouni et al. (Eds.): AFRICOMM 2020, LNICST 361, pp. 234–252, 2021.
https://doi.org/10.1007/978-3-030-70572-5_15

1   Introduction

Holding productive assets such as properties and buildings comes with economic and societal benefits. Financially, assets contribute to a productive economy, generate revenue, and are useful as collateral for bank loans or other transactions. However, the asset benefits are only fully realizable with the details of ownership adequately documented and managed. Credible asset record management requires a system where the asset details accurately reflect the legal owner and permit an efficient and trustworthy transfer of ownership rights.

In Ghana, ownership of assets, particularly land and buildings, is acquired and transferred according to the Land Title Registration Act, 1986 (PNDCL 152), and the Land Registry Act, 1962 (Act 122) [1]. Besides these legal systems, traditional chiefs and local governments in Ghana are still active in the distribution and trading of land and buildings due to their role as the primary actors in the customary land tenure system [2,3].

Buying land in Ghana is arguably a complex and rigorous process for a buyer [3]. When buying a land or a building in Ghana, one local authority has cautioned that an investor or a buyer undertake at least four different levels of checks to avoid fraud [1]. Similarly, a paper on land acquisition in Ghana exposes the indiscipline, lack of trustworthy registration authority, and attendant insecurities in buying land, highlighting that it is common to sell a single property to more than one buyer [4]. According to the World Bank, several African countries besides Ghana have inadequate asset management systems [5]. Irregularities aside, even more highly developed countries such as the Republic of Georgia and Sweden are exploring how blockchain technology is useful for greater efficiency, transparency, and accuracy when validating property-related transactions [6].

1.1   The Paper-Based Land Registration System in Ghana

Ghana's asset registration and management process is primarily a paper-based, not digital, system [7]. Paper records, also known as land certificates, are issued to any citizen who registers his or her property with the Lands Commission. This certificate bears the name of the current owner, the date of registration, the buyer, and the Commission's office's official details.

Storage of all registered land information is in a centralized database within the Lands Commission and subsidiary offices. This centralization of land records and issuance of paper-based land certificates has several implications. It makes it difficult for buyers and investors to track the historical records of a property. Also, financial institutions, particularly banks and insurance companies, cannot verify the validity of a land certificate used as collateral security or an asset to be insured. Additionally, a problem in the paper-based system is the ease of fabrication and tampering with the original ownership document, often with the intent to defraud a buyer. As a result of the ease of fabrication of ownership certificates, it is often possible to sell the same asset to more than one buyer, leading to crime, lack of trust in the real estate market, and inefficient use and transfer of assets.

The main problem to be addressed in this project is the issue of preventing illegal selling of the same land or building to more than one person at a time. This problem is akin to preventing *double spending* on a cryptocurrency platform, which is the primary problem solved by the creation of the original blockchain.

1.2 Project Objectives

The objective of this project is to answer the question, "How can we implement a blockchain smart contract solution to bring greater trust, transparency and efficiency to Ghana's land registration system?" This goal is to create a blockchain-enabled smart contract platform that allows users to register, track, and verify a property on a public ledger, achieving provenance and transparency.

Actors involved in this ecosystem include the Lands Commission officials (to register lands officially on decentralized servers), buyers and sellers, the Ethereum blockchain network (to maintain records and verify that a record is unaltered), and third parties like banks and insurance companies (to verify the authenticity of any asset used as collateral security or insurance). Records of physical assets are stored on the blockchain platform, making it easy for the public to verify and validate the authenticity of property ownership. Additionally, there will be a complete history of asset ownership from creation to depletion.

By connecting the Lands Commission, banks, and other financial institutions to a blockchain network, assets more reliably tracked, and transparency and efficiency are improved. The goals of the project are:

- Improve transparency in buying and selling assets.
- Eliminate dependence on middlemen such as brokers and agents, who add cost and friction to the transaction process.
- Protect buyers from being defrauded.

1.3 Scope

This project focuses primarily on the technical implementation of a proposed solution to the issues identified. However, delivery is within the context of Africa's social, regulatory, and economic conditions as a developing continent. In particular, it relies upon the use of the existing Ethereum blockchain infrastructure with services that can be affordably purchased as needed and requiring little additional investment beyond a computer or smartphone and an Internet connection.

2 Background and Other Work

Having a database or platform that keeps track of property ownership would not only provide transparency for government institutions and business organizations but may also have the potential to unlock economic opportunities for citizens [8]. Several countries have developed technological and legal systems to register properties. However, there remain inefficiencies in the registration of assets, especially in the less developed countries. According to the World Bank's Ease of Doing Business score, it takes approximately 51, 107, and 71 days to register a property in sub-Saharan Africa, South Asia, and East Asia, respectively [5]. These statistics highlight the bureaucracies that exist in these economies. Blockchain technologies are emerging as an alternative to traditional methods for the provenance of assets.

Blockchain, which was introduced in 2008 by the pseudonymous Satoshi Nakamoto, is defined as a chain of blocks of transactions stored on a distributed ledger using a peer-to-peer network to provide a tamper-proof history of transactions [9]. Variations of the original blockchain have been created. For instance, the original peer-to-peer network was public and open, but private or permissioned blockchains have emerged where participation in the network is limited to selected or known entities. Cryptocurrencies, such as Bitcoin, are one of the earliest applications of blockchain technology. The invention of Bitcoin created a revolutionary system for digital cash and payments, allowing two or more parties to make transactions without a centralized authority or trusted third party such as a bank or credit card company [10]. The original blockchain, designed to support Bitcoin, allowed a relatively limited set of functions, while some newer blockchains are fully programmable. We base this work on the Ethereum platform, a so-called *blockchain 2.0* application that is Turing-complete and, therefore, able to support any computable function. Blockchain technology is now applicable to a range of disciplines.

One of the most exciting uses of new blockchain technologies is for *smart contracts*. A smart contract, being programmable, can automate and automatically enforce contract provisions. The supply chain industry has made significant efforts to utilize smart contract technology to enable the transfer of digital assets to a recipient upon the fulfillment of the stated contract [11]. For instance, a buyer and seller can electronically sign a smart contract that automatically releases payment to the seller for goods once they are delivered and accepted at the buyer's warehouse. Blockchain technology, and smart contracts, can be used in a wide range of e-governance tasks, such as digital identity management and secure document handling [10]. The implications for transparency and efficiency in e-government provide compelling reasons to continue exploring blockchain applications.

Blockchain applications have been proposed in the land registration system to improve the transfer and registration process. In 2015, the government of Honduras partnered with Factom, a startup company based in Texas, to develop a permanent and verifiable land title using blockchain technology [12]. The goal of this pilot project was to address the poor record-keeping of the Honduran land registration system. In this implementation, a public blockchain ledger remains updated and secure based on traditional blockchain techniques, where the majority of nodes on the network verify transactions and maintain consensus on the state of the ledger [13]. A similar solution has been implemented in India to address what has been called incoherent and inconsistent land title records in the government institutions [14]. Another project was undertaken in the Republic of Georgia. In the early 2000s, buying and selling land in Georgia was not only a long process but also prone to bribery [15]. In April 2016, the government of Georgia piloted with BitFury, a blockchain firm based in San Francisco, to fight corruption and develop a private permissioned blockchain platform that would improve transparency in property-related government transactions [15]. Despite some success, the project has limitations as the blockchain is not integrated with the country's official land title registration application, but rather is an "add-on" service [16].

Early efforts at registering property on a blockchain often used the original Bitcoin blockchain because of its widespread use and large community. However, because the original blockchain was only designed to register Bitcoin transactions, property registration solutions were limited and required creativity. Bitland, based in Ghana and started in 2016, was an early entrant into the blockchain land registration space. They used the original Bitcoin blockchain and a concept called *colored coins* [17]. The Bitcoin blockchain, while limited, allowed small bits of metadata such as title, GPS coordinates, size, and contact address to be encrypted and attached as metadata to Bitcoin digital tokens [17]. Because each Bitcoin digital token is unique, and unique users can use their private key to encrypt the digital token, only users with the private key had access permissions to perform transactions related to a unique digital token [18]. This process is no different from the control and transfer of a Bitcoin. To expand the metaphor, tokens (or coins) were the same in the way that a US dollar bill has the same value as any other dollar bill, but they were unique (or colored, compared to other coins) in that they were identified by a unique token/metadata combination, much like each US dollar bill has a unique serial number. By associating unique property data with a unique token, possession (or private key cryptographic control) of the token represents possession of the physical land or building. However, any user on the Internet can view and track the ownership history of an asset. As with any asset that is not natively digital, this scheme relied on a trusted third party (Bitland) to verify the correspondence between a digital token and a physical property. Bitland has gone on to develop their own Bitshares blockchain network using similar principles and has had some success partnering with the government of Ghana to digitize and record property deeds while also expanding to other countries [19].

Despite having a goal similar to this project and being based in Ghana, our solution takes a different approach by using the Ethereum platform. This approach is cost-effective from an infrastructure standpoint, compared to developing a custom solution due to economies of scale. Bitland issued a custom digital currency (colored coin) called Cadastrals to facilitate transactions on its blockchain platform. Cadastrals are a new digital currency and require the public to subscribe via initial coin offering (ICO). The value of a digital currency is largely dependent on people's trust in the system and is difficult to bootstrap for a newer and relatively under-subscribed coin. Given that blockchains are not well known in Ghana, any complex solution that does not leverage existing infrastructure will face more significant challenges to acceptance, adoption, and credibility. Our solution, rather than creating a new coin infrastructure, leverages Ethereum's blockchain and Ether to facilitate the transfer of digitized assets. The platform is widely used in the blockchain community, tested, and has more comprehensive support and adoption than a proprietary solution.

Bitland has also come to focus more on related services such as drone mapping and ownership verification, and the details of their blockchain implementation are not open.

Many African countries have yet to adopt blockchain technology, despite the benefits that could come with implementing a blockchain-based asset registration system. The work reviewed in this section highlights certain system features that could make adoption more feasible. As mentioned in the Republic of Georgia implementation, they have a standalone application that does not integrate into the national land title registration system. A successful solution must itself be sufficiently understood, transparent, and reliable to integrate with or replace existing systems. Proprietary or boutique solutions, therefore, are less likely to be accepted. The solutions proposed in [12–14, 19] are limited to land deeds and titles registration only. Stated differently, they do not support the trading and transfer of ownership from one user to another directly on their blockchain platform. In *The Mystery of Capital*, Hernando de Soto emphasizes the importance of converting dead assets into live capital [20]. It is only by allowing owners to trade in their digitized assets that the economic value of their assets is fully realized and that these assets can easily move to their highest and best value, uninhibited by the friction and uncertainty of the current system. Lack of a native payment system was identified as a drawback to some existing proposals [15].

Recognizing these gaps, we propose a land transfer, payment, and registration solution that allows users to not only register their physical assets on the worldwide Ethereum platform but also to facilitate trading and transfer of ownership using smart contracts and Ethereum's native digital currency, Ether.

3 Methodology

This section highlights the approach or methodology followed to build the asset-based transaction blockchain system.

3.1 System Design Process

The system design is categorized into two processes: the asset digitization process and the asset transaction process. Explanations of each follow.

Asset Digitization Process. To register an asset on the blockchain, a user submits a valid land certificate or building document to the Lands Commission of Ghana for verification. Since the Lands Commission is the only institution mandated to issue land title certificates in Ghana, no user can submit invalid or fabricated land certificates as the office can easily detect modifications to the original certificate. After successful verification, the asset details are recorded and tokenized on the blockchain as follows.

A new piece of land, a building, or other asset is represented as a digital token on the smart contract. Each token is given a unique address and tagged with metadata such as the GPS of the land or building, size of the property, year built or owned, and other relevant information. The details of the legitimate owner are encrypted using public key infrastructure to provide anonymity. This information is written to the Ethereum blockchain through a smart contract and appended to the previous blocks of transactions. Since the Ethereum blockchain uses a secure hashing algorithm (SHA) to keep track of block pointers and transactions, it is infeasible to fabricate a certificate on the smart contract. This series of activities is shown in Fig. 1.

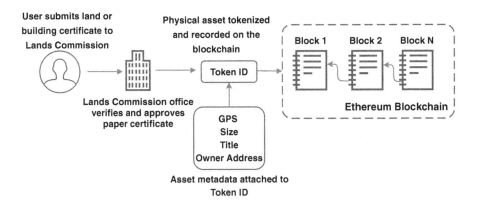

Fig. 1. Tokenization of physical assets on a blockchain.

Asset Transaction Process. After the physical asset is digitally tokenized and published on the blockchain network, the asset owner (or a knowledgeable agent acting on their behalf) can perform future transactions directly on the blockchain. When selling an asset, the smart contract verifies the user is the legitimate owner of the asset through their knowledge of their cryptographic private key. Upon meeting this condition, the owner can securely transfer ownership to a buyer using the buyer's public key. This system is akin to how an email account functions. Anyone can send to an email address because it is (relatively) public, but only the account owner can send from the account because only they know the password.

Upon confirmation of payment from the buyer, ownership details of a token are transferred automatically to the buyer. Payment can take place through the smart contract on the blockchain using Ethereum, again, possibly with the assistance of a knowledgeable agent. Alternatively, the buyer and seller can use traditional payment arrangements, with the seller confirming to the smart contract that payment is satisfactorily received. In the event a user needs a loan from a bank, the blockchain solution will help banks to verify the authenticity and ownership right of the digital asset.

Achieving Consensus. Since our solution leverages the existing Ethereum blockchain infrastructure, our consensus algorithm is the consensus algorithm implemented on Ethereum—Proof of Work (PoW). In the PoW approach, a node competes to be the first to validate transactions on the network and solve a related cryptographic puzzle. The first node to solve the puzzle broadcasts its solution to the other nodes and collects a reward once the other nodes validate the solution. This node subsequently writes the next block of transactions into the blockchain ledger.

There is growing concern regarding the amount of energy expended by nodes to solve the cryptographic puzzle. There is also concern that the massive computing power required compete on the network concentrates the verification and reward, or mining, process, in the hands of a relatively few mining pools. Ethereum is responding to this concern by making a gradual shift from PoW to a newer consensus algorithm called Proof of Stake (PoS). Our solution will take advantage of future developments in the consensus algorithm process without the cost or risk of trying to independently develop an alternative.

Storage of Metadata Chaining Mechanism. We also considered the trade-offs between on-chain and off-chain storage of information, including the limitations of data stored on the blockchain and the cost of executing or committing a transaction. As we aim to develop a cost-effective solution, off-chain storage is the more economical approach given the current capabilities of the Ethereum ecosystem. Instead of converting a hard copy land certificate into a digital copy and saving it directly on to the blockchain, we instead transfer only the essential details that guarantee proof or identification of an asset. These details, such as a hash of the actual document contents, are entered into a smart contract, bundled into a data type, and hashed and stored on the Ethereum blockchain. This approach is cost-effective as it requires less on-chain storage that must be replicated to all nodes participating in the network. Ethereum developers are actively pursuing more economical methods of Ethereum data storage, and we expect to be able to take advantage of future progress.

4   Implementation

This section discusses the implementation of the proposed blockchain digital asset registration system. The architecture of the blockchain system is modelled using the concept of a private permissioned blockchain, where anyone can freely participate on the platform, but only selected nodes are granted the privilege to verify transactions and write them into the ledger. Public blockchains are more common on the Ethereum platform, but permissioned blockchains are supported. Either approach would work from a technical standpoint, but we model a permissioned chain because it is likely more palatable to regulatory authorities.

4.1   The Nodes

The nodes are the actors who are directly or indirectly involved in a blockchain transaction. The identified nodes in the project include:

- Lands Commission: The Lands Commission is the government agency responsible for issuing land certificates to the public. These nodes are given the privilege to validate and verify land certificates presented for registration.
- Buyers and Sellers: These are the direct actors of the platform. The seller can transfer his or her property to the buyer. Also, the buyer can buy an asset and make payment using digital currency.
- Banks: The banks are given permission to deny or approve digital asset transactions in which they have an interest once an asset is created on the blockchain platform. Banks, therefore, have information about the status of assets and their ownership.

4.2   Smart Contracts

The back end code of the blockchain is developed using the Solidity programming language as it supports the creation of smart contracts. The contract classes are as follows.

User Account Contract. This contract contains information about all the buyers and sellers on the blockchain. The properties of this contract are shown in a class diagram in Fig. 2.

Fig. 2. User account class diagram.

In addition to the user account class diagram, below is a code snippet showing the details of the contract in Solidity.

Listing 1.1. User Account Contract

```solidity
contract UserAccount {

        enum Role {User, Institution, LandOfficial}
        event newUserAdded(uint id, address user_address);

        //creates a structure for a user object
        struct User{
                string username;
                address owner;
                Role userRole;
        }
}
```

Asset Contract. This contract will handle all new property registrations. It has the properties and operations shown in Fig. 3.

Fig. 3. Asset class diagram.

Similarly, we show the data structure for the building object in the below code snippet.

Listing 1.2. Asset Contract

```
//structure for a building
        struct Building {
            string size;
            address owner;
            uint token_id;
            uint price;
            string gps;
            string details;
            uint num_rooms;
            uint date_created;
        }
```

Transaction Contract. This contract is the main entry point of interaction between all the nodes identified above. This contract allows users to transfer ownership from one person to another upon confirmation of successful payment, or direct payment in Ether in the Ethereum network, Fig. 4. Likewise, we show a snippet of a constraint that permits digitized assets to be transferred only after receiving the full payment.

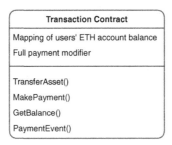

Fig. 4. Transaction class diagram.

Listing 1.3. Full Payment Modifier

```
contract Transaction is Asset{

    //track of the amount of money (Ether) a user has
    mapping(address => uint) private userBalanceMap;

    //a modifier to ensure buyer has made full payment
    modifier fullPayment(uint token_id, uint asset_type,
    uint price)

    {
    uint asset_price = getPrice(token_id, asset_type);
    require( asset_price <= price );
    _;
    }
```

List of Tools and Technologies. The following tools, frameworks and programming language were used to develop the platform:

- MetaMask Ethereum Wallet: This add-in was installed on Google Chrome to allow our web browser to connect to a blockchain network.
- Remix: This is an online editor for writing and managing smart contracts using Solidity.
- Solidity: The programming language used to develop a smart contract. Our Solidity code is available at https://github.com/PeyGis/LandReco.

Simulation Environment. We conducted our simulations on Remix, an online Ethereum and smart contract management platform that enables blockchain developers to develop, test, and deploy smart contract solution on the Ethereum network. We also used the smart contract programming language Solidity to implement our land registry and transfer smart contract solution.

Our simulations used the native Ether payment module available in Solidity. Another option is to explore the use of ERC-721 third-party payment tokens. Unlike most cryptocurrencies, each ERC-721 token is unique and is valued based upon the uniqueness or rarity. Interestingly, they have been used to own and transfer virtual land in the Decentraland virtual world and the related integration of crypto-collectibles in the integration of Cryptokitties and Decentraland.

5   Results and Discussion

We proposed using a blockchain-based asset registration system in Ghana to bring trust and transparency to the system. This section shows how it was implemented.

5.1   How Has the Project Addressed the Problem?

Asset Tokenization. Using public key infrastructure and smart contracts, we found that we could digitize physical assets on a blockchain using a unique token for each asset. Physical assets, ownership, and mapping between physical and digital are verified by integrating a trusted third party into the ecosystem. In this case, Ghana's Lands Commission office. The involvement of a trusted third party helps to validate and verify any document or asset. The asset tokenizing process for registering a land or building on the blockchain network is shown in Fig. 5.

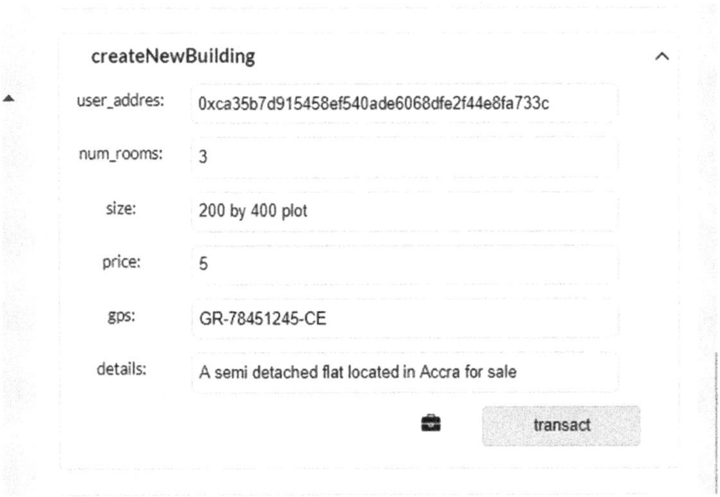

Fig. 5. Creating a new building user interface.

After the property has been created, a unique token is generated for the asset with its associated metadata. This result is shown in Fig. 6.

Asset Transaction. Our simulations show that by digitizing or tokenizing physical assets, a seller cannot sell the same property to more than one buyer, addressing the issue of double selling of an asset. Thus, after a buyer makes a payment for an asset, the asset's ownership details are transferred to the buyer's public key, preventing the seller from selling the same property to a different buyer. Figure 7 shows a simulation of a buyer purchasing an asset and making a payment with Ether cryptocurrency.

The result of this operation is shown in Fig. 8. This operation demonstrates that we could trade or transfer ownership from one user to another on a blockchain platform.

Since the smart contract dynamically transfers ownership rights from one user to another, we mitigate the issue of an asset owner selling the same property to more than one buyer. Figure 9 shows the details of the asset after the makePayment() transaction.

As shown in Fig. 9, the details of the asset (especially the owner's address) have been changed from 0xCA...733c to 0x4B...D2dB. As a result of this oper-

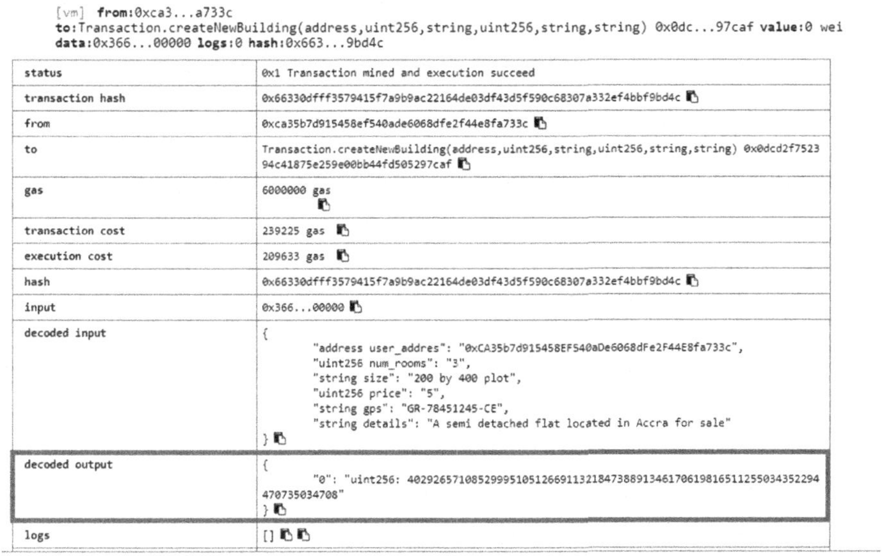

[vm] **from:**0xca3...a733c
to: Transaction.createNewBuilding(address,uint256,string,uint256,string,string) 0x0dc...97caf **value:**0 wei
data:0x366...00000 **logs:**0 **hash:**0x663...9bd4c

status	0x1 Transaction mined and execution succeed
transaction hash	0x66330dfff3579415f7a9b9ac22164de03df43d5f590c68307a332ef4bbf9bd4c
from	0xca35b7d915458ef540ade6068dfe2f44e8fa733c
to	Transaction.createNewBuilding(address,uint256,string,uint256,string,string) 0x0dcd2f7523 94c41875e259e00bb44fd505297caf
gas	6000000 gas
transaction cost	239225 gas
execution cost	209633 gas
hash	0x66330dfff3579415f7a9b9ac22164de03df43d5f590c68307a332ef4bbf9bd4c
input	0x366...00000

decoded input	{
	        "address user_addres": "0xCA35b7d915458EF540aDe6068dFe2F44E8fa733c",
	        "uint256 num_rooms": "3",
	        "string size": "200 by 400 plot",
	        "uint256 price": "5",
	        "string gps": "GR-78451245-CE",
	        "string details": "A semi detached flat located in Accra for sale"
	}

decoded output	{
	        "0": "uint256: 40292657108529995105126691132184738891346170619816511255034352294 470735034708"
	}

logs	[]

Fig. 6. Asset token successfully generated.

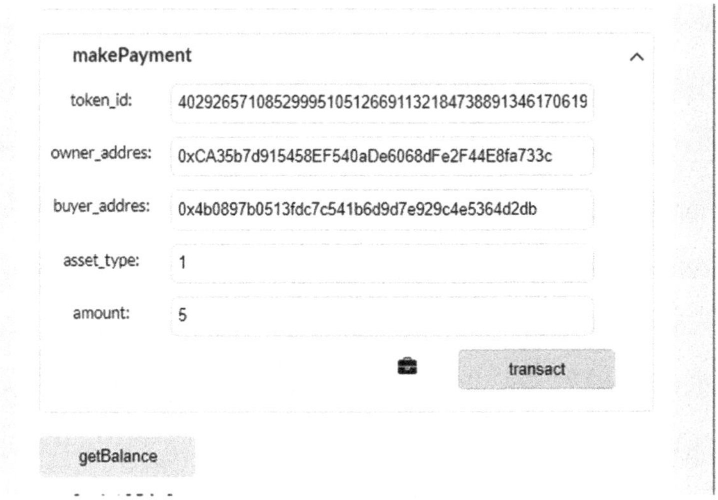

Fig. 7. User making payment for an asset.

status	0x1 Transaction mined and execution succeed
transaction hash	0x89d8b0e4d7a7b328e497fb460248360f6b2f29f93d898b4dfee9e56ae1f0dae9
from	0x4b0897b0513fdc7c541b6d9d7e929c4e5364d2db
to	Transaction.makePayment(uint256,address,address,uint256,uint256) 0x0dcd2f752394c41875e25 9e00bb44fd505297caf
gas	6000000 gas
transaction cost	73442 gas
execution cost	46794 gas
hash	0x89d8b0e4d7a7b328e497fb460248360f6b2f29f93d898b4dfee9e56ae1f0dae9
input	0x67f...00005

decoded input	{
	 "uint256 token_id": "402926571085299951051266911321847388913461706198165112550 352294470735034708",
	 "address owner_addres": "0xCA35b7d915458EF540aDe6068dFe2F44E8fa733c",
	 "address buyer_addres": "0x4B0897b0513fdC7C54186d9D7E929C4e5364D2dB",
	 "uint256 asset_type": "1",
	 "uint256 amount": "5"
	 }

decoded output	{
	 "0": "bool: true"
	 }

logs	[{ "from": "0x0dcd2f752394c41875e259e00bb44fd505297caf", "topic": "0x05666d9673471b289a16b2df77f162a627749ed621e9b78ffedcb38884f4 64db", "event": "PaymentEvent",

Fig. 8. Successful payment receipt.

Fig. 9. Property details after payment.

```
[vm]  from:0x583...40225 to:Transaction.makePayment(uint256,address,address,uint256,uint256) 0x0dc...97<
     value:0 wei data:0x67f...00005 logs:0 hash:0xd47...8106d
```

status	0x1 Transaction mined and execution succeed
transaction hash	0xd478eca0dc9a7b85ecc6c7df7ba7df8327a4fcd887f36c2fba99d42fb768106d 📋
from	0x583031d1113ad414f02576bd6afabfb302140225 📋
to	Transaction.makePayment(uint256,address,address,uint256,uint256) 0x0dcd2f752394c41875e25 9e00bb44fd505297caf 📋
gas	6000000 gas 📋
transaction cost	36707 gas 📋
execution cost	10059 gas 📋
hash	0xd478eca0dc9a7b85ecc6c7df7ba7df8327a4fcd887f36c2fba99d42fb768106d 📋
input	0x67f...00005 📋
decoded input	{ "uint256 token_id": "4029265710852999510512669113218473889134617061981651125503435229447035034708", "address owner_addres": "0xCA35b7d915458EF540aDe6068dFe2F44E8fa733c", "address buyer_addres": "0x583031D1113aD414F02576BD6afaBfb302140225", "uint256 asset_type": "1", "uint256 amount": "5" } 📋
decoded output	{ "0": "bool: false" } 📋
logs	[] 📋📋

Fig. 10. Unsuccessful payment request.

ation, 0xCA...733c can no longer sell or receive payment from this asset. The function above is also made available for banking institutions to validate assets.

The simulation in Fig. 10 shows an unsuccessful transaction for a payment made from 0x58...0225 to 0xCA...733c. This is because 0xCA...733c no longer has control over the asset.

From these simulations, we show that by digitizing physical assets on a blockchain network, we can transfer ownership from one user to another and prevent double-selling of the asset.

5.2 Non-technical Considerations

Legal System. Although proponents of blockchain and smart contracts envision a world where the "code is the law" [12], this requires an evolution of the legal landscape. In the event of a breach of contract, the smart contract must have a mechanism that addresses disputes. It is unlikely that all matters can be settled automatically by the contract, however, and at some point, adjudication of a dispute is likely to enter the traditional legal system. Therefore, legal policies will need to be amended to resolve conflicts and misunderstandings that may arise from a smart contract. "Code as law" may require "coders as lawyers."

Ghana's Data Privacy Act. Given that our proof-of-concept solution is based in Ghana, we considered the laws that govern data access and treatment. In 2012, the Parliament of the Republic of Ghana enacted The Data Protection Act 2012 to protect the privacy of individual's data. One of the critical principles enlisted in this Act is accountability and data security safeguards. Since our proposed solution integrates the land commission to verify paper certificates, we trust that the data provided on our platform is accurate and authentic. The smart contract solution, built on top of the blockchain infrastructure, can provide the level of consistency, security, and privacy required by the Act.

Mapping of Physical Property to Digital Property. The digitalization of physical assets is one means to prevent selling the same asset to unwitting third parties. This correspondence requires accurate mapping of physical assets to digital tokens through a trusted third party. There must also be a mechanism to identify and correct discrepancies or deal with the destruction of an asset.

Context and Practical Concerns. Users will be unfamiliar with Ethereum, blockchain, cryptocurrencies, and the complexity of their functioning and transfer. Use of the Ethereum platform for transactions also requires some minimal fees. A knowledgeable agent will likely be required to assist in facilitating transactions. Many aspects of the traditional property transfer process are complicated and unfamiliar to buyers and sellers, however, and the use of specialized escrow or transfer agents is a well-established custom.

The primary payment method proposed is Ethereum's native Ether cryptocurrency. This method integrates well with the platform and smart contracts. Cryptocurrency payments can be another function undertaken by the escrow agent, as well as transfers that involve traditional payment methods. Ethereum fees can be collected as part of the usual transfer process, similar to fees paid for other services such as notarization. Ethereum fees may also reduce or replace other property registration fees.

Use of the Ethereum platform also depends upon a stable Internet connection, which is not available to many individuals in developing countries. Again, this is an area where an escrow agent can be useful. Many African countries also have district offices where people can conduct government and e-government business in person.

Security of Ethereum and Smart Contracts. The Bitcoin and Ethereum blockchain platforms are grounded on decentralization and the premise that no one entity, or node, can exercise full control over the network. Nodes maximize their chance of earning a reward by participating correctly in verifying transactions, attempting to solve the cryptographic puzzle, and verifying the work of their peers. As there are no shortcuts to solving the cryptographic puzzle and all solutions are peer-verified, there is little incentive to attack the network or propose illegitimate transactions or solutions. Doing so successfully is computationally infeasible unless a malicious entity controls more than 51% of the computing power on the network. Given the decentralized design of the Ethereum network, this is also considered infeasible.

Besides the Ethereum platform's overall security, decentralized apps (DApps) such as smart contracts provide internal security mechanisms. For instance, while developing our smart contract in Solidity, we undertook programming practices to deter successful DApp attacks. Some of the design considerations included using private versus public access, internal versus external, using modifiers to restrict access to a function, and using read-only decorators to prevent unauthorized users from writing or hijacking the contract. These practices enhance the security of the smart contract.

6   Conclusion

Our simulation shows that it is possible to use a well-established open blockchain platform, Ethereum, to create a land transfer, payment, and registration system. Our approach requires little in the way of new blockchain infrastructure beyond writing the appropriate smart contract code. The use of smart contracts creates trust in the transfer process, is efficient, and helps to reduce fraud and corruption.

While we focus on the case of Ghana for details of their current process, our solution is applicable anywhere and is particularly appropriate for Africa because it does not require any new infrastructure. A similar approach may be taken for a variety of e-government services beyond land registration.

References

1. Mate-Kole, E.: What you need to know about land ownership in Ghana, 22 November 2018. https://www.myjoyonline.com/opinion/what-you-need-to-know-about-land-ownership-in-ghana/. Accessed 26 Jan 2020
2. Yeboah, E., Shaw, D.: Customary land tenure practices in Ghana: examining the relationship with land-use planning delivery. Int. Dev. Plann. Rev. **35**(1), 21–39 (2013). https://doi.org/10.3828/idpr.2013.3
3. Antwi-Bediako, R.: Chiefs and nexus of challenges in land deals: an insight into blame perspectives, exonerating chiefs during and after Jatropha investment in Ghana. Cogent Soc. Sci. **4**(1), 1456795 (2018). https://doi.org/10.1080/23311886.2018.1456795
4. Gyamera, E.A., Duncan, E.E., Kuma, J.S.Y., Arko-Adjei, A.: Land acquisition in Ghana; dealing with the challenges and the way forward. J. Agric. Econ. Extension Rural Dev. **6**(1), 664–672 (2018). http://springjournals.net/full-articles/pringjournals.netjaeerdarticlesindex=14gyameraetal.pdf?view=inline
5. The World Bank Group: Registering property, 30 May 2019. https://www.doingbusiness.org/en/data/exploretopics/registering-property. Accessed 02 Feb 2020
6. Shin, L.: The first government to secure land titles on the Bitcoin blockchain expands project. Forbes. Accessed 7 Feb 2017
7. Ehwi, R.J., Asante, L.A.: Ex-post analysis of land title registration in Ghana since 2008 merger: Accra Lands Commision in perspective. SAGE Open **6**(2), 215824401664335 (2016). https://doi.org/10.1177/2158244016643351

8. Carter, L., Ubacht, J.: Blockchain applications in government. In: Proceedings of the 19th Annual International Conference on Digital Government Research: Governance in the Data Age, pp. 1–2, No. 126 in dg.o 2018. Association for Computing Machinery, New York (2018). https://doi.org/10.1145/3209281.3209329

9. Nakamoto, S.: Bitcoin: a peer-to-peer electronic cash system (2008). https://bitcoin.org/bitcoin.pdf. Accessed 01 Feb 2020

10. Ølnes, S., Jansen, A.: Blockchain technology as s support infrastructure in e-government. In: Janssen, M., et al. (eds.) EGOV 2017. LNCS, vol. 10428, pp. 215–227. Springer, Cham (2017). https://doi.org/10.1007/978-3-319-64677-0_18

11. Hasan, H.R., Salah, K.: Proof of delivery of digital assets using blockchain and smart contracts. IEEE Access **6**, 65439–65448 (2018). https://doi.org/10.1109/ACCESS.2018.2876971

12. Lemieux, V.L.: Evaluating the use of blockchain in land transactions: an archival science perspective. Eur. Property Law J. **6**(3), 392–440 (2017). https://doi.org/10.1515/eplj-2017-0019

13. Cong, L.W., He, Z.: Blockchain disruption and smart contracts. Rev. Financ. Stud. **32**(5), 1754–1797 (2019). https://doi.org/10.1093/rfs/hhz007

14. Thakur, V., Doja, M.N., Dwivedi, Y.K., Ahmad, T., Khadanga, G.: Land records on blockchain for implementation of land titling in India. Int. J. Inf. Manag. **52**, 101940 (2020). https://doi.org/10.1016/j.ijinfomgt.2019.04.013

15. Benbunan-Fich, R., Castellanos, A.: Digitization of land records: from paper to blockchain. In: 39th International Conference on Information Systems (2018)

16. Lazuashvili, N., Norta, A., Draheim, D.: Integration of blockchain technology into a land registration system for immutable traceability: a casestudy of Georgia. In: Di Ciccio, C., et al. (eds.) BPM 2019. LNBIP, vol. 361, pp. 219–233. Springer, Cham (2019). https://doi.org/10.1007/978-3-030-30429-4_15

17. Anand, A., McKibbin, M., Pichel, F.: Colored coins: bitcoin, blockchain, and land administration. Annual World Bank Conference on Land and Poverty (2016). https://pdfs.semanticscholar.org/d23e/3b0fecc9f24900a3e3dd4d31dda934c6a88d.pdf

18. Thomas, R.: Blockchain's incompatibility for use as a land registry: issues of definition, feasibility and risk. Eur. Property Law J. **6**(3), 361–390 (2017). https://doi.org/10.1515/eplj-2017-0021

19. Konashevych, O.: Constraints and benefits of the blockchain use for real estate and property rights. J. Property Plann. Environ. Law (2020). https://doi.org/10.2139/ssrn.3520270

20. de Soto, H.: The Mystery of Capital: Why Capitalism Triumphs in the West and Fails Everywhere Else. Basic Books, New York (2000)

Normalized Comparison Method for Finding the Most Efficient DSS Code

Natasa Paunkoska (Dimoska)[1]([✉]), Ninoslav Marina[1], and Weiler Finamore[2]

[1] University of Information Science and Technology (UIST) "St. Paul the Apostle", Ohrid, North Macedonia
natasa.paunkoska@uist.edu.mk, ninoslav.marina@gmail.com
[2] Federal University of Juiz de Fora (UFJF), Juiz de Fora, Brazil
weilerfinamore44@gmail.com

Abstract. Big data is large volume of data produced on a daily basis. Distributed storage systems (DSS) is environment that handles, manages and stores those data. The main drawbacks are the lack of system storage capacity, the network device failures that can appear anytime, on time data processing and the system efficiency. All above mentioned issues can be overcome by applying different coding techniques for data distribution. Till this moment many coding schemes are proposed by the researchers. Determining the most efficient code for usage is still a tricky question, which yields an adequate comparison strategy for code selection. The basic Dimakis comparison method offers analysis between the codes regarding the parameters storage per node and download bandwidth to be repair one node. Total comparison method includes in the analysis the total number of nodes in the system together with the overall storage and total downloaded bandwidth in the repair process, with notation that the file size for all codes must be same. In this paper, we are proposing new method for comparison, called Normalized, that enables consideration of broader spectrum of parameters and not necessarily the same file size of the proposed codes.

Keywords: Comparison methods · Distributed storage systems (DSS) · Efficient DSS system · Reconstruction process · Repair process

1 Introduction

Cloud data centers are very important thread for data management, especially of the 'Big Data' production. These centers acts as distributed storage systems (DSS). DSS is network of many server (nodes) interconnected among them that stores large number of data, keeps the data reliable and safe, and enables fast retrieval of the message for the user. The main function, data storage, is performed as the information (file), of size $|\mathcal{F}|$ bytes, is divided into smaller pieces and then each piece is distributed on physically separated device (node) in the network. The possibility for network/device failure that guarantee data reliability is provided by adding redundancy. Currently, most of the systems use

© ICST Institute for Computer Sciences, Social Informatics and Telecommunications Engineering 2021
Published by Springer Nature Switzerland AG 2021. All Rights Reserved
R. Zitouni et al. (Eds.): AFRICOMM 2020, LNICST 361, pp. 253–268, 2021.
https://doi.org/10.1007/978-3-030-70572-5_16

repetition code for redundancy, i.e, two more copies of each file piece are stored in different locations (nodes). The consequence of this technique is the storage overhead.

Introducing the Maximum Distance Separable (MDS) codes adapted for DSS [1–4] deals the information storage problem by making optimal storage vs. reliability data trade-off. Erasure codes are also interesting for the researchers [5–10]. They are efficient in decreasing the overall system storage. The codes function in a manner that they are taking the entire message $\mathcal{F}$ of size $|\mathcal{F}| = LK$ and parses in blocks of size K. L is number of info-words and K number of symbols within one info-word to be distributed/stored in the DSS system. Then each block K is divided into smaller chunks, with size α, and each chunk is stored in one of the n nodes in the network. The chunk is calculated as $\alpha = \frac{K}{k}$, where k is number of info symbols for the encoding/storage process. Knowing that the DSS system is defined as network of n nodes (servers), the parameters n and k depends of the code $[n, k]$ chosen for data storage. Later, the value $k(k < n)$ is used for determining the number of nodes to which the Data collector (DC) connects in order to retrieve the original stored information. This process in a sense of DSS is known as *reconstruction*.

Another issue in the DSS network is a node failure and losing everything stored on it. In this situation if node i fails, a new node i' (newcomer) that will replace the failed one is programmed to connect to any k surviving nodes, to download from them everything what is stored, by α amount of data, and by proper computation to restore the lost information. This process is known as *repair*. For completing of this process, a lot of unnecessary data going to be downloaded and just few of them will be used in the computations. This means inefficiently high download repair bandwidth that the erasure codes can not handle with.

Interesting solution that deals this problem is introduced by Dimakis et al. [11,12]. There, the authors offer new kind of codes known as regenerating. The code characterization is done by the primary parameters $[n, k, d]$ and secondary parameters $[\alpha, \beta, K]$. The meaning of n, k and α is same as the one mentioned above, $d(d \geq k)$ shows the number of nodes that need to be contacted to be finish the repair process and $\beta(\beta < \alpha)$ is the amount of data downloaded from those d nodes. Precisely, during the *repair process*, a newcomer contacts d alive nodes and downloads from them β quantity of information, unlike in erasure codes, where contacts k nodes and downloads from there everything what is stored α. Thus, the *repair bandwidth* is $\gamma = d\beta$ symbols and is used to recover what was lost. Some researches that are based on the regenerating codes can be found in [13–17].

Till now, there are lot of code constructions proposed that will work efficiently in DSSs. How to choose which one performs the best, is an open question in this area. The simplest solution is to compare the codes. But, finding a suitable comparison method to do that is a problem. The first attempt is made by Dimakis et al. in [12]. Their method use two parameters for comparison, either will be measured by the storage per node, α, or repair bandwidth for one node, $d\beta$.

Later, in [18] is introduced the Total method that extends the comparison to a total system storage and a total repair bandwidth for more failed nodes. In this paper, we are proposing new method for comparison, called Normalized, that gives more realistic output than the existing ones. The proposal is upgrade of the Total concept and the normalization is done over the file size. This allows codes comparison with different file size, in contrast to the others where the file size must be the same. The validity and efficiency of our approach is done through examples, where we compare four various codes (Regenerating, Repetition, Reed-Solomon based DSS and Clay) using the three above mentioned methods.

The paper is organized as follows, in Sect. 2 are given the theorems that describe the trade-off curves of the Dimakis, Total and the new proposed comparison method. In Sect. 3 is given description of the codes involved in the comparison procedures. Section 4 analysis the results from the comparison processes and Sect. 5 concludes the paper.

2   Trade-Off Curve for DSS

Coding for DSS is a process that first parses the input-string $\mathcal{F}$, of size $|\mathcal{F}|$, into L info-words $\underline{u}^{[\ell]}$ each K symbols (q-ary symbols) long. Next, the data from each info-word $\underline{u}$ (focusing on one block, thus drop the index ℓ) is mapped into a code-matrix $\underline{C}$ of dimensions $n \times \alpha$,

$$
\underline{C} = \begin{pmatrix} \underline{C}_1 \\ \vdots \\ \underline{C}_i \\ \vdots \\ \underline{C}_n \end{pmatrix},
\tag{1}
$$

where the content of each $\underline{C}$ row is stored in one of the n nodes in the network.

In general the encoder is a vector function, $\underline{\mathcal{E}} = (\mathcal{E}_1 \ldots \mathcal{E}_i \ldots \mathcal{E}_n)$ which yields the code-matrix $\underline{C} = \mathcal{E}(\underline{u})$. Thus, $R = \frac{k}{\alpha n}$ is the code rate. The reconstruction process happens when the data collector (DC) wants to reconstruct the original information $\mathcal{F}$ stored in the system. During this process, the DC connects to any $k(n > k \leq d)$ nodes and downloads from them by α quantity of symbols. Overall collects $k\alpha$ data and from them obtains the entire original message of size $|\mathcal{F}| = LK \log_2 q$ bytes. Mathematically, the reconstruction process can be described as

$$
\underline{u} = \mathcal{D}(\underline{C}_{i_1} \ldots \underline{C}_{i_\ell} \ldots \underline{C}_{i_k}).
$$

The repair process happens when a node fails, and the trigger is prompted by a new node (newcomer), which connects to $d(n - 1 \geq d \geq k)$ alive nodes in the network and downloads from them by $\beta(\beta \leq \alpha)$ symbols. The total downloaded bandwidth is $\gamma = \beta d$ symbols that is used to recover the lost data previously stored in the failed node. In other words

$$
\underline{u} = \mathcal{R}(\underline{C}_{j_1} \ldots \underline{C}_{j_\ell} \ldots \underline{C}_{j_d}).
$$

Authors in [11] proved that code with parameters (k, d, α, β) of a q-ary regenerating code that reliably stores one info-word of size K must satisfy the following condition

$$K \leq \sum_{i=0}^{k-1} \min \{\alpha, (d-i)\beta\}. \tag{2}$$

The download-bandwidth and the amount of storage can not be minimized in a same time, therefore, a tradeoff between the repair bandwidth, $\gamma = d\beta$, and the storage per node, α, exists and is made explicit in Theorem 1.

Theorem 1 (Storage-Bandwidth Tradeoff curve [11]). *For any value $\alpha \geq \alpha^*(n, k, d, \gamma)$, the points $(n, k, d, \alpha, \gamma)$ are feasible, and linear network codes suffice to achieve them. It is information theoretically impossible to achieve points with $\alpha < \alpha^*(n, k, d, \gamma)$. The threshold function $\alpha^*(n, k, d, \gamma)$ is the following:*

$$\alpha^*(n, k, d, \gamma) = \begin{cases} \frac{K}{k} & \gamma \in [f(0), +\infty] \\ \frac{K - g(i)\gamma}{k-i} & \gamma \in [f(i), +f(i-1)] \end{cases} \tag{3}$$

where

$$f(i) \triangleq \frac{2Kd}{(2k-i-1)i + 2k(d-k+1)}, \tag{4}$$

$$g(i) \triangleq \frac{(2d-2k+i+1)i}{2d}. \tag{5}$$

where $d \leq n-1$. ♦

The storage-bandwidth tradeoff theorem in [11], here refer as Dimakis, establishes that no code exists with pairs of values that are under this curve.

In [18] authors made modification of the previous Dimakis trade-off curve and relates the total storage in the system and the total bandwidth needed for the repair process. Definition of this trade-off curve is given in following.

Theorem 2 (Total Comparison [18]). *Let $(n, K, k, d, \alpha, \beta)$, when $d \leq n-1$, be a set of parameters for a DSS code. The Total-downloaded-data and the Total-storage-data trade-off curve $S^{total}(B^{total})$ joining the points $(B_i^{total}, S_i^{total})$ $i \in \{0, \ldots, k-1\}$ is given by*

$$B_i^{total} = \frac{2dKL}{(2k-i-1)i + 2k(d-k+1)}, \tag{6}$$

$$S_i^{total} = \frac{n}{k-i}(KL - g_i' B_i^{total}), \tag{7}$$

in which

$$g_i' = \frac{(2d-2k+i+1)i}{2d}, \tag{8}$$

is, by definition, the Total Storage-Bandwidth Trade Off Curve *for codes with the given set of parameters.*   ♦

Proof. The Total comparison extends the Theorem 1 idea introducing wider picture of the DSS system. Precisely, takes care not only on one-node repair bandwidth, $\gamma = d\beta$, and storage per node, α, but also counts the number of nodes in the DSS and potentially the necessity of having more nodes for repairing. Thus, modifying Eq. (4), (3) and (5) by multiplying with L and Ln, accordingly, are obtained (6) and (7).

Theorem 3 (Total Storage-Bandwidth Feasible Region). *A DSS code with parameters* $(n, K, k, d, \alpha, \beta)$, $d \leq n - 1$, *has Total Bandwidth,* $t_\beta = \beta dL \log_2 q$, *and Total Storage,* $t_\alpha = \alpha nL \log_2 q$, *such that*

$$t_\alpha \geq S^{total}(t_\beta) \quad \text{if } B_{k-1}^{total} \leq t_\beta \leq B_0^{total} \tag{9}$$

$$t_\alpha \geq S^{total}(B_0^{total}) \quad \text{if } t_\beta \geq B_0^{total} \tag{10}$$

no DSS code exists with $t_\beta < B_{k-1}^{total}$.   ♦

Proof. One node repair bandwidth is defined as number of nodes, d, contacted during the repair process of one failed node and downloaded from them by β quantity of information, or $\gamma = d\beta$. Storage per node, α, is the amount of data stored on each node in the DSS. The Total concept considers also all nodes in the system, the info-word, file size and all potential simultaneously failed nodes. So, calculating now the overall DSS storage the obtained Total Storage is $\alpha nL \log_2 q$, and the whole downloaded bandwidth or Total bandwidth becomes $\beta dL \log_2 q$. The total storage-bandwidth tradeoff theorem establishes that no code exists with pairs of values (t_α, t_γ) that are under the curve S^{total} versus B^{total}, defined with Theorem 2. Because those two values are interdependent, means that the Total Storage value must be above each point that lies on the curve with correspondence to the Total Bandwidth.

In this paper, the main contribution is introduction of new comparison method. The proposed method is a variation of both the storage-bandwidth tradeoff theorem and total storage-total downloaded data tradeoff theorems. A similar tradeoff curve is established relating the quantities Normalized Storage and Normalized Download-bandwidth, defined as follows.

Definition 1 (Normalized Storage). *Let $\mathcal{F}$ be a file to be stored in a Distributed Storage System. The ratio of the total number of bytes stored on n nodes of the network, $\alpha nL \log_2 q$, to the size of the file, $|\mathcal{F}| = LK \log_2 q$ (bytes), or, in other words,*

$$\eta_\alpha \triangleq \frac{\alpha nL \log_2 q}{LK \log_2 q} = \frac{\alpha n}{K} \tag{11}$$

is defined as Normalized Storage.   ♦

Proof. Normalizing the Total Storage, $t_\alpha = \alpha n L \log_2 q$, over the file size, $|\mathcal{F}| = LK \log_2 q$, is obtained Eq. (11).

Definition 2 (Normalized Download-bandwidth). *Let $\mathcal{F}$ be a file to be stored in a Distributed Storage System. The ratio of the total number of bytes downloaded from d nodes of the network (when the procedure to repair one node out of the n nodes is activated), $\beta d L \log_2 q$, to the size of the file, $|\mathcal{F}| = LK \log_2 q$ (bytes), or, in other words,*

$$\eta_\beta \triangleq \frac{\beta d L \log_2 q}{LK \log_2 q} = \frac{\beta d}{K} \tag{12}$$

is defined as Normalized Download-bandwidth.   ◆

Proof. Normalizing the Total Bandwith, $t_\beta = \beta d L \log_2 q$, over the file size, $|\mathcal{F}| = LK \log_2 q$, is obtained Eq. (12).

The trade-off function relating S^{nor} (the normalized storage) and B^{nor} (the normalized bandwidth) is described by the theorem stated next.

Theorem 4 (Normalized Storage-Bandwidth Tradeoff curve). *Let a set of parameters for a DSS code be $(n, K, k, d, \alpha, \beta)$, when $d \leq n-1$. The piecewise linear curve $S^{nor}(B^{nor})$ joining the points (B_i^{nor}, S_i^{nor}) $i \in \{0, \ldots, k-1\}$ is given by*

$$B_i^{nor} = \frac{2d}{(2k - i - 1)i + 2k(d - k + 1)}, \tag{13}$$

$$S_i^{nor} = \frac{n}{k - i}(1 - g_i' B_i^{nor}), \tag{14}$$

in which

$$g_i' = \frac{(2d - 2k + i + 1)i}{2d} \tag{15}$$

is, by definition, the Normalized Storage-Bandwidth Trade Off Curve for codes with the given set of parameters.   ◆

Proof. The Normalized comparison extends the Theorem 2 idea by normalizing the outcomes with the number of symbols stored in the system, K, derived form Eq. (11) and (12). Precisely, normalizing Eq. (6) with K is obtained (13) and normalizing Eq. (7) with K is obtained (14).

Theorem 5 (Normalized Storage-Bandwidth Feasible Region). *A DSS code with parameters $(n, K, k, d, \alpha, \beta)$, $d \leq n - 1$, has Normalized Bandwidth, η_β, and Normalized Storage, η_α, such that*

$$\eta_\alpha \geq S^{nor}(\eta_\beta) \quad \text{if } B_{k-1}^{nor} \leq \eta_\beta \leq B_0^{nor} \tag{16}$$

$$\eta_\alpha \geq S^{nor}(B_0^{nor}) \quad \text{if } \eta_\beta \geq B_0^{nor} \tag{17}$$

no DSS code exists with $\eta_\beta < B_{k-1}^{nor}$.   ◆

Proof. Normalized Storage is defined with Eq. (11) and Normalized Bandwidth with (12). The normalized storage-bandwidth tradeoff theorem establishes that no code exists with pairs of values $(\eta_\alpha, \eta_\gamma)$ that are under the curve S^{nor} versus B^{nor}, defined with Theorem 4. Because those two values are interdependent, means that the Normalized Storage value must be above each point that lies on the curve with correspondence to the Normalized Bandwidth.

The main motivation behind Theorem 5 is its ability to allow comparison of diverse DSS coding schemes (having disparate parameters). Let say, if we compare two codes by the storage per node parameter, then the code with smaller storage is better. This approach have unfair output, because for example doesn't care about the overall system storage and in this sense may give worse performance. Hence, the coding scheme comparison based on the normalized-storage versus normalized-bandwidth tradeoff curves is file size independent, unlike Dimakis and Total methods described in Theorem 1 and Theorem 2. To make this point clear we examine and illustrate the quality of the tradeoff curves using three diverse codes. The chosen codes are defined with values as: first one $(n, K, k, d) = (14, 1, 8, 13)$, second $(n, K, k, d) = (10, 1, 6, 9)$ and third $(n, K, k, d) = (15, 2, 10, 14)$. Figure 1 is based on Theorem 1, Fig. 2 on Theorem 2 and Fig. 3 on Theorem 4. The plots give the trade off curves applied on the chosen codes together with their achievable regions.

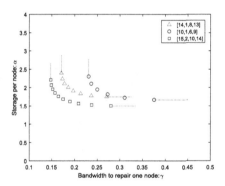

Fig. 1. Trade-off curve Storage-per-node vs. Total-repair-bandwidth for parameters $(n, K, k, d) = (14, 1, 8, 13)$ (marked with a triangle), $(n, K, k, d) = (10, 1, 6, 9)$ (marked with a circle) and $(n, K, k, d) = (15, 2, 10, 14)$ (marked with a square).

From the graphs we can conclude that all three comparison methods gives different outputs. Dimakis method take into consideration only two parameters: storage per node and bandwidth to repair one node and claims that square code is the best. Total method includes plus the number of nodes in the system yielding the overall storage and total downloaded bandwidth for the repair process and favors the circle code. And the normalized concept gives broader picture of parameters by allowing choosing arbitrary code file size and demonstrate that the triangle code is best.

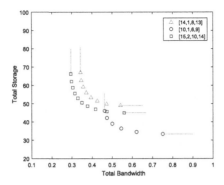

Fig. 2. Trade-off curve Total storage vs. Total repair bandwidt considering fair comparison procedure for parameters $(n, K, k, d) = (14, 1, 8, 13)$ (marked with a triangle), $(n, K, k, d) = (10, 1, 6, 9)$ (marked with a circle) and $(n, K, k, d) = (15, 2, 10, 14)$ (marked with a square).

3   Overview of DSS Codes

This section elaborates the construction of four diverse DSS codes that will be used in the comparison analysis. Precisely, gives description for the functioning and efficiency of the Regenerating Code, Repetition, Reed-Solomon based DSS and Clay code.

3.1   Regenerating Code

The general Regenerating code construction is presented in [11]. Here, we will give explicit construction through an example.

Example 1. The parameters of the code $\mathcal{C}[n, k, d]$, are $n = 4$, $k = 2$, $d = 3$. The file size $|\mathcal{F}|$ is arranged as a vector $\underline{u} = (u_1, \ldots, u_K)$ of $K = k\alpha = 4$ q-ary symbols, where $\alpha = 2$. Further, the vector $\underline{u}$ is arranged in a matrix M given as,

$$M = \begin{pmatrix} u_1 & u_2 \\ u_3 & u_4 \end{pmatrix}. \tag{18}$$

Then the matrix M is multiply by encoding matrix Ψ with properties explained in [11] and a code-matrix is generated,

$$\underline{C} = \begin{pmatrix} u_1 & u_2 \\ u_3 & u_4 \\ u_1 + u_2 + u_3 + u_4 & u_1 + 2u_2 + u_3 + 2u_4 \\ u_1 + 2u_2 + 3u_3 + u_4 & 3u_1 + 2u_2 + 3u_3 + 3u_4 \end{pmatrix}, \tag{19}$$

with dimension $(\alpha \times n) = (2 \times 4)$. The number of distinct blocks or vectors $\underline{u} = (u_1 \ u_2 \ u_3 \ u_4)$ in $\mathcal{F}$ is L, then, $|\mathcal{F}| = LK \log_2 q$. In this example, for $|\mathcal{F}| = 4$ symbols, means $L = 1$.

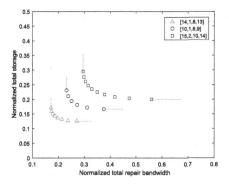

Fig. 3. Trade-off curve Normalized total storage vs. Normalized total repair bandwidth for parameters $(n, K, k, d) = (14, 1, 8, 13)$ (marked with a triangle), $(n, K, k, d) = (10, 1, 6, 9)$ (marked with a circle) and $(n, K, k, d) = (15, 2, 10, 14)$ (marked with a square).

The reconstruction of the original message is done by downloading $\alpha = 2$ data from any $k = 2$ nodes (choosing any two rows from the code-matrix $\underline{C}$). The vector $\underline{u} = (u_1 \; u_2 \; u_3 \; u_4)$ then is obtained by solving four equations with four unknowns.

For the repair process if node $i = 4$ fail, the new added node, $i' = 5$ (the repair-node), contacts $d = 3$ nodes and downloads from them by $\beta = 1$ data. The collected data is represented by the parity-information $\underline{P}$ matrix of dimension $d \times \beta$ given as

$$\underline{P} = \begin{pmatrix} p_1 \\ p_2 \\ p_3 \end{pmatrix} = \begin{pmatrix} c_{1,1} + 2c_{1,2} \\ 2c_{2,1} + c_{2,2} \\ 3c_{3,1} + c_{3,2} \end{pmatrix}$$
$$= \begin{pmatrix} u_1 + 2u_2 \\ 2u_3 + u_4 \\ 4u_1 + 5u_2 + 4u_3 + 5u_4 \end{pmatrix}. \tag{20}$$

With these information the newcomer regenerates the lost vector by proper combination of the parity vector components. In this example the regenerated vector would be

$$(c_{5,1} \; c_{5,2}) = (5u_1 + 7u_2 + 8u_3 + 7u_4, \; 6u_1 + 9u_2 + 6u_3 + 6u_4),$$

obtained with multiplication among $\underline{P}$ and

$$\begin{pmatrix} 1 \; 2 \\ 2 \; 1 \\ 1 \; 1 \end{pmatrix}. \tag{21}$$

Thus, the newly stored repaired information in the network would be

$$\underline{C} = \begin{pmatrix} u_1 & u_2 \\ u_3 & u_4 \\ u_1 + u_2 + u_3 + u_4 & u_1 + 2u_2 + u_3 + 2u_4 \\ 5u_1 + 7u_2 + 8u_3 + 7u_4 & 6u_1 + 9u_2 + 6u_3 + 6u_4 \end{pmatrix}. \tag{22}$$

3.2 Repetition Code

Repetition code construction given in [5] takes the original message to be stored in the system and represents as a vector $\underline{u} = (u_1 \ u_2 \ \ldots \ u_{LK})$. What is distributed in the system is depicted by the matrix $\underline{C} = (\underline{C}^{[1]}; \ldots; \underline{C}^{[n]})$, where $\underline{C}^{[n]} = \ldots = \underline{C}^{[1]} = \underline{M} = \underline{u}$ is seen as multiplication of $1 \times n$ matrix with all elements equal to one's and the input vector $\underline{u}$, i.e.

$$\underline{C} = (1 \ldots 1) \underline{M}. \tag{23}$$

Example 2. To create a repetition example we take $n = 3$, $k = 1$. Knowing that $d = k$, we have $d = 1$, and $n = \alpha = \beta$, $\alpha = \beta = 3$. For $K = 1$, $L = 1$, and message matrix $M = u_i$ for $i = 1, \ldots, n$ we get

$$\begin{aligned} \underline{C}^{[i]} &= (1 \ 1 \ 1) \ M \\ &= \begin{pmatrix} u_i \\ u_i \\ u_i \end{pmatrix}. \end{aligned} \tag{24}$$

The reconstruction and repair processes are simply done by contacting k or d nodes, accordingly, and downloading from them by α or β data.

3.3 Reed-Solomon Based DSS Code

Reed-Solomon (RS) based DSS codes introduced in [4], which are MDS codes, are better alternative then the repetition codes. Each input block is a vector of k q-ary symbols. Hence, the elements of the code-matrix are belonging to a Finite Field $\mathbb{F}_q$. The file of size $|\mathcal{F}^{RS}| = K^{RS} L^{RS}$ is stored by parsing into L^{RS} vectors of size $k = K^{RS}$, then, they are encoded into a vector of size αn. For *reconstruction* of the original file, the DC contacts k distinct nodes and downloads from them k vectors of size $\beta = \alpha$ data. Next, it performs proper data decoding and obtains the wanted file. For the *repair process* new node contacts $k = d$ vectors of size α and downloads from them $\beta = \alpha$. Then, performs proper decoding and encoding, and the content of the failed node is regenerated.

Example 3. A RS based DSS-code $C[n, k, d]$ with parameters $[7, 3, 3]$ is obtained by taking the vector $\underline{u} = (u_1, u_2, \ldots, u_k)$ and using a RS-code generating matrix,

$$G = \begin{pmatrix} g_{1,1} & g_{1,2} & \cdots & g_{1,n} \\ g_{2,1} & g_{2,2} & \cdots & g_{2,n} \\ \vdots & \vdots & \ddots & \vdots \\ g_{k,1} & g_{k,2} & \cdots & g_{k,n} \end{pmatrix}. \tag{25}$$

Every block $\underline{u}$ will give rise to a RS-codeword $\underline{w} = (w_1, \ldots, w_j \ldots, w_n)$. With $K = k = 3$, $\beta = \alpha = 1$ and $d = k = 3$ we have the code-matrix

$$\underline{C} = \begin{pmatrix} w_1 \\ \vdots \\ w_\ell \\ \vdots \\ w_n \end{pmatrix}. \tag{26}$$

3.4 Clay Code

Clay (short for CoupledLayer) codes represents a subset of the MSR (Minimum Storage Regenerating) codes. They have simpler construction for the decoding repair process, achieved by pairwise coupling across multiple stacked layers of any single MDS code [19]. Using this way of code construction it can be decreased the normalized repair bandwidth by increasing the value of $(d - k + 1)$.

Example 4. The example for Clay code have the parameters: $[n, k, d, \alpha, \beta, K] = [4, 2, 3, 4, 2, 8]$. After the encoding process the data is distributed across $n = 4$ nodes, from which $k = 2$ are data nodes and $n - k = 2$ are parity nodes. On each node is stored a superbyte consist of $\alpha = 4$ bytes. This makes the storage overhead $\frac{n\alpha}{k\alpha} = \frac{n}{k} = 2$ that is the ratio between the total number $n\alpha = 16$ of bytes stored to the number $K = k\alpha = 8$ of data bytes. When there is a failed node, the data downloaded from each of the $d = 3$ helper nodes are $\beta = 2$ bytes, which results in a normalized repair bandwidth of $\frac{d\beta}{k\alpha} = \frac{d}{k(d-k+1)} = 0.75$.

Data distribution process is done in several steps explained in [19]:

- A pair of coordinates to represent a layer are used
- Pairing of vertices and bytes
- Transforming from uncoupled to coupled-layer code
- Encoding the clay code
  - Load data into the 2 data nodes of coupled code
  - A pairwise reverse transformations used to be obtained the data stored in the 2 data nodes of uncoupled code
  - A MDS code is used in layer-by-layer fashion for determining the data stored in the parity nodes of uncoupled code
  - A pairwise forward transformation is used for obtaining the data to be stored in the parity nodes of coupled code

4 Analysis of the Different Comparison Procedures

This section gives analysis of the different comparison methods efficiency and validity. The four already described examples of codes Regenerating, Repetition, Reed-Solomon based DSS and Clay are considered in the comparison processes. The emphasis is put on the various chosen codes parameters and different file sizes, this is done to be more evident the meaning of the usage of an adequate comparison method. The focus is put on the comparison technique that includes normalization of the total storage and total downloaded bandwidth with respect of the file size. The normalization operation enables comparison of codes with different file sizes and different parameters concerning the bandwidth and the storage.

Precisely, normalization is done over the file size defined as $|\mathcal{F}| = LK \log_2 q$, concerning the total bandwidth and the total storage given with,

$$T_\gamma = \beta dL \log_2 q, \tag{27}$$

$$T_\alpha = \alpha nL \log_2 q. \tag{28}$$

Thus, the axes on the graph to determine Normalized-Repair-bandwidth and Normalized-Total-storage, the Eqs. (27) and (28) need to be normalized over the file size and to become

$$N_\gamma = \frac{T_\gamma}{KL \log_2 q} = \frac{\beta dL \log_2 q}{KL \log_2 q} = \frac{\beta d}{K}, \tag{29}$$

$$N_\alpha = \frac{T_\alpha}{KL \log_2 q} = \frac{\alpha nL \log_2 q}{KL \log_2 q} = \frac{\alpha n}{K}. \tag{30}$$

4.1 Regeneration Code

Following *Example* 1 the regeneration code scheme has bandwidth of $\gamma = \beta d = 3$ symbols and storage-per-node of $\alpha = 2$ symbols, where $n = 4$ nodes and $k = 2$. Considering a file $\mathcal{F}$ of size $|\mathcal{F}|$ bytes (or $|\mathcal{F}|/\log_2 q = KL$ symbols), which is parsed into $L = 1$ blocks of $K = 4$ symbols then we get

$$N_\gamma^{Reg} = \frac{\beta d}{K} = \frac{3}{4} \text{ bytes}, \tag{31}$$

$$N_\alpha^{Reg} = \frac{\alpha n}{K} = 2 \text{ bytes}. \tag{32}$$

4.2 Repetition Code

Following *Example* 2 the repetition code has parameters defined as, an amount of downloaded data to repair a failed node $\gamma = \beta d = 3$, where $d = k = 1$ and $\beta = 3$ symbols and storage-per-node $\alpha = \beta = 3$ symbol, where $n = 3$. Considering a file of size $|\mathcal{F}| = LK \log_2 q$ bytes, where L is parsed into blocks of q-ary symbols and each block is with size of $K = 1$, we get

$$N_\gamma^{rep} = \frac{\beta d}{K} = 3 \text{ bytes}, \tag{33}$$

$$N_\alpha^{rep} = \frac{\alpha n}{K} = 9 \text{ bytes}. \tag{34}$$

4.3   RS Based DSS Code

By *Example* 3 the scheme bandwidth is given by $\gamma = \beta d = 3$, $k = 3$, $K = k = 3$, $d = k = 3$ and $n = 7$. The storage-per-node is $\alpha = 1$ symbol and the download bandwidth is $\beta = 1$.

With both measured in bytes, we get

$$N_\gamma^{RS} = \frac{\beta d}{K} = 1\,\text{byte}, \tag{35}$$

$$N_\alpha^{RS} = \frac{\alpha n}{K} = \frac{7}{2}\,\text{bytes}. \tag{36}$$

4.4   Clay Code

Using *Example* 4 the bandwidth is $\gamma = \beta d = 6$, $k = 2$, $K = 8$, $d = 3$ and $n = 4$. The storage-per-node is $\alpha = 4$ symbol and $\beta = 2$.

With both measured in bytes, we get

$$N_\gamma^{Clay} = \frac{\beta d}{K} = \frac{3}{4}\,\text{bytes}, \tag{37}$$

$$N_\alpha^{Clay} = \frac{\alpha n}{K} = 2\,\text{bytes}. \tag{38}$$

4.5   Comparison

In this section four codes Regeneration, RS based DSS, Repetition and Clay given in *Examples* 1, 2, 3 and 4 are compared. The set of values for each code are chosen to be different to show that the new proposed method does not depend on them to give real picture. Unlike the other, if we not care which parameters we compare, then the results might be unreliable. Three comparison methods Dimakis, Total and Normalized are applied on the same codes. All codes follows its unique code construction using various parameters, and most important all of them uses different file size $|\mathcal{F}|$. Dimakis comparison method compares the codes using only two parameters, α and γ, and the results from Fig. 4 shows that RS DSS is the best code and Clay worse. Total method adds two more values, n and L, providing a wider picture. According this method, RS DSS is the best, but the worst one now is the Repetition code. Normalized method normalize the values form the Total with respect of the code file size. With this approach now, the figure depicts that Clay and Regenerating code are the best. Analysing Fig. 4 we can see the difference among the various comparison methods and we can conclude that the Normalized method is the best choice for having an adequate result.

Figure 5 compares the same codes, just a little bit adjusted to have same file sizes. It is noticeable that all three comparison methods gives different outcomes.

Code Comparison - different file size

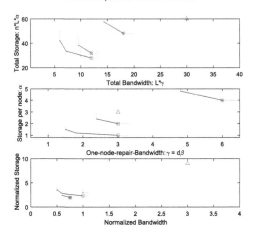

Fig. 4. Dimakis, Total and Normalized comparison methods for codes with different file size $|\mathcal{F}|$ bytes. Regeneration code (square) $(n = 4, k = 2, d = 3, \alpha = 2, \beta = 1, K = 4, L = 4)$, Repetition-DS-code (triangle) $(n = 3, k = 1, d = 1, \alpha = 3, \beta = 3, K = 1, L = 10)$, RS DSS-code (circle) $(n = 7, k = 3, d = 3, \alpha = 1, \beta = 1, K = 3, L = 4)$, and, Clay code (asterisk) $(n = 4, k = 2, d = 3, \alpha = 4, \beta = 2, K = 8, L = 3)$.

Code Comparison - same file size

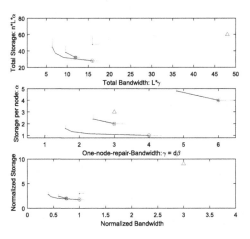

Fig. 5. Dimakis, Total and Normalized comparison methods for codes with same file size $|\mathcal{F}|$ bytes. Regeneration code (square) $(n = 4, k = 2, d = 3, \alpha = 2, \beta = 1, K = 4, L = 4)$, Repetition-DS-code (triangle) $(n = 3, k = 1, d = 1, \alpha = 3, \beta = 3, K = 1, L = 16)$, RS DSS-code (circle) $(n = 7, k = 4, d = 4, \alpha = 1, \beta = 1, K = 4, L = 4)$, and, Clay code (asterisk) $(n = 4, k = 2, d = 3, \alpha = 4, \beta = 2, K = 8, L = 2)$.

Dimakis says RS-DSS is best, and Clay worst code. Total method agrees with the best code, but in contrast says repetition is the one with poorest results. Normalization comparison claims that Regeneration and Clay code are better than the others, and Repetition is the worst.

Observing Figs. 4 and 5 we can see that changing the file size parameter in the codes affect the comparison methods Dimakis and Total by obtaining different results, unlike Normalized that doesn't change the final outcome.

5 Conclusion

A crucial challenge for distributed storage systems is the vast data generation, their processing and managing. Many researcher's work focuses to discover an efficient data management way to produce functional distributed storage networks. Various solutions in a form of data code constructions are proposed till now to deal this problem. Each newly developed code outperforms in some particular aspect of the DSS functioning, either it is the storage overhead, repair bandwidth, data distribution process or some other characteristic. Thus, in a general sense its very hard to say which code performs the best. Therefore, in this paper we are proposing a new comparison method, called Normalized, which allows more convenient approach for picking the best data code construction, despite the differently chosen codes parameters. The new approach produce more realistic results compare to the Dimakis and Total methods, while achieving good DSS efficiency. The comparison experiments are done using four different type of codes: Dimakis DSS, Repetition, Reed-Solomon based DSS and Clay code.

References

1. Moon, T.K.: Error Correction Coding: Mathematical Methods and Algorithms. Wiley-Interscience, Hoboken (2005)
2. MacWilliams, F.J., Sloane, N.J.A.: The Theory of Error-Correcting Codes. North Holland Mathematical Library, Amsterdam, The Netherlands (1983)
3. Rawat, A.S., Tamo, I., Guruswami, V., Efremenko, K.: MDS code constructions with small sub-packetization and near-optimal repair bandwidth. Trans. Inf. Theory IEEE **64**, 6506–6525 (2018)
4. Guruswami, V., Wootters, M.: Repairing Reed-Solomon codes. Trans. Inf. Theory IEEE **63**, 5684–5698 (2017)
5. Weatherspoon, H., Kubiatowicz, J.: Erasure coding vs. replication: a quantitative comparison. In: Proceedings of 1st International Workshop Peer-to-Peer System (IPTPS), pp. 328–338 (2001)
6. Sathiamoorthy, M., et al.: Xoring elephants: Novel erasure codes for big data. Proc. VLDB Endow. **6**, 325–336 (2013)
7. Memorandum of understanding for the implementation of the COST Action, European Cooperation for Statistics of Network Data Science (2015)
8. Dimakis*, A.G., Prabhakaran, V., Ramchandran, K.: Decentralized erasure code for distributed storage. Trans. Inf. Theory IEEE/ACM Netw., (2006)

9. Rawat, A.S., Koyluoglu, O.O., Silberstein, N., Vishwanath, S.: Optimal locally repairable and secure codes for distributed storage system. Info. Theory IEEE Trans. **60**, 212–236 (2013)
10. Rashmi, K.V., Shah, N.B., Kumar, P.V.: Regenerating codes for errors and erasures in distributed storage. In: Proceedings of IEEE International Symposium on Information Theory (ISIT) (2012)
11. Dimakis, A.G., Godfrey, P.B., Wu, Y., Wainright, M.J., Ramchandran, K.: Network coding for distributed storage systems. IEEE Trans. Inf. Theory **57**(8), 5227–5239 (2011)
12. Dimakis, A.G., Godfrey, P.B., Wainright, M., Ramchadran, K.: Network coding for distributed storage systems. In: Proceedings of 26th IEEE International Conference on Computer Communications, Anchorage, AK, pp. 2000–2008, May 2007
13. Han, Y.S., Zheng, R., Mow, W.H.: Exact regenerating codes for byzantine fault tolerance in distributed storage. In: INFOCOM Proceedings, pp. 2498–2506 (2012)
14. Han, Y.S., Pai, H.T., Zheng, R., Varshney, P.K.: Update-efficient regenerating codes with minimum per-node storage. In: Information Theory Proceedings (ISIT), pp. 1436–14406 (2013)
15. Goparaju, S., Tamo, I., Calderbank, R.: An improved sub-packetization bound for minimum storage regenerating codes. IEEE Information Theory Transactions, pp. 2770–2779 (2014)
16. Rashmi, K.V., Shah, N.B., Kumar, P.V.: Optimal exact-regenerating codes for distributed storage at the MSR and MBR points via a product-matrix construction. IEEE Trans. Inf. Theory **57**(8), 5227–5239 (2011)
17. Paunkoska, N., Finamore, W., Karamachoski, J., Puncheva, M., Marina, N.: Improving DSS Efficiency with Shortened MSR Codes. ICUMT (2016)
18. Paunkoska, N., Finamore, W., Marina, N.: Fair Comparison of DSS Codes. In: Future of Information and Communication Conference (FICC 2018) (2018)
19. Vajha, M., et al.: Clay codes: moulding MDS codes to yield an MSR code. In: Proceedings of the 16th USENIX Conference on File and Storage Technologies (FAST 2018), USENIX Association, USA, pp. 139–153 (2018)

Predictive Policing Using Deep Learning: A Community Policing Practical Case Study

Omowunmi Isafiade(✉)(ID), Brian Ndingindwayo, and Antoine Bagula(ID)

Department of Computer Science, University of the Western Cape, Cape Town,
South Africa
oisafiade@uwc.ac.za

Abstract. There is relentless effort in combating the issue of crime in South Africa and many parts of the world. This challenge is heightened in under-resourced settings, where there is limited knowledge support, thus resulting in increasing negative perceptions of public safety. This work presents a predictive policing model as an addition to a burglar alarm system deployed in a community policing project to improve crime prevention performance. The proposed model uses feature-oriented data fusion method based on a deep learning crime prediction mechanism. Feed-Forward Neural Network (FFNN) and Recurrent Neural Network (RNN) models are employed to predict the amount of calls made to police stations on a monthly basis. Device installation and census data are used in the feature selection process to predict monthly calls to a police station. Coefficient of correlation function is used to isolate the relevant features for the analysis. To provide a viable way of achieving crime reduction targets, the models are implemented and tested on a real-life community policing network system called MeMeZa, which is currently deployed in low-income areas of South Africa. Furthermore, the model is evaluated using coefficient of determination function and the accuracy of the predictions assessed using an independent dataset that was not used in the models' development. The proposed solution falls under the Machine Learning and AI applications in networks paradigm, and promises to promote smart policing in under-resourced settings.

Keywords: Public safety · Resource-constrained settings · Deep learning · Memeza · Predictive policing

1 Introduction

There is evidence that South Africa(SA) has a high rate of crime [1], as seen in the ten-year trend presented in Fig. 1. Hence, combating crime is still a top priority for stakeholders [2]. Moreover, high crime and violence levels not only

© ICST Institute for Computer Sciences, Social Informatics and Telecommunications Engineering 2021
Published by Springer Nature Switzerland AG 2021. All Rights Reserved
R. Zitouni et al. (Eds.): AFRICOMM 2020, LNICST 361, pp. 269–286, 2021.
https://doi.org/10.1007/978-3-030-70572-5_17

place a heavy burden on the criminal justice system, but also on health care and state expenditure, amongst others. Notably, preventing crime has been a priority for the government since *1994* [3]. Many aspirations to curb crime and achieve crime reduction goals are embodied in several national laws and international agreements, including several provincial and national community outreach campaigns [4]. Community safety receives particular attention in South Africa's primary strategic framework for development, according to the National Development Plan (NDP) 2030 [6]. The program sets out recommendations aimed at improving the functioning of the criminal justice system and at protecting vulnerable women and children.

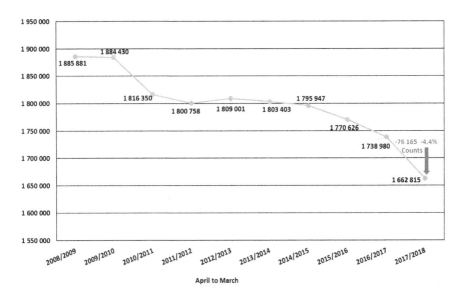

Fig. 1. Trend of crime in South Africa over a ten year period [1]

Despite the efforts by the government, crime trends still remain high in South Africa with only a small portion detected as a result of police action. In general, random patrol activities have not been very effective [7]. Furthermore, police to citizen ratio in South Africa is at *1:450*, and that means one police officer is expected to protect *450* people, which is a near impossible task [4]. Hence, the need for efficient systems that can assist the police [5]. Currently, there is limited or no real-time analysis on crime at source and this hampers service delivery [1,2]. Moreover, residents have not always been predisposed to being policed by the state due to the inherent socio-political terrain of high crime spaces in South Africa, and the poor response time and intervention perceived from the police. Clearly, efficient service delivery has been hampered by massive shortage of resources, which include real-time analysis and knowledge support. There is obviously a need for the government to devise more strategies to combat crime, and encourage more community policing initiatives. One of such initiatives is the MeMeza community policing network, which provides community safety solution to the most vulnerable people of the society.

1.1 MeMeZa Community Policing Platform

MeMeza is a South African initiative that offers innovative solutions to combat crime in vulnerable communities, ensuring that the poor can lead a safe and fulfilling life [8]. The aim of the organization is to provide community-based approaches to crime eradication by running campaigns and providing tools that offer easy access to the police and citizens. The organization provides an alarm system and also tries to fight crime by offering counselling services, addressing topics such as gender-based violence, bullying and crime prevention. This work focuses on the alarm system component of MeMeZa as depicted in Fig. 2.

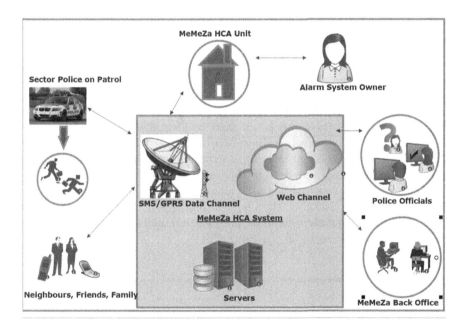

Fig. 2. A depiction of the Memeza community policing project deployed in low-income areas in SA.

The Memeza alarm system is used to mobilize established communities with low-income to fight crime [8]. The system consists of (i) the home community alarm (HCA) unit, which is installed at a subscriber's home, and (ii) the HCA system, which consists of the server that manages all communications within the system. The HCA unit communicates with the system, and vice versa, using a client-server handshake. The subscriber sends a panic message to the police through the system by activating, for example, a *"silent police panic"*, among others, which alerts the police on the need to respond to the location where such panic alert is initiated. A user initiates a panic mode on the alarm system by pressing a red button. The call is then immediately logged to a database in the back-end, to alert the police of the need for intervention. Figure 2 summarises the structure and functionality of the Memeza crime prevention and community mobilisation system.

1.2 Summary of Gaps and Opportunities

According to a report by Memeza and SAPS [8], the following have been achieved as a result of the Memeza pilot project:

1. SAPS response time measured within the pilot area was relatively faster, as opposed to the previous longer (almost 24 h) response time.
2. A migration in the crime hotspots, with a high prevention rate in houses that have the alarm system installed.
3. A reduction in serious crime within the region.

However, while acknowledging this success, it also points out that there are still challenges and that more could be done to address certain problems that still exist. For example, the preliminary analysis we conducted on the MeMeZa data confirms that some incident calls were not responded to by the police as seen in Fig. 3, which shows the top 5 police stations identified with missed incident calls. This means that even when the subscribers initiated a "police panic" call, there was no police presence or reaction as expected or anticipated. This is rather wanting as such experience tends to further reduce public (victim's) confidence in the police, and consequently defeats the intended goal of suspects' apprehension and crime deterrence. Notably, the under-utilised plethora of data archived by the MeMeZa back-end system could be analysed and used for knowledge support. Hence, this research aims to fill the gap.

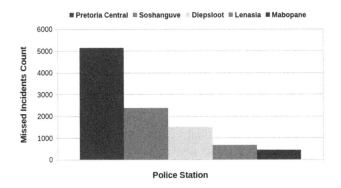

Fig. 3. Top 5 police stations with missed incident calls

Concretely, the unanswered (missed or "distressed") calls could be attributed to a number of factors, such as: (i) insufficient police resources (for example, man power); (ii) repeated calls, perhaps induced by continuous or uncontrollable panic attack by the victim; and (iii) technological constraint such as network infrastructure issues, amongst others. The first factor (i.e. limited police resources) identified is a more general concern [9] that requires some strategic intervention. Moreover, we note that an earlier investigation and research has highlighted limitations that hamper effective policing in resource-constrained environments such as in South Africa [2]. The highlighted limitations have elicited limited policing resources as a major challenge in these under-resourced communities. Hence, any research effort that promotes the effective and strategic use of these limited resources will greatly alleviate the problem.

1.3   Research Problem and Focus

The MeMeza alarm system is rather reactive than proactive and there is not enough evidence of calls decreasing over time. Whilst efforts have been made to increase the number of police stations in the country in the past year [1], it is important to note that this may not be sufficient. There is a need to understand the trend of crime per precinct (or municipality) and leverage technological solutions to improve policing in such areas. Concretely, the plethora of data archived by the MeMeZa system can be explored and analysed so as to alleviate some of the current challenges faced by the police. Hence, this research uses machine learning (deep learning) to predict crime calls in order to inform the police on trend of crime across precincts at different periods of time. This work presents a crime prediction system that is anchored on the well-established correlation between offenders and their target environment [10]. Historical datasets from MeMeZa are used to train two machine learning algorithms and the best performing one identified based on prediction accuracy and computation performance. With a prediction accuracy of up to 90%, this solution serves as an advancement on MeMeZa and has great potential in contributing to the fight against crime in resource-constrained environments.

The rest of the paper is organised as follows: Sects. 2 and 3 present the related work and models, while the implementation and experimental results are documented in Sect. 4 and 5. Section 6 summarises and concludes the research.

2   Related Work

In recent years, there have been various studies on the prediction and control of crime occurrences [10–15,17]. Crime prediction techniques have shifted from simply extrapolating historical data or trend using basic statistical techniques [19] to more advanced techniques that are scalable [20,21] and incorporate intelligence such as machine learning techniques, which thrives in the big data spectrum [14,16,18]. Previous approaches were limited in their computational power. However, current trends involving machine learning techniques have paved the way for the development of proactive measures that can make the police more efficient in combating crime [10]. Such trend lies at the intersection of predictive policing, data mining and information dissemination [13,15,18]. Wang *et al.* [14] addressed a foundational problem of crime rate inference using large-scale crowd-generated point-of-interest and taxi flow data, in order to provide new insight into causal and social factors on crime rate inference relating to the city of Chicago. Mookiah *et al.* [12] conducted a review on crime prediction techniques, while noting lack of cohesion in some previous research. Authors noted lack of extraction of patterns using multiple heterogeneous data attributes, such as crime news stories, user profiles, and social media. McClendon *et al.* [22] analysed crime with various machine learning techniques such as, Linear Regression, Additive Regression, and Decision Stump algorithms using the same finite set of features on crime dataset. In another research [23], the authors use 2010 California burglaries data to find the relationship between week, time of the day, repeat victimization, connector and barriers by plotting the occurrence of a crime on a map. Whereas Lin *et al.* [24] incorporate the concept of a criminal environment in grid-based crime prediction modelling and establishes a range of spatial-temporal features based on different types of geographic information by applying Google API to theft data for Taoyuan City, Taiwan.

Furthermore, Nurul *et al.* [13] reviewed current implementations of crime prediction methods with the aim of highlighting their strengths and possible areas for improvement. Fuzzy theory, support vector machine (SVM), multivariate time series and artificial neural network (ANN) were methods considered as those, among others, that can assist crime intelligence in fighting crime. In recent times, the deep learning approach, which is based on artificial neural network (ANN), has become a trendy technique in crime prediction [11,25,26]. A feature level-data fusion based deep learning model was used by Kang *et al.* [11] to predict crime for the city of Chicago, being the largest city with a high crime density. Stec *et al.* [26] also used a deep learning approach for making future crime occurrence predictions within city partitions, using Chicago and Portland crime data. Hence, this research also explores this trendy technique, using appropriate feature tuning and enhancement with census data as a means to introduce some intelligence into the MeMeZa network system. Two architectures of the deep learning model were explored, which are Feed-Forward Neural Network (FFNN) and Recurrent Neural Network (RNN). While Stec *et al.* [26] used joint recurrent and convolutional neural network for the purpose of predicting crime, our approach differs as it considers FFNN and RNN, and is implemented on a real-life community policing network.

3   Deep Learning Models

Tapping into the potential and success of deep learning in data-driven decision support, this work explores two models based on a deep learning crime prediction mechanism. These are Feed-Forward Neural Network (FFNN) and Recurrent Neural Network (RNN) approaches [27].

3.1   Feed-Forward Neural Network (FFNN)

The feed-forward model is a simple neural network model as depicted in Fig. 4, wherein connections between the nodes are not cyclic [26]. The size of the input layer corresponds to the size of the features in the data and the output layer consists of the possible predictions. The hidden layers are called hidden because they are not directly connected to the data and usually determined experimentally. When the hidden layer in a neural network is greater than one, then it is referred to as deep neural network (deep learning). Hence, the more the number of hidden layers, the more the complexity of the network and its ability to learn. However, too many hidden units could result in a complicated model with high variance and low bias, thus causing over-fitting [27]. In the network, each unit is connected to the previous and the next layer by a weight $(w^{(i)})$, where i denotes each corresponding layer as shown in Fig. 4. Each record is fed into the input layer, and then the values are fed forward using some weight (w) through the network. This sequence continues, where the values are fed forward from one layer to the next through intermediate computations, using an activation function. In this research, the number of input layers is four. Also, rectified linear units (ReLU) is used as the activation function in the hidden layer, while the softmax activation is used for the output layer. The ReLU function overcomes the vanishing gradient problem and often achieves better performance. ReLU is a piecewise linear function that outputs the input if it is positive and zero otherwise.

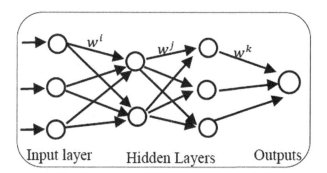

Fig. 4. Feed forward neural network

3.2   Recurrent Neural Network (RNN)

Recurrent neural network(RNN) differs from FFNN by a feedback loop which is connected to their past decisions. RNN usually have two sources of input, which is the current and past recent input [27]. These two sources of input combine to influence how they respond to produce output for the new data. Hence, the decision reached at time step t influences the decision it will reach at time step

$t + 1$ as depicted in Fig. 5. Long Short Term Memory (LSTM) is a special and the most common type of RNN as it solves the vanishing gradient problem that is inherent in RNN. The LSTM have the ability to remove or add information to the cell state, which is carefully regulated by structures called gates. Gates are a way to optionally let information through [25]. They are composed out of sigmoid neural layer and pointwise multiplication operation. A sigmoid layer outputs numbers between zero and one, describing how much of each component should be let through. A value of zero means let nothing through while a value of one means let everything through. An LSTM has three of these gates, to protect and control the cell state.

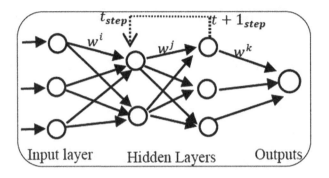

Fig. 5. Recurrent neural network

4   Model Implementation

4.1   Data Used: MeMeZa Data

The data used for the experiment consists of 44,043 records derived from the MeMeZa community policing project in 2017. The original data is stored in two separate (Excel) main files, which are referred to as "People" and "Incidents" files. Table 1 presents a description of some features and subjects associated with the files. The table shows a high level summary of the different categories of data features archived on the MeMeZa system. The Incidents file stores or reports on the amount of calls made by a device to a particular police station at a specific time from a particular location, while the "people" file consists of information regarding the alarm system and corresponding subscriber.

The end goal of the experiment is to predict with high level of certainty that the police can rely on the amount of burglaries per unit area so that the police can focus on the area and plan accordingly. Table 1 depicts the nature of the data sets used in this analysis and Fig. 6 depicts the data cleaning and preparation process. The selected attributes are the relevant ones or the key attributes for our analysis purpose.

Table 1. Different categories of data features considered

Features	Category
Victim ("people") information (subscriber)	device_id, installation date, gender, device_status subscription_bill
"Incidents" information	location, time device_id, device_descr, suburb

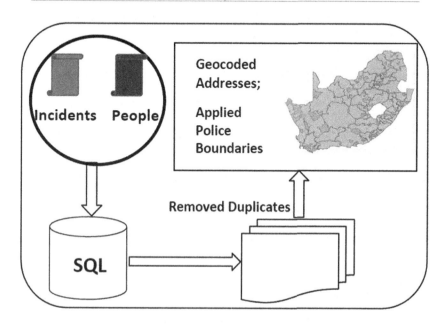

Fig. 6. Data cleaning process

The two data sets are combined by a unique identification (device_id and person_id) for further processing. This combination helps to identify the address of each device. The MeMeZa data contains loosely typed addresses, and for further processing it became necessary to locate the point at which the crime occurred. To achieve this, the Google API which is an online tool for mapping addresses is used to search the address and compute the longitude and latitude at which the event occurred. Police station boundaries are then applied to determine the associated records for corresponding police stations. However, it is noted that *5, 698* records have no addresses and cannot be used for analysis, hence, these were ignored in the experiment. Furthermore, we identified duplicate records (see Fig. 6). *18,074* records are marked as duplicates from the database using these two conditions: (i) if the previous record had the same address as the current one; and (ii) if the time frame between the calls is less than *5* minutes. These duplicate records were assumed to be distressed calls from the users when police were probably not responding to their calls. Eventually, the data set with sample depicted in Table 2 is used, by performing a "join" on the people and incidents table.

Table 2. MeMeza incidents data set sample

Id	Date	Longitude	Latitude	Police_Station
5497	2017-10-07 12:54	28.268015	−25.748704	BROOKLYN
5498	2017-10-07 12:54	28.268015	−25.748704	BROOKLYN
5500	2017-10-07 13:49	28.268015	−25.748704	BROOKLYN
5507	2017-10-07 14:20	28.268015	−25.748704	BROOKLYN
5501	2017-10-07 14:46	28.268015	−25.748704	BROOKLYN

4.2 Feature Selection and Data Fusion

The number of calls made from a certain location is the target and this is computed by summing the calls made in a period of every one month - this gives a fairly randomly distributed data to work with. For further processing and to strengthen the analysis, we combined demographic features from the South African Census data in the features selection process as used in previous research [26]. Certain features in the census data such as unemployment rate, literacy level and age demographics have been found to be very useful in crime prediction. Hence, this data fusion (crime and census dataset) assists our analysis to improve prediction performance.

In order to coordinate and select the best features that will assist the model, the correlation coefficient function was used. The correlation coefficient expresses the statistical measure of the mutual relationship between quantities. Hence, the function helps to filter features that are highly correlated and those that are not correlated in order to remove non-informative or redundant predictors from the model. The formula for computing the correlation, often referred as Pearson r is presented in Eq. 1:

$$r = \frac{1}{n-1} \sum \frac{(x_i - \overline{X})(y_i - \overline{Y})}{s_x s_y} \tag{1}$$

- n is the sample size
- x_i, y_i are the individual sample points indexed with i
- $\overline{X} = \frac{1}{n} \Sigma_{i=1}^{n} x_i$ (the sample mean for features)
- s_x is the standard deviation of x feature

Features with the Pearson whose magnitude is greater than 0.02 are selected in the experiment (Fig. 7). The features used in the analysis are:

– number of installations in that month
– month of the year
– tertiary value from the census data for that location cell
– uneducated value from the census data for that location cell

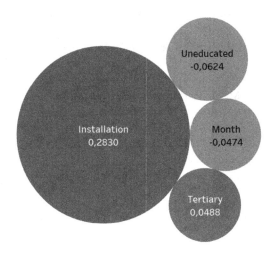

Fig. 7. Pearson values between call count and features

For the experiment, the data was randomised and then split into *80%* training set and *20%* test set. This helps to avoid over-fitting the model and improve its performance. The analysis was conducted on the rest of the police stations. It is noted though that some of the police stations have very few entries, so a filter was applied to get only those police stations with incidents that are more than *350* in a year. The filtering process resulted in twenty police stations for the analysis. The two models are used in predicting crime per unit month across police stations in the precincts by iterating through them and saving the results of the predictions in a database table in SQL. The number of nodes in the input layer is four. The number of hidden layers for FFNN is sixty-four, while that of LSTM is fifty. ReLU, Softmax and linear activation functions were used in the models.

4.3 Evaluation Metric

The R^2 function, depicted in Eq. 2, is used to evaluate the model. The function finds the relationship between the predicted outputs and the actual crime counts. The R^2 function, which is also referred to as Coefficient of determination, gives an indication of the goodness of fit. It gives a visual output of how the predicted crime count compares with the actual values. R^2 is a proportion, hence it ranges between 0 and 1. If $R^2 = 1$, this means that all of the predicted outputs correspond to the actual crime counts (i.e. perfect fit), while $R^2 = 0$ indicates that none of the predicted outputs is anywhere close to the actual values. Hence, an R^2 value closer to one (1) is more desirable.

$$R^2 = 1 - \frac{\sum_{i=1}^{n}(x-y)^2}{\sum_{i=1}^{n}|x-y|^2} \qquad (2)$$

5　Experimental Results and Discussion

To provide a viable way of achieving crime reduction targets, the model is implemented and tested on MeMeZa dataset. The research used the tensor-flow open source-libraries for deep learning, based on the keras high level neural network API, since it allows for convenient and fast prototyping. The rectified linear unit (ReLu) and softmax activation functions from the Keras framework were considered for the experiment. We present prediction results for three stations having relatively high incident calls. Figures 8 and 9 show prediction results for Diepsloot station using FFNN and LSTM respectively, while Fig. 10 presents FFNN result for Pretoria Central station.

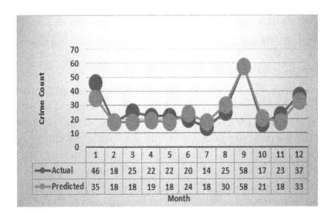

Fig. 8. FFFF diepsloot prediction results.

Figures 11 and 12 present prediction results for Tembisa station, while Fig. 13 presents the result for Roodepoort station. From the visualisation, it is clear that the algorithm predicts the crime for the particular period examined (on a monthly basis) with a high level of accuracy with respect to the actual crime observation. It is observed that there are lots of calls at the beginning of the year for both Diepsloot and Tembisa stations. This is partly due to the fact that many installations of the MeMeZa alarm system were observed to have been implemented at the beginning of the year, until the month of May or thereabout. The number of installed alarm units were noted to be one of the

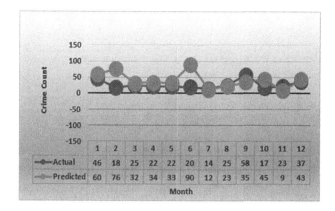

Fig. 9. LSTM diepsloot prediction results.

Month	1	2	3	4	5	6	7	8	9	10	11	12
Actual	46	18	25	22	22	20	14	25	58	17	23	37
Predicted	60	76	32	34	33	90	12	23	35	45	9	43

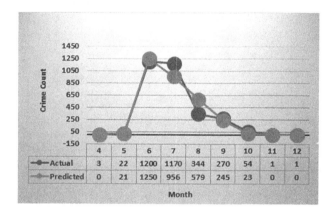

Fig. 10. FFNN pretoria central prediction results.

Month	4	5	6	7	8	9	10	11	12
Actual	3	22	1200	1170	344	270	54	1	1
Predicted	0	21	1250	956	579	245	23	0	0

factors responsible for raising the number of calls made to specific police stations, which relatively makes sense. DiepSloot achieves R^2 of 0.8368 with the FFNN, which is fairly good since it is close to 1. LSTM has an R^2 of 0.0014 which is very poor. Calls were generally on the decline in 2017 except for the month of September. It is noted that three(3) of the calls were from the new installations, and four of the calls in the month of September were from a particular device with device_id 9066, which was activated in March 2016.

There were no calls until the month of April since no installations were done in Pretorial Central until the 3rd of May 2017. The R^2 is at 0.9464 for the FFNN, indicating a very good fit of the model, and that for the LSTM is 0.6418 which is good. As the number of installations increases, so did the calls. It can also be noted that in the month of June alone, 135 calls went unanswered by the police. This shows that installations were done, but probably no co-ordination was made with the police to manage the expected calls. Hence, a reality of

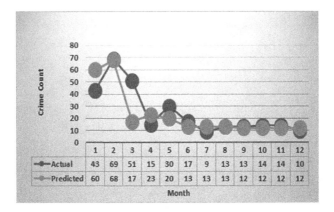

Fig. 11. FFNN tembisa prediction results.

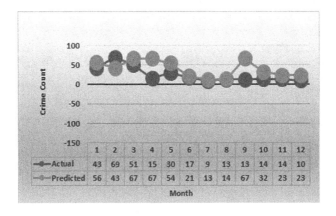

Fig. 12. LSTM tembisa prediction results.

resource shortage. However, in June, there is relatively an increase in the number of calls that the police responded to.

Tembisa has an R^2 of 0.5998 for FFNN which is fairly good, but not perfect. The LSTM has an R^2 of 0.4426. There are many calls at the beginning of the year dropping to about 10 calls a month for the subsequent months. Most of the installations are done at the beginning of the year until the fifth month, that is why there is a higher number of calls in the first quarter of the year. The number of installed units is noted to be a major factor that is increasing the calls made to the police for the stations.

R^2 for the FFNN is 0.9808 for Roodepoort police station which is almost a perfect fit for the model. The LSTM R^2 is 0.9475. There are many calls at the beginning of the year, dropping to about 10 calls a month for the subsequent months. Most of the installations are in the second month, about 1337 of them, the number of actual calls remain low throughout the year.

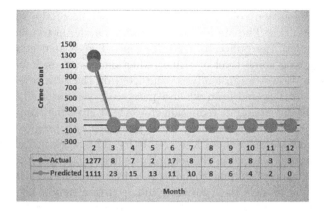

Fig. 13. FFNN roodepoort prediction results.

FFNN is noted to have higher values of R^2 for most of the police stations considered, this means the model gives a better fit for the stations. Figure 14 shows the performance evaluation of the models on the respective police stations. This work shows potential in advancing the MeMeZa system to improve performance on fighting crime.

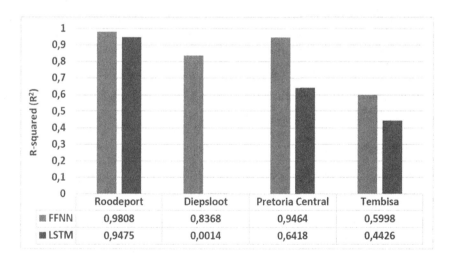

Fig. 14. FFNN vs LSTM results with R^2 across different stations.

6   Conclusion and Future Work

Combating crime in South Africa is an ongoing effort. This culminated in the launch and implementation of the MeMeZa community policing platform, which provides safety solution to the most vulnerable people of the society in low-resource communities. The MeMeZa system allows a victim to initiate a "police panic" call to alert the police to a crime scene. The system is noted to have helped in achieving some level of crime reduction in certain low-income areas of South Africa. However, an analysis conducted on the data reveals that some calls remained unanswered even when a panic call was initiated. High level of unanswered calls defeats crime reduction efforts as it gives the criminal an opportunity to escape. Moreover, this may cause more negative public perceptions of public safety and MeMeza could lose credibility. This work unlocked the value of incorporating intelligence in the form of predictive policing into the existing MeMeZa public safety system, to improve crime prevention. The study used two deep learning models (feed forward and recurrent neural network) to predict crime across different police stations in various regions in South Africa. The paper examined the two models and combined census (demographic) information in the feature selection process to identify the model that gives the prediction with the best accuracy. Coefficient of correlation function was used to isolate the relevant features for the analysis. The main projected benefits of this newly proposed solution is in strategic resource management and predictive policing in the MeMeZa network system.

As a future extension of this work, there is more that can be explored in terms of building an efficient cloud storage capacity using object oriented database that will facilitate efficient operational support, as well as mining streaming crime data from the current MeMeZa system for real time knowledge support, among others. Furthermore, applying more classification models to increase crime prediction accuracy, identifying hotspots and enhancing the overall performance of the system are aspects that could be considered.

Acknowledgment. Authors gratefully appreciate resources made available by the MeMeZa foundation, South Africa.

References

1. South African Government: Crime report. In South African police service annual crime report 2017/2018. https://www.gov.za/sites/default/files/gcis_document/201809/crime-stats201718.pdf. Accessed June 2020
2. Isafiade, O., Bagula, A.: Fostering smart city development in developing nations: a crime series data analytics approach. In: Proceedings of the ITU-Kaleidoscope: Challenges for a Data-Driven Society, pp. 89–95. IEEE, Nanjing, China (2017)
3. Du Plessis, A., Louw, A.: Crime prevention in South Africa: 10 Years After. Can. J. Criminol. Crim. Justice/La Revue canadienne de criminologie et de justice pénale **47**(2), 1–20 (2005). https://doi.org/10.3138/cjccj.47.2.427
4. South African Police Service: Together squeezing crime to zero. J. Strateg. Plan **3**(1), 3–21 (2014)
5. Isafiade, O., Bagula, A.: CitiSafe: adaptive spatial pattern knowledge using Fp-growth algorithm for crime situation recognition. In: Proceedings of the IEEE International Conference on Ubiquitous Intelligence and Computing (UIC-ATC), pp. 551–556, December 2013

6. National Development Plan 2030: Our Future - make it work, pp. 1–70. https://www.gov.za/sites/default/files/Executive%20Summary-NDP%202030%20-%20Our%20future%20-%20make%20it%20work.pdf. Accessed June 2020

7. Mohler, G.O., et al.: Randomized controlled field trials of predictive policing. J. Am. Stat. Assoc. **110**(512) (2015)

8. MeMeZa crime prevention and community mobilisation project: Memeza shout crime prevention Diepsloot pilot results summary. http://memeza.co.za/wp-content/uploads/2016/05/Memeza-Diepsloot-Pilot-Report-2015.pdf. Accessed September 2018

9. Wilson, J.M., Weis, A.: Police staffing allocation and managing workload demand: a critical assessment of existing practices. J. Policing **8**, 1–13 (2014). https://doi.org/10.1093/police/pau00. Advance Access-Oxford University Press

10. Isafiade, O., Bagula, A.: Data mining trends and applications in criminal science and investigations, pp. 1–386. IGI Global, USA (2016)

11. Kang, H.W., Kang, H.B.: Prediction of crime occurrence from multi-modal data using deep learning. J. PLOS-ONE **12**(4), 1–19 (2017)

12. Mookiah, L., Eberle, W., Siraj, A.: Survey of crime analysis and prediction. In: The Twenty-Eighth International Flairs Conference, pp. 440–443 (2015)

13. Mohd Shamsuddin, N.H., Ali, N.A., Alwee, R.: An overview on crime prediction methods. In: Proceedings of the 6th ICT International Student Project Conference (ICT-ISPC), pp. 1–5, Malaysia (2017)

14. Wang, H., Kifer, D., Graif, C., Li, Z.: Crime rate inference with big data. In: Proceedings of the International Conference on Knowledge Discovery in Database, pp. 635–644. ACM (2016)

15. Isafiade, O., Bagula, A.: Series mining for public safety advancement in emerging smart cities. Future Gener. Comput. Syst. **108**, 777–802 (2020)

16. Almanie, T., Mirza, R., Lor, E.: Crime prediction based on crime types and using spatial and temporal criminal hotspots. Int. J. Data Min. Knowl. Manage. Process (IJDKP) **54**, 1–19 (2015)

17. Isafiade, O., Bagula, A., Berman, S.: A revised frequent pattern model for crime situation recognition based on floor-ceil quartile function. Procedia Comput. Sci. **15**, 251–260 (2015)

18. Isafiade, O., Bagula, A., Berman, S.: On the use of Bayesian network in crime suspect modelling and legal decision support. In: Data Mining Trends and Applications in Criminal Science and Investigations, pp. 143–168, USA (2016)

19. Greenberg, D.: Time series analysis of crime rates. J. Quant. Criminol. **17**(4), 291–327 (2001)

20. Flaxman, S., Chirico, M., Pereira, P., Loeffler, C.: Scalable high-resolution forecasting of sparse spatiotemporal events with kernel methods: a winning solution to the NIJ Real-Time Crime Forecasting Challenge. Mach. Learn. **13**, 1–30 (2018). https://arxiv.org/abs/1801.02858

21. Isafiade, O., Bagula A: Efficient frequent pattern knowledge for crime situation recognition in developing countries. In: Proceedings of the 4th Annual Symposious on Computing for Development, pp. 1–2, ACM (2013)

22. Mcclendon, L., Meghanathan, N.: Using machine learning algorithms to analyze crime data. Mach. Learn. Appl. Int. J. (MLAIJ) **2**(1), 1–12 (2015)

23. Almanie, T., Mirza, R., Lor, E.: Crime prediction based on crime types and using spatial and temporal criminal hotspots. Int. J. Data Min. Knowl. Manage. Process **5**(4), 1–9 (2015)

24. Lin, Y.-L., Yen, M.-F., Yu, L.-C.: Grid-based crime prediction using geographical features. ISPRS Int. J. Geo Inf. **7**(8), 298 (2018). https://doi.org/10.3390/ijgi7080298
25. Azeez, J., Aravindhar, D.J.: Hybrid approach to crime prediction using deep learning. In: Proceedings of the International Conference on Advances in Computing, Communications and Informatics (ICACCI), pp. 1701–1710. IEEE, Kochi (2015)
26. Stec, A., Klabjan, D.: Forecasting crime with deep learning. arXiv preprint arXiv:1806.01486l, pp. 1–20 (2018)
27. Zhang, Q., Yang, L.T., Chen, Z., Li, P.: A survey on deep learning for big data. J. Inf. Fusion **42**, 146–157 (2018)

DNS Resilience and Performance

On QoE Impact of DoH and DoT in Africa: Why a User's DNS Choice Matters

Enock S. Mbewe$^{(\boxtimes)}$ and Josiah Chavula

University of Cape Town, Cape Town 7701, WC, RSA
{embewe,jchavula}@cs.uct.ac.za

Abstract. Internet security and Quality of Experience (QoE) are two antagonistic concepts that the research community has been attempting to reconcile. Internet security has of late received attention due to users' online privacy and security concerns. One example is the introduction of encrypted Domain Name System (DNS) protocols. These protocols, combined with suboptimal routing paths and offshore hosting, have the potential to negatively impact the quality of web browsing experience for users in Africa. This is particularly the case in edge access networks that are far away from essential infrastructures such as DNS and content servers. In this paper, we analyse the QoE impact of using open public DoH and DoT resolvers when resolving websites that are hosted in Africa versus those hosted offshore. The study further compares the performance of DoT and DoH under different network conditions (mobile, community network, Eduroam and Campus wired network). Our results show that high latency and circuitous DNS resolution paths amplify the performance impact of secure DNS protocols on DNS resolution time and page load time. The study further shows that users' DNS resolver preferences hugely determine the level of QoE. This study proposes wider adoption of Transport Layer Security version 1.3 (TLSv1.3) to leverage its latency-reduction features such as *false start* and *Zero or One Round Trip Time* (0/1-RTT). The study further proposes the localisation of content and secure DNS infrastructure. This, coupled with peering and cache sharing recommended by other works, will further minimise the impact of secure DNS protocols on Quality of Experience.

Keywords: Networks · Network performance · Internet security · DNS privacy · QoE

1 Introduction

Domain Name System (DNS) [1] is one of the fundamental components of the Internet which maps the human-readable names to their respective IP addresses of Internet resources. For most of the Internet's history, these services have been delivered in plaintext providing a fertile ground for attackers to exploit this

© ICST Institute for Computer Sciences, Social Informatics and Telecommunications Engineering 2021
Published by Springer Nature Switzerland AG 2021. All Rights Reserved
R. Zitouni et al. (Eds.): AFRICOMM 2020, LNICST 361, pp. 289–304, 2021.
https://doi.org/10.1007/978-3-030-70572-5_18

vulnerability and compromise Internet users' security and privacy online. Some governments, Internet Service Providers and other players exploited this vulnerability by using DNS for pervasive monitoring, Internet censorship, content control and other attacks as reported in RFC 7258 [2]. As a result, various efforts have been developed to encrypt cryptographically sign the DNS queries. These efforts have resulted in the development of different protocols such as DNS over TLS (DoT) [3], DNS over DTLS, DNS over QUIC, DNS over HTTPS (DoH) [4] and DNSCrypt [5]. Although these protocols are relatively new, there has been increased adoption of some by service providers, OS vendors and software vendors. Lu et al. [6] collectively call these DNS encryption protocols *DNS over Encryption (DoE)* the term we use in this paper. Amongst these protocols, DoT and DoH are two standardised which are gaining grounds in the industry and research communities. Our study, therefore, focuses on these two protocols as measured from Internet user's networks and devices.

Much as these are desirable developments that provide essential security goals, Internet users should be willing to bear the extra QoE costs that come with security [7–9]. Generally, DNS-over-Encryption can incur performance overhead for DNS clients due to an extra delay TLS session setup and encryption [6]. Measuring the real impact of DoE would help the users make a rational decision and correctly estimate their QoE expectations. The Internet research community has tried to measure the impact of DoE on DNS resolution and page load time. However, none of the measurement studies has focused on edge access networks commonly found in developing regions such as Africa. Therefore, the findings from these studies cannot be generalised.

This paper presents the results of Internet security measurements study taken from different edge networks in Africa. We specifically aimed to find out the extent to which DoE coupled with latency and offshore content hosting would impact overall Quality of Experience. To ably achieve this aim, we carried out measurements from end-user networks in seven (7) African countries: Madagascar, Malawi, Nigeria, Kenya, Uganda, South Africa and Zambia. We measured the impact of DoE provided by the open DNS recursive resolvers on DNS resolution time (DRT) and page load time (PLT). To correctly estimate the impact of DoE, we measure the cost of resolving with regular plaintext DNS (hereafter referred to as Do53) from both the user network, which we call local Do53 and remote Do53 measured from each of the open public DNS recursors. The following is a summary of our major findings:

   i. *We find that unencrypted DNS transport is by far faster than the encrypted DNS transport in high-delay, lossy edge networks.*

  ii. *We find that network conditions, user's DNS resolver choice, webserver and DNS resolver geolocation hugely determine the QoE (DNS response times, page load times and success and failure rates of Secure DNS resolution).*

 iii. *Comparably, we find that providers having their caches in Africa have a higher probability of successfully resolving names than distant recursors. Therefore, we motivate for the implementation of local DoE infrastructure by the Internet Service Providers (ISPs) to further reduce the DNS response time and page load time hence improving QoE for Internet users.*

2   Background

Unreliable, slow, insecure, expensive or non-existent Internet access remains a big problem for billions of people in the developing world where the physical infrastructure is still underdeveloped. Bandwidth is generally an expensive resource for developing regions with low user densities [10]. Despite the recent development of the internet infrastructure in these regions, Quality of Experience for users is often impacted by high latencies resulting from circuitous name resolution as observed by Formoso *et al.* [11]. Recent studies [12,13] report that African content is normally hosted in North America despite the availability of some Content Delivery Networks in the region. This may be attributed to the cost of hosting and unreliability of power in most of the underdeveloped countries. Apart from bandwidth, latency is caused by a number of factors including lossy links and lack of peering between the networks, preventing the sharing of CDN servers, as well as poorly configured DNS resolvers [14]. Besides these works, this study has especially been inspired by the study conducted by Calandro *et al.* [13]. The authors surveyed the type of content commonly produced and consumed in Africa. They further conducted active latency and traceroute measurements to locate webservers hosting the African content. They found that most of the content is hosted outside the countries owning such content and most often, offshore. In this study, we measure how these observations combined secure DNS resolution would impact DNS response time and page load time.

Given the recency of DoT and DoH, the research community is yet to establish the real performance cost of these protocols. At the writing of this paper, we know of very few measurement studies on the performance cost of DoT and DoH. An early preliminary study by Mozilla[1] found that DoH lookups are only marginally slower (6 ms) than conventional, unencrypted DNS over port 53 (Do53). Bottger *et al.* [15] studied the DoH ecosystem to understand the cost of the additional DNS security. Their findings indicate that the impact is marginal and does not heavily impact the page load times. In their works, Hounsel, et al. ([16] and [17]), compared the cost of DoT and DoH measured from campus network and Amazon ec2 instances. Their results show that although the resolution times of Do53 is better than that of DoT and DoH, both protocols can perform better than Do53 in terms of page load times. Lu *et al.* [6] conducted end-to-end DNS-over-Encryption measurements and found that that generally the service quality of DNS-over-Encryption is satisfying, in terms of accessibility and latency and that the added latency is worth it. DoH, in particular, is attracting the attention of the research community due to its current centralised implementation. Some fear to entrust valuable browsing information to a few providers. As such, some works are focusing on de-centralising DoH so that no single provider has all the browsing information. Hoang *et al.* [18] propose K-resolver to slice user information to different decentralised DoH resolvers. This,

---

[1] See https://blog.nightly.mozilla.org/2018/08/28/firefox-nightly-secure-dns-experimental-results.

however, suffers from increased latency when the servers are geographically separated. A similar study is conducted by Hounsel *et al.* [19] which proposes a distributed DoH server architecture called M-DNS.

In this paper, we measure and compare DNS response and page load times to websites hosted within Africa versus websites hosted in America and Europe respectively. We conduct measurements from edge network (3G/4G mobile networks, community wireless network and home broadband) vantage points in Africa. We perform these measurements against open public DNS recursive resolvers such as Google, Cloudflare, Quad9, CleanBrowsing and AdGuard. We also measure latency to each of the recursors and websites to provide a context for our findings.

3   Methodology

In this section, we describe the metrics used and how we measure these metrics using our experiment setup.

3.1   Metrics

This study aimed to understand how Do53, DoT and DoH impact browsing Quality of Experience (QoE). The study considered network-level and browser-level metrics. These metrics are latency, DNS response time (in this paper referred to as DRT), DNS success and failure rates and page load time (PLT).

Latency. Several studies have pointed out that African networks suffer higher latencies. Recent studies [11,13,14] have attributed these latencies to suboptimal routing, lack of peering and cache sharing. Other studies have attributed these latencies to offshore hosting and misconfiguration of DNS. However, none of these works has looked at the impact of latency on security protocols in the region. Latency determines the kind of applications that can run on affected networks. For example, VoIP and video conferencing may allow latency of not more than 400 ms and online gaming, not more than 200 ms. Therefore, it is important to understand the extent to which the secure DNS protocols add on to the already high latency in order to inform Internet users of what applications may run on a given network condition. Also, it is important to show which public DNS providers respond with reasonable latency as this would aid users in the choice of DNS recursive resolvers. We also perform latency measurements to resolvers and websites in order to explain the source of delays in our results. We conduct ping measurements to each of the recursors and domains using different DNS configurations. We then calculate the median RTT for each latency measurement.

DNS Resolution Time. DNS query response time is one of the major factors that affect the speed of page rendering in the browser. A web page normally contains several objects fetched from different servers. In this study, we measured DNS resolution time firstly for the main page, and thereafter, for each domain, we collected all the unique domains for components (i.e. images, JavaScript, CSS etc.) and measured their respective DNS Response time. We use *getdns* and *libcurl* C libraries to issue Do53, DoT, and DoH queries. *Getdns* provides an API that allows developers to perform DNS Do53 and DoT requests using different programming languages. Libcurl supports POST requests to be sent via HTTPS. This capability enables us to measure DoH DNS response time. We could have gotten the DNS response times from the collected HARs, however, we noted that some of the timings were not correct and decided to use the *getdns*. It is important to note that the DNS responses were not cached by the browser used in the measurements to make sure that the subsequent transaction is not affected by the cache.

DNS-Related Failure Rates. Failures within DNS can have a dramatic impact on the wider Internet, most notably preventing access to any services dependent on domain names (e.g. web, mobile apps) [20]. Recent studies on Do53, DoT and DoH have found that encrypted queries tend to fail more than the regular DNS. Hounsel et al. [16] found that in lossier conditions, such as 3G, DoH experiences higher failure rates compared to Do53. This work seeks to establish DNS failure rates from real 3G and 4G conditions. We argue that understanding the prevalence of errors resulting from a particular DNS protocol is essential in informing the users' choice of DNS protocols given their network conditions.

Page Load Time. Page load time is an important metric of browser-based QoE. It represents the amount of time a user has to wait before the page is loaded in a browser. In this study, Firefox was used in headless mode to visit a set of HTTPS-enabled websites. For each website, we collect HAR files in JSON format containing timing information, including blocking information, proxy negotiation, DNS lookup, TCP handshake, SSL, Requests, Waiting and Content download. From the HAR files, we record the *onLoad* timing - the time taken to completely load the page together with its components.

3.2 Experiment Setup

We begin by describing how we collected the dataset that we analyse in this study. The study uses Alexa top 50 global websites for African countries[2] and top 50 Alexa local websites[3] for each African country (hosted locally or operated by local entities). The local websites were particularly included to represent the

---

[2] https://www.alexa.com/topsites/countries.

[3] https://www.alexa.com/topsites/category/Top/Regional/Africa.

websites serving African content and observe how DoT and DoH impact the browsing QoE on the local websites. These websites are normally not heavily cached in different public DNS recursive resolvers. We managed to get 2294 unique websites altogether. We then used *pshtt* modules of domain-scanner[4] application to find the websites that were online and responsive on port 443. This process gave us 1583 websites.

We then used MaxMind to geolocate 1206 websites. Of the 1206 websites, we found that 55.7% of the websites are hosted in North America, 27.6% in Europe, 14.4% in Africa, 1.7% in Asia, $0,5\%$ in Oceania and 0.1% in South America. We then selected the first three continents which served the most websites in our dataset. We randomly selected an equal number (173) of websites from America and Europe datasets. The 173 value came from the lowest number of websites in the selected continents, which is Africa in our case. This gave us 519 websites which we use in this study. We did this to have a common denominator for on which to base our results and discussion. For each of these continents, we looked at the common TLS protocols negotiated. We found that America had the highest number of websites that negotiated TLS1.3 (84%) and the remaining 16% negotiated TLS1.2. Africa had 84% TLS1.2, 15% TLS1.3 and 1% TLS1.0 while Europe had 87% TLS1.2, 12% TLS1.3 and 1% TLS1.0.

To replicate web browser actions when a user visits a website, we follow a methodology used in a study by Hounsel *et al.* [16]. We use automated Firefox 67.0.1 to randomly visit the websites in our list in headless mode. This is a clean instance without any ad or pop-up blockers. We, however, install a plugin to export HTTP Archive objects (HARs) from each visited website. We store these HARs in a PostgreSQL database as JSON objects. The study also aimed at measuring how the selection of DNS recursive resolver and DNS transport affect browser performance which, in turn, affects user's QoE. As such, we use 5 DNS recursive resolvers each offering Do53, DoH and DoT. Additionally, we used default Do53 at each vantage point. It is important to note that the default resolvers only support Do53 and this serves as a baseline for the performance over Do53. Table 1 lists resolvers used in this study. Of the five resolvers, three (Google, Cloudflare and Quad9) negotiated TLS1.3 while CleanBrowsing and AdGuard negotiate TLS1.2.

Firefox web browser natively supports Do53 and DoH. On the other hand, DoT has to be configured on the user's machine outside of the browser. As such, we use Stubby for DoT resolution, a stub resolver based on the getdns library. Stubby listens on a loopback address and responds to Do53 queries. All DNS queries received by Stubby are then sent out to a configured recursor over DoT. We modify /etc/resolv.conf on our measurement systems to point to the loopback address served by Stubby. This forces all DNS queries initiated by Firefox to be sent over DoT.

Between the measurements, we were not able to control the caches of the recursive resolvers. We, therefore, randomised the order of arguments that were presented to the browser in the form of a tuple comprising websites, DNS

---

[4] https://github.com/18F/domain-scan.

Table 1. Compared DNS resolvers

Configuration	Do53/DoT address	DoH URI	Marker
Local	Default Do53	None	Local
Cloudflare	1.1.1.1	https://cloudflare-dns.com/dns-query	CF
Google	8.8.8.8	https://dns.google/dns-query	GG
Quad9	9.9.9.9	https://dns.quad9.net/dns-query	Q9
CleanBrowsing	185.228.168.168	https://doh.cleanbrowsing.org/doh/security-filter	CB
AdGuard	176.103.130.131	https://dns.adguard.com/dns-query	AG

recursive resolvers and DNS protocols. This was done to avoid biasing results due to network quiet and busy times, as well as the potential effect of a query warming the recursor's cache for subsequent queries from the other protocols tested.

This measurements study was done from February 2020 to 21 May 2020. The measurements were done from 14 vantage points located in 7 countries; Malawi, Madagascar, South Africa, Kenya, Zambia, Nigeria and Uganda. This study aimed at measuring the impact of DoT and DoH on user's Quality of Experience hence the measurements were conducted at network edges. As such we used our contacts from 5 of these seven countries. These countries are (with their respective networks we measured from enclosed in brackets after the country name): Madagascar (Widecom), Zambia (MTN, Liquid telecoms), Uganda (Airtel, Orange), Kenya (Airtel) and Nigeria (MTN). The researchers had access to two countries; Malawi (TNM, Airtel, wired Campus network) and South Africa (Vodacom, Eduroam, Campus wired network, Community network). The participants were compensated with extra Internet data bundles.

At each vantage point, we conducted two sessions of measurements; one under 4G and another under 3G. Measurements were also conducted on a wireless community network and two University campus networks (Wired and Eduroam) in South Africa. The community networks are becoming more prevalent in the region as a low-cost Internet access network managed and operated by communities to meet their communication needs [21]. The campus networks represent the well connected, higher resourced networks which we use to benchmark our results.

We ran the measurements on computers running Ubuntu 18.04 desktop version. We packaged the Firefox browser in a docker container for portability. The tools ran on i5 computes with 8 GB of RAM except for one PC which had 16 GB RAM.

4   Results

In this section, we present findings from the measurements conducted. We start with an overview of the data collected from all vantage points, and thereafter, we highlight vantage points and protocols that show peculiar results. We focus the discussion on comparing the performance of different DNS configuration from 4G networks. The evaluation is also based on the continent in which the websites are hosted. We then benchmark these findings against measurements from university campus networks, representing the high-end networks. It is important to note that in the dataset we have timings longer than four seconds. However, using boxplots we can identify the distribution of the data and comfortably cut off outliers. As can be seen from the results in this section we place a cut-off point at 2000 ms for latency and DNS response time. We further use the median difference for page load time.

4.1   Transport Delay

Following our findings in terms of DNS response time and page load time, we deep-dived into other determinants of Internet performance, such as latency and DNS resolution paths. To do this, we conducted ICMP ping measurements and traceroute measurements.

Latency Measurements: Each time we performed a page load test, we performed ICMP five ping tests to each resolver. We observe that Quad9, Local, Cloudflare, Google, Cleanbrowsing, and Adguard have median round trip times (RTTs) of 229.4 ms, 328.8 ms, 333.8 ms, 381 ms, 443.4 ms and 1296 ms respectively. On the median case, we see that Quad9 has lower latency than the Local resolver. We note that AdGuard has the highest RTT. Zooming into the performance of providers in different countries, we observe varying results. Figure 1 shows the average latency from different countries to public DNS resolvers. From this figure, we observe that generally, Local resolver outperforms the remote DNS resolvers. This can be observed in Kenya, Madagascar, South Africa, Uganda and Zambia. This can be attributed to good peering enabled by Internet Exchange points available in the countries. On the other hand, Malawi's Local median RTT is almost equal to that of Google and Cloudflare. This suggests that the networks use either Cloudflare or Google as default resolver(s). However, Malawi's networks would have experienced lower latency (median 250 ms) if Quad9 is used as a default resolver. A similar pattern is observed from Nigeria, where the default resolver had minimum RTTs of >200 ms and hence outside our cleaned data. Nigeria's MTN network would have experienced lower latencies if it used Google ($\approx$250 ms) as a default resolver. This is unsurprising since Google has a cache in Nigeria.

Network wise, we found that the RTTs vary from one network type to another. For example, in South Africa, we conducted measurements under 3G, 4G, community wireless network, Eduroam and Campus wired networks. Comparing the RTTs under these network types, we found that campus networks had lower RTTs. We found that $\approx$90% of latency to Cloudflare resolver from campus networks was under 20 ms. In the same range of 1 ms–20 ms, from 4G, 3G and community networks, no transaction was recorded. The RTTs to Cloudflare, under 3G, ranged from 140 ms to 210 ms with $\approx$90% of the transactions under 200 ms. On the other hand, under 4G, RTTs were in the range of 90 ms–110 ms

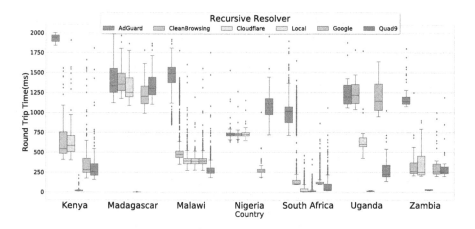

Fig. 1. Round Trip Time (RTT) to the public recursive resolvers from seven countries

with ≈96% of the transactions under 100 ms. We further categorised the RTTs based on DNS type. Interestingly, we observed that all the three protocols Do53, DoH and DoH had comparable RTTs suggesting that DNS resolvers (i.e. Do53, DoH and DoT) from the same provider are co-located.

We note in our dataset that a greater percentage of webservers in Africa (84%) and Europe (87%) negotiated TLSv1.2, a protocol that expends Two Round Trip Time (2-RTT) during TLS handshake. This implies that higher latency networks would experience even higher page load times (PLTs) and DNS response times when lower versions of TLS are used. We find that, in general, DoT performed better than DoH for websites hosted in Africa, with PLT average difference of 650 ms, even though 84% of such websites used TLSv1.2. We expect that QoE for websites hosted Africa and Europe would improve if webservers in these regions negotiated TLSv1.3, which uses 0/1-RTT when performing TLS handshake.

Traceroute Measurements: To understand the reason behind higher latencies to resolvers form some countries, we conducted traceroute measurements to geolocate the DNS recursors. We performed traceroute to each of the resolvers in our measurement tool. The findings show that the paths to some resolvers are longer than others. For example, looking at the previous host before the final destination, we notice that for DNS providers have their presence in South Africa. However, the paths taken from various countries to South Africa differ, even between two ISPs from the same country. For example, from a vantage point in Malawi, Airtel network had lower RTTs than Telkom Networks Malawi (TNM). To understand the reason behind these varying RTTs in these networks, we conducted traceroute measurements from our vantage points to the DNS resolvers. We notice that all the paths to the resolvers pass through South Africa; however, the traceroute measurements revealed that these networks use different network paths to the same destination. For example, Cloudflare resolver (1.1.1.1) is one hop (ASN) away from Airtel subscribers compared to three hops (ASNs) under TNM.

4.2 Pageload Success and Failure Rates

Table 2 shows the success and failure rates for the page loads. It also presents error types we encountered during our measurements. Generally, Do53 has higher success rates compared to DoT and DoH under all the network conditions in all the three continents. DoH has the lowest success rate across networks when resolving websites hosted in all the three continents. A closer look to at the individual recursive resolver's performance, we observe that DoH is affected much with deteriorating network conditions and distance to the resolver. The worst DoH success rate is observed when resolving websites hosted in Europe on 3G with 24% success rate and 43% DNS error rate. This can be attributed to caching issues; users in Africa mostly consume content hosted in North America, which suggests that most of the American hosted content exist in African caches.

We noted that the *Other Errors* are quite high compared to *Selenium* and *Pageload timeout*. This prompted us to look into what might be these errors which included *refused, DoT stub errors* and *nss* errors.

We observe that the success or failure rates depend on the network conditions and DNS protocol. We note in our results that the rates are directly proportional to network conditions; the better the network conditions (bandwidth, delay), the higher the success rate and vice versa. For example, we note (Table 2) failure reduction as we move from 3G, 4G and Eduroam. These observations further indicate that the success of connection depends on the users' choice of DNS protocol.

4.3 DNS Resolution Delay

Overall, as expected, we find that Do53 has a lower DNS resolution time (DRT) compared to DoT and DoH across all the resolvers. It should be noted that we have two kinds of Do53; local and remote (provided by the open public resolvers). Figure 2 shows a category plot for DNS response times for different recursive resolvers grouped by continent and DNS protocol. This implies that users have to bear some substantial cost to benefit from DNS security. The difference between DoE and Do53 on the same DNS provider is substantially wide. We note from the latency results that DoE and Do53 from the same DNS provider were colocated except AdGuard which showed a median RTT difference of ≈200 ms. This RTT difference translates to a median response time difference of ≈750 ms between AdGuard's DoE and Do53 as shown in Fig. 2. We observe a marginal difference between DoE from the same DNS provider with DoH having lower response times than DoT except for Google which displays the opposite when resolving domains hosted in Europe and North America. However, Google's DoE seems to perform uniformly when resolving sites hosted in Africa. We further observe that Quad9's DoT has way higher than its DoH despite having comparable median.

Table 2. Success and Error rate for Do53, DoT and DoH to websites hosted in Africa, Europe and North America respectively under 3G, 4G and Eduroam networks.

Continent	Network	Protocol	Successful (%)	DNS error (%)	Pageload error (%)	Selenium error (%)	Other errors (%)
Africa	3G	dns	61.33	11	0	10.33	17.33
		doh	47.88	35.45	0	4.55	12.12
		dot	58.63	12.2	0	11.61	17.56
	4G	dns	79.37	2.73	1.02	1.26	15.63
		doh	61.14	23.63	0.7	1.17	13.37
		dot	79.52	2.64	1.14	1.39	15.31
	Eduroam	dns	85.98	2.49	1.85	2.12	7.56
		doh	65.06	24.9	1.08	2.16	6.8
		dot	77.3	11.93	1.41	2.32	7.04
Europe	3G	dns	54.7	4.27	0	14.53	26.5
		doh	24.62	43.85	0	18.46	13.08
		dot	55.3	5.3	0	15.15	24.24
	4G	dns	77.78	2.61	1.63	0.79	17.18
		doh	62.14	19.5	1.43	0.76	16.18
		dot	76.72	2.86	1.76	1.3	17.35
	Eduroam	dns	86.29	2.8	0.8	1	9.11
		doh	72.16	20.54	0.63	1.17	5.5
		dot	80.02	12.06	0.72	0.81	6.39
North America	3G	dns	64.22	7.33	0.43	17.67	10.34
		doh	49.22	31.01	0	12.4	7.36
		dot	60.38	8.46	1.15	17.69	12.31
	4G	dns	84.09	0.91	0.37	1.42	13.21
		doh	67.78	17.57	0.29	1.28	13.09
		dot	82.43	0.86	0.58	1.32	14.81
	Eduroam	dns	88.67	2.42	0.11	0.99	7.81
		doh	73.66	20.5	0.1	0.89	4.85
		dot	82.28	10.89	0	0.89	5.94

Much larger differences can be seen when we compare DNS providers against each other. From Fig. 2, we note that four of the five public resolvers (Clean-Browsing, Cloudflare, Google and Quad9) have ≈750 ms as their 3rd quartile. Surprisingly, CleanBrowsing shows even lower response times than Google and Quad9. We posit that the filtering performed by CleanBrowsing makes it skip some domains hence making it perform faster. As expected, AdGuard reports the highest DNS response times across the vantage points. This is as a result of the higher latencies to the resolvers. Cloudflare Do53 provides lower DNS response times than the ISP's (Local) resolvers in Fig. 2, cases. We mostly observe this from Zambia, Nigeria and Malawi (Fig. 3). It should be noted that Cloudflare does not support EDNS Client Subnet which scopes the cache per subnet which gives it the ability to aggressively cache DNS responses. Continent wise, we observe that cumulatively DoH reports lower response times for content hosted in Africa compared to content hosted offshore.

Figure 4 shows CDFs response times for Google, Cloudflare and Quad9 under 4G (Fig. 4a) and Campus wired network (Fig. 4b). We observe a noticeable difference between these networks. Of greater interest is the performance of Cloudflare's DoT on a wired network under 100 ms response time; it performs better than DoH and comparable to local Do53. For response times longer than 100 ms, DoH outperforms DoT. At response times longer than 400 ms, DoH seems to perform better than local Do53. This result concurs with the findings found by Hounsel *et al.* [16].

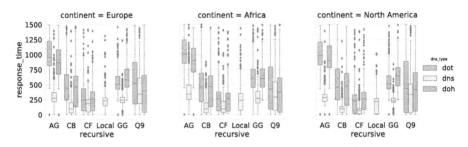

Fig. 2. DNS response time for different open public recursive resolvers when resolving websites hosted in Europe, Africa and North America from across the vantage points under 4G

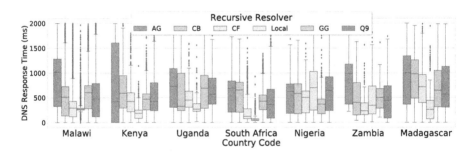

Fig. 3. DNS response time for each DNS recursive resolver across the vantage coutries under 4G

4.4   Page Load Times (PLT)

Pageload time is a more direct indication of how users experience web browsing. We have already seen the differences in query response times among the various DNS protocols under different network types across African vantage points. In this section, we show the relationship between the DNS response times and the page load times.

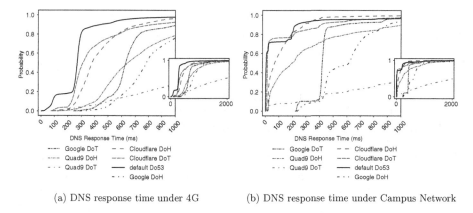

(a) DNS response time under 4G   (b) DNS response time under Campus Network

Fig. 4. DNS timings for local Do53 vs DoE from major DNS providers (Google, Cloud-flare and Quad9) under 4G and Campus network

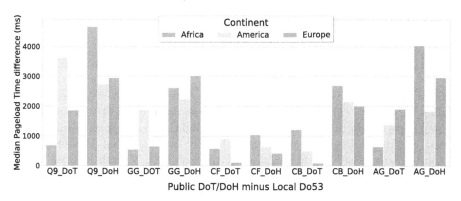

Fig. 5. Median pageload time differences between DoE and local Do53 when resolving websites hosted in Africa, North America and Europe measured from 4G networks

Figure 5 shows PLT differences between DoE resolvers (Google (GG), Cloud-flare (CF), Quad9 (Q9), CleanBrowsing (CB) and AdGuard (AG)) and default Do53 when resolving websites hosted in Africa, America and Europe. The difference is calculated by taking the median page load time for a website/user using one secure resolver minus the median page load time of the same website/user using local resolver. The difference, therefore, is indicative of extra cost a user would bear when using secure DNS protocols provided by public DNS resolvers as compared to default Do53. From the graph, the lower PLT difference on the secure DNS resolvers implies that the performance is almost closer to that of default Do53.

Our first observation is that, unlike the pattern observed in DNS response times (Fig. 2) where DoT had relatively higher response times than DoH, Fig. 5 shows that generally, DoT has lower median response times than DoT. From Fig. 5, we note that DoT performs much better than DoH on websites hosted in

Africa, with a difference of less than 1000 ms. This behaviour can also be observed on the websites hosted in Europe except for CleanBrowsing's DoT which has a difference of ≈2000 ms. On the other hand, DoH has poorer performance in all DNS configurations for websites hosted in all continents, with a difference of more than 2000 ms. Quad9 DoH and AdGuard DoH, however, have the most impact, with PLT differences above 4000 ms. This implies that if 4G users configure DoH in place of default Do53, they should expect performance overhead of up to 4000 ms. We note that Cloudflare's DoT and DoH PLT differences are consistently lower across continents.

Zooming into Google's DoT and DoH PLT differences, we note an interesting result; Google's DoT PLT difference is ≈700 ms while DoH is ≈4700 ms. However, we expected Google to perform better in the region by the mere fact that Google has caches in several countries on the continent. This disparity could be due to protocol implementation issues, such as caching and ENDS Client Subnet support. Unlike Cloudflare, Google supports EDNS Client Subnet [22], which scopes the caches per subnet. This means that Google DoH would steer cache to ISPs' network, whereas Cloudflare cannot.

5   Limitations

This study has potential limitations which may affect the generalisation of our results. Firstly, we conducted the measurements from only 14 vantage points located in seven countries. Secondly, we conducted the measurements using automated Firefox on Ubuntu environment. Finally, we only used Maxmind as a geolocation database, which might affect the accuracy. Nonetheless, we argue that our findings provide an overview of DoT and DoH performance in Africa and their impact on the quality of browsing experience.

6   Conclusion

In this paper, we investigated the performance impact of public Do53, DoH, DoT on the websites hosted in Africa, North America and Europe. We also measured DNS resolution success rates and failure when local Do53, public Do53, DoT or DoH are used. While it is well understood that encrypted DNS protocols and systems are desirable for a safe and reliable Internet, these protocols have also been shown to negatively impact the quality of experience for web users. This is particularly true in higher-delay networks edge networks that are far away from critical infrastructures such as DNS resolvers and content servers. The negative impact is even more severe in developing regions such as Africa due to the prevalence of sub-optimal routing paths and offshore hosting. This paper has looked at the extent to which high latencies between users and resolvers, as well as offshore web hosting, impact the performance of secure DNS resolution and the overall web browsing performance.

Recent studies [11,13,14] have reported that networks in the region experience high latencies due to lack of local peering. Fanou *et al.* [14] further found that African countries hardly share caches leaving cacheless countries with no option but to fetch the content using longer paths. Our results show this pattern, where different countries show different results for the same recursive resolver. In addition to localisation of content and cache sharing proposed by these and other authors, this study recommends that ISPs should consider implementing local DNS over Encryption infrastructure to reduce DNS resolution path, which, in turn, will improve the Quality of Protection and Experience to their customers. We noted in the results that DoH was affected by network conditions and latency – implementing local DoH servers would improve its performance and success rate. We further recommend the wide adoption of newer security protocols such as TLS1.3, which is designed to reduce the latency impact of the older versions of TLS.

Acknowledgements. The authors are grateful for the financial support received from the Hasso Plattner Institute for Digital Engineering, through the HPI Research School at the University of Cape Town. The authors would like to thank Nick Feamster and Austin Hounsel for their help and inspiration in this study.

References

1. Mockapetris, P.: Domain names - concepts and facilities, RFC 1034, IETF, November 1987
2. Farrell, S., Tschofenig, H.: Pervasive monitoring is an attack, RFC 7258, IETF, May 2014
3. Hu, Z., Zhu, L., Heidemann, J., Mankin, A., Wessels, D., Hoffman, P.: Specification for DNS over Transport Layer Security (DoTLS), RFC 7858, IETF, May 2016
4. McManus, P.H.P.: DNS queries over HTTPS (DoH), RFC 8484, IETF, October 2018
5. dnscrypt.info: DNSCrypt version 2 protocol specification. DNSCrypt, 14 July 2019. https://dnscrypt.info/protocol. Accessed 22 Aug 2019
6. Lu, C., et al.: An end-to-end, large-scale measurement of DNS-over-encryption: how far have we come?. In: Proceedings of the Internet Measurement Conference (2019)
7. Radmand, P., Talevski, A.: Impact of encryption on QoS in VoIP. In: 2010 IEEE Second International Conference on Social Computing, pp. 721–726, August 2010
8. Mohammed, H.A., Ali, A.H.: Effect of some security mechanisms on the QoS VoIP application using OPNET. Int. J. Current Eng. Technol. **3**, 1626–1630 (2013)
9. Spyropoulou, E., Levin, T., Irvine, C.: Calculating costs for quality of Security service. In: Proceedings 16th Annual Computer Security Applications Conference (ACSAC 2000), pp. 334–343, December 2000
10. Chen, J., Amershi, S., Dhananjay, A., Subramanian, L.: Comparing Web interaction models in developing regions. In: Proceedings of the First ACM Symposium on Computing for Development, ACM DEV 2010, pp. 6:1–6:9. ACM, New York (2010)
11. Formoso, A., Chavula, J., Phokeer, A., Sathiaseelan, A., Tyson, G.: Deep diving into Africa's inter-country latencies. In: IEEE INFOCOM 2018 - IEEE Conference on Computer Communications, pp. 2231–2239, April 2018

12. Fanou, R., Tyson, G., Francois, P., Sathiaseelan, A.: Pushing the frontier: exploring the African Web ecosystem. In: Proceedings of the 25th International Conference on World Wide Web, WWW 2016, pp. 435–445. International World Wide Web Conferences Steering Committee, Republic and Canton of Geneva (2016)

13. Calandro, E., Chavula, J., Phokeer, A.: Internet development in Africa: a content use, hosting and distribution perspective. In: Mendy, G., Ouya, S., Dioum, I., Thiaré, O. (eds.) AFRICOMM 2018. LNICST, vol. 275, pp. 131–141. Springer, Cham (2019). https://doi.org/10.1007/978-3-030-16042-5_13

14. Fanou, R., Tyson, G., Fernandes, E.L., Francois, P., Valera, F., Sathiaseelan, A.: Exploring and analysing the African Web ecosystem. ACM Trans. Web **12**, 22:1–22:26 (2018)

15. Böttger, T., et al.: An empirical study of the cost of DNS-over-HTTPs. In: Proceedings of the Internet Measurement Conference, IMC 2019, pp. 15–21, Association for Computing Machinery, New York (2019)

16. Hounsel, A., Borgolte, K., Schmitt, P., Holland, J., Feamster, N.: Analyzing the costs (and benefits) of DNS, DoT, and DoH for the modern web. In: Proceedings of the Applied Networking Research Workshop (2019)

17. Hounsel, A., Borgolte, K., Schmitt, P., Holland, J., Feamster, N.: Comparing the effects of DNS, DoT, and DoH on web performance. In: Proceedings of The Web Conference 2020, WWW 2020, pp. 562–572. Association for Computing Machinery, New York (2020)

18. Hoang, N.P., Lin, I., Ghavamnia, S., Polychronakis, M.: K-resolver: towards decentralizing encrypted DNS resolution. ArXiv, vol. abs/2001.08901 (2020)

19. Hounsel, A., Borgolte, K., Schmitt, P., Feamster, N.: D-DNS: towards re-decentralizing the DNS, 02 2020

20. Yang, D., Li, Z., Tyson, G.: A deep dive into DNS query failures. In: 2020 USENIX Annual Technical Conference (USENIX ATC 20), pp. 507–514, USENIX Association, July 2020

21. Rey-Moreno, C.: Supporting the creation and scalability of affordable access solutions. Annual report, Internet Society, May 2017

22. Contavalli, C., van der Gaast, W., Lawrence, D., Kumari, W.: Client Subnet in DNS Queries, RFC 7871, IETF, May 2016

A First Look at the African's ccTLDs Technical Environment

Alfred Arouna[1], Amreesh Phokeer[2], and Ahmed Elmokashfi[1(✉)]

[1] Simula Metropolitan CDE, Oslo, Norway
{alfred,ahmed}@simula.no
[2] African Network Information Centre (AFRINIC), Ebene, Mauritius
amreesh@afrinic.net

Abstract. Leveraging multiple datasets, we evaluate the current status of African ccTLDs technical environment with regard to best practices. Compared to the top 10 ccTLDs, African ccTLDs appear to have enough IPs to maintain service availability while handling authoritative DNS queries. With regard to the early stage of IPv6 deployment in the AFRINIC region, it is interesting to note that 94% of African ccTLDs support IPv6. This is due to the huge adoption of *out of region* or *offshore* DNS anycast provider. The majority (84%) of African anycast traffic is handled by non-profit foundations and/or organisations using resources from other RIRs such as RIPE-NCC and ARIN. Furthermore, less than 30% (16) of African ccTLD have signed their zone. From this group, the majority is using the recommended algorithm RSASHA256 (Algorithm 8) as suggested by BCP 14. Strangely some African ccTLDs lack basic DNS configuration such as missing PTR records, lame delegation, EDNS compliance and consistent serial numbers. These misconfigurations can be easily fixed with consistent monitoring or the use of modern automated registry software which comes with internal checks. Overall, African ccTLDs are characterised by the usage of *out of region* resources.

1 Introduction

The Domain Name System (DNS) is a global hierarchical and decentralized distributed directory service. The DNS maps a resource to a value. The Internet Assigned Numbers Authority (IANA) is the global coordinator of the DNS Root, which is the highest level in the DNS hierarchy. As for other regions, all African countries have country code Top Level Domain (ccTLD) assigned by IANA. ccTLDs are very central as they remain the main way to clearly indicate that content is targeted to a particular region or country. Of course, many African users/organisations are using generic Top Level Domain (gTLD) to provide their services in the AFRINIC region. But collecting data related to each African ccTLD from these gTLD require time and collaboration of gTLD managers. Moreover, with the new gTLD program, it becomes harder to identify all gTLD that are used by end-users in a specific country.

The African ccTLD DNS ecosystem is led by the Africa Top Level Domain Association (AFTLD) [1]. As key performance indicators, it is expected to have

R. Zitouni et al. (Eds.): AFRICOMM 2020, LNICST 361, pp. 305–326, 2021.
https://doi.org/10.1007/978-3-030-70572-5_19

90% of African automated registry systems with IPv6 and 50% with DNSSEC by 2020 [2]. In the 2016 Africa Domain Name System Market Study Report [3], the Internet Corporation for Assigned Names and Numbers (ICANN) recommended among other things, to simplify, automate and expedite domain registration processes. In 2018, Africa ccTLDs posted strong registered domains growth of 9% compared to 6% in 2017 [4], which illustrates the rapid development of the Internet in the region. This growth increased by 6% in 2019 [4] but volumes remain low (1.7% in 2019) of the international market share. As explained in [3], the DNS market is clearly dependent on the availability of infrastructure and access to service providers. Thus, many studies have focused on African Internet topology (Interdomain routing, IXP, IPv6, intra-Africa latency, etc.) while only a few targeted services like the web or the DNS.

In this paper, we take a closer look at the technical environment of African ccTLDs. Using several data sources, we assess whether African ccTLDs meet best practices and recommendations from ICANN and IETF. We also examine the hosting of these ccTLDs and investigate them for misconfigurations.

Through active African ccTLDs data collection, we correlate results from different datasets and find that most African ccTLDs follows minimum best practices and only 16 have DNSSEC enabled. We also find that African ccTLDs meet the minimum requirement for zone management and widely support IPv6 at the transport level.

2   Related Work

Internet topology in Africa has received a lot of attention recently with the interest of the use of IXPs and IPv6. Most research are related to interdomain routing [5], IPv6 adoption [6], latency, intra-africa and inter-country Internet traffic [7–10]. These studies address only a subset of African Internet challenges, by focusing mainly on topology and its impact on Quality of Service (QoS). For instance, a few works have targeted the DNS and more specifically, the technical environment of African ccTLDs.

Liang et al. highlighted that root DNS servers latency from Africa and South America were 3 to 6 times worse than Europe and North America [11]. This latency to root DNS servers is an element of the overall latency from the end-user's point of view. The capabilities and locations of the servers for each service also have a huge impact on overall latency. Nakahira et al. have found that 80% of web servers using African ccTLDs are offshore (out of home country) and more than half of these are located in Europe [12]. They add that offshore servers constitute a significant aspect of the digital divide problem. Not only do they provide little benefit to the African Internet ecosystem, but also, they heightens the risk of a African ccTLDs being unable to apply their own policies and regulations.

Furthermore, Zaki et al. observe that, rather than bandwidth, the primary bottleneck of web performance in Ghana is the lack of good DNS servers and caching infrastructure [13]. They show that the use of well-known end-to-end latency optimizations like simple DNS caching, redirection caching, and SPDY can yield substantial improvements to user-perceived latency.

Recently, Fanou *et al.* [14], by exploring and analysing the African Web Ecosystem, found that top African websites prefer to host their content abroad. According to them, major bottlenecks to host content in Africa are the lack of peering between networks, as well as poorly configured DNS resolvers. They recognise that improving connectivity in Africa is only one part of the equation. But it is required to ensure the quality of services provisioning.

Pappas *et al.* [15] evaluated the impact of configuration errors on DNS robustness. They noted that the degrees of misconfiguration vary from zone to zone. They indicated that the DNS, as well as any critical system, must include systematic checking mechanisms to cope with operational errors.

In the same vein, Phokeer *et al.* [16] focused on one of the DNS server misconfiguration that affect the responsiveness of the DNS service which could lead to delayed responses or failed queries: lame delegation. Basically, a delegation is lame when the delegated server did not respond to DNS queries. They discover that 40% of AFRINIC region reverse DNS present misconfigurations related to lame delegation and their work has been used to implement a policy in AFRINIC region[1].

This paper differs from these works by targeting African ccTLDs technical environment. The goal is to identify trends or key characteristics (good and bad) to make a couple of recommendations on how to improve the resilience of the DNS ecosystem in Africa. We take a broad perspective, looking at several different datasets and DNS parameters. The rest of this paper explores these parameters to understand the current technical state of African ccTLDs.

3   Methodology

To characterise the African ccTLDs technical environment, this work used active measurements to collect data from several sources during one month. We assume this period is sufficient since, to maintain consistency, IANA data and nameservers IP and/or name changes very little over time: they are used as baseline for DNS resolution. We were not able to detect inconsistent data during the collection period across all our daily measurement.

IANA Whois [17] provide main reference data for TLD nameservers. To evaluate nameservers set consistency, we use `getdns` to collect nameservers records as provided by each African cctTLD and compared them with IANA Whois records. Moreover, to identity *out of region* resource usage, we map each nameserver IP to its related Regional Internet Registry (RIR) by taking advantage of NRO's delegation [18] dataset. Therefore, combining NRO data with Anycast one, we can identify Anycast providers and their use by African ccTLDs.

IANA Whois also provide DNSSEC related data in the DS record (ds-rdata). Combined with the DNSSEC Deployment Maps project from Internet Society,

---

[1] AFRINIC Lame Delegation Policy - https://afrinic.net/policy/2017-dns-001-d2.

we have evaluated Domain Name System Security Extensions (DNSSEC) zone signing by African ccTLDs. Going further, we use Zonemaster tool to test African ccTLDs nameservers configuration against a set of well-defined requirements.

Taking advantage of Zonemaster misconfiguration report and previous datasets, we were able to get a better view of the African ccTLDs technical environment and we can provide some recommendations and guidelines following best practice to African ccTLDs. The scripts and data used in this study are publicly available[2].

3.1 Datasets

IANA WHOIS: For the purpose of this study, we have collected data for 54 [19] African member states of the United Nations from IANA Root Zone Database using WHOIS protocol. Currently, Somaliland did not have a ccTLD and Sahrawi Arab Democratic Republic (Western Sahara) with the ccTLD EH did not have records in IANA database. Saint Helena (SH), Ascension (AC) and Tristan da Cunha are British overseas territory managed by the British registry Internet Computer Bureau Limited (ICB Plc). Réunion (RE) and Mayotte (YT) are overseas department and regions of France managed by the French registry Association française pour le nommage Internet en coopération (AFNIC). From the IANA WHOIS server and for each ccTLD, we have selected nserver (i.e. nameservers records) and ds-rdata (i.e. DNSSEC Delegation Signer (DS) record) if available. Each nameserver can have multiple IPs (IPv4 and/or IPv6). This data will be used as a reference for all analysis.

NRO Delegation: The Number Resource Organization (NRO) is a coordinating body for the Regional Internet Registries (RIRs): AFRINIC, APNIC, ARIN, LACNIC and the RIPE NCC. The NRO provides a consistent and accessible Internet number resource statistics. One of these is the consolidated RIR Extended Delegated file [18]. This dataset is a daily updated report of the distribution of Internet number resources: IP (IPv4, IPv6) address ranges and Autonomous System Numbers (ASNs). The RIR statistics will be used to identify nameservers IPs' corresponding region by filtering *assigned* prefixes only. For this paper, we do not take into consideration the use of unassigned resources by African ccTLDs. In addition, we were able to identify related RIRs for all African ccTLD prefixes and ASN. It seems like African ccTLDs resources are legitimate ones, but a new study focusing on the unlawfully used of non-assigned prefixes is welcome.

Anycast: In 2015, Cicalese *et al.* [20] provided a *near*-ground-truth dataset of IPv4 anycast prefixes. More recently in 2019, Bian *et al.* [21] updated their results by using passive BGP routing information. They discovered that anycast routing has been entangled with the increased adoption of remote peering.

---

[2] https://github.com/AlfredArouna/AfTLDTechEnv

But these datasets do not contain any anycast IPs like those from the African DNS support programme[3] (AfDSP), RIPE-NCC Authoritative DNS (AuthDNS) project[4], DNSNODE from Netnode[5] or ironDNS[6] or from other anycast DNS services from private companies. Additionally, these data only cover the IPv4 space. Although RFC 2526 [22] recommends the use of reserved IPv6 anycast addresses within each subnet prefix, this recommendation is barely put into practice. Therefore, we use a combination of these research results added with AFRINIC, PCH, NetNode anycast prefixes (IPv4 and IPv6) and our heuristics: anycast namservers name may contains strings like *afrinic*, *pch*, *dnsnode*, *ripe* or *any* to determine whether an **nserver** is anycast or not. Four (`ML`,`GA`, `CF` and `GQ`) African ccTLDs are managed by the same registry, Freenom[7], which uses anycast under the service name "OpenTLD AnyCast Cloud".

DNSSEC Deployment: The Domain Name System Security Extensions (DNSSEC) is a suite of specifications to ensure *authenticity of origin* and *data integrity* of DNS data. DNSSEC adds several new resource records (RR) such as the DS (Delegation Signer), DNSKEY, RRSIG and NSEC or NSEC3 [23]. The parent zone stores the child zone DS record. The latter, which is a hash of the Key Signing Key (KSK), is used to check the child zone records' signature validity while also enabling the chain of trust up to the root zone, which IANA manages as the parent of all TLDs. The child DS records of the TLDs can be found in the IANA database (if available) in the `ds-rdata` field. The DNSSEC Deployment Maps[8] is an Internet Society project to provide a view into global DNSSEC deployment. It breaks the deployment status of TLDs out into the following five categories: (1) `Experimental` (Internal experimentation announced or observed), (2) `Announced` (Public commitment to deploy), (3) `Partial` (Zone is signed but not in operation, no DS in root), (4) `DS in Root` (Zone is signed and its DS has been published) and (5) `Operational` (Accepting signed delegations and DS in Root). As of writing this paper, the latest raw data is from 6 Jul 2020 [24]. For the rest of this paper, we will only consider `Operational` and `DS in Root` categories. Those categories take into account the `ds-rdata` from IANA database and will help to compare IANA database with the DNSSEC Deployment Maps result.

3.2 Tools

`getdns` **for Nameservers Set:** Once a ccTLD `nserver` information is saved in IANA database, it is supposed to be consistent and persistent. But daily management of a ccTLD may require changes in nameservers: improving performance,

---

[3] https://afrinic.net/dns-support.
[4] https://www.ripe.net/analyse/dns/authdns.
[5] https://dnsnode.netnod.se/.
[6] https://www.irondns.net.
[7] https://www.freenom.com/en/freeandpaiddomains.html.
[8] https://www.internetsociety.org/deploy360/dnssec/maps/.

response to an attack, change of registry, etc. Here, we use the `getdns` python bindings to collect NS records for all 54 African ccTLDs. `getdns` [25] is a modern asynchronous DNS API that simplifies access to advanced DNS features. With `getdns` as a stub-resolver, we use three different public DNS resolvers: Google Pulic DNS, Quad9 and Cloudfare to compare nameservers set consistency across resolvers and measurements. From our measurements, all public resolvers provide similar nameservers set. Data collected with `getdns` will be used to check consistency between information saved in the IANA database and information delivered by nameservers.

Zonemaster: Zonemaster [26] is a joint project from AFNIC[9] and IIS[10] to develop a new DNS validation tool; taking advantage of DNSCheck from IIS and Zonecheck from AFNIC. Zonemaster aims to check nameservers for configuration errors and generate a report that could help in fixing DNS misconfigurations. The optimal goal is to propose a standard for DNS Operations [27] while testing nameservers configuration against a set of requirements. Zonemaster comprises several components[11], including a storage (database) and a GUI. For this study, we only used the Zonemaster-LDNS, the Zonemaster-Engine and the Zonemaster-CLI. The Zonemaster-CLI v2.0.4 uses 67 requirements (tests cases) classified into 9 categories/modules (Basic, Address, Connectivity, Consistency, DNSSEC, Delegation, Nameserver, Syntax and Zone). Zonemaster is used to validate each African ccTLD nameservers configuration. We filter errors by levels; from highest to lowest: CRITICAL, ERROR, WARNING and NOTICE. For instance, if a ccTLD have CRITICAL and WARNING errors, we will consider CRITICAL only. Doing this, we keep the highest error level for each ccTLD.

4   Analysis

4.1   ccTLDs Reachability

All African ccTLDs have consistent nameservers records as seen from the IANA database and NS records except for Niger (`.NE`). The Nameserver `BOW.RAIN.FR` from the IANA database is not part of the NS records for `.NE` ccTLD, i.e. it is considered as a lame delegation[12].

Figure 1 shows the distribution of number of nameservers IPs for each ccTLD for both IPv4 and IPv6. The black line shows the number of unique nameservers used by each ccTLD. All African ccTLDs nameservers meet the minimum best practice of having at least two IPs to serve their DNS zone [28,29]. The majority of African ccTLDs, 94%, have nameversers with IPv6 addresses except for

---

[9] Afnic is the registry for domain names in.fr.

[10] IIS is the registry for domain names in.se.

[11] https://github.com/zonemaster/zonemaster.

[12] A lame delegation, also known as a lame response, is a type of error that results when a name server is designated as the authoritative server for a domain name for which it does not have authoritative data or is unreachable.

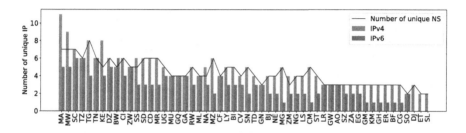

Fig. 1. Number of unique nameservers and IPs per African ccTLD: African ccTLD meet the minimum requirement to maintain service availability.

Ethiopia (ET), Sierra Leone (SL) and Djibouti (DJ). The high support of IPv6 is unexpected given that IPv6 deployment in the region is low [6]. This support of IPv6 on the transport level will be analysed in the next section.

To contextualize the numbers above, we compare with ccTLDs from other continents. According to Verisign's Q1 2020 report [30], top 10 ccTLDs with the highest number of domains were TK, CN, DE, UK, NL, RU, BR, EU, FR and IT. These top ccTLDs use a median of 10 IPs for their nameservers. United Kingdom (UK) has the highest number of IPs (13) while Netherlands (NL) is using the lowest number: 6 IPs. For African ccTLDs, the median is 7 IPs:(4 for IPv4 and 3 for IPv6). Morocco (MA) is using 16 IPs while Ethiopia (ET) and Sierra Leone (SL) are using 2 IPv4 addresses (no IPv6 IP for nameservers). 60% of top 10 ccTLDs are using a number of IPs greater than the median, which is sightly higher than African ccTLDs ratio. We notice that 53.70% (29) of African ccTLDs have a number of IPs (shared by nameservers) higher than the median of the number of IPs used by top ten ccTLDs. Having several IPs to handle DNS traffic, definitively helps, when it comes to scalability and resiliency. These benefits are only realized, if these servers are topologically diverse.

Overall, the African ccTLDs appear to have enough IPs to maintain a reaspnable quality of service, while handling authoritative DNS queries. We assume this traffic to be small, given the size of the DNS market in Africa [4]. Without public statistics of registered domain per African countries, we can only speculate about the correlation between the number of IPs used by a ccTLD and the country local DNS market. Top five African countries with highest Internet users[13] are Nigeria (NG), Egypt (EG), Kenya (KE), South Africa (ZA) and Algeria (DZ). It is expected that these countries probably host most local content and require more resilient infrastructure. But, from Fig. 1, it seems that this assumption is not always true. NG, EG, ZA are using few IPs while KE and DZ are using 4 or more IPs. It seems like the availability of resilient DNS infrastructure is not enough to stimulate local hosting.

---

[13] https://www.statista.com/statistics/505883/number-of-internet-users-in-african-countries/.

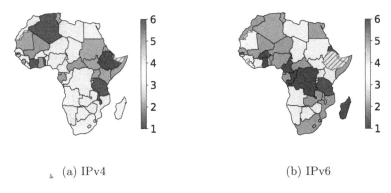

    (a) IPv4   (b) IPv6

Fig. 2. Unique ASN usage per ccTLD: except one extreme case, best practices are more followed in IPv4 than in IPv6

The two panels in Fig. 2 show the number of Autonomous systems, ASNs, that are associated with each ccTLD for IPv4 and IPv6, respectively. Except for Ethiopia (**ET**) with one ASN, all African ccTLDs running over IPv4, are served from two or more ASNs. We also note that the number of African ccTLDs using 2 or more ASNs is also lower for IPv6 than for IPv4.

Comparing to IPv4, African ccTLDs are less resilient on IPv6. A disruption affecting one ASN (for 10 ccTLDs) or two ASNs (for 17 ccTLDs) on IPv6 traffic can make some African ccTLDs unavailable (at least for IPv6 transport).

Takeaways. Overall, the African ccTLDs appear to have enough IPs to handle authoritative DNS queries. This definitely helps when its comes to scalability and resiliency. Compared to IPv4, African ccTLDs are less resilient on IPv6. But, these benefits are only realized, if these servers are topologically diverse.

4.2 Prefix Origin of NS

Using the NRO delegation database, we can retrieve prefixe allocations per region. We can then check if African ccTLDs are using IPs from multiple regions as recommended or not.

Figure 3 shows the ratio of number of namerservers IPs used by African ccTLDs per region. The color range from white to red indicates the ratio of IPs used from each RIR. The white color shows that no IP is used from the respective RIR, while red implies that all IPs in use come from the respective RIR. Green indicates a good balance in term of usage of IPs from different RIRs, while yellow shows a tendency to use more IPs from a specific region.

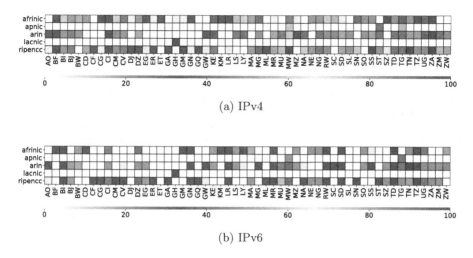

(a) IPv4

(b) IPv6

Fig. 3. RIR resources usage per ccTLD: for historical raison, African ccTLD mostly rely on RIPE-NCC and ARIN resources (Color figure online)

We record that African ccTLDs use IPs from several RIRs more on IPv4 than IPv6. Six ccTLDs are associated with IPv4 addresses from a single RIR compared to 16 on IPv6. Comoros (KM) and Freenom[14] customers (ML, GA, CF and GQ) are consistently using IPs (IPv4 and IPv6) from one RIR. Comoros is using AFRINIC only while Freenom customers are using RIPE-NCC only. Ethiopia (ET) is not using IPv6 and rely only on AFRINIC IPv4 allocations. We have 11 more African ccTLDs with 100% IPv6 usage from one RIR: Burkina Faso (BF), Democratic Republic of the Congo (CD), The Gambia (GM) are using IPs assigned by AFRINIC. Ghana (GH) is relying on IPs assigned by LACNIC. Madagascar (MG) and Seychelles (SC) are using resources from ARIN. Republic of the Congo (CG), Cameroon (CM), Eritrea (ER), Senegal (SN), São Tomé and Príncipe (ST) are using RIPE-NCC IPs only. These African ccTLDs have one-point-of-failure type of infrastructure: a problem that can lead to service unavailability (at least on IPv6).

In general, Fig. 3a shows that most *out of region* IPv4 are from RIPE-NCC, followed by ARIN. Likewise, Fig. 3b shows, the use of resources from theses RIRs for IPv6. LACNIC and APNIC resources are less used by African ccTLDs. This could be explained by the historical relation between AFRINIC and RIPE NCC or AFRINIC and ARIN. The AFRINIC region resources were initially managed by ARIN (south of the equator regions in Africa) and RIPE-NCC (north of the equator regions in Africa) until the creation of AFRINIC in 2005[15].

As seen in Sect. 4.1, African ccTLDs support IPv6 on transport level by mostly using *external* DNS providers. This assumption is confirmed by the high *out of region* IPv6 ratio while IPv6 deployment is at the lowest in AFRINIC

---

[14] https://www.freenom.com/en/freeandpaiddomains.html.
[15] https://www.nro.net/development-of-the-regional-internet-registry-system/.

region. We can conclude here that some African ccTLDs are either hosted out of the AFRINIC region by using IPv6 from *external* DNS providers. Not only this could have a negative impact on DNS resolution time for users in the country, but it suggests that the local ecosystem in not mature yet to host IPv6 services.

Takeaways. Overall, the African ccTLDs have good balance of resources usage from other RIR (topologically diverse) in IPv4 compared to IPv6. IPv6 adoption by African ccTLDs is driven by the use of *out of region* providers. RIPE NCC and ARIN appears to be the most use *out of region* RIRs resources for historical reasons.

4.3 Anycast

With anycast, the same prefix can be announced (by the same ASN) from multiple locations around the globe and clients are directed to the topologically-nearest replica. Hence, anycast allows registries to provide DNS content delivery from multiple sites that are, usually, physically distributed. Using anycast, African ccTLDs inherently increase their scalability and resiliency.

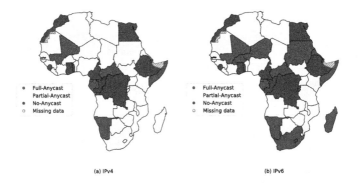

(a) IPv4   (b) IPv6

Fig. 4. Anycast is widely adopted by the African ccTLD. This adoption is driven by the use of *out of region* providers.

Figure 4 shows the ratio of discovered anycast nameservers. Namibia (NA), Somalia (SO), and the Freenom customers has 100% anycast ratio for both IPv4 and IPv6. This is correlated to the 100% out of region ratio as seen in Sect. 4.2. 11 African ccTLDs (20%) including Morocco (MA), Egypt (EG), Sierra Leone (SL), Togo (TG), Ethiopia (ET), Djibouti (DJ), Cameroon (CM), Democratic Republic of the Congo (CD) do not seem to use an anycast service. Half of African ccTLDs have an anycast ratio greater than 50%. This indicates that most African ccTLDs are opting for anycast.

Figure 5 shows that, apart from the African DNS support programme (AfDSP) from AFRINIC and the PCH DNS Anycast service, all other anycast providers are *out of region*. Note that the special provider NO ANYCAST is used here to show ccTLD which seems not to use anycast.

PCH Anycast Domain Name Service is by far the most popular, followed by RIPE-NCC AuthDNS and private companies. AFRINIC (29%), RIPE-NCC (12%) and PCH (35%) together manage more than 75% of anycast DNS traffic in AFRINIC region. If we add Netnode DNSNODE (8%), the majority (84%) of African anycast traffic is handled by non-profit foundations and/or organisations. However, the advantages given by the use of anycast seems not to target African Internet users. More than 70% of African ccTLD anycast traffic are *out of region*.

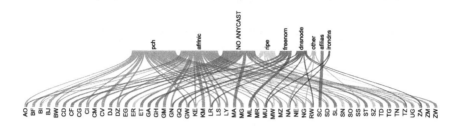

Fig. 5. The majority of African ccTLDs anycast traffic is handle by non-profit foundations and organisations: PCH, AFRINIC, RIPE-NCC, etc.

Moreover 16 African ccTLDs rely only on one anycast DNS provider. Zimbabwe (ZW), Zambia (ZM), Madagascar (MG), Cape Verde (CV) and Benin (BJ) are using PCH only. FREENOM customers ML,GA, CF and GQ rely on their provider anycast service. Seychelles (SC) is doing the same with AFILIAS. Senegal (SN), Eswatini (SZ) and Eritrea (ER) are using only RIPE anycast service. AFRINIC anycast service is uniquely used by Comoros (KM), The Gambia (GM) and Burkina Faso (BF).

The number of African ccTLD increase to 17 when it comes to using two anycast providers between PCH, AFRINIC, DNSNODE and RIPE. Ten African ccTLD are using the maximum number of anycast providers in the region. These African ccTLD are mostly sharing their anycast traffic between three anycast providers. Uganda (UG), Tanzania (TZ), South Sudan (SS), Sudan (SD), Rwanda (RW), Nigeria (NG), Namibia (NA), Mauritius (MU), Kenya (KE) and Burundi (BI) are using a combination of 3 anycast providers from AFRINIC, PCH, RIPE, DNSNODE, IRONDNS and UNKNOWN anycast provider.

With 80% of African ccTLD using it, anycast is popular in AFRINIC region. However, when correlating with Sects. 4.1 and 4.2, it is clear that the targeted market is not the African one. According to ICANN DNS Purchasing Guide for Government Procurement Officers [31], the use of IPv4 and IPv6 is an element on the checklist to select a TLD. Most African ccTLD meet this requirement.

Takeaways. Overall, Anycast is widely adopted by the African ccTLD. The majority of African anycast traffic is handled by non-profit foundations and/or organisations. However, with more than 70% of African ccTLD anycast traffic flagged as out of region, the advantages given by the use of anycast seems not to target African Internet users.

4.4 DNSSEC Zone Signing

The DNSSEC is a suite of protocols to further enhance DNS security. DNSSEC strengthens authentication in DNS using digital signatures based on public key cryptography. An authoritative DNS manager can sign their zone and resolvers can follow a chain of trust to validate the signed data. Due to the DNS hierarchical structure, each child who has signed his zone, must inform his parent by means of a specific resource record: Delegation Signer (DS) [23]; the parent zone store the child zone DS. IANA as managing the Root zone is the parent of all TLDs. The DS is the glue that creates the chain of trust from Root zone to the zone to be validated. DNSSEC by taking advantage of public key cryptography uses several algorithms: some for signing zones, some for validation on resolver side, and some can do both.

Table 1. Signed ccTLDs as seen by IANA and DNSSEC Deployment project

Countries	IANA	Deploy360		
		Operational	DS in root	Not available
Tanzania, Kenya, South Africa, Botswana, Namibia, Seychelles	Yes	Yes		
Botswana, Senegal, Mauritania, Guinea, Guinea-Bissau, Liberia, Tunisia, Algeria, Morocco, Uganda	Yes		Yes	
South Sudan	Yes			Yes
Zambia, Ivory Coast, Mauritius	No	Yes		
Madagascar	No		Yes	

Table 1 shows signed ccTLDs status from IANA database and from the DNSSEC Deployment project. The signed ccTLDs are mostly similar except for 4 ccTLDs: Zambia (ZM), Ivory Coast (CI), Mauritius (MU) and Madagascar (MG). According to the DNSSEC Deployment project, Zambia (ZM), Ivory Coast (CI) and Mauritius (MU) DNSSEC status are Operational and Madagascar (MG) has DS in root. But none of these ccTLDs have ds-rdata records in IANA database. We Contacted the DNSSEC Deployment project but they were not able to justify all their result for these four countries. Zambia (ZM) had published DS in root starting October 8, 2015 while Madagascar (MG) did the same starting March 18, 2016[16]. However, at the time of writing, the reasons for the removal of these DS from the Root are unknown. We have contacted both ccTLDs, but only Madagascar (MG) replied to our email and explained that they have removed their DS record temporally for internal reasons. Ivory Coast (CI) and Mauritius (MU) cases are related to *forward-looking* entries: the DNSSEC Deployment project trust TLD registry announcement to deploy DNSSEC on a certain date. If the

---

[16] http://rick.eng.br/dnssecstat/.

registry failed to meet this date, it had to be manually push out to some future time.

Less than 30% (16) of African ccTLD have signed their zone: Tanzania (TZ), Kenya (KE), South Africa (ZA), Botswana (BW), Namibia (NA), Senegal (SN), Mauritania (MR), Guinea (GN), Guinea-Bissau (GW), Liberia (LR), Tunisia (TN), Algeria (DZ), Morocco (MA), Uganda (UG), Seychelles (SC) and South Sudan (SS). This number is similar to the count done by the dnssec-africa[17] project as of July 2020 and there is no clear relation between signed zones and high *out of region* ratio. For instance, Namibia (NA) has 100% *out of region*, Kenya has 57% while Morocco (MA) has 18% *out of region* ratio. This result breaks our assumption that DNSSEC signing is driven by external DNS providers.

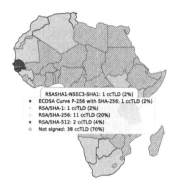

Fig. 6. The majority of signed African ccTLDs are using recommended DNSSEC signing algorithm. This algorithm is used worldwide and considered to be strong

Figure 6 shows DNSSEC signing algorithms used by these ccTLDs. Algorithms 5 (RSASHA1), 7 (RSASHA1-NSEC3-SHA1) and 10 (RSASHA512) are NOT RECOMMENDED [32] for DNSSEC signing. Namibia (NA), by using deprecated RSASHA1, is subject to efficient collision attack: *SHA-1 is a Shambles*. Thus, an attacker can spoof the DNS despite DNSSEC [33]. RSASHA1-NSEC3-SHA1 is used by Seychelles (SC) and RSASHA512 is used by Tanzania (TZ) and Guinea-Bissau (GW). These algorithms are widely deployed, but it is recommended to switch to other algorithms like 13 (ECDSAP256SHA256). According to [32], ECDSAP256SHA256 provides more cryptographic strength with a shorter signature length than either RSASHA256 or RSASHA512, therefore, it is now at MUST level for both validation and signing. Senegal (SN) is the very first and only one African ccTLD using Algorithms 13. RSASHA512 is not widely deployed hence, it requires RSASHA512 on DNSSEC validation to ensure interoperability. The majority (10 over 16) of African ccTLDs are using recommended algorithm: algorithm 8 (RSASHA256) which have a MUST level (BCP-14 [34]). It is used worldwide and considered to be strong.

---

[17] https://dnssec-africa.org/index.html.

Like IPv6, African ccTLDs DNSSEC signing is in an early stage. DNSSEC requires an additional workload through constant monitoring, while the insecure DNS *just works* and requires attention only in case of a failure. The weak DNSSEC uptake may hint at a lack of incentives.

Takeaways. Overall, DNSSEC zone signing is in an early stage in the AFRINIC region. Unlike IPs, ASNs and Anycast usage, DNSSEC signing is not driven by external DNS providers. Moreover, from the 30% of African ccTLDs that have signed their zone, the majority is following best practices.

4.5 Misconfigurations Report with Zonemaster

Zonemaster is a tool for investigating the state of the domain in a comprehensive way. It examines DNS from the Root (.) to the corresponding domain by checking the specified domain nameservers. Zonemaster aims to check nameservers for configuration errors and generate a report that will help in fixing misconfigurations. It has a predefined list of test cases that are organised into several categories (see Table 3). Each test has a severity level as described in Table 2. From highest to lowest, we have: CRITICAL, ERROR, WARNING, NOTICE and INFO.

Table 2. Zonemaster errors severity levels [35]

Severity level	Comment
CRITICAL	Zone being tested has one or more problems that are so severe that it is not possible to even test it
ERROR	A problem that is very likely (or possibly certain) to negatively affect the function of the zone
WARNING	Something that will under some circumstances be a problem, but that is unlikely to be noticed by a casual user
NOTICE	Something that should be known by the zone's administrator but that need not necessarily be a problem at all
INFO	Something that may be of interest to the zone's administrator but that definitely does not indicate a problem

Using Zonemaster, we have checked all 54 African ccTLDs for misconfigurations. The result of the testing of all 54 African ccTLDs with Zonemaster is organised into two levels of misconfigurations: 22 ERROR and 27 WARNING. There is no CRITICAL error: this is a proof that African registries meet the minimum requirements for operating a TLD as stated in BCP-16 [28].

Figure 7 shows the distribution of errors categories (Table 3) and tests cases grouped by severity levels. All misconfigurations messages are explained in the Mapping test messages to test module documentation [36].

Table 3. Zonemaster tests categories [36]

Categories	Usage
Basic	Initial tests: input validation, parent and child checking, etc.
Delegation	Parent and child nameservers properties
Consistency	All name have consistent answers
DNSSEC	Algorithms, secure delegation
Address	IP addresses properties
Name server	Authoritative DNS server checking
Connectivity	UDP/TCP, same AS, etc.
Zone	Data controlling the zone sane
Syntax	Illegal hostnames and characters

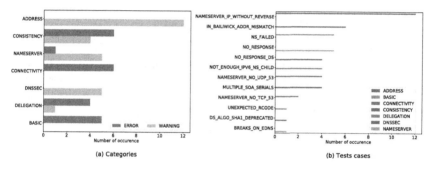

Fig. 7. Discovered misconfigurations categories and tests cases: missing PTR, lame delegation and badly configured nameservers are top three errors reported by zonemaster.

The most common misconfiguration is missing PTR records. It seems like African ccTLDs are not configuring `in-addr.arpa` or `ip6.arpa` "reverse" DNS. We can see here that most African ccTLDs did not follow RFC1912 [37]: for every IP address, there should be a matching PTR record. The PTR record is also critical for some services like mail. It is well known that to verify a mail server identity, one step is to check the matching of PTR records. If the nameserver did not have a PTR record, such a check can not be carried out. A mail from a server without a PTR record will mostly be directed to Spam or Junk folders. The quality of deployment will not be acceptable to end user, which will prefer popular working mail services.

The second most common misconfiguration is inconsistency between the glue records in the delegation and authoritative. Compared to IANA as parent, some African ccTLDs nameserver do not provide consistent NS records (glue record) with IANA database. Some NS records in the root zone for some ccTLDs are not present in the corresponding ccTLD response to an NS query. From an end-user point of view, the DNS resolution to an African ccTLDs will start with the

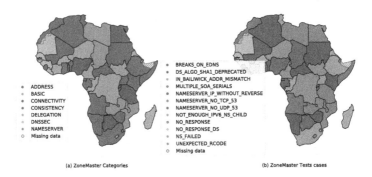

(a) ZoneMaster Categories   (b) ZoneMaster Tests cases

Fig. 8. Repartition of misconfigurations categories and tests cases across the African continent: misconfigurations did not follow any sub regional pattern

root DNS server. It will then try to reach the first available child NS record and continue the resolution process. Since there is a mismatch between parent and child, root DNS can provide a set of NS-es that the child (African ccTLD) do not recognize. The end-user's resolver will try each of NS in the set from root and continue with the first with positive result. Consequently, the first resolution process will take more time than expected and will increase the latency to the requested service.

NS_FAILED and NO_RESPONSE are the third most common misconfigurations. Some African ccTLDs nameserver response codes to DNS queries are: REFUSED and SERVFAIL. REFUSED means that some African ccTLDs refuse to act like DNS authoritative server. SERVFAIL indicate a misconfiguration on the server side. As result, these African ccTLDs nameservers did not respond to the DNS queries. Many factors can cause these (no) responses, but they can be easily fixed by simply monitoring DNS server request/response. Monitoring will help to find the root cause of misconfigurations, which can then be fixed. Like the inconsistency error, resolver will try several nameservers before finding a *working* one; adding latency to DNS resolution process.

The fourth most common misconfigurations is related to missing DS records, not enough IPv6 IP, nameservers not responding to DNS request on UDP or TCP and multiple serial numbers. Some African ccTLDs nameservers involve 2 or 3 different serial numbers from the SOA records. This is a sign of the lack of usage of well known DNS synchronization zone techniques such as AXFR or IXFR between nameservers. As a result, two users can get two different responses, if their resolvers reach separately one of these nameservers with a different serial number. This inconsistency in serial numbers can induce an inconsistency in DNS records as seen by the resolver. From the user perspective, the respective website or service is not available, since the user is not directed to the correct resource value (IP in most case) to connect to it. This is also true when nameservers do not respond. By default, a DNS server must respond to UDP and TCP queries on port 53. Some African ccTLDs nameservers do not meet this requirement.

This misconfiguration has been linked to the 3rd common ones, but the impact is worse.

EDNS support, unexpected response code and the use of deprecated SHA-1 signing algorithm are the last range of misconfigurations. Namibia (NA) by using RSASHA1 did not meet BCP 14 [34] recommendations. Basically, EDNS allow to add more data in the DNS than before. These servers may be using very old implementations of DNS.

Overall out of 2109 tests, only 697 fall into ERROR and WARNING levels. This relatively low rate of error 33% is a sign that African ccTLDs configurations mostly follow best practices. The misconfigurations did not follow any sub regional pattern. All Africa sub-region have ccTLDs with at least one of these misconfigurations as shown in Fig. 8. Nevertheless, some minimal misconfigurations like TCP or UDP connectivity, EDNS or multiple SOAs can be easily fixed.

Table 4. ICANN TLD Registry checklist

Criteria	Number of African ccTLDs
DNSSEC	16 over 54
IPv4 and IPv6 (both)	51 over 54
Registry lock	Not available
Good reputation	Not available

According to [31], a TLD registry choice should be based on the following criteria: DNSSEC support, IPv4 and IPv6 support, registry lock and good reputation. Table 4 shows the African ccTLDs against the criteria of the ICANN procurement checklist for choosing a TLD registry. Registry lock and reputation data are not currently available for African ccTLDs and it will be interesting to analyse results from another research focusing on these two topics. For the rest of criteria, few African ccTLDs have DNSSEC enabled and *out of region* IPv6 is widely use. Thus, only a fraction of African ccTLDs meets the checklist.

Takeaways. Overall, African ccTLDS meet the minimum requirements for operating a TLD as stated in BCP-16. According to Zonemaster misconfiguration report, all Africa sub-region have at least one ccTLD presenting one or more misconfigurations. Moreover, a part from IPv6, African ccTLDs did not meet ICANN TLD registry checklist. Nevertheless, some minimal misconfigurations such as TCP and/or UDP and/or EDNS compliance or multiple SOAs can be easily fixed.

5   Limitations

This research could be improved if we were able to overcome following limitations.

Dataset. This research is based on publicly and freely available datasets. We were not able to get any kind of publicly and/or freely available data from African ccTLDs as the opendata[18] from Afnic for instance. Moreover Namibia (NA) is the only African ccTLD participating to OpenIntel[19] project. Thus, we were not able to collect the data directly from African ccTLDs registries. Of course, having access to anonymized registry data or logs will definitely improve our analysis and help to find the root cause of some misconfigurations. In addition, we have collected data during one month. We assume this period is sufficient since, to maintain consistency, IANA data and nameservers IP and name changes vary little over time: they are used as baseline for DNS resolution. Moreover IANA database changes are not predictable over time and we were not able to detect inconsistent data during the collection period. Finally, our measurements are run from an *out of region* server which may introduce bias in our collected dataset.

Other Services. This research did not take into consideration other registry services such as whois/Registration Data Access Protocol (RDAP), Extensible Provisioning Protocol (EPP), Multi-language support & Internationalized Domain Name (IDN), etc. The whois/RDAP service features recursive results for all associated objects from the registry database. The main advantage of RDAP is to process queries using a RESTful web services and to provide response as a standard, machine-readable JavaScript Object Notation (JSON) format. The registrars communicate with the registry using the EPP and IDN is the core of modern registry that allow UTF-8 domains registration. A study on these topics will require publicly and freely available data from African ccTLD registries.

6   Recommendations

African ccTLDs technical environment can be improve by implementing best practices and taking into account the following proposals.

Data Availability. *Data culture* is not at all popular in the African DNS ecosystem. According to AfTLD, the African DNS ecosystem seems not mature enough for research, but at the same time, this community needs researchers to be able to deploy an African DNS observatory. Strangely, African ccTLDs share their raw data with *out of region* provider, but are reluctant to provide public data for research. We clearly encourage AfTLD on its effort to increase *data culture* withing the African DNS ecosystem by organising training on this topic.

---

[18] https://www.afnic.fr/en/about-afnic/news/general-news/9522/show/opendata-data-from-the-fr-tld-to-serve-innovation.html.

[19] https://www.openintel.nl/coverage/.

Misconfigurations. From a technical point of view, African ccTLD can easily fix some misconfigurations. Niger (NE) lame delegation may require to follow IANA *change requests*[20] process in case the lame server is not use anymore. If the lame server is still in use, but was not working for any reason, this server has to be (re)deployed as soon as possible. The use of automated registry system can solve most of discovered misconfiguration. Modern registry systems comes with internal checks. Theses checks are invoked regularly at a configurable interval and evaluate registry services status. Following the DNS Flag Day project, TCP and/or UDP and or EDNS compliance can be easily fixed by upgrading DNS software and/or switching to a modern authoritative DNS software like NSD, KNOT DNS, PowerDNS or Bind.

Security. Namibia (NA), the only one African ccTLD participating to an DNS data collection project, still uses deprecated RSASHA1 for DNSSEC zone signing. Changing KSK/ZSK or CSK is well documented and we assume Namibia (NA) as the first in the African DNS ecosystem to sign a ccTLD, has all necessary expertise to rollover to RSASHA256 or ECDSAP256SHA256. SHA-1 is nowadays a Shambles and no longer guarantees DNSSEC integrity.

AfTLD Feedbacks. According to AfTLD, this research is more than welcome and more research on this topic should be done for the perspective of deploying an African DNS observatory. Most African ccTLDs are facing administrative and technical challenges that may explain some of our results.

Beside AfTLD offering training to enforce technical knowledge in the region, most African ccTLDs are not able to retain or maintain their employee once trained. Thus, the mean of number of employees of African ccTLDs is 3 and the ccTLD management is a part time activity. The lack of dedicated team working for the ccTLD can explain some misconfigurations such as TCP/UDP/EDNS compliance and multiple SOA as reported by zonemaster.

7   Conclusion and Future Work

Using several data sources, this paper has taken a first look at the African ccTLDs technical environment. We have found that all African ccTLDs meet the minimum requirement of having at least two IPs to serve their zones. Most African ccTLDs have nameservers with IPv6 support. This is related to the reliance on *out of region* DNS providers. Those *out of region* DNS provider offer anycast service and indeed use their respective RIR IPs delegation. Many African ccTLDs rely on *out of region* DNS providers to activate DNSSEC signing for their zone. However, DNSSEC uptake, at 16 ccTLDs, remains low. In general, signed African ccTLDs use recommended algorithm but there are some misconfigurations. Nevertheless, with the high *out of region* ratio and the use of *external* DNS provider, most African ccTLDs infrastructure do not target African Internet users.

---

[20] https://www.iana.org/domains/root/manage.

According to BCP-16 [28], most African ccTLDs by using multiple name-servers spread the name resolution load. Except extreme case from DJ, SL and ET, all African ccTLDs has 2 or more secondary nameservers. Many African ccTLDs do not meet BCP16 recommendations by placing namerservers at both topologically and geographically diverse locations, to minimise the likelihood of a single failure disabling all of them. This is more evident on IPv6.

We also record several issues that impact the reliability and stability of African ccTLDs. For instance, some African ccTLDs nameservers do not provide the same serial number for primary and secondary servers. Inconsistent serial numbers implies that some secondary nameservers are not able to connect to primary for many reasons: IP connectivity, misconfiguration, bad TSIG keys, abandoned nameservers, etc. In any of these case, it is fairly simple to fix this issue and maybe upgrade nameserver software to a standards conforming implementation.

In the future, we plan to conduct a long term study of the dynamics of African ccTLDs using OpenINTEL for instance. We also plan to take a closer look at zone files to identity orphan and abandoned records.

Acknowledgment. We would like to thank our shepherd and the anonymous reviewers for their valuable detailed feedback. We are indebted to Barrack Otieno from AfTLD for his detailed comments on how this work fits into AfTLD research strategy.

References

1. The DNS Forum's Journey, June 2020. https://dnsforum.africa/history-and-future/
2. The DNS Forum's Journey, July 2020. https://dnsforum.africa/history-and-future/
3. The 2016 African Domain Name System Market Study, June 2020. https://www.icann.org/en/system/files/files/africa-dns-market-study-final-06jun17-en.pdf
4. The Global Domain Name Market in 2019, June 2020. https://www.afnic.fr/medias/documents/etudes/2020/Afnic-The-global-domain-name-market-in-2019.pdf
5. Gupta, A., Calder, M., Feamster, N., Chetty, M., Calandro, E., Katz-Bassett, E.: Peering at the internet's frontier: a first look at ISP interconnectivity in Africa. In: Faloutsos, M., Kuzmanovic, A. (eds.) PAM 2014. LNCS, vol. 8362, pp. 204–213. Springer, Cham (2014). https://doi.org/10.1007/978-3-319-04918-2_20
6. Livadariu, I., Elmokashfi, A., Dhamdhere, A.: Measuring IPv6 adoption in Africa. In: Odumuyiwa, V., Adegboyega, O., Uwadia, C. (eds.) AFRICOMM 2017. LNICST, vol. 250, pp. 345–351. Springer, Cham (2018). https://doi.org/10.1007/978-3-319-98827-6_32
7. Chavula, J., Feamster, N., Bagula, A., Suleman, H.: Quantifying the effects of circuitous routes on the latency of intra-Africa internet traffic: a study of research and education networks. In: Nungu, A., Pehrson, B., Sansa-Otim, J. (eds.) AFRICOMM 2014. LNICST, vol. 147, pp. 64–73. Springer, Cham (2015). https://doi.org/10.1007/978-3-319-16886-9_7

8. Fanou, R., Francois, P., Aben, E.: On the diversity of interdomain routing in Africa. In: Mirkovic, J., Liu, Y. (eds.) PAM 2015. LNCS, vol. 8995, pp. 41–54. Springer, Cham (2015). https://doi.org/10.1007/978-3-319-15509-8_4

9. Chavula, J., Phokeer, A., Formoso, A., Feamster, N.: Insight into Africa's country-level latencies. In: 2017 IEEE AFRICON, pp. 938–944. IEEE (2017)

10. Formoso, A., Chavula, A., Phokeer, A., Sathiaseelan, A., Tyson, G.: Deep diving into Africa's inter-country latencies. In: IEEE INFOCOM 2018-IEEE Conference on Computer Communications, pp. 2231–2239. IEEE (2018)

11. Liang, J., Jiang, J., Duan, H., Li, K., Wu, J.: Measuring query latency of top level DNS servers. In: Roughan, M., Chang, R. (eds.) PAM 2013. LNCS, vol. 7799, pp. 145–154. Springer, Heidelberg (2013). https://doi.org/10.1007/978-3-642-36516-4_15

12. Nakahira, K.T., Hoshino, T., Mikami, Y.: Geographic locations of web servers. In: Proceedings of the 15th International Conference on World Wide Web, pp. 989–990 (2006)

13. Zaki, Y., Chen, J., Pötsch, T., Ahmad, T., Subramanian, L.: Dissecting web latency in Ghana. In: Proceedings of the 2014 Conference on Internet Measurement Conference, pp. 241–248 (2014)

14. Fanou, R., Tyson, G., Fernandes, E.L., Francois, P., Valera, F., Sathiaseelan, A.: Exploring and analysing the African web ecosystem. ACM Trans. Web (TWEB) 12(4), 1–26 (2018)

15. Pappas, V., Wessels, D., Massey, D., Songwu, L., Terzis, A., Zhang, L.: Impact of configuration errors on DNS robustness. IEEE J. Sel. Areas Commun. 27(3), 275–290 (2009)

16. Phokeer, A., Aina, A., Johnson, D.: DNS lame delegations: a case-study of public reverse DNS records in the African region. In: Bissyande, T.F., Sie, O. (eds.) AFRICOMM 2016. LNICST, vol. 208, pp. 232–242. Springer, Cham (2018). https://doi.org/10.1007/978-3-319-66742-3_22

17. IANA WHOIS Service, July 2020. https://www.iana.org/whois

18. NRO Extended Allocation and Assignment Reports, June 2020. https://www.nro.net/wp-content/uploads/apnic-uploads/delegated-extended

19. Member States, June 2020. https://au.int/en/member_states/countryprofiles2

20. Cicalese, D., Augé, J., Joumblatt, D., Friedman, T., Rossi, D.: Characterizing IPv4 anycast adoption and deployment. In: Proceedings of the 11th ACM Conference on Emerging Networking Experiments and Technologies, pp. 1–13 (2015)

21. Bian, R., Hao, S., Wang, H., Dhamdere, A., Dainotti, A., Cotton, C.: Towards passive analysis of anycast in global routing: unintended impact of remote peering. ACM SIGCOMM Comput. Commun. Rev. 49(3), 18–25 (2019)

22. Deering, S.E., Johnson, D.B.: Reserved IPv6 Subnet Anycast Addresses. RFC 2526, March 1999

23. Rose, S., Larson, M., Massey, D., Austein, R., Arends, R.: Resource Records for the DNS Security Extensions. RFC 4034, March 2005

24. TLD DNSSEC deployment maps and CSV files as of 13-07-2020, July 2020. https://elists.isoc.org/pipermail/dnssec-maps/2020-July/000337.html

25. Overview of get DNS, June 2020. https://getdnsapi.net/documentation/readme/

26. Zonemaster, June 2020. https://www.zonemaster.net

27. Wallstrom, P., Schlyter, J.: DNS Delegation Requirements. Internet-Draft draft-wallstrom-dnsop-dns-delegation-requirements-03, Internet Engineering Task Force, October 2016. Work in Progress

28. Patton, M.A., Bradner, S.O., Elz, R., Bush, R.: Selection and Operation of Secondary DNS Servers. RFC 2182, July 1997

29. Domain names - concepts and facilities. RFC 1034, November 1987
30. The Verisign Domain Name Industry Brief, March 2020. https://www.verisign.com/assets/domain-name-report-Q12020.pdf
31. DNS Purchasing Guide for Government Procurement Officers, July 2020. https://www.icann.org/en/system/files/files/octo-013-24jul20-en.pdf
32. Wouters, P., Surý, O.: Algorithm Implementation Requirements and Usage Guidance for DNSSEC. RFC 8624, June 2019
33. SHA-1 chosen prefix collisions and DNSSEC, June 2020. https://blog.apnic.net/2020/01/17/sha-1-chosen-prefix-collisions-and-dnssec/
34. Bradner, S.O.: Key words for use in RFCs to Indicate Requirement Levels. RFC 2119, March 1997
35. Severity Levels, June 2020. https://github.com/zonemaster/zonemaster/blob/141fc8db548f2afe33756350c56a0098392ebabd/docs/specifications/tests/SeverityLevelDefinitions.md
36. Mapping test messages to test module, June 2020. https://github.com/zonemaster/zonemaster/blob/141fc8db548f2afe33756350c56a0098392ebabd/docs/specifications/tests/TestMessages.md
37. Barr, D.: Common DNS Operational and Configuration Errors. RFC 1912, February 1996

African Nameservers Revealed: Characterizing DNS Authoritative Nameservers

Yazid Akanho[1], Malick Alassane[2], Mike Houngbadji[1],
and Amreesh Phokeer[3(✉)]

[1] IGBANET, Abidjan, Ivory Coast
{yazid,mike}@igbanet.bj
[2] World Internet Labs, Porto-Novo, Benin
a.malick@worldinternetlabs.org
[3] AFRINIC, Ebene, Mauritius
amreesh@afrinic.net

Abstract. The Domain Name System (DNS) is one of the most critical services for daily operation of the Internet. It is used to primarily resolve names to IP addresses and vice versa on the Internet through a distributed hierarchical system. This work aims at characterizing the authoritative DNS nameservers of two categories of domain (1) publicly available *in-addr.arpa* and *ip6.arpa* reverse zones managed by AFRINIC, (2) 57 ccTLDs in the African region. We study several aspects such as the number of nameservers, the geographical and topological distribution, EDNS and TCP compliance. Overall, the authoritative servers of reverse zones of IP addresses allocated by AFRINIC to their members are 75% EDNS compliant and 72% TCP compliant while the authoritative servers of Africa ccTLDs are respectively 46% and 43.6% compliant for EDNS and TCP. The study also revealed other important information such as the clear domination of some authoritative nameservers, which represents a potential risk of service disruption should these servers become unavailable. Similarly, the geographic location of the authoritative nameservers may potentially have an impact on response times to DNS resolutions and affect user experience. Therefore, a series of efforts must be done in those areas to ensure the optimal functioning of the Internet in the region.

Keywords: DNS · EDNS · TCP · UDP

1 Introduction

The *Domain Name System* (DNS) [1,2] is one of the critical services for Internet to work. DNS is used in almost all transactions that we carry out on the Internet, whether it is visiting a website, transferring data between two remote hosts, performing online banking transactions, or simply sending or reading an email.

R. Zitouni et al. (Eds.): AFRICOMM 2020, LNICST 361, pp. 327–344, 2021.
https://doi.org/10.1007/978-3-030-70572-5_20

The DNS makes it possible to resolve domain names into IP addresses and vice versa on the Internet through a distributed hierarchy involving several servers, each playing a specific role. Systems that store information about the domain name space are called *authoritative nameservers*. A nameserver can be authoritative for several zones, for which, they have information and can provide definitive answers to queries about the zone. To ensure proper redundancy, a zone must have several authoritative servers; Best Current Practice (BCP) 16 recommends a minimum of two nameservers connected to different networks and located in different physical locations and on topologically different networks [3].

The DNS protocol was standardized in Request for Comment (RFC) 1035 [2] and it was originally designed atop the UDP protocol with a maximum packet size of 512 bytes. Since then, the protocol has evolved with new additional resource records (RR) such as TXT [4] and DNSSEC [5]. To overcome this limitation, RFC 2671 [6] and its replacement, RFC 6891 [7], have defined an extension mechanism for the DNS called EDNS: *Extension Mechanisms for Domain Name System*. EDNS is a mechanism for ensuring the scalability of the DNS and its uses on the Internet. Thanks to this mechanism, DNS messages larger than 512 bytes can still be transported over UDP. Furthermore, EDNS also introduced new fields for the transport of additional data. Thus, in a DNS request, the client informs the server of its ability to use EDNS (0), and therefore to receive UDP messages of size greater than 512 bytes without obligation to split the message or even switch to TCP mode. This means that DNSSEC data of considerable size, for e.g. AAAA records (IPv6), DNSSEC RRSIG data or simply long TXT data, can be sent over UDP between a server and a client. EDNS thus makes it possible to maintain the use of UDP for transporting DNS messages without switching to TCP.

In this paper, we collect two publicly available datasets of authoritative nameservers namely (1) the list of reverse delegations that AFRINIC[1] manages, which we shall refer to as *reverse DNS* (rDNS), and (2) the list of 57 country code top-level domain in the African region, which we shall refer to as ccTLDs. The reverse domains are associated to the IP blocks allocated by AFRINIC based on the octet boundaries, i.e. /16 and /24 for IPv4 or /32 and /48 for IPv6 address block. For example, if AFRINIC allocates a /22 IPv4 block, the assignee will need to register four /24 rDNS entries.

We start by characterizing the individual NS records by address type (IPv4, IPv6 or dual-stack) and also by analyzing the distribution of NS records per domain as well as their geographic locations. We then run EDNS compliance checks on both datasets.

---

[1] AFRINIC is the Regional Internet Registry (RIR) for Africa and allocates Internet number resources (IP address blocks and Autonomous System Numbers) to ISPs and end-sites.

2   Related Work

The original design of DNS restricts the total packet size to 512 bytes using UDP transport protocol, which effectively does not leave any space for a "location extension", or any other extension like DNSSEC. The EDNS (Extended DNS) standard solves the problem in a backward-compatible way, i.e. if two communicating DNS servers support EDNS, they can exchange packets larger than 512 bytes over UDP, and if not—they fall back to the traditional DNS. New implementations of the EDNS protocol were launched in 2013 and documented under a new RFC 6891 (which obsoletes RFC 2671 that introduced EDNS in 1999). Thanks to the EDNS standard, DNS servers are now able to communicate with other EDNS-based servers, that allowed bypassing the 512-byte package limit.

Several studies have characterized the DNS ecosystem on specific aspects. In a recent paper, Stipovic et al. examined the level of compatibility of EDNS for a number of public DNS servers for some popular Internet domains and explored behaviour of some contemporary DNS implementations such as Microsoft Windows 2012, 2016 and 2019 as well as Linux-based BIND in regards to the EDNS [8].

Furthermore, Ota et al. carried out a survey on the measures against IP fragmentation attacks on DNS [9]. For this research, the authors surveyed the authoritative servers that manage TLDs to determine whether they can be affected by IP fragmentation attacks. They investigated the fragmentation status of ICMP and DNS responses using PTB (Packet Too Big) and showed that out of 3127 hosts surveyed, 1844 hosts (58.97%) replied with fragmented responses.

Finally, in 2016 Phokeer et al. focused their study primarily on detecting lame delegations in the AFRINIC reverse tree and detected 45% of nameservers recorded were lame, i.e. either not responsive or not authoritative for the zone queried [10].

As opposed to the previous studies, our work performs a characterization of DNS authoritative nameservers evaluating a set of different criteria on both AFRINIC reverse zones and Africa ccTLDs.

3   Methodology

We first proceeded with retrieving the IP addresses of the authoritative servers for both the AFRINIC reverse zones and the ccTLDs. To obtain NS and A/AAAA records for rDNS, we simply parse the text files[2], extract the NS records and perform an nslookup. For ccTLDs we used dig, a Unix command line client to query DNS servers and then again we performed an nslookup to get the IP addresses. All the results are recorded in a Postgresql database. We used the RIPE APIs [11] for various tasks such as identifying the geographic location (country) of the server. While the latter provides some hints on where servers are physically located, because of DNS anycast nameservers, it is difficult to get an accurate geolocation of nameserver. It's possible to infer the location of DNS

---

[2] http://ftp.afrinic.net/pub/zones/.

anycast nameservers by running traceroutes from the country of operation and geolocating anycast servers will be considered for future work.

Secondly, in order to assess the overall EDNS compliance of an authoritative server, the latter must be subjected to several tests from [12] and described in detail in Appendix 1.A. The Internet System Consortium [13] has developed and published a set of tools allowing among other things registries and registrars to check the DNS protocol compliance of the servers they are delegating zones to. See Appendix 1.A for the list of tests required.

With regards to EDNS compliance as a means to avoid fragmentation of DNS response, we are interested to know the EDNS buffer size where a value between 1220 and 1232 bytes is recommended; the main reason being that the MTU on an Ethernet link is 1500 bytes. IP fragmentation is considered fragile and harmful by many specialists; an IETF draft describes IP fragmentation and explains its negative impact on Internet communications [14]. The organizers of the DNS Flag Day 2020[3] recommend 1232 bytes as the optimal value for the EDNS buffer on authoritative servers.

4   Datasets

In this section we describe the two datasets we have analyzed (1) rDNS and (2) ccTLDs. For both of the two datasets we characterized the NS records in terms of address family (IPv4, IPv6 or dual-stack) and we see the distribution of the number of NS records per domain seen in the DNS. This allows us to evaluate the redundancy and therefore the resilience of a domain. BCP-16 stipulates that a zone must have a least two nameservers, placed in two different networks and geographically spread [3].

AFRINIC rDNS. AFRINIC maintains a list of reverse domains corresponding to the prefixes delegated to their members. This list is publicly available on the registry website at https://ftp.afrinic.net/pub/zones. This is an example of the reverse zone for the 2001:db8::/32, as it would appear in the AFRINIC rDNS zone files:

```
8.b.d.0.1.0.0.2.ip6.arpa.        NS        ns1.example.net.
8.b.d.0.1.0.0.2.ip6.arpa.        NS        ns2.example.net.
8.b.d.0.1.0.0.2.ip6.arpa.        NS        ns3.example.net.
8.b.d.0.1.0.0.2.ip6.arpa.        NS        ns4.example.net.
```

It is updated by AFRINIC on the basis of technical information provided by its members. Reverse resolution is the mechanism for retrieving the name assigned to a host from its IPv4 or IPv6 address. To do this, the special domains named *in-addr.arpa* and *ip6.arpa* have been defined. Each reverse domain is associated with a list of authoritative servers which serves requests on the corresponding zone. Pointer records (PTR) are good example of reverse DNS entries:

---

[3] https://dnsflagday.net/2020.

```
$ host 196.216.2.6
6.2.216.196.in-addr.arpa domain name pointer www.afrinic.net.

$ host 2001:42d0:0:200::6
6.0.0.0.0.0.0.0.0.0.0.0.0.0.0.0.0.0.0.2.0.0.0.0.0.0.d.2.4.1.0.0.2.ip6.arpa
domain name pointer www.afrinic.net.
```

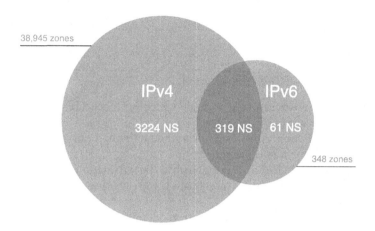

Fig. 1. For all of the reverse zones declared at AFRINIC, we found 3224 unique NS serving 38,945 IPv4 reverse domains and 61 unique NS serving 348 IPv6 reverse zones

As of June 15, 2020, 38,945 IPv4 reverse zones and 348 IPv6 reverse zones were known to AFRINIC. These zones are defined by members who have been allocated IP prefixes from the Registry. A total of 3604 distinct authoritative nameservers provide reverse resolution for the global IP address space (v4 and v6) administered by AFRINIC: 3224 NS manage IPv4 space, while 61 NS manage IPv6 space and 319 NS provide reverse resolution for both IPv4 and IPv6 reverse domains of the Regional Internet Registry (see Fig. 1).

African ccTLDs. To obtain the list of nameservers for African ccTLDs, we queried each country-code individually and requested for the NS records. We could have queried IANA database directly but IANA database is usually not accurate because many registries perform changes in their authoritative nameservers without informing IANA to commit the change in the root zone. For the 57 country-code queried, we obtained 254 NS records, 167 NS (66%) are IPv4-only and the remaining 87 NS (36%) are reachable both over IPv4 and IPv6. Below is an example of a query to retrieve the NS records of the .za ccTLD.

```
$ dig ZA. NS
...
; ANSWER SECTION:
ZA. 48665    IN   NS   za1.dnsnode.net.
ZA. 48665    IN   NS   za-ns.anycast.pch.net.
ZA. 48665    IN   NS   nsza.is.co.za.
...
```

5   Results

We characterize both datasets in terms of:

1. **A/AAAA distribution** to determine which protocols (IPv4/IPv6 or both) the nameservers support.
2. **Number of NS per zone** to determine how many nameservers are acting as authoritative for a specific zone.
3. **Nameservers location and geographic distribution** to determine potentially where the nameservers are hosted and whether they are geographically/topologically spread.
4. **Zone distribution by nameserver** to determine which nameservers are most used
5. **EDNS compliance** to determine which nameservers are correctly supported the Extensions to DNS (EDNS) protocol
6. **TCP compliance** to determine which nameservers are correctly supported the TCP protocol

5.1   AFRINIC Reverse Zones Authoritative Nameservers

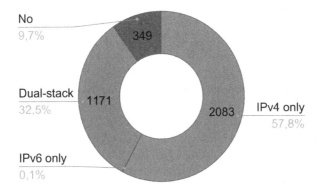

Fig. 2. AFRINIC reverse zone Nameservers A/AAAA records distribution.

A/AAAA Distribution. Out of total of 3604 distinct nameservers (NS records), we found out that 2083 NS have an IPv4 address (IPv4 only), i.e. 57.80%, 1171 NS are dual-stack, i.e. they have both an IPv4 address and an IPv6 address: 32.50% (see Fig. 2). Additionally, we found only two NS that are IPv6 only: *ns1.ipv6.yattoo.com* and *ns2.ipv6.yattoo.com*, which represents only 0.01%. Finally, no type A (IPv4) or AAAA (IPv6) record has been identified in the DNS system for 349 servers, which is 9.70% of the NS declared to AFRINIC by the members. This could be due to *lame delegation* as previously highlighted by Phokeer *et al.* in a study on lame delegations on AFRINIC rDNS entries [10].

Number of NS per Zone. An important recommendation contained in BCP-16 is to have at least two NS for a zone: a primary and at least one secondary. In our rDNS dataset, 1236 zones (1224 IPv4 zones and 12 IPv6 zones) are defined on a single NS. Therefore, those reverse zones do not comply with the recommendations of BCP-16. A direct consequence is that reverse DNS query resolution for those zones can potentially fail should the only one server where there are defined are unreachable, affecting services that usually use rDNS (Fig. 3).

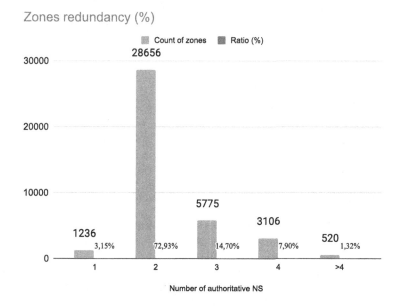

Fig. 3. Reverse zones nameservers redundancy.

Nameservers Location and Geographic Distribution. Using the IP address, we identify the geographic location of the nameservers using RIPEStat [11]. Thus, apart from servers whose location could not be obtained because their IP address could not be determined (name resolution failed), USA, South

Table 1. AFRINIC reverse DNS authoritative NS distribution by country

Hosting country name	Number of authoritatives	Ratio (%)
United States	1060	29,42%
South Africa	706	19,59%
#N/A	352	9,77%
Nigeria	98	2,72%
Egypt	74	2,05%
Kenya	72	2,00%
Angola	70	1,94%
United Kingdom	68	1,89%
Tanzania	68	1,89%
Ghana	55	1,53%
Morocco	54	1,50%
France	49	1,36%
Uganda	40	1,11%
Mauritius	38	1,05%
Botswana	36	1,00%
Bulgaria	35	0,97%
Cameroon	34	0,94%
Germany	33	0,92%

Africa, Nigeria, Egypt and Kenya are the top five countries hosting the biggest chunk of authoritative NS for AFRINIC reverse zones with the following proportions respectively: 29.42% (US), 19.59% (ZA), 2.72% (NG), 2.05% (EG) and 2.00% (KE). More than 35% of NS were located outside of the African region. See Table 1 for full details.

Reverse Zone Delegation Distribution on Authoritatives. Two servers clearly concentrate the maximum of AFRINIC reverse zones. Out of the 39293 reverse zones, more than five thousand, almost 15% of AFRINIC allocated address space, are delegated to *ns1.mweb.co.za* and *ns2.mweb.co.za*. As shown in the Table 2, other authoritative servers like *ns1.afnet.net*, *ns2.afnet.net*, *ns1.jambo.co.ke*, *ns3.jambo.co.ke*, *dns1.angolatelecom.com* and *dns2.angolatelecom.com* are also major actors with around thousand reverse zones they are each delegated to. The top five of main authoritative servers that manage AFRINIC allocated reverse zones are located in Africa. While *ns1.mweb.co.za* and *ns2.mweb.co.za* are both located in two different ASN from the same company in South Africa, *ns1.afnet.net* and *ns2.afnet.net* are located in different networks of the same ASN in Ivory Coast, same for *ns1.jambo.co.ke* and *ns3.jambo.co.ke* in Kenya or *dns1.angolatelecom.com* and

Table 2. AFRINIC reverse DNS zone delegation distribution on authoritatives

Date	NameServer	Count of Zones	Ratio (%)
2020-06-15	ns2.mweb.co.za.	5499	13,99%
2020-06-15	ns1.mweb.co.za.	5454	13,88%
2020-06-15	ns2.afnet.net.	1273	3,24%
2020-06-15	ns1.afnet.net.	1273	3,24%
2020-06-15	ns3.jambo.co.ke.	1169	2,98%
2020-06-15	ns1.jambo.co.ke.	1169	2,98%
2020-06-15	dns2.angolatelecom.com.	1036	2,64%
2020-06-15	dns1.angolatelecom.com.	1034	2,63%
2020-06-15	ns1.link.net.	744	1,89%
2020-06-15	ns2.link.net.	742	1,89%
2020-06-15	dns1.menara.ma.	592	1,51%
2020-06-15	dns.menara.ma.	592	1,51%
2020-06-15	abidjan.aviso.ci.	560	1,43%
2020-06-15	yakro.aviso.ci.	560	1,43%
2020-06-15	ns2.kenet.or.ke.	553	1,41%
2020-06-15	ns3.kenet.or.ke.	553	1,41%
2020-06-15	ns1.kenet.or.ke.	553	1,41%
2020-06-15	pns11.cloudns.net.	538	1,37%
2020-06-15	pns12.cloudns.net.	538	1,37%
2020-06-15	ns1.host-h.net.	532	1,35%
2020-06-15	ns1.dns-h.com.	531	1,35%
2020-06-15	ns2.host-h.net.	531	1,35%

dns2.angolatelecom.com in Angola. However, *ns1.link.net* and *ns2.link.net* are located in the same network in Egypt.

However, we note some discrepancies in the number of zones served by nameservers. We can see a misalignment on the count of zones defined on some couple of servers like: *ns1.mweb.co.za* and *ns2.mweb.co.za* serve 5454 zones and 5499 zones respectively. The same is to be noticed with *dns1.angolatelecom.com* and *dns2.angolatelecom.com*, *ns1.link.net* and *ns2.link.net* while *ns1.afnet.net* and *ns2.afnet.net* or *ns1.jambo.co.ke* and *ns3.jambo.co.ke* are well aligned. Several zones could be defined on one NS only, increasing the risk of unavailability of the zone if the server goes down or is unreachable. The potential root cause may be replication issue or zone transfer issue or human error. In all cases, there is a higher risk of reverse dns resolution failure for such zones. We have already seen above that 1236 zones (1224 IPv4 zones and 12 IPv6 zones) are defined on a single NS.

EDNS Compliance. Almost 75% of the AFRINIC reverse zone servers that have been tested support EDNS0 with a buffer between 512 and 4096 bytes. 25.4% of the servers do not seem to support EDNS extension (Fig. 4). As we shall see in Sect. 5.2, the percentage for non-compliance for ccTLDs is double, around 54%. In both cases, these are servers which are probably running an outdated software version or the EDNS parameter is disabled in the configuration, which is not recommended.

TCP Compliance. An important element of DNS is that authoritative servers must be able to process DNS requests in TCP mode. In fact, RFC1035 specifies that an authoritative server must be able to handle DNS queries via TCP or UDP on port 53. That said, UDP has historically been preferred because it is faster and simple. However, with the introduction of DNSSEC particularly, the need to communicate over TCP has grown as DNSSEC responses can quickly be greater than 512 bytes. Based on the tests done, we received answers on requests in TCP from 71.7% of authoritatives handling AFRINIC reverse zones. It is difficult to clarify whether it is the server that is not configured to respond to TCP requests or a firewall located between the client and the server rejects this type of traffic (unfortunately, several engineers still consider that DNS works only in UDP).

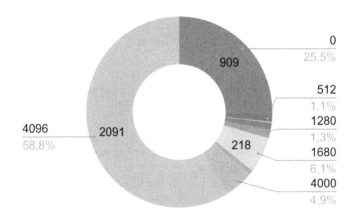

Fig. 4. EDNS Buffer size (Byte) on AFRINIC reverse zone

5.2   African ccTLDs Authoritative Nameservers

A/AAAA Distribution. As of June 15, 2020, 57 ccTLDs were served by 225 NS have been identified on the African continent. One of the NS from .cm ccTLD (*benoue.camnet.cm.*) appears to have neither an A or AAAA record in DNS. Figure 5 shows the IP addressing distribution of those servers: 36% of them are IPv4 only while 63,6% are dual stack. This seems to be a good trend, however efforts must be maintained such that all NS servers are dual-stacked in the near future. None of the servers have been identified to be IPv6-only.

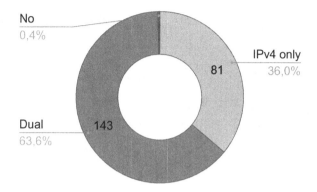

Fig. 5. Africa ccTLD IP addressing.

Number of NS per Zone. As for the number of NS per ccTLD, we found that none is running with only one authoritative server (Fig. 6). Actually, 40.0% of ccTLDs have more than four NS, 26.5% have four, 28.5% have three, and 5.0% have 3 NS configured. The number shows a rather commendable level of redundancy for ccTLDs in Africa.

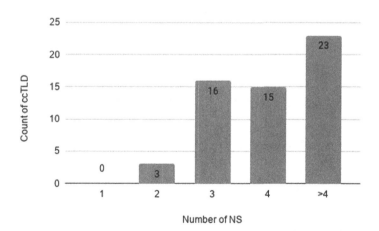

Fig. 6. Africa ccTLD Name servers redundancy.

Geographic Distribution of CcTLD Authoritative Servers. While trying to identify where (countries) the authoritative servers of Africa ccTLDs are hosted using RIPEStat [11], we notice that many of them are located outside

Table 3. Geographic distribution of ccTLD authoritative servers

Hosting Country	Number of NS	Ratio (%)
USA	68	30,22%
South Africa	54	24,00%
#N/A	53	23,56%
France	10	4,44%
Cameroon	5	2,22%
Morocco	5	2,22%
Sweden	4	1,78%
Australia	2	0,89%
Burundi	2	0,89%
Egypt	2	0,89%
Japan	2	0,89%
Kenya	2	0,89%
Libya	2	0,89%
Togo	2	0,89%

Table 4. Same authoritative nameservers

Authoritatives	Number of ccTLD
rip.psg.com.	7
fork.sth.dnsnode.net.	5
censvrns0001.ird.fr.	5
phloem.uoregon.edu.	4
ns.cocca.fr.	2
e.ext.nic.fr.	2
f.ext.nic.fr.	2
h.dns.pt.	2
d.nic.fr.	2
g.ext.nic.fr.	2
sns-pb.isc.org.	2
auth02.ns.uu.net.	2

Africa (see Table 3). USA is on top with 68 nodes which is worth approximately 30% of those servers. France and Sweden host respectively 10 and 4 servers, that is 4,44% and 1,78% of the total. South Africa comes on top of African countries with 54 nodes which represents 24% of the list. See Table 3 for the full list. Note that many ccTLDs used DNS Anycast service such as from PCH and AFRINIC. PCH uses AS42 which is geolocated in the US. As earlier mentioned, DNS anycast can skew the geolocation even if the server are located in Africa.

Africa ccTLD Distribution on Authoritatives. The study reveals that several ccTLDs share the same node as an authoritative server. In fact, there are 12 servers which manage at least 2 ccTLDs and "rip.psg.com" is on top with .eg (Egypt); .gn (Guinea); .lr (Liberia); .mw (Malawi), .sz (Eswatini), .tn (Tunisia) and .tz (Tanzania). See Table 4 for more details.

EDNS Compliance. As explained above, while RFC 6891 defined a maximum size of 4096 bytes for the EDNS buffer, there is no fixed value specified. However, a value between 1220 and 1432 bytes is commonly recommended in the industry to avoid DNS answer fragmentation due to Ethernet MTU size [15].

With regard to the overall EDNS compliance of the authoritative nameservers of Africa ccTLDs, 1.4% are fully compliant, i.e. all tests returned exactly the expected responses and the size of the EDNS cache is between 512 and 1232 bytes; while 7,5% of them have EDNS size within the recommended range. See Fig. 7 below.

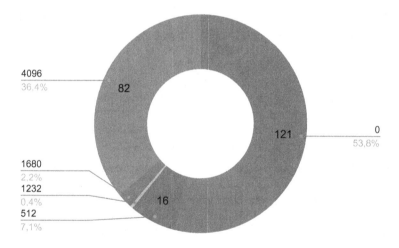

Fig. 7. EDNS Buffer size (Byte) on ccTLD Name Servers.

An alarming number of servers (53.8%) do not have EDNS active, those systems are probably running an outdated software version or the EDNS parameter is disabled in the configuration. There is therefore important work to be done with African Registries for the application of good practices related to the EDNS extension.

TCP Compliance. It is quite difficult to accurately evaluate the real number of authoritative nameservers of Africa ccTLDs that can respond to DNS requests using TCP. This is mainly because firewalls sitting somewhere on the path to that servers can filter DNS requests/response in TCP port 53. Unfortunately, this is still an existing practice in networks because several engineers still consider that DNS works only in UDP. However, we were able to receive answers from 43.55% of those servers using TCP.

6 Discussion

EDNS Compliance Impact: DNS has historically relied on UDP. The maximum size of a normal DNS message over UDP is 512 bytes. However, as stated in the RFC 6891 "Many of DNS's protocol limits, such as the maximum message size over UDP, are too small to efficiently support the additional information that can be conveyed in the DNS (e.g., several IPv6 addresses or DNS Security (DNSSEC) signatures)". DNS implementation and specification document (RFC 1035) does not specify any way to advertise capabilities between the actors that interact in the system. RFC 2671 added extension mechanisms to DNS and a number of new DNS uses and protocol extensions depend on the presence of these extensions. Moreover, IP fragmentation is unreliable on the Internet today, and can cause transmission failures when large DNS messages are sent via UDP. Even when fragmentation does work, it may be insecure; it is theoretically possible to spoof part of a fragmented DNS message, without easy detection at the receiving end [14, 16, 17] and [18]. A recent technical report by Koolhaas *et al.* has also shown that the safe EDNS buffer size is 1232 bytes for IPv4 DNS servers [19]. An EDNS buffer size of 1232 bytes will avoid fragmentation on nearly all current networks. All DNS authoritative servers that do not comply with this recommendation (have EDNS configured and buffer size not exceeding 1232 bytes) will not work optimally because they will cause fragmentation which may lead to transmission failures as mentioned above.

TCP Compliance Impact: The DNS assumes that messages will be transmitted as datagrams (UDP) or in a byte stream (TCP) carried by a virtual circuit. While TCP can be used for any DNS activity, UDP is preferred for queries due to their lower overhead and better performance [2]. when a DNS response is too big to fit in the EDNS limited buffer size, it is important to allow the communication between DNS server and client to switch to TCP mode. Failing to do that can cause some clients not being able to receive answers from DNS servers. Such a scenario could cause an Internet user not being able to browse some web sites and more generally access some Internet services because the resolver they are using is not able to get answers from DNS authoritative servers. In simple words, blocking TCP or failure to support TCP may result in resolution failure and application-level timeouts. On the other hand, TCP normally implements Path MTU Discovery and can avoid IP fragmentation of TCP segments.

Geographic Distribution Impact: More than 35% of authoritative NS of AFRINIC reverse zones are located outside of the African region. The value is almost the same while talking about Africa ccTLDs authoritative NS with USA on top of the list in both cases (30%). Internet is composed of a large set of distributed services. However, their geographic distribution can have a variable impact on the RTT (Round Trip Time) and can therefore affect their performance. As revealed by several previous studies on network performance [20–23], having servers located offshore (usually several hundreds ms away) is inefficient as it impacts the DNS resolution time and ultimately the page load time.

7 Conclusion and Future Work

The DNS is one of the key elements of Internet and the DNS protocol has evolved over the years to meet Internet development. This study has explored several important aspects of authoritative servers on the reverse zones of AFRINIC allocated address space and authoritative servers of African ccTLDs. Some metrics observed clearly show that several DNS standards and good practices are implemented. This is for example the case of dual-stack implementation and redundancy of NS servers in African ccTLDs. However, several indicators are alarming and call for a wide awareness sessions on the one hand and corrective actions from ccTLD managers and ISPs on the other hand in order to contribute to global efforts to make the Internet more secure and resilient. In fact, 54% of the NS of African ccTLDs do not have EDNS activated and more than 35% of the NS of AFRINIC allocated address space reverse zones are hosted outside the continent. In addition, more than 1000 reverse zones have been identified at risk because they are defined on a single NS and only 30% of the NS of AFRINIC allocated address space reverse zones support both IPv4 and IPv6. Additionally, we found that approximately 10% of the servers declared to AFRINIC by its members do not have any A or AAAA record in DNS, which could affect resolution for the zones they manage.

All those findings can potentially have a negative impact on the end user's experience. In worst cases, the user may never be able to access a resource on Internet (while others are able to) because DNS fails to resolve the name or DNS resolution takes longer than expected because server does not support EDNS or communication between client and server cannot switch to TCP for large packet size.

In terms of future work, we intend to run active measurements in a longitudinal manner to see the trends in terms of EDNS compliance of both ccTLDs and rDNS nameservers in the African region. Additionally, we would like to understand the impact of using DNS anycast service and quantify the impact on DNS resolution time and accurately locate the placement of nameservers.

Finally, based on our current findings, we recommend AFRINIC to develop a periodic reporting process that can provide an overview of the NS of the reverse zones provided by their members for the resources they have been allocated.

Acknowledgments. We would like to thank AFRINIC for giving us this opportunity to conduct this study as part of the AFRINIC Research Collaboration (ARC) programme 2019. Many thanks go to the reviewers and to our shepherd for their important reviews and suggestions.

1.A Appendix

See Table 5

Table 5. List of EDNS test using the "dig" command [24]

Test	Command	Expected results
Plain DNS	dig +norec +noedns soa zone @server	- expect: SOA record in the ANSWER section - expect: status is NOERROR
Plain EDNS	dig +norec +edns=0 soa zone @server	- expect: SOA record in the ANSWER section - expect: status is NOERROR - expect: OPT record with EDNS version set to 0 (See RFC6891)
EDNS - Unknown Version	dig +norec +edns=100 +noednsneg soa zone @server	- expect: status is BADVERS - expect: OPT record with EDNS version set to 0 - expect: not to see SOA record in the ANSWER section
EDNS - Unknown Option	dig +norec +ednsopt=100 soa zone @server	- expect: SOA record in the ANSWER section - expect: status is NOERROR - expect: OPT record with EDNS version set to 0 - expect: that the EDNS option will not be present in response
EDNS - Unknown Flag	dig +norec +ednsflags=0x80 soa zone @server	- expect: SOA record in the ANSWER section - expect: status is NOERROR - expect: OPT record with EDNS version set to 0 - expect: Z bits to be clear in response
EDNS - DO=1 (DNSSEC)	dig +norec +dnssec soa zone @server	- expect: SOA record in the ANSWER section - expect: status is NOERROR - expect: OPT record with EDNS version set to 0 - expect: DO flag set in response if RRSIG is present in response
EDNS - Truncated Response	dig +norec +dnssec +bufsize=512 +ignore dnskeyzone @server	- expect: status is NOERROR - expect: OPT record with EDNS version set to 0
EDNS - Unknown Version with Unknown Option	dig +norec +edns=100 +noednsneg +ednsopt=100soa zone @server	- expect: status is BADVERS - expect: OPT record with EDNS version set to 0 - expect: not to see SOA in the ANSWER section - expect: that the EDNS option will not be present in response

References

1. Mockapetris, P.V.: Domain names-concepts and facilities. Internet Engineering Task Force, RFC1034 (1987). http://www.ietf.org/rfc/rfc1034.txt
2. Mockapetris, P.V.: Domain names-implementation and specification. Internet Engineering Task Force, RFC1035 (1987). http://www.ietf.org/rfc/rfc1035.txt
3. Elz, R., Bush, R., Bradner, S., Patton, M.: Selection and operation of secondary DNS servers. Internet Engineering Task Force, RFC2182 (1997). http://www.ietf.org/rfc/rfc2182.txt
4. Rosenbaum, R.: RFC 1464-using the domain name system to store arbitrary string attributes (1987). http://www.ietf.org/rfc/rfc1464.txt
5. Arends, R., Austein, R., Larson, M., Massey, D., Rose, S.: RFC 4033: DNS security introduction and requirements (2005). http://www.ietf.org/rfc/rfc4033.txt
6. Vixie, P.: Extension mechanisms for DNS (EDNS0). Internet Engineering Task Force, RFC2671 (1999). http://www.ietf.org/rfc/rfc2671.txt
7. Damas, J., Graff, M., Vixie, P.: Extension mechanisms for DNS (EDNS0). Internet Engineering Task Force, RFC6891 (2013). http://www.ietf.org/rfc/rfc6891.txt
8. Stipovic, I.: Analysis of an extension dynamic name service-a discussion on DNS compliance with RFC 6891. arXiv preprint arXiv:2003.13319 (2020)
9. Ota, K., Suzuki, T.: A survey on the status of measures against IP fragmentation attacks on DNS (2019)
10. Phokeer, A., Aina, A., Johnson, D.: DNS lame delegations: a case-study of public reverse DNS records in the African region. In: Bissyande, T.F., Sie, O. (eds.) AFRICOMM 2016. LNICST, vol. 208, pp. 232–242. Springer, Cham (2018). https://doi.org/10.1007/978-3-319-66742-3_22
11. NCC RIPE: Ripestat: BGP looking glass. https://stat.ripe.net
12. DNS violations: DNS flag day 2020. https://dnsflagday.net/2020/#how-to-test
13. ISC: Itesting EDNS compatibility with dig. https://kb.isc.org/docs/edns-compatibility-dig-queries
14. Bonica, R., Baker, F., Huston, G., Hinden, B., Troan, O., Gont, F.: IP fragmentation considered fragile. Technical report, IETF Internet-Draft (draft-ietf-intarea-frag-fragile), work in progress (2018)
15. Arends, R., Austein, R., Larson, M., Massey, D., Rose, S.W.: Protocol modifications for the DNS security extensions RFC 4035. Technical report (2005)
16. Huston, G.: IPv6, large UDP packets and the DNS, August 2017
17. Fujiwara, K.: Measures against cache poisoning attacks using IP fragmentation in DNS, May 2019
18. Fujiwara, K.: Avoid IP fragmentation in DNS, September 2019
19. Koolhaas, A., Slokkker, T.: Defragmenting DNS - determining the optimal maximum UDP response size for DNS. Technical report, July 2020. https://rp.delaat.net/2019-2020/p78/report.pdf. Accessed 25 Oct 2020
20. Formoso, A., Chavula, J., Phokeer, A., Sathiaseelan, A., Tyson, G.: Deep diving into Africa's inter-country latencies. In: IEEE INFOCOM 2018-IEEE Conference on Computer Communications, pp. 2231–2239. IEEE (2018)
21. Calandro, E., Chavula, J., Phokeer, A.: Internet development in Africa: a content use, hosting and distribution perspective. In: Mendy, G., Ouya, S., Dioum, I., Thiaré, O. (eds.) AFRICOMM 2018. LNICST, vol. 275, pp. 131–141. Springer, Cham (2019). https://doi.org/10.1007/978-3-030-16042-5_13

22. Chavula, J., Phokeer, A., Formoso, A., Feamster, N.: Insight into Africa's country-level latencies. In: 2017 IEEE AFRICON, pp. 938–944. IEEE (2017)
23. Phokeer, A., et al.: On the potential of google amp to promote local content in developing regions. In: 2019 11th International Conference on Communication Systems & Networks (COMSNETS), pp. 80–87. IEEE (2019)
24. ISC: ISC EDNS compliance and tester. https://ednscomp.isc.org/

Correction to: Towards new e-Infrastructure and e-Services for Developing Countries

Rafik Zitouni⬤, Amreesh Phokeer⬤, Josiah Chavula⬤,
Ahmed Elmokashfi⬤, Assane Gueye⬤, and Nabil Benamar⬤

Correction to:
R. Zitouni et al. (Eds.): *Towards new e-Infrastructure*
and e-Services for Developing Countries, **LNICST 361,**
https://doi.org/10.1007/978-3-030-70572-5

In the original version of these proceedings, the affiliation of the volume editor Assane Gueye displayed in the frontmatter was incorrect. This has been corrected.

The updated version of the book can be found at
https://doi.org/10.1007/978-3-030-70572-5

Author Index

Printed in the United States
by Baker & Taylor Publisher Services